THE SPIRAL PATH

Contributors

Mother Tessa Bielecki
Venerable Tenzin Dechen
Sarah Eagger, M.B.B.S., M.R.C. Psych.
Brooke Medicine Eagle
Mary E. Giles, Ph.D.
Rabbi Lynn Gottlieb
Dorothy Hale
Abbess Koei Hoshino
Anne Lamb
Erminie Huntress Lantero, Ph.D.
Vivian Jenkins Nelsen
Reverend Keiju Okada
Theresa King O'Brien
Chandra Patel, M.D., F.R.C.G.P.
Qahira Qalbi
Swami Shivananda Radha
Bernadette Roberts
Irina Tweedie
Sister Sue Woodruff
Charles Bates
David Fish, D.O., M.R.O., M.B.Ac.A.
Justin O'Brien, Ph.D.

THE SPIRAL PATH

Essays and Interviews
on Women's Spirituality

Edited by

Theresa King O'Brien

YES
INTERNATIONAL
PUBLISHERS

St. Paul, Minnesota

Specified excerpt of 23 lines abridged from "The Thunder, Perfect
Mind (VI, 2)" pp 271-272 translated by George W. MacRae, edited
by Douglas M. Parrott from THE NAG HAMMADI LIBRARY, James
R. Robinson, General Editor. Copyright 1978 by E.J. Brill. Reprinted
by permission of Harper & Row, Publishers, Inc.

Erminie Huntress Lantero, Feminine Aspects of Divinity. Pendle Hill
Pamphlet #191, Pendle Hill Publications, Wallingford, PA 19086, USA

1988
YES International Publishers
562 Holly Avenue
Post Office Box 75032
St. Paul, MN 55175-0032

Printed in the United States of America

Library of Congress Cataloging in Publication Data

The Spiral path.
    Bibliography: p.
    1. Women--Religious life. 2. Spirituality.
I. O'Brien, Theresa King.
BL625.7.S65 1987   291.4'088042   87-5082
ISBN 0-936663-01-4 (pbk.)

Contents

Preface

All my life I have been purposefully engaged on a spiritual path. I attended sixteen years of Church-run schools, lived a vowed life in a monastery for eight years, studied Christian theology with my philosopher husband, spent ten years in a yoga ashram, and traveled around the globe exploring Zen, Hinduism, Yoga, Buddhism, Shintoism and other forms of religion and spirituality. Truths abound; I have been deeply touched. Yet always I was aware that something was missing; some connection to an integral part of myself was not being made. Others felt it as well. After retreats and lectures a few women would tentatively ask, "Are there any women spiritual teachers?"

And slowly other questions grew: Why are all the scriptures written by men? Why are the naves of churches filled with women while the sanctuaries are peopled with men? Why are women excluded from the lawmaking bodies of religions? Over the last decades courageous women theologians have publicly explored these political-religious issues and set us all on a course of discovery--enough of a discovery for the questions to continue. What can we learn from the ancient worship of the Goddess? Do women image God in a different way from men? Do the great male and female saints tread the same spiritual paths? Do they speak about enlightenment and mysticism in the same terms? Is there a difference between women's spirituality and men's? What is the difference?

In asking the questions I was early met with amusement and then with definite annoyance. "The spiritual path is the same for men and women!" But how could it be the same? If female history is different, if female biology is different, if female psychology is different, if

all the hundreds of little responses to life's daily occur-
rences are different, how can the spirituality be the same?
Is it the same because male teachers say that it is? I was
always reminded of the woman in the audience of the
great eighth-century Indian Vedantist, Shankara, who challenged him to prove his statements about women through
experience rather than through rhetoric.

Women have been given their steps to spirituality by
the same patriarchal groups that have given them their
place in society, in politics, in the arts, in the workplace.
Her spirituality was developed for her alongside her subjugation and invalidation. Masculine values have been taught as
the norm in spirituality as well as in every other art and
science in our culture. Women have so internalized these
concepts that they themselves guided young women in
those same male norms. The most elemental reading in
feminist literature will overwhelm the reader with stagger-
ing evidence of the determined and successful efforts of
the male system to invent a place for women and keep
them in it at all costs. Philosophy and psychology have
studied men and boys to develop a universal norm and
then measured women against it with the result that women
question their own feelings and responses, doubting their
experiences, and altering their judgments in the effort to
force themselves into the masculine norm. Religions, meant
to be vessels for the celebration of life, have told women
that they are inferior, the origin of humankind's fall, the
temptation to man's purity, the source of his sin. Her
own body, in its life-giving cycles, is called "unclean."

The resultant pain of women throughout the ages,
the loss of the gifts in spiritual literature and service that
they might have given humankind, can only be mourned.
But after our mourning, we must begin again the process
of discovery. There is much to discover. Spiritual development is, after all, development into full human maturity.
It is ultimately the complete integration of our body,
mind, emotions, tendencies, actions, values, aspirations,
and intuition into the perfect being matching the idea of
original manifestation or creation. Obviously all members
of the human family share stages of growth and maturation.
Obviously we can all reach a point where differences will
vanish, and individuation will dissolve into pure consciousness, bliss, the Beatific Vision, or the Void. But until we

realize that state of being, we exist in parts--as a woman or a man, having these particular circumstances, these particular physical and emotional needs, this particular history, existing in time and place with others living through their particular histories, needs, circumstances. Eventually we must embrace ourselves as total human beings, but we seem to reach integration step by step, experience by experience. We can only begin from where we are right now. True spirituality, then, incorporates and infuses every aspect of our life, from our tenuous first steps to our final enlightened union.

For many of us spirituality is a hard word. It conjures up dusty images, ephemeral feelings and old responses from hours spent in the churches of our childhood. It jogs our memory for forgotten saints, bits of memorized prayers and all that is mysterious. It also seems to carry connotations of the spoilsport: disdain for fun and comfort, wealth and physical beauty. The word is often misused to cover superstitions and dogmas that can be, and often are, antithetical to real spiritual growth. Yet by using the word spirituality we are also put in touch with the experiences of all those who have preceded us on the perennial search for ultimacy. We use the term in the sense of the search for reality, in the discovery of what it means to be fully human.

Women's spirituality must be truly holistic. It must speak to all those parts of us that make us women as well as the parts that make us human. We need a spirituality that guides our emotions and instincts as well as our thinking, and shows us meaning in our everyday lives as well as the life to come. Women need to find such a spirituality, and probably we must develop one. This task requires courage, of course, and brutal honesty to question what we have been taught to believe, to reinterpret truths on which we have been raised, and to examine our ideas to see if they really "fit," if they are indeed leading us to self-enlightenment and full maturity.

In *Beyond Good and Evil,* Nietzsche wrote, "In the end, when we read what women write about 'woman' we are justified in a good measure of distrust that woman really want--really can want--enlightenment about themselves." In this scorching statement we are not entirely blameless. We err by our silence. It is by sharing our insights with each other and communicating our steps to growth that women express this want. Enlightenment is our birthright as women, but we must claim it to live it. By sharing with each other and hearing of other's insights into life, meaningful rituals, states of ecstasy, and wisdom from altered consciousness, we can recognize those experiences in ourselves and validate them as women's ways. We may need to develop a new languaging so that women's concepts will not be superceded by the traditional male usage of terms. But whether charting an entirely new spirituality or growing in the midst of the world's great religions, women assist each other by strengthening our confidence in ourselves and acknowledging our own inner light as the sure and right guide.

This book is an attempt to add to that growing dialog. The women who speak are all extremely individual; they represent several cultures and age-groups, religions and lifestyles and viewpoints. Some have long trodden the mystical path and are honored teachers; others have quietly integrated spiritual concepts into their lives of work. But common to all is a deep personal commitment to enlightenment. Each speaks from the flowering of her own spiritual practice and her purposeful striving for real human maturity.

Three men have been included in this volume to give us another perspective of ourselves. They have been selected because of their continued respect for women's issues and their keen insights gained through many years of deep spiritual practice and exploration.

The writers speak in their own voices. When I lived in Nepal and India, I often heard God referred to as "She." When I asked for the preferred pronoun in Japan, my co-workers and friends were astounded: "But of course God is male!" Many of the writers have wrestled with the dilemma of naming God in their essays, but I have left the final decision to each of them.

Dogen, one of the patriarchs of Zen Buddhism, counseled, "Do not overlook one drop in the ocean of virtue." And so I have tried to include in this volume all aspects of a woman's life: self-image, health, marriage, motherhood, nurturing, her connection to nature, solitude, and community life, her relationships with men, her place in society and the work world, her sexuality, her seeking for

God in scripture and in prayer, mysticism and prophecy and wisdom. The writers show us new ways to know God, and illumine the old ways with fertile, new meaning. They gather our richness as women into a harmony of love and service, and help us to identify and follow that inner guide urging us on to perfect fulfillment.

My deep appreciation is given to all those who helped in bringing this volume to publication. Particular thanks is due to Rebecca Kratz Mays and the Quaker community of Pendel Hill who very kindly gave permission to reprint Erminie Huntress Lantero's work. I am indebted to my dear friends Mahya Kim and Charles Thorpe of Tokyo, Japan for their invaluable assistance in the Japanese translations; to Hugh Bennewitz for getting the concept just right; to Veena Bates and Deborah Willoughby for their practical assistance; and to Patricia Condle Richter for her encouragement. Words fall far short in attempting to acknowledge my husband, Justin O'Brien, as well as Charles Bates, and Sri Swami Rama for their support and blessings.

TKO

Going on means going far,
Going far means returning.
                        Tao Te Ching

The Spiral Path

Theresa King O'Brien

Have you ever watched, from the vantage point of a quiet hill, the slow meanderings of a river snaking its way through a valley? Or do you remember, as a child, being mesmerized by the bath water flowing down the drain, faster and faster, until its powerful vortex threatened to carry your bath toys along with it? Water shows us in many ways a vital principle--the archetypal principle of Being wanting to realize itself, regardless of all circumstances. In many ways, quietly yet incessantly, it shows us the journey of our own self on our quest for fulfillment.

Water always tends to take on the form of a sphere, to become an image of the whole cosmos. It falls as a drop, forms on our skin as round globes of perspiration, builds up as shimmering spheres of dew on the morning grass. Yet it is also constantly forced to move along. Gravity pulls and prods, fighting for ascendency, setting water in motion, determined to make it follow a linear course in spite of its innate tendency to return to its round form. The compromise that water makes to maintain a harmonious balance between these two forces is a spiral. That is why all flowing water, from the tiny trickle to the broad rivers, to the mighty currents of the oceans, never moves straight ahead, but flows spiraling forward, revolving as well around its own axis.

Like water, many forms in nature follow the pattern of the spiral. From unicellular creatures to human beings, the spiral manifests in our bodies and in our psyches. In *Sensitive Chaos* Theodore Schwenk tells us that all of nature, "every living creature, in the act of bringing forth its visible form out of its archetypal idea, passes through a liquid phase. All reveal in their forms that phase . . . Not only creatures swimming in water, but also organs through which water flowed are inclined to be spirally formed."[1]

We have all collected the beautiful spiraling shells of sea animals and garden snails; we admire the whorls of grain in polished wood; we sit dreamily over curiously spiraling steam from our cup of tea, or the blue-grey funnels of smoke from a lighted cigarette; we marvel at the spiral unfurling of a leaf or a flower; we admire the tall spiraling horns of antelope; we watch longingly as birds glide upwards on vast, twisting columns of air; and stand in fear and awe at the powerful spiraling vortex of a tornado.

Like the archetype of water and the many manifestations of those whose cycles pass through it, the human body follows the pattern as well, from the prints of our fingers, to the spiral twisting of muscles and nerves and bones, to the mysteriously spiraling fibers of our heart which cause it to beat.

Is it any wonder, then, that our spirit also travels the path of the spiral? In its essence a perfect image of perfection, the soul manifests by pulling itself outwards like gravity acting on the sphere of water. It reaches out to touch creation, to experience time and space, relativity, relationships, separateness, growth. And like water, the soul compromises its journey into a spiral path by its constant seeking for the return to Self and its yearning for knowledge of all reality.

Physicists now tell us that matter consists of its own movement. A spiral originates from and returns to its own source. So does the spiral path consist of its own spiraling; our search for spirituality is a search for our own true self.

It cannot be a straight path--this seeking for ourselves in the midst of reality--for life itself is cyclic. Time is cyclic. Nature, in its seasons of conception, birth, maturation, and death is cyclic. The spiral is nature's own form; its beginning and its end are one and the same. It spirals up to spiral down; it spirals out to spiral in. We, too, return again, at the very last, to the place where we began. Eventually we all must learn the two truths that the spiral teaches, the same truths that Siddhartha learned from the river: Everything changes; everything returns.

On our way through life the universe gives us the same situation again and again, until finally we master it. It can be a situation of dependency, or one which produces

anger, or requires compassion, strength, fearlessness, or
generosity. Each time we encounter the situation and
recognize the symptoms from a higher round of the continuing spiral of experience, we are given another opportunity
to integrate the learning which will move us forward in
our personal evolution. In like manner we all collectively
have another learning. The seemingly endless wars, the
religious bigotry, the genocide, the destructive nationalism,
reoccur throughout history with only minor changes until
finally one generation will recognize the pattern, see the
symptoms, and learn the lesson.

The spiral measures our growth. It is like the row
of little notches Grandpa made on the door frame each
birthday to mark how high we grew in that year. Each
turning on the spiral path is another place from which to
survey our maturity as so many little notches carved by
life's events. Each notch is so familiar, so comforting: We
have gotten through that, and look how we've grown! Only
what lies ahead, the mysterious unknown, looms sometimes
challenging, sometimes frightening, until turn by turn, it
also becomes one more notch on the door frame.

I remember well a spiritual pilgrimage I made in
the Himalayas of India and Nepal. Part of it was the
thirteen-hour trek from Gangotri, high above the plains,
up to the sacred spot called Gomukh, "Mouth of the Cow,"
the place where the River Ganges bubbled up, icy and
silvery, from the cave deep within an enormous glacier.
We began in early morning, clothed in our jackets and
hats and scarves against the cold mountain air. Our foot
path was a ribbon of sand and dirt five feet wide. It
wound its way along the cliff edges overhanging the river
in a long view which disappeared around a bend in the
next hill. We trudged upward to the bend only to find
another long view spread before us, the path again disappearing behind another bend. All day long as we shed our
layers of clothing beneath the fierce sun, as we drank our
ration of water in guilty, desperate gulps, as we ate our
cold boiled potato and fried bread from our backpack,
that ribbon of trail kept teasing us with one long disappearing view after another. Always we thought the road must
surely end just there, beyond that next steep turning. But
always there was another turning, and another after that,
all seemingly the same, all equally difficult.

At last we were rewarded with the longed-for source of the Mother Ganges at the spot where the trail ended at the very last turn in the road. But so intrigued was I with the mysterious disappearance and reappearance of the sections of road that I decided to count them on my way down the mountain. How many turns in the path did we actually climb? How many turnings would our feet retrace on our five hours down? And why did it seem so easy now? The spiritual number 108 was just uttered in my counting when there before me the last long view spiraled down to the temple at Gangotri at the end of our journey-- the place where we began.

Such is our own development. We follow the path of the spiral throughout life. It is the route we take to reach the same point on another winding. Like the trek on the mountain, we see the events just completed from a differ- ent perspective. They take on a new look on the spiral of time and experience. An early failure, when walked around and seen from slightly above, no longer looks a failure, but a learning experience, a definite step along our way. We spiral around the same point, yet each time we do, we have gained something, we have expanded our awareness just a bit so that our hindsight gives us a little wisdom. We can see ourselves from another angle, returning to the place we were before, noticing our growth. On life's spiral, we will return again and again to the same situation, seeing it slightly altered each time until finally we grasp its full meaning.

For women, especially, the spiral is an apt symbol. Women experience in their bodies the rhythms of life and growth and death. Our whole existence, acknowledged or not, is intricately involved in nature's cycles. Month after month, following the moon, we actualize in our bodies the circle of building up and tearing down, of preparation and cleansing away. Whether or not we actually give birth, we are linked to our mothers and grandmothers and great- grandmothers in the endless cycle of nurturance, the rituals of caring for the sick, and the mysteries of the dying. On the continuum of time we are a child birthing a child, watching our child birth a child.

Women in traditional roles--mothers and teachers and nurses and secretaries and homemakers--share in the tedium of repetitive tasks. We labor in the seemingly endless cycle of cooking, cleaning, picking up toys, washing clothes, typing forms, correcting papers, knowing that tomorrow we will do it all again, and the next day, and the day after that. We answer children's questions over and over again. We read a story knowing that we must read the same story, without the slightest change in expression, for days on end. "My life is so ordinary, so boring, always the same old thing."

But it is not quite the same. The spiral shows us that each ordinary step on the path changes us so that if we look back to see the way behind us and chart where we have been, we will realize that we are not exactly the same person even if the task is the same. And the task itself does not seem so mundane when it also has the power to lead us to personal development and self-realization.

What is the central point around which all this turning occurs? What is that core from which we begin and to which we will inevitably return? It is our own innate wisdom, the wisdom of our own pure self. Wisdom is there from the beginning. It guides our steps even when they seem to be faltering. It leads us forward. It returns us again to itself, older, more confident, more able to see what we really are.

Like the curious phenomenon of water's spiral vortex, we move slowly along, unaware of the swiftness at our core. At any one point on our path we may see ourselves as powerless, but like the gradually increasing speed of the whirlpool, we are urged on as we are pulled to our center--that incredible power capable of drawing all things in and sending them out again with new impetus. And from that central point of wisdom and power and consciousness, our steps lead up or down or out or in, always guided by the centering force which is the image of God.

For better understanding of the spiral path, we will divide it into the four types of spirals possible from the central point. Each movement, while looked at here separately in time and space, can actually be seen to proceed simultaneously also with just a slight change in focus. Going down can also be going out or in or indeed even up with just a little push. Going out is also going down or up or even eventually back in. The beauty of the spiral path is the hope it gives its follower: it is perfectly correctable. Everything changes; everything returns.

The Downward Spiral: Obstacles

Many years ago as a newly professed nun, I entered the large community room of my order for the half hour of daily talking, sharing, and sewing known as "recreation." The room was fitted with a very long table, both sides lined with wooden chairs. The original Rule ordained that nuns sat at the table (as well as walked into the dining room, knelt in the chapel, received their food, and everything else in the community), in a strict ordering of seniority from oldest to youngest. That sometimes beloved, sometimes scorned rule had just recently been changed and now the nuns were free to sit wherever they wished. That evening as I entered the room, I saw a shocking event: Two old nuns, each nearly fifty years in the convent, were engaged in a violent argument. One sat, bent over on a chair, her old veined hands tightly grasping the edge of the table, screaming, "I always wanted this place . . . I can sit here if I WANT!" The other had hold of the back of the chair, jerking it and trying to unseat the other, yelling, "This is MY place. I sat here for forty-six years. This is MINE!"

Years later I asked my teacher what he thought was the single greatest obstacle for women on the spiritual path. Without hesitation he replied, "Attachment."

The downward spiral, unwinding from order into chaos, is a symbol of the obstacles we encounter on our spiritual journey. The obstacles are many, but they generally fall into three major areas: attachment, dependency, and self-negation. These are the sins of woman against herself. They are the stones upon which she trips and thinks she cannot regain her footing. Each obstacle is a paradox because each is also an important aspect of growth. Any virtue taken to its extreme becomes dysfunctional. The qualities women need for profound growth are often those traditionally suppressed within her through socialization, and the developmental characteristics which lead to her maturation can also become stumbling blocks for further development. We can become imprisoned by our own faithful servants.

Such is the case with attachment. The psychological development of the baby girl is one of defining boundaries between herself and her mother while maintaining a sense of identification with mother. She learns to see the world in terms of sameness to herself rather than in terms of difference, as do boys. Females are thus more able to identify strongly with others, develop rapport, experience sympathy and compassion, and become open to mystical states. This is in contrast to male development which more easily produces strong ego, a sense of personal power, and a strong sense of self. Psychologist Carol Gilligan tells us that "The elusive mystery of women's development lies in its recognition of the continuing importance of attachment in the human life cycle."[2]

The fact that attachment is so necessary for our development and is the basis of our interaction with others is confused by the bad press that attachment receives in spiritual literature. The paradox can be clarified somewhat through language. Let us call the developmental aspect of attachment 'bonding,' while the dysfunctional aspect will be called 'attachment.' It is when the bonding principle is over-emphasized or over-used in our lives that it can become the obstacle of attachment. Bonding is life-giving and expansive; attachment is the nun who would not let go.

On one level, attachment has to do with material things. It means being addicted to our possessions and dependent on them for our very identity. Swami Rama says, "The danger lies not in having natural possessions; it lies in becoming attached to them or craving more."[3] Things are actually not our own. We are merely custodians for the things of the earth, and that only for a while. We are like travelers passing through. A traveler may insist on the best of everything--accommodations, entertainment, food, leisure activities, traveling companions--yet she always has in the back of her mind the idea that she will be moving on. The things she has at the moment are only that: momentary. She would not think of being obsessed with her hotel room in Verona, or the restaurant in Kathmandu. She enjoys them while she is there, knowing full well that she will be elsewhere tomorrow or next week.

Attachment becomes an obstacle for women because it limits our ability to have something else. Women's spirituality is always concerned with freedom. There must be freedom to explore our image of ourselves, to establish connections to those aspects of society from which we

have been excluded, to develop what Carol Christ calls
'new namings' through stories and myths.[4] And there must
be freedom to make mistakes and try something else. But
as Frederick Franck, the visionary and artist said, "If I
hold onto my identity of the person I was, it hangs as a
great millstone around my neck."[5]

In Ransoming the Mind, Charles Bates says,

> In attachment one becomes so identified with his environ-
> ment that he becomes limited to the potency of that
> which he has become. He loses himself, because upon be-
> coming the creation, he forgets that he is the creator.
> He thus relinquishes access to his full power. . . . When
> one thoroughly identifies with something and is unable to
> release attachment to it, one gives up access to potency
> in other areas.[6]

So attachment is really our unwillingness to find
ourselves. It is an inability to distinguish our self from
those we serve or nurture. It is to forget our connectedness
to all creation, while grabbing onto a single object--a
person, possession, lifestyle, place, or role--thinking it is
our identity. Attachment is a kind of false love. It is
total identification with, and absorption in, another being
to the exclusion of all else, even one's own needs and self-
worth.

Love always expands and gives freedom, while attachment contracts and brings bondage, both to the one who
is attached and to the object of her so-called devotion.
Such attachment always brings anxiety along as a companion. One who is attached to another is constantly expecting
something; the beloved's attentions are never enough. In
contrast, love is given freely, not asking for anything in
return. Kahil Gibran says it this way:

> Love gives naught but itself and takes naught but from
> itself. Love possesses not nor would it be possessed; For
> love is sufficient unto love.[7]

Realizing that we are harboring attachment in our
heart and freely choosing to let it go expands our field of
awareness. It widens our view and changes our love from
something weak into a strong, mature love. Without negative
attachment, women's positive bonding characteristics will
lead to happier relationships and set our foot more firmly
back on the path. Irina Tweedie's meditation group has a

motto which speaks to such love: Give me freedom to sing without an echo; give me freedom to fly without a shadow; and love without leaving traces.

Attachment, of course, leads to dependency, another obstacle for women. Often we are obsessed with another person, not through love, but through fear. We fear being unloved, being alone, being responsible for ourselves, being abandoned. And so when we find someone to love us, we become desperately attached and completely dependent.

Many women really fear independence. We tend to search for someone to take care of us and protect us from whatever is difficult or hostile. We are quite willing to attain that psychological protection through submission and subordination to our protector. This behavior, especially for the 80's woman, is largely unconscious. It falls under what Colette Dowling calls the Cinderella Complex: "The network of largely repressed attitudes and fears that keep women in a kind of half-light, retreating from the full use of their minds and creativity. Like Cinderella, women today are still waiting for something external to transform their lives."[8]

Females are fed dependency with their mashed bananas, and their dependent behavior is unconsciously reinforced by well-meaning parents, even when they think they are treating their boy and girl children equally. In a life where her husband may be the only independent choice she will ever make apart from her clothes, young women are encouraged to choose partners who will "take good care" of them. That is the basis of the time-honored ritual question asked of the fiancé-to-be by the stern father: "Can you take care of my daughter in the fashion to which she is accustomed?" Nowadays the questioning may be disappearing, but the underlying attitude of parents towards their 'little girl' is the same.

Society's traditional treatment of women has only reinforced their early dependence. Women often continue the habits of seeking approval and asking permission well into adulthood. We are so busy trying to please parents, teachers, bosses, lovers, husbands, children, doctors, (even the delivery man!), that we never have a chance to please ourselves, nor do we really know how to go about it.

The switching of signals in society after the impetus

of the women's movement has left many women in worse straits than before. Now we must appear outwardly independent while inwardly fighting with our unconscious acceptance of, and loathing for, the dependency role we were taught. One day we chide our partners for keeping us dependent, the next day we are upset because he won't do something in our place. We may be happy with our job, but underneath the contentment is the conviction that we can quit any time it becomes too difficult because our partner will always support us. And unmarried women secretly search for someone to marry so he can take up their burden of personal responsibility.

Beyond the obvious, the real problem of psychological dependence is that its captives never get to know themselves. We remain weak if, untested, we are not aware of our strength. It is through the independent making of decisions, along with the mistakes decisions inevitably bring, that we learn about our personal goals, our inner guidance, the way we are directing our life. There can be no growth, nor any real happiness, without the knowledge that we are responsible for ourselves totally, even when we choose to be dependent. Ultimately there is no one to fall back on but ourselves. We alone are responsible for our spiritual development. We all face death alone; we all find God in our own way. The ultimate questions of life are answered individually; dependency only puts off the answering for awhile.

On the positive side, it is true that dependency makes the idea of trust in God and the concept of divinity as loving parent very easy for one trained to look to others for care. One of the most highly regarded of spiritual states by mystics and saints is surrender to the divine, guiding force. Women do not seem to have the great problems that men on the path have with this concept. But dependency exists as a very definite block when that trust in God is used as a substitute for personal development in independence, self-confidence, and trust in our innate power. There is no escape on the spiritual path; we cannot run from ourselves. We will have to understand that we cannot hide behind Christ's dictum to "become like little children" because on the path of spiritual maturity that dictum refers to openness to divine grace rather than clinging in fear to a protector, even a divine one.

The first step is to find out what it is we are afraid of and face that fear. When looked at squarely, fear loses its dreamlike proportions and slowly becomes manageable. The next steps are many. They are the successive steps of insight and awareness into our own powers and personal goals so that finally we can surrender to divinity as mature, independent women, confident in our ability to succeed, standing before God as fulfilled and whole persons.

The third obstacle on the path of women's spirituality is perhaps the most destructive. It is woman's sense of self-negation. It is her feeling of worthlessness, her acceptance of social defeat, her self-hatred, her conviction that "there must be something wrong with me."

From the continuous seeking after approval from others in order to identify our self-worth, we fall into self-loathing when that approval is not forthcoming. The sense of worthlessness is often deeply ingrained from our childhood by our experiences: our accomplishments are not really important, our strength and speed and agility will never quite measure up, our future careers are not very valuable for society, at least not as important as any boy's.

> Parents and teachers rarely will tell a girl that she is less important than her brothers and other boys, for that would contradict the American ideal of equality and justice for all. The message of her inferiority will be communicated in more subtle ways: by lack of concern, by failure to fully nurture her potential for growth and development, by not expecting her to succeed at difficult tasks. And because the messages are mixed, a woman may then feel that her mother's, father's, or teachers' lack of attention to her stems from some specific failing of her own. Internalizing the voices of her oppressors, the currents of her feelings of inferiority and self-hatred run strong and deep.[9]

Even in the traditional area in which women find approval and appreciation--physical beauty--we are not secure. We are never beautiful enough. Most women are quick to point out several 'serious flaws' in their bodies, and as those bodies age, their tenuous self-approval fades with it.

Feelings of worthlessness set the stage for our victimization that others are quick to recognize and fulfill.

Women are easy victims because we think so little of ourselves. Even in criminal cases of violence against us we are apt to blame ourselves.

For most of us the experience of self-negation manifests in our failure to appreciate ourselves. It is the light mockery we make when someone praises our work or our appearance or compliments our ideas. It is our vague feeling that we live a wasted life. It is the sense of inadequacy we experience before any new undertaking. It shows up in eating disorders, in our put-downs of other women, our discourtesy to shop assistants, our fleeting thoughts of harming ourselves.

How do we get out of this trap of self-hatred? By taking another look, looking sharply, and seeing clearly. We must awaken to what is really there: the intrinsic power and beauty and uniqueness of every woman. When we realize that society has not spoken truthfully to us, we can re-evaluate what was said, and come to new definitions about ourselves. We can learn to recognize that the experiences of our lives are steps to maturity and thus are of immense value. We can choose to develop in new areas where we formerly did not dare trespass. We must stop the self-defeating comparison of ourself to others, but rather acknowledge others' power and selfhood while not denying our own. We must reaffirm that which is good in us, in our training, in our traditional roles, in our relationships, in our service, while maintaining the right to change those things when they are no longer meaningful or helpful to us. We can see ourselves with new eyes.

Seeing more clearly on the spiral path allows us to look back and notice that women's self-negation, when it is a step to new self-worth, is very close to an important stage of the mystical life. Contemporary spiritual writers have noted[10] that women's experiences of nothingness and worthlessness often precede an awakening to new sources of power and spirit. They compare it to the dark night of the soul of mysticism, a time of darkness and emptiness when ties to conventional sources of value are broken just before new, profound insight is achieved. In this view, women's insights from their experience of self-negation can be the impetus for their spiritual awakening to new realizations about themselves, leading to a true sense of their real worth and a genuine caring for all their sisters.

The downward spiral, then, serves as a useful tool on our journey. We only need to look down its windings to learn where it leads and recognize its pitfalls. We already know that the eternal spiral always returns, and so with a shift of energy provided by a friend, a prayer, a ritual, a book, or sometimes a painful event, we will turn the obstacles to learnings, and find ourselves once again on the upward route to self-realization.

The Outward Spiral: Expansion of Awareness

On a hot, sunny day last summer, I climbed Mt. Fuji, Japan's sacred peak. During the climb I met two young women, missionaries from America, who came to the country to convert the Japanese people to Christianity. We chatted as we trudged along, talking about many things and growing closer in the shared experience through the afternoon and long night. Four o'clock in the morning found us on the mountain top waiting in the dark, and huddled close together against the fierce, cold wind. And then, accompanied by shouts of "Bansai!" from the hikers on the slopes, the sun arose. It was so beautiful, cracking open the horizon and painting gold the sea of clouds at our feet, that I could not help but exclaim, "What a glorious world the Divine Mother gives us!" With a sharp intake of breath, my companions pulled away murmuring, "Oh, you're one of those! . . ." and began their downward trek without me.

The outward spiral is a symbol of our expansion of consciousness. It is a sign of our growth in awareness--our relationship to creation, our connectedness to each other, and to all of life. Its outer-winding coils guide us out of our narrowness to embrace new concepts, understand divergence of beliefs, accept variety in lifestyle, and realize that all is one and that all is holy.

Patriarchal spirituality dicotomized the sacred and the profane, the spiritual and the physical, the supernatural and the natural. Because women are so wrapped up in nature, they have often been excluded from things spiritual: spirituality has traditionally been reserved for those who dwell in realms of the mind, not for those so closely connected with the earth. This has led some women to question whether notions of the sacred and the divine are compatible with their lives.

The mystics who live in both worlds have, through the ages, told us that the dichotomy is false. They have whispered through spiritual literature that every phase of life is sacred, that all actions can lead us to total integration, and that there is not only one way to know God.

The path of spirituality is intimately connected with every aspect of life. It *is* life, in fact. To deny our spiritual self is to destroy our psychosomatic unity as human beings. A young woman I spoke with said, "Oh, I'm not at all interested in that," as if spirituality were merely a topic for discussion along with old movies and the antics of her cat. Actually, spirituality is a part of each of those things because it is the basic stuff of life. We mature as humans from needs for self-preservation, food, sleep, and sex through needs for security and safety, to needs for love and relatedness and esteem, and finally to needs for self-actualization, meaningfulness, perfection, and spiritual goals. We are always drawn to the beautiful, the good, and the true whether it be in the forms of old movies or old theological tracts. We cannot really separate spirituality from the rest of our growth. Trying to do so will produce lopsided individuals, our lives wobbling in the constant efforts of lying to ourselves.

The world of external reality is a textbook for our spiritual quest. One cannot really see and understand nature without learning lessons of relationship and inter-dependence. The connections within nature are incredible. Ecologists have been making us aware of the damage done to hundreds of species by the removal of only one link in the life chain. We have learned from Eastern methods of medicine that our feet and hands and ears and faces have nerve connections to every organ of our body, and that by caring for a point on our foot, for example, the corresponding organ will be soothed. Iridologists tell us that all our body parts are represented in like manner in the iris of our eye. Biofeedback shows the mind's control over parts of our body previously thought to be uncontrollable. Scientists report that clones of ourself can be grown from every one of our cells, and physicists experiment with individual and group intent on the psychic level affecting physical matter. We have long been aware of the connection of our minds and bodies to the phases of the moon, and thus the tides of the seas, and probably the movements of the other heavenly bodies. Indian scriptures say that the body is a microcosm of the larger solar system and that each influences the other.

A woman seems to feel that connectedness that exists at the center of reality. She is always interested in the relationship of one thing to another; her body reminds her of it. "We are born remembering; we are born connected. The thread of personal myth winds through the matriarchal labyrinth, from womb to womb, to the faceless source which is the place of origination." [11]

What is needed in our spiritual life is to expand that feeling. We should know how the world works as well as we know the workings of our body. It is necessary for us, who have been taught to fear nature or wonder about our place in the vast systems of constructed order, to gain many experiences there. The more we know about external reality, the more we know about ourselves, and the more we know God. Knowledge of nature and structures and our relation to them gives us glimpses of the vastness of life. It expands our consciousness to tap realms of ourself--conscious, unconscious, and superconscious--that we can only guess at now. Our expanding awareness of the wonders of creation leads us to the core of every being and from there to the universal core of all being. Our spiritual development is for society as well as for ourself. "The first step toward appropriating this spirituality is to attend closely to our own feelings and responses to the world and to each other. This attention to our feelings and responses is the root of our connectedness with others and, as such, the root of our power to change the world." [12]

To transform the world we must first transform ourselves; to transform ourselves, we must first know who we are. It is not sufficient to accept another's image of ourself and live through that image. To all of us the Sibyl's message, "Know Thyself," is personally given. Expanding our awareness multiplies the possibilities for self-knowledge; there are many more chances for us to recognize ourselves in each new experience of reality, so many opportunities to gain insight into who we are in relation to what others have learned and shared with us. And when we have paid attention to our experiences of reality, we must question them, and our responses to them, in order to find their real meaning. How do these experiences show me who I am? How do they connect with my other life experiences? How do they relate to others and to the larger world? How do they help me to achieve my goal of oneness with all the parts of myself?

I do not like to hear women say, "I am not very feminine. I have no womanly virtues; I'm really more like a man." Sometimes it is said apologetically, sometimes smugly, but always it smacks of self-loathing and lack of awareness. Why don't we see that women are capable of, and indeed have, many various aspects? By making such statements we are accepting the false notion that a 'real' woman is only one style and can have only one dimension. We are narrowing our consciousness and limiting God's manifestation as female. The fact that many very different women say, "I'm not feminine" means that they as women are expressing many strong womanly characteristics which, although not necessarily matching the usual female myth, are nonetheless feminine.

Jean Shinoda Bolen, in *Goddesses in Everywoman,* lists a whole range of female characteristics--from vulnerability to self-sufficiency, from sensuousness to innocence, from nurturance to destruction--as archetypes within all women. Together they encompass all human qualities. Yet she points out that these archetypes, or goddesses, are all parts of the one Great Goddess, the representation of a whole female person living in the soul of each woman. Learning who we really are means accepting all these parts of ourself. Our reaching out and stretching towards fulfillment encompasses, one after another, the many behaviors and personalities of this Great Goddess. It is by acknowledging that "all this is me" that we connect ourself with all of life and learn much about the undiscovered parts of ourself.

Swami Rama has said that life is like an iceberg: only a small portion is visible.[13] Most of life, as most of our own self, is concealed below the surface. Even though we try, we cannot confine our self to what is manifest alone. We are not so small, so insignificant, nor so facilely known. When we have explored all that is visible, the huge task of the invisible waits to be discovered. Denying what is beyond our current consciousness would be to deny most of our being. Those mystics who have attained an inroad into further levels of awareness write that the experience is overwhelming, and that all knowledge pales before such wisdom.

It would seem that our greatest sin is to limit ourselves to a single image. As we limit ourselves, so do we limit God, the limitless one. We are formed in God's image, but forgetting that, we form God into our image instead, and then worship that. How can we do otherwise? How can we imagine what we have not experienced?

And so our task in spirituality is to constantly expand our awareness of our self. As our knowledge of who we are takes on new facets and ever-widening expression, so will our image of the divine. And as we see our connections with all of life, we may possibly come to the realization that God is also all forms.

The outward spiral, imitated by the whirling of dervishes in ecstasy, models the spiraling expansion of the universe as well as the expansion of the human heart. As we spiral outwards we expand our awareness from old stereotypes to new strengths and new qualities of genius until the spiral once again turns inward and we realize that each turning is but another view of the perfect whole within.

The Inward Spiral: Introversion

The inward spiral is a symbol of introversion--our seeking within, a turning of our mind and heart to solitude, meditation, and contemplation. In our spiritual life we often are drawn inward to peace and rest and recollection. After actively gathering knowledge and truth as so many jewels, we feel the need to withdraw in order to contemplate our treasures. In the midst of daily events and interactions we are reminded often of Justin O'Brien's words: Genuine spirituality induces a tranquil mind. [14]

And so the spiral of our awareness is gently pulled toward introversion and recollection. All expansion leads to contraction, and the one who expands conscious awareness also contracts awareness to a single, inner point. When we still our outer mind we follow the inner mind, and slowly withdraw from everything external to allow our psyche to become peaceful and strong. We stop to drink from the font of joy and tranquility, from water unrippled by the changing externals of everyday life, so we can continue on, refreshed, to take up our work in community again.

The saints and mystics have always spoken of the need for introversion of the mind and heart, the need to turn away from life's activities and personalities to replenish spiritual strength and wisdom. In *The Feminist Mystic*, Mary Giles reminds us of the charming analogy used by Teresa of Avila who said that the soul of one practicing recollection can be "compared to a hedgehog curling up, or a turtle drawing into its shell."[15] The image of a chambered nautilus also comes to mind with its pearly entrance leading gradually into smaller and smaller enclosures until the central, quiet, secret point of origin is met--the place where one would meet oneself and be totally captivated and totally secure.

Introversion is the source of our spiritual life as well as its refreshment. It is the hallmark of those on a purposeful spiritual path. The mystic needs introversion the way the rest of us need air; and as we progress on the path ourselves, we continually feel the increasing need to go within and find what is hidden there.

There are many methods of recollecting the mind, emotions, will, and spirit. Meditation and contemplation are the most perfect forms. In the historical development of meditation in the West, however, an unfortunate confusion of terms has ensued so that the words contemplation and meditation in Christian writings are used to mean the opposite of their Eastern counterparts.[16] For our purposes here we will use meditation and contemplation interchangeably to mean the broad process of introversion.

Meditation leads us to silence. It is both the method of exploration and its final goal. It is the quieting of body, thoughts, desires, sensations, and emotions, as well as the resultant state of complete rest. We pierce through the levels of conscious and unconscious mind to the source of mind itself where our thoughts, will, and emotions become fused and concentrated into one conscious point. Here we seek, and find, that hidden essence of our being which manifests to us only when our mind is sufficiently stilled to recognize it. Here we encounter the ultimate.

This state of meditation, we are assured by yogi and saint alike, is the experience of direct knowledge and perfect bliss. It is a state beyond time, space, and causation, beyond any needs of the body or senses, beyond any distractions of perception or thought. By such complete concentration we reach the place where we know, without intermediary, the essence of all being--that which dwells as a flame within the lotus of the heart. Some call that the Self and others name it God.

In the fourth century, St. Augustine voiced his lament: "Late have I loved you, O Beauty ever ancient, ever new; late have I loved you. For behold, you were within me, and I outside, and I sought you outside!"[17] Our heart weeps with him for all his lost time, searching for his love in the wrong place, only to find it hidden and waiting deep within himself. Many of us have that same lament at some point in our lives. There is an inner longing in the depths of us all and the pull to go within is very strong. Yet some of us fight it and try to escape its insistence with ever more dedicated external activity. Others of us do not recognize the call, thinking our yearning is for something or someone else. Perhaps behind all our strivings for beauty and joy and loveliness, for truth and generosity and purity, is the voice of One who calls. Perhaps that is the One we search for in every friendship, the Beloved we seek in every lover. Sooner or later we must all heed the incessant, nameless longing and acknowledge, "Thou hast made us for thyself, and our hearts are restless until they rest in thee."

For those women who speak of their own religious awakenings, we learn that we are compelled to total commitment to a spiritual life by either of two things. One impetus is pain; the other is love. For some, the tarnishing of ideals once held, the crushed hopes for society, the failure of relationships become too much to be borne and so, disappointed with all external life, they are impelled to turn within for meaning and guidance. Others are drawn to seek the experience of oneness because of their love and admiration for someone else on the path. Many nuns enter religious life because of their love for a teacher or a sympathetic priest whom they want to emulate. Many women join ashrams and spiritual communities because of their devotion and attraction to the spiritual master there.

Once I met with a group of Buddhist nuns and residents of a yoga ashram to talk about their initial attraction to an intense life of discipline and contemplation. All were united in the opinion that the spiritual master was most influential, and possibly the sole reason, for their acceptance of the rigors of a difficult path. They spoke of great yearning when in the presence of the teacher, who was often physically beautiful, kind, courteous. They remembered years of obedience to his every word, complete devotion to his person, and the keen desire to be like him.

One said, "He seemed to embody everything I always wanted and everything I imagined God to be."

Another said, "We become obsessed with the beloved person, needing to fill our emptiness, our senses, our eyes, our ears with him. When our emptiness meets with the pure master, he uses it: he fills our emptiness with his own fullness."

Eventually this longing is recognized as a pull from within. Sometimes the master helps in the recognition: when he knows your love is strong and one-pointed and total, he pushes you away. He will not speak to you nor allow you in his presence. Then it is that you learn that to be close to the master you must seek him in your heart. It is a growing process similar to a mother bird pushing her cherished offspring out of the nest. Without this cruel step the devotee would harm herself; after years of closeness to the teacher she would be completely drained, rather than fulfilled. And so without his presence the powerful yearning for the teacher will be replaced by that which the teacher represents. The longing she thought was for him will be felt to be for one much greater; the emptiness she originally experienced will be filled with God.

The remarks of this group parallel the experiences of many mystics who spoke of intense yearning for an external lover (sometimes in the form of Christ) only to find at last total union with the One who waits, unchanging and formless, in the center of themselves. And there contemplation begins in earnest.

Evelyn Underhill says that "contemplation is the mystic's medium."[18] It is a state of constant awareness of God's presence where we are content to absorb and be absorbed, rather than think or speak. It is being lost in the Beloved in that quiet place where heart speaks to heart: *cor ad cor loquitur.* It is resting in love in the presence of that which is our source and our power. It is the point, as Underhill says, where human life and divine life meet. We reach that place when we empty ourselves of all that is not real, when we discard all negative and self-serving interests, when we simplify our life by clearing away all that is not divine. It requires new sight and great honesty.

The spiral path draws us inward to this beginning and end point. By following its turnings, we go out to activity, return in to stillness; we go out to others, come in to Self; we go out to learn, come in to know, winding ever tighter and tighter to the very source of being until, carried inward by love's vortex, we are finally pulled into mystic union with the divine Indweller.

The Upward Spiral: Transcendence

The upward spiral is a symbol of transcendence. Transcendence is defined as "exceeding usual limits; extending or lying beyond the boundary of ordinary experience." Throughout the centuries women and men have sought transcendence in many ways. Challenged by that which is beyond, humankind has sought to soar like a bird, walk on the moon, climb the highest mountains, see God. There seems to be within a force that both pushes and pulls us out of ourselves to reach for that which lies farther than our current grasp--whether materially or spiritually. We feel instinctively that there must be more to life than the mundane, that something must be out there worth having.

It is this force that keeps us striving for the mysterious which will open new vistas to our mind and spirit. Transcendence is the goal of all our strivings for self-unfoldment and self-transformation. We all have a desire to know ourselves fully and are constantly drawn towards objects that show us, unconsciously, glimpses of our perfect self. In the all-knowing depths of our soul we realize that the object holds, even partially, that for which we have been striving. Often we are not aware of the fact that we yearn for, and seek after, transcendence. We call it other things: falling in love, a religious vocation, artistic purity, business drive. Even self-destruction, by a rather circuitous route, is ultimately extreme dissatisfaction with what we

are because we know there is something else to be. All
the learning and building and improving that we do in life
are steps to that unknown self which lies beyond.

Self-transformation--that continuous growing towards,
and assimilation of, a further step of development--is
what spirituality is all about. Once grounded in who we
are right now, and loving that self, we are impelled to
spiral up to the next level, reaching for transcendence.
The upward spiral is a symbol of that reaching. From
ancient days it reminded women and men to "raise hearts
and minds to God." Early worshippers made their holy
places raised ground surrounded by naturally spiraling
ridges. Later, towers of churches and minarets of mosques
were built to spiral upwards, lifting eyes and spirits to
the mysterious Unreachable.

In Jewish mysticism the serpent of wisdom spirals
up through the Tree of Life bringing knowledge; in yoga
the sleeping serpent of kundalini, coiled around the base
of the spine, unwinds upwards to open seven centers of
consciousness. From the primitive spirals scratched on cave
walls in Siberia to the perfection of Bernini's twisting
columns in St. Peter's basilica, the spiral takes our awareness past ourselves and frees it to soar above all things
temporal.

We strive to touch that mystic place in some way,
to revive those fleeting feelings we know in our best moments; we have a desire to transform ourselves into our
purest form. We do this in stages of development, step by
step, absorbing each stage before reaching out for the
next. We begin in the domain of experience, in what is
real to us, and progress toward the transcendent until bit
by bit the transcendent also becomes real to us. Spirituality
is the quest for the transcendent to become immanent.

Our spiritual path aims to put us in touch with the
transcendental aspects of our being as surely as we know
the empirical. The spiral path winds towards that which is
above, not by ignoring what is below, but by joining both.
It shows us to live not in abstraction, ignoring the real,
but rather to make the unknown known. It connects the
pairs of opposites; it unites mundane and mystical, rational
and intuitional, individual and social, natural and constructed, spirit and body, life and death. It strives for the same
familiarity with the realms of our divinity as we have

with the coverings of our humanity. We should live the mystical life as naturally as we shop for groceries.

There is a real need for us to take care, however, that we are not misled by simplistic solutions. Ours is a spirituality of experience, not merely one of words. The transcendent realm beckons to us to continue our strivings for knowledge of God. As we must discover who we are through our own searching, so must we discover who God is in the same way. Religion can guide and inspire and advise us, but finally for our relationship with divinity to be a living, transforming state, the fruits that are shared by God's intimates must be gathered alone.

In their efforts to "make God meaningful" in our lives, religions and moralists have translated the Universal Source of Existence, the Pure Ground of All Being into a simple person--sometimes meek and kind, sometimes fierce and powerful--but always perfectly knowable and, more importantly, perfectly controllable. From pulpits and classrooms come images of God that leave little to the imagination. God is spoken of casually in terms that convey a vision of the Supreme Being at our beck and call: "God really wants you to . . . You are hurting God by . . . God will punish you if . . . God loves us when we . . ." We have put God into little boxes. We open a box and pull out the appropriate God for the right occasion. We know all there is to know about the Final Cause: sex, likes and dislikes, wants and needs, schedule, fears and sorrows, expectations and hopes, weak spots to touch for mercy, and touchy sides to steer clear of.

But when we open the Vedic scriptures we read, *"Neti, neti,"* "Not this, not this." God is not this. The mystics stumble over words in their attempt to name what they have experienced. They speak of God in wonderful terms: 'The One' says Plotinus; 'Eternal Light' says Dante; 'The Energetic Word' says Bernard; 'Pure Love' says Catherine; 'The Naked Abyss' says Ruysbroeck; 'The Void' says Tweedie; 'Divine Mother' says Rama; 'The Reality' says Rolle; 'Divine Darkness' says Dionysius; 'Still Wilderness' says Eckhart; 'The Bridegroom' says John; 'Supreme Beauty and Sovereign Good' says Angela; 'That Which Is' says Augustine.

As we learn about ourselves throughout life we are awed at our greatness, our diversity, our own multi-faceted beauty. We marvel at our light and our hidden darkness, both reflections of the incomprehensible divinity whose likeness we are. All of life is the playground of that One; every image a glimpse of its vastness; every speck a light from that Light. Such is the One we mirror; to that One does our spiral ascend:

For I am the first and the last.
I am the honored one and the scorned one.
I am the whore and the holy one.
I am the wife and the virgin.
I am the mother and the daughter.
I am the members of my mother.
I am the barren one and many are my sons.
I am she whose wedding is great, and I have not taken a
    husband.
I am the midwife and she who does not bear.
I am the solace of my labor pains.
I am the bride and the bridegroom and it is my husband
    who begot me.
I am the mother of my father
and the sister of my husband
and he is my offspring. . .
I am the silence that is incomprehensible
and the idea whose remembrance is frequent.
I am the voice whose sound is manifold
and the word whose appearance is multiple.
I am the utterance of my name.[19]

The spiral path gathers up all the aspects of our life, all the manifestations of our being, all our sets of opposites and seeming contradictions and spins them into unity. Our growth and development are repeated countless times through other beings, in other times. We all are joined, like children's beads, by the thread of divinity which hangs around the neck of God. As Jill Purse beautifully writes, "The entire universe, with all its spatial and temporal states, is but the spiral manifestation of the still center; as it rotates it expands, and while still rotating it contracts and disappears to the source from whence it came."[20]

Our entire life is the eternal motion of the double spiral. We begin metaphysically as a point, an idea of consciousness, the longing of divine love for itself. Physically we begin also as a point--a tiny fertilized egg. We spiral outwards from that point, growing in awareness as in size as the spiral opens wider. The idea is outgoing; the child becomes an individual. As we grow we explore farther and farther afield learning about life, discovering how to control our environment, meeting and influencing and assimilating more and more beings. And at the apex of our career, at the widest point of the spiral, a curious thing happens: we begin slowly to withdraw back into ourselves. We become more interested in what is inside rather than what is outside. As our body slows, our psyche pulls in to make philosophical relationships about all the things we have studied and to marvel at the basic simplicity of all life. In the tighter windings of the continuing spiral we renounce our activities, our ambitions, and our body, finally giving up that breath we first took in, and actualizing our relationship with God--Lover and Beloved merging--and returning again to the single point of consciousness in the sea of divinity from which we came.

Theresa King O'Brien has backgrounds in education, music, and publishing. She worked as a Montessori directress, as a teacher in primary schools and special education, as a choir director, and as one of the founders and managers of the Himalayan Press. A long-time student of spirituality, she has lived a semi-cloistered religious life for eight years, served as personal assistant to yoga master, Swami Rama, for seven years, and continued her studies in India, Nepal, Japan, and Europe. She currently lives in London with her husband where she writes and studies.

*She is clothed with strength and dignity and she laughs
    at the days to come.
She opens her mouth in wisdom
And on her tongue is kindly counsel.*

Proverbs

Women's Steps to Spiritual Life

Swami Shivananda Radha

My spiritual training took place in the foothills of the Himalayas, where I was initiated into *sanyas*, renunciation, by Swami Sivananda in 1956. I was one of only five women to be initiated in the whole of India. I am a very practical person, as was my Guru, who was a medical doctor before taking to the path of renunciation. He realized that many things begin in the mind, and he would not tolerate any display of emotion--tears didn't impress him--which to him showed you were unfit for the high office of *sanyas*. He demanded of me ruthless honesty. This rigorous training is necessary in order to rid oneself of illusions, assumptions, and projections, and to develop awareness.

As a woman comes in contact with her spiritual search, she needs to ask herself many questions, even if the answers are not immediately forthcoming. Your own reflection on each question will bring you one step closer to realizing your goal in life. Just in posing these questions to yourself, it becomes obvious that the demands of spiritual life are very tough.

What is the Purpose of my Life?

In reflecting on your life, where have you placed the greatest emphasis? What has been the motivating force that has sustained you through the years? Was it to be accepted? There are a lot of things that hold women back, but the main one is emotional dependence. A woman may have all the financial security she could want, yet still struggle in her competition with men. Women's faces show the tension and anxiety of this struggle, and their eyes beg, "please accept me." It won't work. You will have to accept yourself first. That is a big job because women have never looked into themselves, nor met themselves on the gut level. While women have often been accused of being very talkative (which is true), have you ever thought why this is so? It could be that women think no one listens to them, so it doesn't matter what they say. But they have also not listened to themselves, and that is where you have to be ruthlessly honest.

There is an interesting book by Otto Rank, called *Beyond Psychology,* which it would be helpful for Western women to read because it is from our tradition. What he wrote in 1930 is very much in harmony with Eastern teachings. He says that women are not hysterical; they act "peculiarly" because the men do not accept them the way they are. Is that true in your own life? Do you feel that you are accepted as you really are? Look at the tremendous efforts women make to get men's attention--nine billion dollars alone is spent in the cosmetic industry. Look at the birth control methods. It is you as women who are putting your health on the line by using them. Why don't you have the courage to say no? Is it because you are so eager to live and complete yourselves through somebody else? I do not mean to speak against men. Men would prefer to have companionship, rather than assume the heavy burden of someone who has to be carried piggyback.

What did women do historically, when they found they were not accepted by men nor given any recognition? The man became their Father in heaven. This happened because, at the time the Lord's prayer was introduced, the father was a symbol for great power. The Jewish husband had power over the family, so uneducated people could understand it in this way. If their human father didn't accept them, women could pray to their Father in heaven. But to those who could understand more, the close disciples, Jesus said the kingdom of heaven is within, and made no reference to a father.

It would be a tremendous step forward for women to look to the kingdom within their own heart, instead of to a father image. I do not criticize any religion, but wish only to bring to your attention that changing your image of God can be important, since there is no real human being sitting up there anyway. If you have a spiritual or religious affiliation, you will only find a true response to it if you can discover your own divinity within. That divinity does not depend on the kind of religious faith you hold, but it will help you to become a better Catholic, Christian, Jew, Muslim, or whatever. It is we who give the neutral spiritual power a shape and form, based on our own understanding.

Sometimes people criticize the religions of the East, saying they are based on the worship of graven images. But the image of the Father in heaven is no different. Also, the pictures that people buy or create of Jesus arose from the imagination of the artist who created the picture. Jesus came from the East, yet we often see pictures of him with blond hair and blue yes, wearing a long wavy robe with a golden belt. These are symbols that indicate something important to us. We live by symbol and metaphor and we are at liberty to choose the symbols that help us accomplish what we want to do. Women can help themselves by replacing the symbol of the father with something else that has meaning. Jesus has said, "I am the light of the world (John 8:12)." You can choose the Light as your symbol, so that you do not have to deal exclusively with male images. Eventually that symbol can become your own inner light.

The image that the Christian has of Jesus is the greatest rival of what Jesus really is--Christ consciousness. Similarly the image that a woman holds of her husband is his greatest rival, and prevents her from ever truly knowing him. Couples have to help each other diminish the old images so they don't get caught in outdated roles, but continue to grow together. The image you are putting out is also your greatest rival. If you cannot go beyond that image you will never know who you are. Can you get beyond your own image?

Has the purpose of your life thus far been to find your dream lover? For women, there is a lot of pain and many lost hopes, because they have been trained to indulge in illusions and fairy tales and, of course, advertising and society reinforce this. Women pursue the illusion of their fairy-tale prince--the dream lover who one day will come and rescue them. I have met many women for whom that dream lover is still alive even when they are in their 60's. They are motivated by the false promise of a dream that cannot be fulfilled. Why do we have such a dream? There is an answer to this question, but no one can give it to you; you will have to dig it out of your own life. Each person has her own way of awakening to the truth and in every life it is quite different.

The demands of the spiritual path are tough. Many dreams, illusions, and hopes must be abandoned in order for you to become well-grounded, with both feet firmly on the earth. You have to look at who you are and where you are. Most of all you have to look at your strengths. Women really are powerful and it is a pity that they do not recognize and use the strengths they have.

What Makes my Life Worth Living?

How do I fulfill myself? Do I look to other people to make my life worth living? Women often look to men to gratify their emotional needs. Look carefully at what you feed your emotions. Consider your emotional needs like the branches of a fruit tree. Fruit trees are trimmed each year so they will produce more fruit, rather than using the sunlight and fertilizer to sustain non-fruitbearing branches. Women must trim the branches of their emotions so they will not take all the available nourishment. Instead, women must find out what truly sustains them and investigate how they can nourish that. Anything that does not further their psychological growth should be trimmed back. That trimming is necessary before any spiritual development can take place.

Emphasize those things that make life worth living. Bring quality into your life so that whatever you do, you feel good about. You have a right to be proud of the things that you do well or that reflect your standard of quality. Most of the time a woman takes pride in the accomplishments of the man she is with. She tries to live through him in the hope that some of his glamour will rub off on her. Wives of politicians often have no choice. They need to be a source of strength and inspiration for their men, but unless they stand on their own feet, they can end up having a problem with alcohol, or sex, which can then be a source of embarrassment and shame. They, too, have to find their own way and their own place in life. Women cannot be just a nice decoration in a man's lapel, but must prepare themselves for their life and know the contribution they can make.

Life has become too complex for simplistic roles. A woman cannot look to a man to take care of her. If there is a place for women in today's world, they must decide what their place will be without waiting for someone else to put them there.

To What Degree Do I Accept Responsibility for Myself?

There are many factors in life that reinforce a state of emotional dependence in women. It starts, of course, in the family, with the roles that are learned there. The mother will say, "Well, father wouldn't like that. Ask your father. Get your dad's permission." This creates a reinforcement that is difficult to overcome unless the father is a very mature person who knows how to guide a daughter into life. But most of the time he has neither the training nor the awareness in himself of the dependence.

Mothers, also, are not trained. Generally women become mothers without knowing that instinct is the basis for their actions. Animals are carefully bred, but human beings are still wild. For instance, we do nothing to avoid having retarded children. A young woman who wants to get married may be so caught in her emotions and illusions of love and marriage that she doesn't seek any training or education, nor does she find out how healthy she is and what her chances are for having a healthy baby. She rarely thinks of the contribution of the man she wants to marry to the health of a baby.

We still operate from many old cultural traditions. Why was a son more desirable than a daughter in many cultures? A son could fight and defend the food or animals that were needed for survival. These old traditions are still with us. Today you can meet a woman who has two or three doctorates, but when somebody says, "There is a mouse!" she climbs on the table. This is not because she is afraid that the mouse will bite her, but tucked away in the recesses of human memory there is still the lingering fear of starvation. When there was no means of preservation, grains were the only way for human life to survive the severe winters. The first rat or mouse meant there would be thousands following to eat all the grain. Those old memories create inexplicable responses, and it is help-ful to find out what lingers within your unconscious mind.

In ancient times, the king used his daughter as a

bribe so that neighboring kings would not attack. Women became objects of trade. Today women are not used so explicitly as trading objects, but this is the origin of dowries and the idea that women are the property of men.

We have acquired many customs and traditions from history. There are leftovers that we have to deal with, but we can only do so by learning to recognize them. This means reflecting on why you react a certain way. When you entertain a few women friends along with only one man, watch the faces and the eyes of the women. Prior to the man entering the room, the women may be relaxed and casual. But when he comes in they all sit up, their eyes bright. He is the focus of their attention because he is a potential conqueror. Every woman must recognize these games and decide when she is going to stop playing them.

The sociobiologist says we are all programmed by our genes. That might be so, but if that were the only way of operating available to us, there could never be any advances to take us beyond our own programming. Consider the great scientists of our time. Are they only working on the basis of the genes? Or is there a way to bypass the programming of the genes?

In the Eastern tradition there are said to be six stages of human beings. The first stage is called mineral man, and represents a very primitive state in which a person is not likely to learn anything from life. The next stage is vegetable man, which is a little more advanced. But vegetables do not live long and their roots prevent them from moving to new places. The third stage is animal man who lives by instincts. The fourth stage means to be truly human and recognize the need for greater awareness. Then the fifth stage consists of those who are aware; you may call them spiritually developed. The sixth stage of human beings is beyond description.

In my opinion the sociobiologist is referring to the human being in the first three stages of development. But beyond these first three stages there are other realms of possibility that are achieved through awareness. The people who develop beyond the first three stages are sometimes called saints; I refer to them as geniuses in a very specific field. Just as the genius in science goes beyond his past scientific programming, so the saint is a genius in the spiritual field. We are all geniuses in the making, and all of us achieve our own level of genius through awareness.

It is important for women to become aware to what extent they are the product of their environment and genetic programming, but also to recognize what is entirely their own, and for which they have to take complete responsibility. It is often convenient to shift responsibility to the family or to biological makeup, but to find her own place each woman must look for a way to reprogram herself. For awhile, one program may be substituted for another, but, I assure you, finally you can go beyond all programming and all game playing. At first you will play each game a little more masterfully, until eventually you can drop all of them.

Where Am I Ruled by Emotional Responses?

Emotions play a very important part in everyone's life so do not condemn yourself for having them. What is necessary is to find a channel where they can work for you instead of against you. There is a variety of ways in which you can do this.

First of all, acknowledge your emotions. They are there. Do not deny them--that is the way you feel. Do not judge them as "terrible," saying, "I want to be saintly and here I am with these awful emotions." Acknowledge their presence and try to get hold of the power of the emotions. Watch them carefully and ask yourself, Where do they come from and where do they go?

After some practice of that, you can watch your emotions arising. For example, with anxiety or anger you can feel them welling up. Direct your attention to yourself. If you focus on the subject or what makes you angry, you will miss it. Here is the anger rising up--catch it like a ball right in the middle of the situation. Learn to say without fear, "Oh, never mind. I don't want to finish that sentence. Forget about it." In this way you cut off the compulsory force that the emotions have over you.

The great yogis in the East have always said that pain is self-created. When I first came to India I questioned this statement. What could it mean? Surely I would not create any pain for myself. But it took only three weeks for me to find out. People have the choice whether to be hurt or not if things don't go their way. If, for example, a friend does not show up for an appointment, are you really hurt or is it your self-importance that wants to bask in that feeling? You always have the option of admitting that you have just been inconvenienced, not hurt. This choice determines whether one is in control of the emotions or ruled by them. Discrimination makes the difference. Women have to learn to be aware and discriminate. So before you make up your mind about what someone has done to you, find out if the choice you have made is born out of your need for self-importance.

Can You Identify Your Personality Aspects?

One of the biggest obstacles to increased awareness is that everyone has many unacknowledged personality aspects. There is the personality aspect of the wife, the mother, the college teacher, the musician, the painter, etc., and each one has its own ego and its own powerful emotions. Each wants to survive. Shifting from one personality aspect to another does not solve the problem. You have to go down to the gut level and uproot the aspect that you have discovered to be your worst enemy. Learn to free yourself from these enemies.

To gain that freedom you have to be courageous and slaughter those aspects or they will ruin your life. When you reach down into your gut level, do not be afraid. You may think you will find terrible things there but, in fact, you will find your greatest treasures buried under all the garbage. Then you can truly have a dialog with yourself and you will not need to talk all day to everybody else in order to avoid facing yourself. As for the garbage, you can easily be rid of it. You have only to decide.

In the workshops I give I say to people, "If you want to cry because you have so much pent-up emotion, fine, go ahead. But do not cry just because you feel pain. Instead, this is the time to be happy to be getting rid of this garbage. Do not indulge in self-pity. That is another of women's great obstacles, and it comes from the feeling of being controlled by others."

The problem most people have with authority arises because the ego itself is the most merciless taskmaster.

Any woman who can understand that will find that authority problems will drop away; she will be able to have mercy on herself. Then, as understanding grows, compassion for others will also grow. That will make any woman the most lovable and desirable companion, for other women as well as for men.

Our culture tends to value the rational process over the irrational. However, although women are usually accused of being irrational, they do not have to drop that irrationality; rather, they must learn to balance the rational and the irrational aspects within themselves. Men also use the irrational approach. Businessmen have admitted in workshops that their best successes come through their hunches, or their irrational mode of thinking. In stockmarkets and investments, people go by their hunches--they cannot explain why they invest in certain stocks at a particular time, because it is an irrational process. Women need not feel excluded by their use of the irrational, and by male emphasis on logic. They can find out where men are not rational, then invite them to look at their own irrationality. Women do not have to fight, but make it known that they are not inferior simply because they use a different mode of thinking. Self-acceptance will help a woman to learn to stand up for herself in male company.

As a Woman, What Makes me Worthy to Pursue the Spiritual Path?

Where does my sense of self-worth come from? Is it related to my physical appearance? In the world, tall, slim, beautiful women are more readily accepted than the average plain-looking ones.

What are my reasons for a spiritual search? Am I just dissatisfied? Do I seek glamour in a different kind of life? Are spiritual women of the past an inspiration to me? Has the life of any saintly woman inspired me to shift my view of life? How did these women reach the steps of their Inner Temple?

Is my wanting to be spiritual coming from a deep desire for change in myself that I sorely need? Up until now I may have spent a lot of time trying to change the world. Maybe I will try changing myself so that I can find my place in the world.

Spiritual Tools Needed for the Path

(1) Spiritual Diary

What tools are required to gain emotional independence? First of all, keep a daily diary. Reflect on what happened during the day and what you could have done better. Do not criticize yourself if you did not "make the grade," or if you are not quite clear. Clarity will come. You have to begin somewhere. You might be stumbling around like a baby and fall on your bottom, but you can pick yourself up. Nobody else can. Nobody else will.

Criticism really does not get you anywhere. There is a difference between seeing the facts of a situation, and judging yourself or others. If you are impatient, recognize the fact that you are impatient but do not sit in judgment of yourself. If you feel your impatience has gotten you into trouble a lot of the time because of its strong nature, then you can decide to deal with it directly. Put all your will behind your decision in the same way you do when you want to control other people to get your own way. If you learn to control your own life and your own emotions first, you are bound to succeed. You can anticipate most of the issues that stir up your emotions. Do not let them become a barrier between you and your friends, loved ones, sons, daughters, husbands.

Every evening, at the end of the day, write the story of your life in a book with empty pages. If you are ruthlessly honest with yourself you will get a very clear picture of your behavior. You may lock the book away. It is not for anybody else to see. It is your book of life and learning. At the end of the week, read your whole story again and take a couple of colored highlighters and mark all the emotional incidents. Those that you feel you have conquered to the degree that they no longer run your life can be marked in a different color. Say thank you to the divinity within yourself for giving you that awareness. Whenever you can say thank you to the divinity within, it will cooperate with you much more intensely than you would ever dream. You will be surprised at all the hidden talents you discover.

(2) Workshops

Workshops, in conjunction with your spiritual diary,

are a great help in discovering the illusions you still carry. Go to some workshops where you are challenged, where you are really pushed, and see how you survive. That will help you to find out if you are hiding behind the image of your career or place of business. You may have the proper haircut, the business suit, the briefcase, but if you are sitting in a big meeting and are attacked by half a dozen businessmen who have been used to interacting with each other and you have to choke back your tears, you have lost. Appearances mean nothing.

You need to sit down and find out what your illusions are. Discover which of them have a reasonable possibility of being experienced in life and which, like your dream prince or dream lover, are impossible to achieve. If you are in trouble in a marriage, look for your dream lover image first, and then find out how your husband compares. He will, of course, always fall short in that comparison because he is human. Your dream lover is an invention of your mind, mainly created by the little girl in you. This immature aspect has to go.

(3) Finding a Support Group

If you are determined to become aware of your illusions, join an ongoing study group that deals with such work, or a kundalini yoga class. In the yoga classes given at my ashram, or any of the ashram's satellite centers, you write many papers to clarify what you mean by the words you use, such as love, mind, energy, higher consciousness, meditation, or nirvana. You also investigate the five senses because it is through them that you perceive the world. The papers are read out in class and are discussed as a group because the interaction of the group is very helpful. It allows people to discover that they are not alone in their difficulties, nor is truth the property of any one person. Everyone has valuable input.

In looking for a group to join, find a small organization where it is easier to become part of the activities, to know what is going on and hence to learn to trust. The woman who does not appreciate her own sex would be better off not choosing a spiritual organization headed by a woman. However, she must be careful that her choice of a man as her teacher is not based on a non-spiritual attraction. By choosing such a man, a woman may be

trying to protect herself from her own sexuality, and that
is not a good basis for choosing a spiritual teacher. However, even disappointment in spiritual leadership has to be
seen as a test of whether one is truly committed to spiritual life.

(4) Mantra Practice

The root *man* in the word *mantra* means in Sanskrit
"to think." *Tra* comes from *trai* meaning "to protect or
free from the bondage of samsara or the phenomenal
world." Therefore mantra means "the thought that liberates
and protects." A mantra is a combination of sacred sylla-
bles that forms a nucleus of spiritual energy, serving as a
magnet to attract or a lens to focus spiritual vibrations.

"Om Namah Sivaya" is a mantra. Om is the Sanskrit
letter for the divine without shape, form, or image. Namah
means "great name." Siva is one of the three aspects of
the Hindu trinity of Brahma, Vishnu, and Siva. Brahma is
the creator aspect of the divine; Vishnu is the preserver,
and Siva is the destroyer. Destroying, in this context, does
not mean killing, but destroying everything that is between
you and the divine. Sometimes blessings come in disguise.
An illness may give us time to be holy, time to think and
to reflect on the purpose and direction of our life. Destruction on any level means turmoil and this is especially true
on the spiritual level. But the old form of the ego needs
to be destroyed in order to make room for new insights.

It can be very helpful and supportive to join a group
that practices mantra regularly, along with doing papers
and other spiritual work.

(5) Watch Your Dreams

Pay attention to your dreams. At my ashram we
follow the Eastern approach to the analysis of dreams,
which helps you to know your own symbolism. The characteristics of the animals, individuals, landscapes, or houses
in the dream tell you something about yourself. Many
things can be worked out in the seven or eight hours that
you sleep, but the dream needs to be recorded very accurately. Watch your emotions when you write the dream
down and when you are tempted to change a little here
and there. When you do this you are judging yourself. You
have to stop all that judgment. Criticism of yourself is

unjust most of the time. You will tend to use this same criticism toward others and that stands in the way of a healthy relationship.

Women have a lot of power, and the tools to discover that power. Do you accept this responsibility or would you rather sit in your armchair, watch TV, and dream your impossible dreams? It is a bitter pill to swallow, but it is your choice whether you want to be entertained or help yourself to grow. You can learn to be a different woman, so that eventually it will make no difference if people like you or not. You have to like yourself and hold your position--your rightful place in today's world.

Swami Sivananda Radha was born in Germany and lived there until after World War II when she came to North America. A visionary experience led her to her guru, Swami Sivananda Sarasvati, in Rishikesh, India. There she received an intense training in the philosophy and practices of yoga and the spiritual life. She chose to dedicate her life to the service of others and, in 1956, was initiated into the sacred order of sanyas, becoming a swami. At her guru's behest, she returned to bring the teachings of yoga to the West. She founded an ashram and several affiliates in

Canada and the United States. She has lectured extensively throughout the world especially on university campuses, for the Institute of Transpersonal Psychology, and at the parapsychological institutes of Europe. She has written many pamphlets and books, among them: *Radha: Diary of a Woman's Search; Kundalini: Yoga for the West; Mantras: Words of Power; Seeds of Light: Aphorisms of Swami Sivananda Radha; Gods Who Walk the Rainbow.*

Lead me from the unreal to the real;
Lead me from darkness to light;
Lead me from mortality to immortality.
Upanishads

Discovering Spirituality:
From Nothing to Everything

Dorothy Hale

Embarking on the spiritual path is not an easy undertaking. The path is often long and twisting, filled with subtle obstacles. Yet spiritual practice has the power to bring new awareness and clarity in life not obtainable any other way. My own practice of hatha yoga and meditation has revealed the age-old secrets to self-knowledge and have led me on a joyful spiritual journey.

At first spirituality seemed to me to be a discipline, something a wise and loving teacher told me would be good for me to do. So I did it. As I practiced over and over and over each day, it became a joy and a personal strength which I looked forward to. As time continued and I found deeper joy and well-being in what I was doing, my practice ceased to be a discipline, ceased even to be a practice, and became a worship. It was not a worship of God, it was not a worship of anything, it was just a feeling of worship-full-ness. There was a deep sense of gratitude, not for any thing, but just a gratitude of being--a gratitude in my heart, in my mind, even in my body, as though it were feeling well for the first time and saying, "Thank you."

I have heard it said that enthusiasm means "with God," (*en* means "in"; *theos* means "God"). I certainly had great enthusiasm in my practice, but controlling my mind was a challenge. I was a typical Type A, single parent with two children, no money, a full-time job, and no belief in any god. A beautiful experience changed my life and began my search into yoga and meditation.

At the request of a friend, I accompanied her to church one Sunday. I sat in the back row with my coat collar turned up, my arms folded protectively across my chest, staring challengingly at the minister. During the sermon, he spoke of prayer and meditation, saying that prayer was an outward-going thought to God, and that meditation was an inward-flowing of the mind as one sat respectfully in silence to listen. He implied that praying and then jumping up to vacuum the carpet might cause us to miss something. "If there was a God," he said, "perhaps in his wisdom and majesty he had a plan that would be worth listening to." Meditation was being still. It was hard for me to imagine closing down the hurrying intellectual mind and being still to allow the intuitive mind to open and receive. Skeptical but interested, I knew I could use some quiet in my mind and in my life so I decided to try it. "Be still and know that I am God" was a phrase the minister had used. It was too much for me to consider in its wholeness, so I took the first two words for a few years and tried to be still.

I continued to attend the church and to enjoy the vibrant spirituality and the minister who seemed so sure that God existed. I just basked in the sunlight coming through the stained glass windows and the warmth flowing from all the loving people who gathered after service for coffee and sweets. My heart melted at their sincere greetings and their wonderful welcome to one and all.

One sunny morning we stood outside sipping our steaming cups of coffee and engaged in happy conversation. I kept apart from the crowd and watched. Suddenly a feeling surged in me that took form as a thought. "That's what God is! God is the love in the faces of all these people." God isn't a "he" or a "she" because if God were one, God wouldn't be the other. God is everything, including the love they were feeling for each other. It was an overwhelming, joyful discovery. "There is a God," I thought. For me, that has existed without a doubt ever since. An unusual experience helped to confirm my new faith.

The minister had told us that if we wished to meditate, we needed to do it at the same time every day and in the same place. Being regular about our meditation time in a hectic lifestyle was important, he said. I chose ten o'clock at night because my family chores were done-- supper was finished, dishes were washed, children were in bed or doing homework, and no interruptions should disturb the silent sitting. So every night for a year I sat to meditate at ten o'clock.

One night I asked a question in my mind: "Lord, now that I have found you, I want to share you with others; I

want them to come to my home and talk about you. I
know I should not pray for anything material, but I am
really embarrassed at my shabby living room furniture.
Could I have your permission to reupholster the furniture,
please?" It was to take much longer than a year to realize that the One who answers is within, the very Self.

My sons and I lived in a big, old house. For many
years we had played and rough-housed on the furniture, so
now its upholstery was worn and dirty. We didn't entertain
anyone so we had let it go and didn't mind. But now that
had to change. We had no money, no savings, and many
debts. Still, I was determined to tell people about God
and to have a nice place where they would like to come.
Very quietly, I thought the thought again, "Lord, I know I
should not pray for anything material, but you know we
have no money for such an expensive purchase. If I have
your permission to upholster the furniture, I will do it.
OK?"

How shall I describe the feeling of "Yes" that
came back? It was not a word. It was a deep, inner knowing that yes had been given. I asked again, just to be
sure. "Yes" again. So I thought I would trick God. I altered
the thought to: "Is that just my lower mind wishing to
buy something new and nice?" I felt the answer: "No." I
smiled and tested: "Are you sure?" "Yes." So I got up
and went to the children. "God says we can reupholster
the furniture." They looked amazed. I went back to my
seat. Thinking that my abrupt interruption would ruin my
chances, I tested again. "Lord are you sure I can do the
impossible and reupholster all the furniture?" "Yes."

The next day I called the department store and
chose the fabrics. Upholsterers came and took the furniture
away. Six weeks later, it was brought back and arranged
in the living room. Awed, we stood and admired it. It was
beautiful.

A few days later I went to the mailbox and found
the bill: $1,269.49. Undaunted, I wrote out a check for
the full amount. I had only $7.00 in the bank, no savings,
and not a prayer of ever getting $1,200. I thought I would
go to jail. Nevertheless, I walked to the mailbox, put the
check and bill inside, and lifted the red flag. Then I dropped the matter from my consciousness entirely and went
about my work.

Three days later, while bringing in the mail again, I noticed two strange envelopes. One contained a check for $900.00 from a man who had owed us money for many years; the other was an income tax refund check. Both checks totaled $1,269.00. Just forty-nine cents off!

There is a universal fund, an unceasing supply for the demand, and while there are days of seeming financial poverty, the wealth is constant and the way is always made clear whenever the need is selfless. The goal is ahead of us until we realize that we are one with the goal.

After being supplied from this fund, I knew I had to practice meditation in earnest, and went in search of a teacher. Asking everywhere, I was finally directed to a loving teacher who patiently tried to slow me down rather than speed me up. My intensity was my greatest stumbling block both spiritually and physically. He taught me in many ways on many levels and brought me closer to understanding the role of women in spirituality and spirituality in women.

All women reflect divinity as Divine Mother. All women are the embodiment of a gentle, strong, loving light which affects all whom they meet and guides those whom they know. The practice of yoga and meditation allows that light which is within to show forth. After centering and practicing only a few postures, some breathing and meditation, a woman becomes more youthful and beautiful, strong and self-assured. To watch the inner and outer beauty grow day by day encourages one to continue these practices.

The old cliche, "The hand that rocks the cradle rules the world" has deep meaning. Since they are architects of society, the more women meditate, the finer the world will be. The very act of meditation is a refining, gentling process which makes a woman stronger and more effective in her roles.

To be healthy spiritually, to be on the path, it is helpful to be healthy both physically and mentally. As one thinks one becomes. A healthy body with a disturbed, frivolous mind cannot remain centered on the goal of life, to know God. A strong mind in an infirm body will be distracted from the goal by the demands of that body. Body and mind are inter-related so intimately that where the one goes, the other is sure to follow.

Nevertheless, I was shocked one day when my meditation teacher told me to study hatha yoga. "Yoga!" I replied with a sneering condescension. "Exercises?" I wasn't prepared for this betrayal, but he knew how to reach me: "It will help your meditation." So I went to see the yoga teacher and asked if I could just observe one of his classes. I didn't want him to know I couldn't do the yoga postures, so I just took notes in my lap about the postures he taught in class and then rushed home to practice them, trying to remember which hand went over the knee and which arm went behind the back. I grunted and groaned and thought, "Oofdah!" But I went again. And again.

Then, a great Indian sage came to Minneapolis, and I learned that he would instruct some hatha yoga teachers. I asked to sit in the back of the room and observe. It was an extraordinary experience to be in his presence and to see all those people doing amazing things with their bodies. Mostly, however, I was struck by the deep spiritual and physiological benefits of the yoga and breathing exercises and the fact that the meditation afterward was the most profound I had ever experienced. Yoga was not for sissies, I decided; it was part of the spiritual path. With the same intensity and determination which had plummeted me into meditation, I decided to study the whole path. I enrolled in a hatha yoga class.

As a woman, a mother, a business person, a teacher, a friend, I found that hatha yoga and meditation helped in my everyday life as well as in my spiritual life. When the children were young, I often would come home tired and cross from the office and have to prepare a balanced, hot meal for us, help with homework, wash the dishes, and appear to be cheerful and rested when I was not. One of the lessons yoga taught me was the art of witnessing--having the presence of mind to observe events as they occurred, and not to identify with my mistakes or those of others which could adversely affect me.

One night I was particularly upset with the way things had gone at the office, and felt outraged and frustrated because I had not expressed myself properly to my colleagues. As I came into the house, it was late and dark, and I was angry. My sons, then about eight and nine years old, were sitting at the kitchen table doing their homework. They had come home to a dark, empty house; they, too, might be tired from their day at school; they had work to do, and probably were hungry. Realizing that supper would be late, I felt guilty and more angry, not at them, but at life in general and at my own weakness. I knew I would soon be yelling at the boys for no reason, so I said sternly, "You would be safer upstairs in your room until I have had a bath and a glass of juice." Knowing my temper, they scrambled out of the kitchen and ran upstairs. I cooked supper and dragged myself upstairs to take a bath. The children were jumping up and down on the beds, giggling and chanting, "Mommy had a bad day, Mommy had a bad day . . ." I laughed to myself, sliding into the hot bath. After a few minutes, there was a knock at the door. "Come in." A small hand reached around the shower curtain and put a glass of juice on the edge of the tub. Then he ran out to the accompaniment of more squeals and jumping. Later, rested and secure, I called them to supper. "What happened, Mommy?" they asked. "Nothing, really, and it doesn't matter now." "OK."

Their ability to not react negatively to my negative mood helped us pass through a time of frayed nerves and shakey emotions. The concept of witnessing, seeing my anger arising, and knowing it was not directed at them, was possible because of the love we shared for each other and the knowledge that we had learned that anger is an emotion arising, like a bubble in a glass of champagne, but it is not our identity.

Yoga reminds us that "it doesn't matter now." Living in the here and now, with the mind withdrawn from other times and places, we come to know that in the now there is no disturbance. Witnessing teaches us to view past and future neutrally, without attachment, to view emotions as separate from ourselves. This helps eliminate the guilt of thinking, "I'm bad" or the pride of thinking, "I'm good" judged on what we have done rather than what we innately are.

A modern-day issue for both men and women is feeling out of control as life and circumstances whirl around us. The practice of yoga and meditation teaches us: "I am not this body, for I am moving the body; I am not the breath, for I can control the rhythm of breathing; I am not the mind, for I am watching my thoughts." We come to experience control of the body, breath, senses, and conscious mind. This gives us the assurance that we can be in control of other aspects of life, both within and without.

The conscious realization that we are in control releases us from feeling like a victim. Instead, we become the witness and the architect of our life. We come to know that the same immortal life force dwells in everyone. If we are the same as everyone else, then the issue of equal rights becomes an issue of equal awareness. Freedom and self-respect are in the mind. They are as near as one's next thought.

In today's world we women need new guidelines by which to chart the course of our lives. Times are changing; the old roles have been expanded and modified, and women are no longer content to be stereotyped. It is not a matter of where we are creative but of how we see the world around us and within us that makes us successful. Staying at home and raising a family is good; going out and raising money is good; but in order to be fulfilling, both require a certain attitude of mind. There is always some pain in change. Leaving the old ways and leaping forward into more dynamic, assertive roles is a growing experience and brings with it a certain anxiety. "Who am I really?" "Am I okay this new way?" It is like being very fat and losing much weight: we are used to being one way and wonder if people will like the new me.

In the home or in the marketplace, we need to keep our personal center of integrity and balance. Diet and exercise alone will not keep us happy, healthy, and youthful. The glow of youth is found in the inner joy and peace of being always in love with life and everyone in it. True beauty is first inside, then outside.

We are all familiar with the frequently misused slogan, "A woman's place is in the home." Home means not only a house, but the hub, the center, to which all the radii return for rest after venturing out into the external world. Such is the great strength of a woman that she is the hub or center to which everyone can return for nourishment. She, then, must be centered to receive them. A woman is a powerful force at home and in society. Each of us has that center within from which to radiate outward into our work, our errands, our entertainment, our relationships and to which we return when we become still. Moving outward is masculine; moving inward is feminine. Where the two meet back at the center is our balance point from which we draw inner strength and stability while the world turns and changes around us. It is natural for a woman to be drawn to the spiritual path, whether she is working in the world, raising a family, or living in seclusion in a monastery. Dressed in this body, we are the immortal spirit, a reflection of the One who is omnipresent and all-pervading throughout the universe. Knowing this, we can settle into the work of improving our body and mind so we are clear and beautiful vehicles for this radiant spirit within.

The Royal Path of Yoga

When the yoga system was codified by Patanjali (approx. 200 B.C.) into eight steps, called *cstanga* or *raja* yoga (the royal path), spiritual restraints and observances were listed before the practice of postures, breathing, and meditation. The principles and practices of this royal path of yoga provide us with a systematic method for feeling centered, confident and secure, even when we are threatened with so-called failure. Let us take a brief look at these eight steps.

1.   Restraints (Yamas)

The restraints are non-violence, truthfulness, non-stealing, continence, and non-possessiveness.

Non-violence is similar to the commandment, Thou shalt not kill in the Judeo-Christian tradition. But to abstain from killing is only part of non-violence; it also includes non-harming. During an argument between husband and wife one partner may say something cutting to injure the other, even though not striking with the hands. Parents may say cruel things to children in a moment of anger, ("Mommy won't love you if you do that"). We may find ourselves caught in a gossip session where hurtful remarks are being made. These ways of harming others and ourselves are to be avoided by spiritual seekers. We unconsciously harm ourselves in subtle ways also by overeating, straining at our work, through alcoholism, smoking, doing what we don't believe in, or by injuring others in thought, word, or deed. All this harms the spirit of non-violence.

Violence has no place in the life of a woman, whose energies are its opposite. Of course we can be firm in dealing with children, business associates, tradesmen. But this firmness comes from an inner strength, and weakness in these relationships is a violence against ourselves.

Truthfulness is the second restraint. Exaggerating and not admitting to something we have done are forms of untruth. In the business world it might refer to "creative accounting," juggling things to appear what they are not. Truth is not found in hedging. Truth is truth, always and forever. It is not something for one culture and not for another, for one person and not for the second. Truth is always truth, unchanging in a changing society. Truth is within, and we know it when we seek it within; it cannot be known by asking someone else. It is not that something which your parents believe but you do not, nor is truth that which society insists on and you reject. It exists, whether you believe in it or not. The spiritual seeker counsels within and asks, "What is truth?" That which comes through the higher mind, the conscience, that rightness that is known from inside, is truth.

Non-stealing is to not take that which does not belong to us. To most of us, it is inconceivable to steal a purse or someone's car, but many think nothing of envying another's husband or possessions. To keep something borrowed and delay returning it is another level of stealing. In family life, yoga suggests we not take the blame for the wrong actions of others (including your children) and equally, that we not take credit for their successes. We are not responsible for another person's actions, nor for the results of those actions, and it is self-defeating or self-inflating to take blame or credit for them. Blame and praise are irrelevant for one who rests secure in the knowledge that she owns neither the action nor its fruits for she has given those to others.

Continence is often misunderstood to mean sexual suppression. But yoga is never suppression. Continence means moderation and self-control in everything one does, including sex, eating, speech, sight, and thought. *Brahmacharya*, the Sanskrit word for continence, means "walking in God; there is no need for activity when one is in the presence of the ultimate expression of stillness and love.

Sex and celibacy, as love itself, brings us into a deeper awareness of our true androgynous nature of oneness with the Lord within. The observance of continence makes one self-reliant and strong from within. The physical benefit of continence is long life, increased power and energy. Mental benefits include purity and clarity of mind.

Non-possessiveness means that everything in the world is ours to use, but nothing is permanently ours to keep. People are in the habit of saying, "My husband, my children, my house." We know it is not possible to possess someone else, but when we learn to give up the attachment to the material items of the world as well, such as food, cars, houses, clothes, etc., we learn to relinquish the attachments we feel toward relationships and our fixed ways of thinking. Through the conscious practice of realizing, "This is mine to use but not to keep," we grow in the understanding that everything is meant for all and that at the time of death, even this body will be released. We realize that by letting go of one thing, we always receive the next thing we need.

2.   Observances (Niyamas)

The five observances of yoga are purity, contentment, austerity, study, and surrender to the Supreme.

Purity has many layers. A woman is always cleaning the house, scrubbing the children, washing the clothes. An internal purity is needed on the spiritual path, however, and that comes from proper cooking and eating, digesting wholesome foods in moderate amounts and at proper intervals. Often, taking frequent, long baths or showers is an attempt to remove a dirt that is felt inside and cannot be cleansed by any soap. The only soap for internal purity is love. It prevents unclean speech, thought, and actions, and erases all the dirt that might be thrown onto us from outside.

Contentment. It is easy to feel contentment when everything is going well, but yoga emphasizes contentment which does not depend on worldly status or material possessions but is present while doing a difficult posture or job, or in the midst of financial ruin, misunderstandings, betrayal, or the loss of friends. Contentment is not suppression; it is acceptance. It comes when we can be aware of what is happening, be emotionally neutral toward the event, and remain even in our mind. This neutral observation is always taught with the postures and breathing techniques. The student is asked to maintain a steadiness during the practice of each posture, which will then expand to life's situations. When we are steady, we can experience a setback or an austerity without suffering.

Austerity (in Sanskrit *tapas*) means literally "that which generates heat." It is often translated as austerity, and sometimes misunderstood to mean torturing the body or practicing extreme forms of asceticism. Extremes are not yoga. Yoga is the middle path of moderation where all extremes and opposites are merged into perfect balance and steadiness. In daily life austerity means doing whatever we set out to do with enough energy and enthusiasm to actively create heat; to be not lazy and slothful, but charged with divine energy. To actively live life and serve all is tapas. It means to be consistent and constant in our spiritual practice. Tapas is the practice of spirituality with every breath of life, toward everyone, toward every creature, in everything we do: how we raise the children, prepare the meals, serve selflessly with no thought of personal gain; how we love all and exclude none. It creates a subtle and powerful spiritual benefit for those who practice it. This benefit then graces all.

Study means the study leading to knowledge of the Self. It is the study of scriptures and the lives of great people which leads us to greater awareness of the basic goodness of life and inspires us to remember that if one can become enlightened, all have that potential. Study alone is able to produce the change in us that leads to enlightenment. When working with the body, breath, and mind we notice improvement and change day by day. This awareness flows into our life where we are able to observe our thoughts as they arise and control whether or not they become actions. We must study ourselves without judgment, condemnation or praise. In self-condemnation we feel less worthy than others; in self-praise our ego is inflated, and we feel superior. Study sharpens our power of discrimination and leads to self-realization.

Surrender to the Supreme. Everything leads to surrender. When one surrenders, everything she has tried so hard to do is done. At first, it takes great effort to surrender, but when all effort is dropped, one finds she is there! Mini-surrenders are preparations for the big surrender, death, when we surrender what we have thought of as "me." In that instant, we are apt to think, "Wait! What will become of me?" Yoga helps us to prepare physically, mentally, and spiritually to surrender by learning who and what we are and what becomes of that.

If a drop of water is removed from the ocean, it becomes, for a time, an individual, separate entity. It contains all the properties of the whole, yet it is divided from the whole and appears separate. When it drops back into the ocean, it loses its identity as an individual drop and becomes one with the whole. It becomes, in fact, the ocean. Surrender is the drop finding joy in becoming merged with the ocean from which it came. In life, that same joy and merging occur when one sees in all beings the same source.

3. Postures (Asana)

In the practice of hatha yoga, we begin with the physical, but each posture has an effect on the mental and spiritual levels of consciousness as well. Beautifully and effortlessly, one who practices hatha yoga becomes more aware of her own spirituality and learns to respect and care for the body. If the body is easeful, the mind is peaceful, and a perfect balance of physical-mental-spiritual occurs.

The body is the temple of the soul and should be taken care of with the same respect that one takes care of the altar in any church or temple. A healthy body is at peace with the world outside and with the mind inside. This fosters the awareness of spiritual oneness with all. When we are ill, we feel out of step and isolated; the mind which could dwell on the consciousness of the divine is drawn repeatedly back to the physical body's aches and turmoil.

Unlike some forms of body movement, yoga teaches us to be aware of the internal stillness while observing external movement; to become strong through gentleness. That gentleness is our own inner strength revealed. External strength is nothing compared to the strength which comes from within us.

There are three levels to be aware of when practicing hatha yoga or when living life. First, what is your comfortable capacity? Second, when do you feel a slight stretch? Third is pain. Yoga says to avoid pain by two inches in hatha and by two miles in life. Yoga means "union," union of the outer self with the inner Self. If the body is doing something that the inner Self does not feel is right, one will be in conflict.

Through the practice of a few simple hatha yoga postures every day, it is possible to keep the body and mind healthy, light, flexible, and strong. Forward-bending postures help us become more assertive, while backward-bending postures help us become better able to serve, as in the expression, "She would bend over backward to help people." Spinal twists help to remove toxins stored in the nervous system after anger and other negative emotions have arisen. Inverted postures help restore balance and health to all the systems of the body as well as helping us to see things from another point of view.

Every yoga posture works on many levels. For example, the Lion's Pose, while strengthening the throat muscles is also excellent for removing fear; the Posterior Stretch, or sitting forward bend, brings circulation and awareness to the base of the spine where many fears are stored.

To change physically, or to grow spiritually, we first become aware, then accept, and then alter. We begin by learning to consciously control the external body, moving into the postures properly, and maintaining them without strain. Later, we are directed further inward to observe the breathing, and finally the mind. This inward journey brings us to awareness of the autonomic functionings of the body. Once we are aware, we are able to change.

Body work is the first step in working from the outside to the inside, from the visible to the invisible. When we go in and in and in with our awareness, we cannot help but ultimately become aware of the innermost dimension of being, beyond the body, breath, senses, and mind. All body work, especially that which takes us into stillness and self-awareness as yoga does, leads to heightened spiritual awareness.

4. Breathing (Pranayama)

The study of hatha yoga is the study of the mergence and unity of "ha," which represents the sun and the breath in the right nostril, with "tha," which represents the moon and the breath in the left nostril. In the universe, the micro-moment of balance between the sun and the moon occur at sunrise and sunset. In the body, this union of breath is sought between the two nostrils. At the moment of perfect balance one feels joyful and calm. Body and mind are in complete equilibrium, since opposites have merged into their original oneness.

The special breathing techniques in yoga science make the student aware of the subtle changes in breathing rhythms and teaches how to consciously create a perfect balance between the two polarities. The mind is then balanced and at ease for deep meditation. The science of breath and the control (yama) of energy (prana) within the breath can help relieve anxiety, depression, and other diseases if properly taught by a competent teacher.

Feeling hurried and worried, running in circles, always behind, quick to anger, easily upset with life's events are all signs of a disturbance in one's being which can be relieved by correct breathing. Breathing exercises can also help remove fear and fatigue; they lower blood pressure, and restore a feeling of well-being and clarity of mind, preparing subtle energy channels for meditation.

Beyond the physical and emotional benefits of breath awareness and breathing techniques are those for the mind and spirit. We are intimately connected with other life forms on the earth. If we inhale but do not exhale, we will cease to be. It is the same life breath that flows through all. We are all one but seem to be many. Watching the breath leads us to an awareness that the whole universe is breathing in unison. The inhalation which we receive must be surrendered and released, just as the fruits of our actions are released, to benefit others and to open us to receive that which is eternally and perennially flowing. When we are closed, we do not receive it and think it is not there. When we are open, we receive and realize it was there all the time. Giving and giving up are learned from studying the subtleties of the breath that sustains us, even when we are not aware of it doing so.

5. Sense Withdrawal (Pratyahara)

The ability to meditate depends on the ability to concentrate inward. The ability to concentrate depends on the ability to withdraw awareness from the external stimuli of the world and our responses to those stimuli through the senses. Pratyahara is the practice of this ability to withdraw awareness.

We need to withdraw the mind from two disturbances which arise from within: memories of the past and anticipations about the future. Thought is faster than the speed of light, and we may feel calm one moment and suddenly dejected or apprehensive the next, although nothing has happened. Such a sudden shift in energies can cause us to reach for a cigarette or phone a friend or eat nervously or smile when no one is in the room. In the moment called "now," there is no oscillation, no joy, no sorrow, no expectation, no remorse. As soon as the mind moves off that point, it remembers or anticipates, and there is a disturbance.

Yoga teaches us to not suppress those thoughts or pretend something did not happen that did, but to gently withdraw the mind from those other times and other places and be here now. Withdrawing leads to that concentration called being here now.

6. Concentration (Dharana)

Hatha yoga and breathing techniques teach us to become aware of the body and mind and their disturbances, constantly returning to a steady point of concentration, to dwell as long as possible in the now. When the mind is aware only of now, we experience perfect peace and are united with the divine nature within, which resides ever calm, ever pure, untouched by emotions, thoughts, or actions. As soon as the mind moves into the past or the future, a change occurs, and we experience joy or sorrow, pleasure or pain.

Through withdrawal of the senses from their objects of excitement, we become concentrated; through the practice of remaining concentrated, we discover meditation.

7. Meditation (Dhyana)

Meditation is perfect stillness. When we let go of all our sensory distractions, worldly cares, and thoughts, we become still and know that what lies within is what we have been seeking outside.

All the practices of yoga teach us to let go, to

release and receive on many levels, including the final letting go called death. We die daily. Monday dies so Tuesday can come. Youth is left behind so we can become an adult. A moment ends so the next moment can come. Everything has a cycle: a beginning, a period of being, and its dissolution. In letting go we are able to receive.

Meditation is the greatest gift. It comes when we seek nothing, expect nothing, but are open to receive. This openness without expectation is subtle and feminine and is filled with spiritual power. Meditation increases our awareness of, and ability to use, that spiritual power and focuses it like a laser beam so we can become whatever we want: more beautiful, more nurturing, more dynamic, better mothers, better athletes, better human beings.

The sages have taught for centuries that we are already divine, but need only to become better human beings. Meditation can be practiced in silence or in the midst of our daily activities to achieve that goal.

8. Transcendence (Samadhi)

A yoga maxim states that one should teach what one practices and practice what one teaches. I will not speak about *samadhi* except to say that the student can experience a deep state of tranquility and bliss which is beyond thinking, where there are no more questions and no more thoughts, where a sense of oneness exists, and then even that drops away. As soon as we think, "Ah, this is it," the "it" is lost.

Many runners experience a high in their running; musicians and artists speak of this same inner peak experience. Yoga students describe the different levels of existence, consciousness, and then bliss in meditation, but all words fall short of the reality. It must be experienced and cannot be read about.

The uninterrupted flow of meditation for a sustained period of time leads to *samadhi,* which is absolute bliss.

§

Spirituality is the essence of every woman's being; in truth it is the essence of every being. It is quite easy to develop spiritual characteristics when you are surrounded by people of similar intentions, but it is more difficult to maintain your beliefs and practice them in situations where others are not practicing in the same way. The royal path of yoga offers a simple pattern for use in daily living. It guides us to live in the external and internal worlds both, to love all and exclude none, and to find greater awareness of the peace that lies within us waiting to bring us joy.

The essence of our being is spirituality, and the essence of spirituality is love. Women love to love: to nurse the children, to serve the family, to care for the sick, to share affection, to work in the business realm, to improve the world community. The formula for success is simple. All actions will be successful if they are done according to our true conscience, with a quiet, neutral mind, selflessly, with the results surrendered for the benefit of others.

For this success, we need all the commitments: non-violence in how we approach and deal with the situations of life; truthfulness in thought, word, and deed; non-stealing of material goods or credit or blame; self-control in mind, action, and speech; non-hoarding of what is achieved; purity of mind and purpose; contentment in the action and its results; heated effort toward what we believe in; proper study of our capacity, the situation and our role in it; and surrender of the results and of ourselves to God. Then we are ready to begin, to move out into the world and put into effect that which comes from within, our belief becoming actualized and manifested for the improvement of all.

After taking action we return to our center through withdrawing our senses from their objects and activities; through concentration first on our task and later within ourselves on breathing and silence; and finally through deep meditation to the center of consciousness within. As the drop returns to the ocean, we return to the ocean of bliss within and reunite with our true nature of spirituality.

Again we emerge to act in the world, each time bringing more of that peace with us. Finally we dwell in that peace all the time, even while acting in the world.

I pray that all may come to know this peace and that the deepest peace may be with us always; that we find our way to it daily, hourly, minute to minute, and finally dwell in it forever.

Dorothy Hale is founder and director of the Yoga Meditation Center in Minnetonka, Minnesota. A native of New York City, Dorothy attended the Spence School and worked as administrative assistant at Doubleday and Company. She moved to Minneapolis to work at Honeywell and also attended the University of Minnesota, majoring in Humanities.

Her study of yoga began in 1972 at the Center for Higher Consciousness, Minneapolis. A few years later she opened the Center of Enlightenment in Minnetonka teaching yoga, meditation, and holistic health, resigning her business career of twenty-two years to devote her life to teaching others the benefits of yoga. In 1976 Dorothy attended a two-year residential training program at the Himalayan International Institute of Yoga Science and Philosophy under the guidance of Swami Rama of the Himalayas. She also worked as an administrative assistant at the Institute and assisted in the publications department.

Currently the principal teacher at the Yoga Meditation Center, Dorothy is also a consultant to area physicians. She counsels and lectures on the therapeutic use of yoga, breathing techniques, and meditation as non-drug alternatives for illness and as aids to spiritual awareness and the quest for self-unfoldment.

Perfection of the body consists of beauty, radiant complexion, grace, strength, and virtual indestructibility.

Yoga Sutras

Woman's Body and Spirituality

Chandra Patel

Spirituality, as Carol Ochs writes, means coming into a relationship with reality.[1] It is understanding the meaning of life or realizing the Self. This can occur through religion in its broad sense of belief in divine power manifest either through a system of faith or through insights into the common experiences of everyday life. The lives of saints and sages from the East and West show the latter quite clearly. Buddha's enlightenment began by seeing an old man, a sick man, and a dead man. Most of us have seen these things; they are not extraordinary in any way. They were the instrument to Buddha's enlightenment, however, because in trying to understand what the experiences meant, they sparked his quest for the meaning of life. For St. Ignatius of Loyola it was a severe wound in battle; for St. Augustine it was the death of his beloved mother; for St. Francis it was the feeling of guilt and disgust over his carefree life in Assisi; for Ghandi it was the agony of discrimination and injustice for his people in South Africa; for Mother Teresa it was death and suffering in squalid, poverty-stricken areas of Calcutta. Jesus himself had a critical point when at Gethsemane he was "sorrowful unto death" (Matt. 26:37). Thus spirituality is understanding reality--the value of life and its meaning--through the everyday experiences of our lives.

The traditional concept of spirituality is, however, quite different. From its viewpoint, we are told that the only way to reach spiritual maturity is by living an ascetic life within a religious community. We can thus portray the spiritual being as a man living a celibate life in a monastery, wearing special robes, practicing mortification and fasting in order to escape from the temptations of the flesh. Traditional writings urge denial of life and withdrawal from the world: "Fear not the dead, but flee the living and the things of the world."[2] The common lives of ordinary

men and women, lives of domestic love, work, and social
life are considered temptations of the world and unworthy
of spirituality. Activities like baking, planting, and weaving
can be a part of spirituality provided they take place
within a religious community and are carried out in the
prescribed way for the service of God. Work as it is experienced in everyday life by most people is not recognized
as having spiritual merit or purpose. The religious community and the relationship its members have with its leader
and other members is important, but the community in
which most human beings live cannot be important from
the aspect of gaining spiritual merit. The world itself is
viewed negatively as material, sexual, and a potential trap
for a would-be seeker of God.

On these terms, love can only be a part of spirituality if it is restricted to the love of God or asexually to a
fellow member of the religious community. One may expand
this community to embrace abstract humanity provided,
however, that this 'humanity' excludes most women. In
traditional scriptures women are considered temptations,
not human beings. Their bodies are considered evil, real
obstacles to a true spiritual life. To achieve enlightenment
one must view life not for living and enjoying, but as a
vale of tears, only as a means to a goal beyond itself,
which is a relief from tainted flesh, an achievement of
salvation.

By denying the existence of true spirituality outside
a formal religious community we deny the majority of
humanity the spiritual value of their lives. By denying the
worth of the body and sexuality, we deny the maturing
growth of our everyday experiences. Similarly, the exclusion
of women and women's unique experiences as expressions
of spirituality is likely to be detrimental not only to women
but also to the spiritual life of all people.

Because women in most societies have been relegated
to conditions of powerlessness, servitude and other physical
and psychological disadvantages, they are left frightened,
confused, and vulnerable. Despite recently legalized equal
opportunities, very few top jobs are filled by women.
Although there are more women voters than men voters,
less than ten percent of the members of Parliament or
Congress are women. In less developed countries the plight
of unmarried women is even worse: unescorted women are

not allowed admission to restaurants, hotels, and clubs where single men can enter with pride; facilities like credit cards, mortgages, hire purchase, or bank borrowing are particularly difficult for women who are single, widowed or divorced.

Despite their subjugation and subordinate social status, women remain sober, refined, strong, and attractive. They learn endurance and silent suffering from their alienation. Endurance and suffering themselves represent a triumph that is real. The secret lies in the tremendously potent power of submission. By remaining calm and firm, by surrendering to noble causes with persistence, they conquer adversity. In the end they triumph. Resistance is futile before the power of their endurance. In spite of their undervaluation they remain a real source of strength to society and by their strength become the center around which the family pivots.

The fact of women's subjugation is not just a modern phenomenon. It has pervaded our society through the biblical era for thousands of years. The Bible itself, through its stories of women's mistreatment and humiliation has been used to justify women's subordinate social status. Similar stories in the scriptures of other religions have kept women in a subservient position in many cultures. How should we interpret such stories?

With Ochs, let us examine the story of Hagar, the Egyptian maidservant of Abraham's wife, Sarah. When Sarah realized that she was barren she decided to have a son through her maid. Hagar thus became pregnant by Abraham. As Sarah's self-esteem fell, she started abusing Hagar and treating her very harshly. Eventually Hagar was cast out and left to die. The angel of the Lord found her by a spring of water in the wilderness and told her to go back to her mistress and submit to the harsh treatment. The voice said, "Behold, you are with child and shall bear a son; you shall call him Israel, for the Lord has paid heed to your suffering." Hagar returned to servitude, her son was born, and she called him Ismael. As luck would have it, Sarah also had a son, Isaac, in her old age. Once again Hagar and Ismael were sent away with some bread and water, for Sarah told Abraham, "The son of that slave shall not share in the inheritance with my son, Isaac." Hagar wandered in the wilderness of Bath-Sheba, but when her supply of water had gone, she left the child under one of the bushes and sat down at a distance: "Let me not look on as the child dies." Sitting there alone, she burst into tears. But, as the story goes, the angel of God then called Hagar and said, "Fear not, for God has heeded the cry of the boy. Come, lift him up and hold him by the hand for I will make a great nation of him." Then God opened her eyes and she saw a well of water, and realized that God was with the child.[3]

Even though she was humiliated and mistreated, it is difficult to see Hagar with eyes full of pity. Her endurance and strength command our respect and tremendous reverence. For the sake of her child, she was able to endure and sustain herself even in the most arid times. She was able to live and pass on the gifts of life, love, trust, and faith. She had the capacity to remain open to forces which transformed her.

"Every woman on earth who sincerely desires to discover the truth of her femininity should spend some time in India, the land where God is woman."[4] So writes Meenakshi Devi of Anand Ashram about Mother India. The country is said to have a feminine soul, and it worships God as the Divine Mother who takes many forms. She is fierce, powerful, and vengeful as Kali; benevolent and kind as Durga; a warrior queen as Meenakshi; a seductive temptress as Kamakshi; an eternal virgin as Kanya Kumari. She stimulates knowledge and creativity as Saraswati, and distributes wealth as Lakshmi.

Women are in a position to reveal the nature of reality and shed light on the questions of the meaning and value of life through insights into the experiences of life which are unique to them--like childbirth and mothering--in addition to potential insights which can be gained through experiences common to all human beings: love, fear, joy, loss, trust, despair, ecstasy, birth, and death. What is required is a consciousness that will reflect on these experiences and that will not let go until their meaning has been understood. Carol Ochs suggests that a relationship with reality fulfills our human potential and is open to all who are open to the full human experience. It is important to remember that it is not the experience itself but the insight into experience that leads to spirituality. A life structured so as to leave no time for reflection is a life of flight."[5]

Many scriptures tell us to ignore the body and sublimate it through penance and loathing in the name of spirituality. But the word 'religion' is derived from the Latin *religare,* meaning "to bind together." True religion could therefore be "the conscious self-effort to bind together in ever-expanding states of consciousness the body, the mind, and the soul toward the bliss of God-communion."[5] This definition also comes close to the aim of yoga, the word itself derived from the Sanskrit root *yuj,* meaning "to join or to reunite." In the cosmic plan of evolution, the soul, mind, and body are intended to be in harmonious unity in trinity where the body and the mind should be the temple and vehicle for the soul to express itself. It is interesting to note that the word 'individual' comes from the Latin *indivisus,* meaning "not divided," or "being one in the soul, mind, and body." Thus our body is far from a hindrance to our spiritual life. It is an important and necessary element to it. The image we have of our body reflects and affects our entire being, spiritually as well as culturally.

The remainder of this essay discusses ways for women to gain spiritual experience through their bodies.

Spirituality in Sexuality and Reproduction

Humankind is often a victim of calamity. Natural as well as man-made disasters lead to epidemics and premature deaths. However, the human race has survived the ice age, thousands of years of wars, black death, and millions of other epidemics, and will survive the space age, too, because we have been empowered with a most effective weapon whose custodian is woman.

Women have the primary responsibility for the survival of the human race. Man may feel proud of his dazzling technical achievements and his control over the environment, but no man can reproduce another human being. To ensure that every women devotes herself unceasingly to this vital task, nature has infused her with sexual energy unsurpassed in the animal kingdom. This vital energy is passed from mother to daughter in the embryo. Female sex hormones which pass out of the mother's bloodstream into the fetal circulation develop the female genitals of the embryo. The

all-powerful female hormones prime the ovaries of the
female embryo so that, when the time comes, they can
produce massive amounts of hormones themselves.

At the time of puberty, the girl undergoes dramatic
physical alterations. Even more important are the subtle
and profound emotional changes which evolve and accelerate
over the next few years. The result is a woman. She now
has the ability to create a new human being. Once a man
lends his services for a few moments, the entire process
of reproduction depends on the woman. Using the raw
material of her own body, a unique, new human being is
produced. She converts a few drops of seminal fluid into a
professor, a prime minister, or a saint.

> Through the insight into the experience of women passing
> on the gift of life, we discover that what is deathless is
> not a creation, but participation in the ongoing process
> of creating.[6]

Tremendous changes occur in the woman's body
during the months of pregnancy, and with overwhelming
rapidity. Most of these changes are beyond her control.
She cannot know or control multitudes of factors essential
for the healthy development of her baby, but she surrenders
because she believes and trusts in the reality that a higher
power will take care of her and support her baby's growth
and well-being.

When faced with pain our instincts signal us to
flee. However, Ochs reminds us that pain stimuli can be
interpreted according to the way we are conditioned. Most
women in Western cultures have learned from the Bible
that they must bring forth children in pain; thus they will
most likely interpret all sensations during labor as pain
unless they are reconditioned. The stage of labor called
'crowning' has been described as the most painful experience a woman could have, yet those who are prepared for
natural childbirth and trust their bodies find this experience
intensely joyful. The difference between the prepared and
the unprepared woman is that of attitude, the difference
between trust and fear. Fear heightens the perception of
pain and leads the mother to fight against the process of
labor rather than cooperate with her body. Trust leads to
the reinterpretation of stimuli, letting go of the fight, and
allowing the higher power, which is bringing forth the baby,

to have control.[7]

In a study of several Guatemalan mothers about to give birth, researchers studied the effect of a companion at the birth. Traditionally in Guatemala, as in many other cultures, a mother is accompanied by a female friend who lends moral support during labor and childbirth. Dr. Roberto Sosa and colleagues found that women who were attended by a friend during labor and childbirth had far fewer complications requiring medical interventions than those without companions. Not only did they have fewer complications, but mothers who were accompanied by friends had shorter labor and easier delivery, they stayed awake longer after delivery, and they smiled at, stroked, and talked to their newborn infants more.[8]

It is suggested that stress, fear, and anxiety could aggravate pain and are more likely to complicate labor and childbirth. Whereas trust in God in making her instrumental in this supreme task, or the presence of a trustworthy friend can reduce pain and complications by relieving anxiety.

Mothering as a Spiritual Experience

Women can develop spiritually because of their insights derived from their capacity to bear and nurture children. They can realize through mothering not only what they can give, but also what they must have received. In the awareness that we were mothered, we acknowledge that we too were once helpless and utterly dependent, that we were nurtured and sustained by caring parents and that the life that flows through us is a gift. The result of such recognition is not only gratitude to our mother but a lessening of fear in ourselves and a willingness to pass on the gift to our own children.[9]

Mothering involves deep, unselfish love. And love is the essential soil in which femininity blossoms. Throughout babyhood the mother enjoys special intense intimacy with her baby. She nuzzles its neck, kisses its hands, nibbles its toes. Mothering also involves physically caring for the infant--nourishing, nurturing, cleaning, comforting. It means holding, caressing, petting, and pampering. It means protecting the infant from hostile environments: testing the bath water, keeping it away from a hot iron or a boiling kettle, and ensuring that it doesn't fall off the bed or suffocate under a pillow. It means being aware of the infant's sensitivity and making necessary adjustments for its auditory sensitivity to loud noises, visual sensitivity to bright lights, kinesthetic sensitivity to touch and temperature.[10] Her love pours like a cascade of sunlight into the hearts of the young, enabling them later to pass to the next generation what they themselves received.

The Indian scriptures say that when two people get together to produce a child, they should be in a beautiful place, they should have great love for each other, they should eat nutritious food, and have higher thoughts. Whatever qualities the parents have will automatically be imbibed by the child.[11]

It is also said that mothers can mold their children in whatever way they wish. There is an ancient Indian legend about a queen named Madalasa. Madalasa's father had taught her yoga meditation and wisdom and so whenever she conceived a child she would think about God. As she carried the child in her womb she filled her awareness with the universal God. After the child was born she would sing, "O my child, you are ancient, you are truth, you are consciousness, you are the absolute." Madalasa had seven sons. They all grew up to become yogis and attained enlightenment. After they had all gone the king said to Madalasa, "What have you done? Who will succeed to the throne? After all, I am king and need an heir." She told him not to worry: "One more child will be born." When the eighth son was born, Madalasa began to think differently. She sang, "You are very brave, you are courageous, you will take care of your subjects with great righteousness." When that child grew up he became the king.

Whatever we want our children to learn we should first learn ourselves. We should imbibe it in the essence of our bodies and mind. We should make it alive in the atmosphere of our home. Then our own state will affect our children naturally and we will not have to teach them anything.

It is said that our basic attitude towards the world, as well as towards our bodies, is fashioned early in the way our mother holds us. Ochs reminds us that an infant is not yet an integrated being, and so it is closely bound to the mother in a unique relationship. In many ways being held with care and concern by the mother is an integrating experience for the infant in a world with many confused experiences. Such integration requires the mother to know in depth the infant's experiences and be totally devoted to it.

Loving the child also means loving it for itself and not for what it can give to us. As the infant grows it moves from total dependence to relative independence and the mother must let go of the original closeness to allow the infant to grow and develop physically and psychologically. Any failure of adaptation on the part of the mother can be a hindrance in the child's capacity to become an integrated unit. Thus holding on is essential for the infant's being and well-being, while letting go is essential for its growth.[12]

Even in those cultures where women are treated poorly, the mother is not denied the opportunity to feed her baby every few hours, and thus revel in the intimacy of the bodily contact that the act of breastfeeding brings. In some cultures, the skin contact between mother and infant is prolonged into toddlerhood. African babies are cradled against their mothers' bodies day and night. The observation that they cry far less than European babies has started the fashion of baby slings in many Western countries. In some hospitals this cocooning closeness is being tried against the warm body of the mother instead of in an incubator. We have found that placing premature babies in incubators or hospital nurseries can lead to the failure of bonding between mother and baby, depression in the mother, and at worst, baby battering later on.

Winnicott explains that the baby does not need to be given the correct feed at the correct time so much as to be fed by someone who loves feeding her baby. Without the mother's pleasure the whole procedure is lifeless and mechanical. The baby's needs are not just for food, warmth, shelter, and sleep; it has humanistic needs for relationship. The mother fulfills this need first, but the need for relationship seems to persist throughout life. The pleasure the woman takes in what she does for the infant very quickly lets the infant know that there is a loving human being behind the action.

Ochs says that mothering teaches us about love: its physical, caring, knowing aspects and its letting go aspect.

If we experience ecstasy as our infant falls asleep in our arms after a frenzied crying, then that experience is significant, too. We must not, however, allow an experience to become an end in itself, but an opportunity for understanding and intuition. The insights that occur naturally in the course of mothering are the need to give oneself completely to the physical and spiritual care of the infant, the need to know by empathetic understanding, the need to endure self-discipline, the need to accept the child's development through trial and error, the necessity to love the child not as a possession but as belonging to itself, and the necessity of letting go. These are all spiritual experiences of women which complement and correct the insights of traditional spirituality.[13]

Letting go of our child leads us to think and relate to the world in a non-possessive, non-controlling way. If we really wish to pass on the gift of life and not view our child as a possession, we must let go. The desire to hold on becomes an obstacle to the child's independence and its own enlightenment.

As the mother teaches her child to let go its nightly struggle against sleep she is reminded of her own need to let go. As she helps the shy toddler meet the world halfway, she is reminded of her need to be more open and welcoming. As she teaches her child to deal with conflicts, she is reminded of the lessons she needs to relearn. Motherhood affords the opportunity of consciously reliving childhood--the process which was formerly unconscious.[14]

Spirituality in Disease and Healing

The dominant theory of human function in medicine today is that of Cartesian dualism. In fact, modern medicine views humans in this way: there is a fundamental split between the mind, the spirit, and the body, and as a rule there is no interaction between them. The body works on a mechanical principle. The non-material mind or spirit cannot, even in principle, affect the mechanistic, material body. Since disease is viewed as a mechanical breakdown or a material process, it is confined to the body, and the spirit can neither cause it nor heal it.

As mentioned earlier, it is not enough to mechanically feed a baby; to treat someone in a mechanistic way is to threaten the relationship with that person. Freud stated in his late writings that he was concerned not with scientific knowledge but with empathetic understanding, not unlike the mother's knowledge of her infant. In psychoanalysis, he says, the rational account of etiological factors brought to the surface from the depth of suppressed material in the subconscious may be correct but not therapeutic. This may explain why patients frequently do not get better. Those who do improve do not do so because of the knowledge of the facts; more important is the relationship which develops between the patient and the therapist during the course of analysis. Their relationship of trust, respect, understanding, and empathy is the therapeutic agent.

Similarly, before modern scientific research methods were established, medical practitioners used substances which were of dubious value, if not positively harmful, by today's standards. Yet patients often got better because the patients, as well as the doctors, believed in the treatment and both were able to establish a positive, trusting relationship. Even now there are practitioners using animal, vegetable, and mineral products whose value is doubtful. But because of the positive and trusting relationships between patients and practitioners alternative medicine remains popular. How often have we heard of a recovery when doctors have stepped back and said, "We've done all we can; now it's up to her" and contrary to all expectations the patient musters up her inner strength or faith to pull herself out of a seemingly hopeless illness?

Love of one's self, including love of one's body, seems to be the single most important element in good health. A woman's self-image is the catalyst that triggers her happiness or despair, as well as illness or healing. Strange as it may seem, religious nuns who consider their bodies unimportant and not worth loving, even though they live dedicated lives, have a greater incidence of breast cancer compared to ordinary women who love themselves and are loved.

Dr. Joan Bonysenko reviewed papers on the outcome of cancer patients.[5] In one study from London, it was reported that of women with breast cancer, those likely to live longest are those who love themselves most, who do not become anxious and depressed, and who have faith and inner confidence. They have "fighting spirit." They want to be well and plan to be well. They say from the outset that they are going to do all they can to beat the disease.

In another investigation 75% of all the women who showed the "fighting spirit" after a mastectomy from breast cancer triumphed over their disease and had a favorable medical outcome five years later, compared with only 22% of women who responded with stoic acceptance or a hopeless outlook. Looking at it differently, of all the women who initially reacted with helplessness and hopelessness, 88% were dead within the next five years. On the other hand, of the women who were disease-free after five years only 46% had shown such negative emotions at the start of their illness. In general, those who were least successful in fighting cancer were described as despairing, helpless, or poor copers. Developing coping skills which foster a sense of belief and control has been an important factor in the longer survival of cancer patients.

Doctors Abeloff and Darogatis in a study of thirty-five women with metastatic breast cancer found that long-term survivors asked their physicians a lot of questions and expressed their emotions freely.[16] Because of this they were often considered difficult or uncooperative patients. In fact, they ask questions because they want to understand their illness and want to participate fully in their treatment. They wish to educate themselves to be specialists in their own care. Similarly, Sandra Levy at the National Cancer Institute of America showed that patients with breast cancer who expressed their emotions freely survived longer than those who were passive and apparently showed little distress. Those 'bad' patients who found meaning in their lives fought their disease well and had more killer T cells (the kind of white blood cells that destroy cancer cells) than those docile, 'good' patients. The former found meaning in whatever life thrust upon them and began to look within for the strength to fight and endure.[17]

Dr. Borysenko proposed that elicitation of the relaxation response or meditative techniques might provide unique facilitation of coping for those struggling with cancer. In particular, meditation rooted in a deep faith or strong belief of some sort, may be an excellent tool to help patients keep their spirits up and even live longer.[18]

Doris Schwerin describes her experience in hospital

the night before she was to undergo a radical mastectomy. As usual she was offered a sedative after the last visitor had gone home, but she decided not to take it. She also decided not to distract her mind by watching television or reading a book. Instead she thought about what the next day would bring: pain, change in her body image, and even the possibility of death. In those hours before surgery she was in solitude, not unlike the solitude an ascetic seeks in the mountains or deserts in search of spiritual experience or personal salvation, except that this was thrust upon her by circumstances not of her own choosing. She decided to seek support and strength within herself. After surgery she returned to the world and to her family and her friends enlightened and transformed through what she had learned about herself and life, anxious to pass on the gift to others in need.

Doris describes the circumstances surrounding her mastectomy as leading her to rethink and reshape her relationship with herself and her family. She proclaimed that she felt whole for the first time after her mastectomy. Her healing began while watching a family of pigeons building a nest on a window ledge across the way. Their efforts at building led her to understanding, and then to compassion, and finally to the connection to her own life. The relationships she saw clearly led her to eventually heal herself.[19]

There are numerous examples of women who go through similar experiences courageously confronting adversity head on. Distracting ourselves does not cure. By experiencing pain or grief and working through them, we can gain a strength that fights for control, reason, perspective, and faith that is adequate to meet all there is of life, its pain and delight, its loveliness, and its fractured relationships as well as its joyful and supporting relationships.[20]

Both men and women are subject to hopelessness, but because of their divergent roles, the situations that trigger despair and depression for them are different. Men are generally better able to express anger, while women tend to suppress anger and become depressed. Dr. Bernie Segal reported a case of a woman who developed cancer after her children grew up and left home as saying, "I had an empty space in me and the cancer grew to fill it."[21] He reported that housewives who feel unfulfilled or trapped in an unenjoyable role are more likely to get cancer. He quoted the results of a study showing that housewives get 54% more cancer compared with the general population, and 157% more compared with women who work outside the home and feel more fulfilled.

When Dr. Herbert Benson had an audience with His Holiness the Dalai Lama to request his permission to study mind-body feats of Tibetan monks in the Himalayas, the Dalai Lama requested that Dr. Benson also take a look at Tibetan medicine. In particular he said, "Pay attention to the three main components of Tibetan medicine: the belief of the doctor, the belief of the patient, and the karma [the spiritual force generated by interaction or relationship] between the two." Dr. Benson suggests that in the West, we have been using this powerful effect without acknowledging it. We brush aside the issue by saying it is a placebo effect, as though it is an undesirable effect. If both the patient and the doctor start with a belief in a common spiritual or non-physical curative power, he says, remarkable things begin to happen. The vast majority of patients--about 75%--are helped merely because they visit their doctor, believe in him, and get assurance from him. The trust between doctor and patient can actually alter a patient's physiology and effect the cure or relief of bodily diseases.[22]

Orthodox medicine has made tremendous advancements; many killer diseases can now be cured thanks to scientific discoveries. Unfortunately, it is moving away from basic human requirements. When Prince Charles addressed the British Medical Association on the occasion of its 150th Anniversary in 1982, he reminded the doctors that,". . . through the centuries healing has been practiced by folk-healers who are guided by traditional wisdom that sees illness as a disorder of the whole person. . . I would suggest the whole imposing edifice of modern medicine, of all its breath-taking successes is like a Tower of Pisa, slightly off balance. The health of human beings is so often determined by their behavior, their food, and the nature of their environment."[23]

It is not surprising that holistic medicine which includes practices like relaxation, meditation, and faith healing is making a comeback into the stream of conventional medicine.

Spirituality in Death and Bereavement

Much of the hatred of the flesh stems from the fear of death. However, we cannot achieve spiritual maturity--coming into a relationship with reality--if we are governed by the fear of death. We have to come to terms with death and dying.

The fear of death is common to all who are terminally ill and for those who care for them. This fear creates an unholy distance between the care-givers and the care-receivers. It can take the form of denial of the meaning in life. Facing this fear head-on can not only lessen the fear, but help those who are dying to achieve some meaning in life. When Elisabeth Kubler-Ross asked terminally ill patients if they would submit themselves to an interview attended by medical students, 98% agreed. In analyzing why so many patients were willing to share their experiences, she writes:

> Many patients feel utterly hopeless, useless and unable to find any meaning to their existence at this stage. . . . Another aspect which is perhaps more important is the sense that their communication might be important, might be meaningful, at least to others. There is a sense of service at a time when these patients feel that they are of no earthly use to anybody anymore.

And more than one patient put it:

> I want to be of some use to somebody. Maybe by donating my eyes or my kidneys, but this seems so much better, because I can do it while I am still alive.[24]

The need to give, more than the need to receive, does not diminish even when we are on our death bed. We find even then that we can contribute, that our soul was destined to perform and give to this world, that we could still discover a way of being.

Women's insights into death occur from their roles of caring for the aged and dying--care undertaken with the aim of easing the passage through life, not of conquering death. In some way, women are familiar with the process because in the similar course of seeing their children mature and leave, they have found a way to transcend that loss.

Elisabeth Kubler-Ross summarizes a major insight

she gained from her extensive experiences with the dying:

> It appears that people who have gone through a life of
> suffering, hard work and labor, who have raised their
> children and have been gratified in their work, have shown
> greater ease in accepting death with peace and dignity
> compared to those who have been ambitiously controlling
> their environment, accumulating material goods and a
> great number of social relationships, but few meaningful
> interpersonal relationships which would have been avail-
> able at the end of life. [25]

The quotation reminds us that dying is learning to let go
and let be. Only when we have faced the meaning of
death can be become really free to live. Women's intimate
role in caring for the dying allows them to have a deep
understanding of death and compassion for the bereaved.

Bereavement can be overwhelming. Suddenly the
light is gone and the darkness seems to pervade every
waking moment. Fear grips with intensity and negative
emotions begin to invade. One can no longer think ration-
ally or act with common sense. But even through such
circumstances we can learn compassion and love. As the
Tibetan Dalai Lama says, love and compassion are basic to
any religion. [26]

Ochs reminds us of Buddha's compassion in the
midst of suffering by retelling the parable of the mustard
seed. In the story, a woman's only son has died. In grief
she asked all her neighbors for medicine to revive him.
The neighbors responded by saying that the child is dead
and nothing could revive it. But the woman wouldn't believe
them. She continued to search for medicine to revive her
son. Eventually she came across a man who said that
while he himself could not supply medicine, he knew of a
physician who could and directed her to the Buddha. Buddha
answered her plea by asking for a handful of mustard
seeds to be taken from a house where no one had ever
died--neither child, husband, parent or friend. The woman
went from house to house but found no household in which
a beloved person had not died. She came to realize that
her grief was selfish. She then overcame her grief by
loving others as she had loved her son.

Conclusion

Spirituality defined as coming into a relationship with reality is not reserved for any select group of religious elite, but is available to all. It is the culmination of our natural maturation process, the fulfillment of humanity. Every life is significant and potentially revealing of reality, and a woman's life is especially so. Our bodies, as the first and most basic touch with reality, are necessary in the spiritual developmental process.

Through sexuality and the power to reproduce, women have been made instrumental to the greatest miracle of this world--the creation of new life and sustenance of the human species. The mother's love in caring for the child physically, emotionally, psychologically, and spiritually teaches her when to hold and when to let go, teaches her the value of a child as belonging to itself, and how to love it without possessing it. Mothering thus also offers a major opportunity for spiritual achievement. Similarly, work provides an opportunity to understand shared values and through that understanding, to contribute to full spirituality. Birth, death, illness, joy, grief, pain, and pleasure all provide an opporttnity to gain insight into the meaning and value of life.

It is, however, important to realize that reality is larger than our conception of it. Reality has the capacity to transform our consciousness, but only if we are open to it. If we women structure our experience so that we challenge our narrow conception of reality, then we expand the possibility of gaining insights from our day to day experiences and thus allow reality to transform us.

Chandra Patel, M.D., F.R.C.G.P. is an internationally acclaimed expert on the prevention and control of high blood pressure and the management of heart disease. Born in India in 1931, she received her medical degrees in England. For the last sixteen years she has worked as a general practitioner in Surrey with a special interest in helping patients with heart disease to help themselves rather than be totally reliant on drugs. To this end she pioneered the use of relaxation and meditation in medicine. During this time she was also a member of the executive board of the Southwest Thames Faculty of the Royal College of General Practitioners. In 1980 she was awarded the British Heart Foundation Award, and in 1981 the James Mackenzie Award for her research in cardiovascular medicine.

Dr. Patel is a Fellow of the Royal Society of Medicine, an Honorary Fellow of the Society of Behavioral Medicine (USA), a Trustee of the British Holistic Medical Association, a member of the Biofeedback Research Society of America, the Advisory Council of the Yoga Biomedical Trust Cambridge, a member of the Advisory Council of the Centre for Prevention and Behavioral Medicine (Canada), and other societies too numerous to list. She has written many articles for medical journals and is the author of the new book *Fighting Heart Disease*.

Dr. Patel is currently Senior Clinical Lecturer in the Department of Community Medicine, University College London and Middlesex Hospital Medical School, and is a welcome speaker at professional gatherings throughout Europe and America. She is married and the mother of two grown children.

*In every mystical experience worthy of the name,
animus and anima collaborate in an act of love.*
                                    Henri Bremond

The Spirituality of Marriage

Anne Lamb

Born as individuals, we may or may not marry. Understanding of what marriage involves varies between people in more ways than it would be possible to describe, each having her or his own hopes and history to relate, though there are shared factors.

Marriage is the condition which exists when a man and woman become husband and wife, joined to each other in the expectation of continuing, reciprocal connection and commitment. The married couple join and are joined into a unique, private world of experience accompanied, very often, by keenest public interest and speculation. The exultation and pleasure of wedding is generally common to all concerned, past and present, as the anticipated delights, adventures, and adversities of the new pair are shared, together with hopes for the fruitfulness of their union. Their joining is enjoyed privately and publicly, inwardly and outwardly together.

Social anthropologists who investigate marriage customs report on what is done and go on to conjecture explanations and interpret their significance, thus discovering clues concerning the culture of the tribe. Ordinary travellers observe with interest what they happen to see: Neapolitan couples being photographed near the Sibyl's cave at Cumae; Hindus draped in garlands of scented orange glory; Americans who hold hands and exchange vows in the parental home or garden; Arabs who offer camels as bride price; the symbolic canopy above the heads of bride and groom at Jewish weddings. I am British, and writing in England where we have lately rejoiced with the Queen in the third of her children's marriages. "A princely marriage," wrote Bagehot, "is a brilliant edition of a universal fact."[1] It is local as well as universal, and the scenes at Westminster Abbey (and on an earlier occasion, St. Paul's) were transmitted round the world through the medium of television, directly apprehensible to viewers, and with words and music more or less understood and appreciated. Royalty heightens reality, offering representative action: personification of traditional and archetypal functions of depth and splendor which empitomize its own culture, be it in London or Bangkok, Tokyo, Oslo, or Kathmandu. When a culture expands into a great civilization, the source can be detected in its spiritual inspiration: the essence, the spirit of the thing, the primary impulse of its nature and development.

The conjunction of seen and unseen is symbolized in marriage by the wedding ring: blessed by the officiating parson, given in public, often exchanged each to each, witnessed by the congregation accompanied by the exquisitely disciplined ecstasy of the choir and the prayers of hope and goodwill of every well-wisher, present and absent.

In the *Book of Common Prayer,* the service (in the full sense of creatures offering and rendering service to the Creator) is called 'The Solemnization of Matrimony.' It is personal, social, legal, moral, and spiritual together: whole and complete. It is a condition which brings out the very best and the very worst in us. We can tumble into it by accident of circumstance as well as through careful consideration and decision. We are warned not to enter into it 'lightly or wantonly,' though as often as not we neither hear nor heed nor can digest such precautions. Sometimes the very concept of 'solemnization' is repudiated, commitment evaded, and private life divorced from public, personal from communal experience, losing much-needed support and enrichment from family and friends.

Few, if any, of us reach our fullest potential. Apprehension includes anticipation as well as fear, which is the beginning of wisdom.

Spirituality

If there be aught spiritual in man, the will must be such. If there be a will, there must be a spirituality in man. . . . the will is in an especial and pre-eminent sense the spiritual part of our humanity.   Coleridge [2]

Thy kingdom come, thy will be done on earth as it is in heaven.   Matthew 6:10

The first hurdle is recognizable, that spiritual consciousness enlivens us to the principle of things: the theory
which abstracts form and order from the limits of appearance, and which brings understanding. We approach the
essential nature of things.

If we know what a car is for, and have access to
one, and the desire, we may learn to drive without being
expert mechanics. Once the engine has started, the journey
can begin, to continue until it ends at the destination.
Purpose and activity, object and subject interact interdepen-
dently. In our first world, this unity is our undoubted
being, and decisions follow impulse and inclination with
little hesitation beyond consciousness of danger, difficulty,
and perhaps the reactions of those who matter to us. In
the uncomplicated immediacy of infancy and early childhood, the life of the body is natural, needy, vulnerable,
enjoyable, as well as sometimes painful. Later, we may
develop consciousness which enlightens instinct, as well as
emotions and thought processes. A sensitive conscience
tunes our will, as we grow, towards resolution of conflicts.
Becoming a qualified car driver is one stage, making journeys with confident purpose is another, and the infinite
variety of motives bears comparison with possibilities in
other spheres of life. The instrument of control is the will
of the driver using the car, which is, for the time being,
the vehicle of the journey, disposable yet mobile and flexible within its limits, and itself needing care, maintenance,
and fuel as well as skilled driving.

In making and doing we express our being, our vital-
ity--learning and remembering, thinking and reflecting,
using our minds, responding and feeling with joy and misery
in our hearts. All together, our faculties unite the very
essence of our vital existence. We have, within ourselves,
this potential marriage of flesh and spirit, body and soul.
The well-being of our psyche depends upon its health, and
often the balance is uneasy between the two. Self-denial
and the subjection of the flesh belong to situations where
the union is in danger of imbalance and is uneasy. Some
tend to regard such efforts as inhibiting, repressive reactions
to natural appetites. On the other hand are those to whom
control is as indispensable as training to an athlete, pains-
taking care for detail in the dedication of the scholar, or
the devotion of the loyal and faithful servant, disciple, and

friend--the sovereign spirit which orders our being. The success of our marriage with ourselves will condition, qualify, and influence our marriage with another.

Emotion is constantly confused with and mistaken for spiritual resolution. It is the spark which ignites our will, but if we are subject, we are as likely to be dominated by its undisciplined squads in the pursuit of rapid gratification instead of focusing our efforts to objective purposes. Spiritual purpose is like the refining fire which re-creates and re-forms as it consumes and illuminates those possessed by it. It is like the internal combustion which intensifies as we accelerate our car toward the objective when the way is open.

What is 'spirit'? What is meant by 'spirituality'? Is it nothing more or less than, in Coleridge's sense, pertaining to the will? Beyond the stimuli and storms of emotion are the calmer waters of reflection and judgment: the means through which purposes are considered, formulated, and resolved, and whereby we ponder, wonder, and think. Perception and imagination extend and enhance our vision, clarify hopes, and strengthen feeble knees.

Once this first hurdle is cleared, the next is to introduce ourselves to the variety of experiences traditionally described as 'spiritual.' Only the briefest summary can be attempted here.

The paradox of opposites is paramount--positive opposed to and co-existing with negative, as we value light when we also know darkness. Spiritual pain--guilt, failure, frustration, and defeat--become clearer when we have assumed purposes often unseen by outside observers, but clear aims and realizable aspirations within.

Spiritual life is inward beyond immediate reaction, and may become the source of balance, resolve, and of strength. It has a deeper as well as a higher purpose, extended as well as immediate, and raises our sights towards what may be continuing rather than temporary, eternal as well as temporal.

Alone as individuals, but not necessarily isolated, communal vision and purpose, if available, is a source of nourishment and strength. There is a formidable body of experience: local, national, and international, and increasingly available as our spheres interact, overlap, and depend on one another. An outstanding example of the discovery of ways of ascertaining communal will is the Parliament of England. In its earliest days, representatives of local communities (shires and boroughs) were called by the Crown to meet in Council, together with the Lords, Spiritual and Temporal. This traditional assembly has survived periods of stress and battle with varying degrees of authority and efficiency, depending in the last resort on the competence and conscientiousness of those who make it work: primarily its own members. Its function is to discover and express its will, 'the will of the house.' In Resolutions and Acts, this will is binding upon the whole community. We are expected, indeed obliged, to act accordingly: to obey the Road Traffic Acts, for instance, for the greater safety of all, in other words, for the common good.

The Crown summons, opens, and dissolves Parliament, and respects the will of the electorate in appointing the leader of her Government, and the policies then pursued, though she must be consulted in the sense of being informed, and warning or encouragement is within the conventions. The will of Parliament, approved by the Crown, becomes the law of the land. Like marriage, it is for better or for worse, and the traditional expectation of the coinherence of spiritual and temporal wears thin if 'temporal' is identified with 'secular' or 'worldly' rather than with the reality of practicality that, though qualified by human fallibility and imperfection, is capable of soundness and strength. This is the marriage of spiritual and temporal for public purposes. The nation is the community or greater 'polis' whose politics now accept, at least in principle, the feminine interest together with the masculine: inseparable yet distinct. A Conservative woman Prime Minister was unimaginable to most until it happened. A sovereign lady has notable and proven precedents.

The vision which a community has of itself is potentially realizable through the interaction between the people and the leaders. Testing judgments and purposes is a major function of constitutional democracy. It certainly tends to complicate and retard in the passage through procedures of consultation, but the enrichment of wisdom and, above all, acceptance of will changes the spirit of the community from fear to freedom, from subjection to a sense of responsibility: of participation on one hand and accountability on the other.

A different negative of 'spiritual' is 'carnal': raw and primitive, the physical untempered by considered, civilized, controlled purpose--too positive a negative for easy balance. Attempted marriage between antipathetic positives invites disaster, for their purposes are irreconcilable. Violence and disintegration are the likely result in community and in personal life. Fear and insecurity promote the probability of withdrawal into ineffectual helplessness, or the danger of overly prescriptive defences and rules. Fascism and racism feed on and breed public cruelty. Domestic tyranny and oppression, physical, emotional, and psychological aggression are the domestic counterpart.

The earliest use of 'spiritual' in our language was not always distinct from 'sense.' This is still so: "That idea makes sense. She is a sensible person. I can see the idea makes sense. I can see the spirit of the thing"--meaning what is beyond, or gives sense to, the obvious or physically observable. If 'spiritual' means 'immaterial' it then becomes abstract, and thinking is a process of abstraction and analysis. When 'spiritual' means 'sensible' the manifest interdependence of theory and practice is realized: the art of the possible. Otherwise, we may be like the driver when the gearbox is faulty: there is no motion. Without abstracting and comprehending theory, things may not 'make sense.' It is by the veritable discernment of principle, the recognition of purpose and function, understanding processes, that we begin to grasp the facts of life. At this stage, will emerges to become distinct from instinct. John Wycliffe's translation of St. Paul's comment on our life cycle reads: "It is sown a beastly body: it shall ryse a spiritual body."[3]

Coleridge's observations on will require the qualification that willpower is not quite the same as spiritual power. He goes on to say that "if there be a will, there must be a spirituality in man." Coleridge is looking for insight into the nature of 'spiritual religion,' and his next step is to consider moral science (also known at Oxford as philosophy). There are good and evil spirits, good-will and ill-will, both powerful, and occasionally at war within ourselves, as well as elsewhere. Any pursuit of spirituality which evades the momentous implications of this dichotomy of experience is looking for a refuge from reality. It is no less unbalanced than the dream of romanticized fantasy upon which some matrimonial adventurers set out.

Pure essence of spirit, materially, is alcohol: volatile, explosive, and dangerous unless treated with knowledge, respect, and care for its special dynamic purposes. The French word for gasoline (petrol) is essence, which communicates this essential quality. The French use of 'spirituelle' suggests a closer integration between intelligence, intellect, and evaluation than 'spirituality' in comtemporary English. A remaining part of the Puritan heritage on both sides of the Atlantic sustains some over-reaction to moral precepts as such. Associated with oppressive attitudes and joyless lives, it survives as more than a folk memory. I suspect, too, that feminism draws some of its energy from reaction to occasional masculine claims to a sort of moral authority which is based on precept rather than example, directive rather than co-operative, what might be called 'masculinism.'

The conventional embargo on religion as a topic of social conversation in England has amounted, in some circles, to near prohibition. There are cases where 'intellectual' or even 'serious' interests would substitute for 'religious' but might just as readily mean 'spiritual.' Winston Churchill once heard himself described as a pillar of the church, but demurred that he was not quite a pillar but perhaps a flying buttress. That he was a man of majestic will and spirit is beyond doubt, and in no sense a puritan.

I am approaching the connection between 'spiritual' and 'religious' by way of 'ecclesiastical' which, in English tradition, is the institutionalized form and order of faith. As soon as this is stated, it is necessary to recollect that the letter kills while the spirit gives life. True religion is the spirit in action: in thought, word, and work inseparably. Without the spiritual, the letter is dead. Without works, faith fails to find expression, and 'spirituality' little more than the pursuit of disengaged detachment. There is no marriage unless that condition is directed to the ministry of contemplative prayer.

The gap between emotional involvement and intellectual objectivity is occasionally bridged by refinement of feeling and cultivation of sensibility which is aesthetic rather than spiritual. Here again, the seesaw of emphasis and reaction facilitates exaggerations. The higher faculties of the mind are concerned with beauty as a form of truth as well as with theory and theology. Artists of quality harness sympathy and sensitivity together with clear perception and thought. Their work communicates spiritual quality in their medium: words, music, visual arts. Between the divergent ends of art for art's sake on one hand and academic analysis on the other, the finest critic is deeply appreciative and the genuinely talented artist will value and practice constructive criticism. Very occasionally the gifts co-exist to an exceptionally high degree, as in the case of Coleridge himself and, more recently, in T.S. Eliot. This degree of spiritual vitality is expressed in poetry and criticism which are amongst the treasures of English literature, uniting thought and feeling at the highest intensity.

Quick wits and a sense of humor are included in the French understanding of 'spirituel.' I would as soon praise Shakespeare's clowns as his great tragic heroes; both are manifestations of his vitality, humanity, and artistry.

In a last and most obvious sense, 'spiritual' describes any concern with spirits--angels and devils, witches and wizards, charmers and enchantresses--which reflect unseen powers. Few marriages would begin without the dreams and terrors which surround us in everyday life, and if too much imagination is a danger in any continuing relationship, too little can limit humor, sympathy, and necessary adventurousness. In matters of the heart some (even in this scientific age) turn readily to fortune tellers, astrologers, cults, and rituals in which the frontiers between superstition and enlightenment are opaque, if they exist at all. Our first world of nature is about the struggle for survival in health and wealth. If we grow to physical maturity, the further need for emotional stability and mental balance may bring us to consciousness of the potentialities of the human spirit. Intimations of divinity may lead us to pursue and cultivate the knowledge and experience which are the fruit of faith, and which I have called the inward marriage of body and soul.

Marriage

There is no doubt that marriage suits some people

better than others. It is the extreme case in human relationship, whether in time (of brevity or endurance), in
space (living together intimately or distantly), in fertility
or infertility of body and soul. There may be a friendship,
partnership, a cooperative duet, based on any level of com-
patibility and/or competition, but the bedrock is shared
lives including physical union which normally leads to
parenthood and family life. Polygamy, common among
primitive people but rejected in Christian civilization, has
become more prevalent in practice than recognized in
principle or law. Most western countries acknowledge
monogamy in the sense of not more than one wife (or
husband) at a time. Bigamy is theoretically disallowed.
Divorce increases, as does what is known as 'common law'
marriage.

English literature until comparatively recently has
tended to reflect both the conventions and customs of
marriage, together with exceptions and irregularities, in
the infinite variety, richness, and desolation of experience.
Chastity and fidelity, for centuries the acknowledged ideal
and ethical norm, have seemed to suffer some erosion
with our increased mobility, changing attitudes to widely
available contraception and vacillating values. Contemporary
literature is increasingly conscious of these and other
changes, as comparison of marriage in a novel of Jane
Austen or Charlotte Bronte with, for instance, one of
Margaret Drabble or Iris Murdoch quickly illustrates. You
cannot be unconventional unless there are conventions, and
conventions grow when a society is stable enough to sustain
manners which are in their turn a halfway house between
clear moral criteria and the wish to avoid giving offence.
Furthermore, our eccentricities, uncertainties, and conflicts
are the material of comedy and tragedy and what drama-
tists and novelists write about. Marriage is in a league of
its own.

The married state is also known as wedlock: a word
which exemplifies the binding, continuing nature of the
condition brought about by the vows made upon entering
it. Among the major aims of spiritual education is cultivation of clearer, fuller vision and of a well tuned heart and
will. Marriage is the immediate testing ground in that
either partner tends to be affected by the decisions and
actions of the other. It is concerned with intention and

with long term purpose, a fusion of need, vision, and hope. Each of these is of the self as well as of the other. Joy in marriage lives in the delight of understanding and care through which we express our love, given and received. It is, for most, elemental personal fulfillment, reaching every level of consciousness: physical, mental, moral. When all three are alive and capable of union, then the intensity of the partners enhances the possibilities of the marriage and its spiritual quality. If not, wedlock tends to become deadlock.

In every marriage there are at least two wills. Jewish friends, who tend to have a story for everything, say that the husband makes the big decisions, the wife makes the little decisions and also decides which are big and which are little. A husband may say: "I am the head, but she is the neck." The traditional promise of obedience by wife to husband in the English marriage service has, since 1928, been a matter for each couple to agree to themselves. Coincidentally, in the same year (under the Representation of the People Act), the franchise became equal to all adults--but for the vivid exceptions of peers, lunatics, and felons serving sentence.

"Two minds with but a single thought, two hearts that beat as one" is part of the folklore of lovers and describes the spirit of unity which is an ideal of marriage. Sheridan's advice to a young woman on marriage was always to let her husband have her way.

Beyond the personal, domestic details of a marriage are the family, community, and public aspects. The apparent independence of individuals in prosperous circumstance has given a lead to the idea that these two may be not only separable but separate: that private affairs have nothing to do with public. If spiritual consciousness is undeveloped or immature, there is a tendency to confuse sexuality and spirituality as the most significant reality, since the former is also a prime source of psychic energy. It is a natural but perilous confusion, and I realize at this point that it is no longer possible to avoid more definite reference to the distinction between 'spirituality' and 'religion.'

Religion without spirituality is comparable to marriage without love. Spirituality without religion has something in common with sexuality without marriage. These provocative assertions are useful in steering us away from exaggerated abstractions towards the inescapable paradox that one side of experience intensifies its opposite. We reach for principle amongst the chaos of the practical, only to discover exceptions, eccentricities, extreme cases which appear exempt. Our ancestors who saw celestial bodies gradually found out how they related to terrestrial. Hints were observable and observed, but the secrets of the patterns only slowly unfolded. We are reminded of the interdependence of practical and theoretical, and between different spheres of knowledge. Astronomy, for instance, requires both observation and mathematics, movement in place and time, here and elsewhere; past, present, and future, the very predictability acting as an invitation to predict from the stars more than their apparent movements. So it is with belief and behavior.

Nature cults grew in early searches towards sense beyond the senses, resting on the awe felt when some mystery was elucidated, some puzzle solved, some truth discovered. Linking the patterns of sunlight and heat in ancient Egypt to the rise and fall of the Nile waters, to the coming of Spring on the Eleusian plain in Greece, to celebrating the solstice at Stonehenge, the 'knowing' could be seen as powerful persons, priestly, capable of coordinating seen and unseen, and leading the celebrations of benefits which included rites to invoke beneficence.

Realization of the unity of things, their interaction and interdependence, was disclosed in a dawn of unique splendor to the consciousness of a migrant tribe: creation is all one, there is unity in diversity, diversity in unity, originating from one creating spirit. The human being who seeks, and listens, may hear that voice and may choose to follow or not. Adam and Eve evicted from Eden and losing their paradise, Abraham called to the Land of Promise. The spiritual is apprehended as the source of order and the means of understanding. Then, from theory to theism grows the confidence that this Spirit, the originator or Prime Mover, once known of is knowable. Still more than this, the becoming known which awaits the enquirer reveals the secrets of relations between people as well as with things. The principles which were clarified at Mount Sinai became universal and timeless, and concern creator, creature, and created (God, people, and things).

Having said there are at least two wills in marriage,

then the recognition of unity just described acknowledges the third which, once acknowledged, takes precedence over either one of the pair.

One of the greatest blessings of existence is that we can make use of the discoveries of others in practical and in theoretical matters. Hence our need for and dependence on experts and elders. An infant lives on milk without knowing anything about it. Most of what we need, use, and do in adult life derives from the accumulated understanding of its nature and operation by other people. We do well to become anything approaching expert in any detail of some speciality of a skill or profession, and yet knowledge of transforming benefit, such as antiseptics and electricity, is widely available to our advantage.

The life of the spirit can be seen to be as essential and commonplace as mothers' milk, but to reach for maturer sustenance requires conscious knowledge and will as well as disciplined pursuit. There are vocabularies, of words as well as systems of thought, which approach language, philosophy that includes concepts and ideas, and doctrines associated with faith and religion. These vary between where you happen to live, your native tongue, and the culture to which you were born, or have embraced.

Spirituality rarely develops in a vacuum. Believers attached to the great religions have pursued the path of discipleship according to the insight and vision of the founder. Only people of intense spiritual power and originality offer this degree of inspiration, believing that to share in the essence, the Spirit, is the gift of the creator. Deists discover and disclose their experience of the deity whose will then is precedent. "Thy kingdom come, thy will be done" sums it up. What was seen as the third will in marriage may become the primary source of unity and harmony between the two human beings. Such marriages enjoy the support of the community which shares this outlook and commitment. The Christian ideal, for example, is as demanding as it may be strengthening.

Religious teaching is a formulation of beliefs tested in experience and expressed in the history and doctrine of that particular faith. It is a combining of the knowledge and experience of divinity, within the life, thought, worship, prayer, and praise of the community of believers. Jesus was born into the tradition of revelation through promise and law known in Jewish history, known through patriarchs and prophets who lived in the spirit. He lived the unity of seen and unseen, the healing spirit and redeeming love which make into one things earthly and heavenly. His heart uniting spirit and matter, disclosing sacrament in practice and symbol in theory, like the blood bank which makes the saving transfusions possible. Thus, healing and teaching are at the heart of Christian civilization, as care and understanding, self-giving generosity and sacrifice are at the heart of marriage.

Suffering is inescapable, for we are often so very ill at ease with ourselves, each other and the world. This dis-ease is emotional and moral as much as, if not more than, physical. The animus and anima of our makeup, self and other, matter and spirit are part of the ding-dong rhythm of existence. Dissatisfaction and yearning for unison cause us to fly off, as often as not, into the skirmishes and battles of personal conflict while seeking, through inward struggle, for control, sublimation, and spiritual order. This is only the subjective aspect but, yet again, not always readily disentangled from the objective pursuit of what is true, in fact, in judgment and through faith. Approach to the spiritual means far more than a radical existentialism. It is an ever-increasing recognition of the sovereignty and power of the object--the spirit of the creator. In Christian spiritual life this is disclosed through the word made flesh. It is humbling and penitential. Restoration involves reorientation of both mind and emotion preceding, maintaining, and sustaining the purposes of will. Discipleship is not a self-invented exercise.

Mystics

Faith and devotion lead towards meditation and the contemplative life on one hand, and towards vigorous action on the other: hermits and crusaders, monasteries and missions, solitary study and active ministry together. In England we still sing the hymn, 'Onward Christian soldiers, marching as to war,' but the enemy is evil, and the army the mystical body known also as 'the communion of saints.' The relation between individuals with direct spiritual insight--mystics--and organized communities of believers is a controversial aspect of spirituality. It is rarely straightfowardly and often unsympathetically received. Ignorance, zeal, and pragmatism all have a part in this attitude, but the very definition of sacrament (an outward and visible sign of inward, spiritual grace) can be the bridge. Meditation is practiced to cultivate concentration and develop personal awareness in any sphere. It is the first requirement in training intelligence towards independent perception and for cultivating reflection and contemplation: the essential for inward organization, coherence, and resolution. Suspect when the withdrawal is seen as a disguise for vacillating inaction, but valued and respected when recognized as a ministry of prayer, and the source of inspiration and leadership, as well as healing.

Searchers for the deepest levels of understanding through devotion and self-surrender are to be found where and when they find themselves. Some write, some are written about, some leave no record in words but contribute their wisdom to those fortunate enough to encounter them. Some are nurtured within a religious tradition as were Dame Julian of Norwich and the unknown author of *The Cloud of Unknowing;* but not all. Occasionally there are outbursts of apparently spontaneous interaction when a number of people develop exceptional degrees of mystic vision.

Quiet reflection, increasingly concentrated meditation, the influence of one who can share the inspiration, a systematic regular pattern of life--all can contribute to growth. But technique will not suffice without the wholehearted seriousness of interest and purpose which is the momentum of profession. Without this, the mystic marriage remains unconsummated. Desire is the first movement of emotion, mind, and will. Half measures are insufficient in reaching for the goal.

Central to faith is confidence that we not only explore but use the maps of others to find a route, and that nothing can be compared with the object of the exercise, the journey's completion. This is inward, personal experience, not always sharable even with closest friend, partner, or spouse, but of inestimable benefit in every sphere where there is care and balance. The interaction and interplay of opposites intensifies with ceaseless delight and danger. Tension and relaxation, effort and rest, and the inherent linking together of ancestry and posterity as in family life which searches the past and looks to the future while enjoying the present.

The Analogy of Marriage

Marriage is like life in this: that it is a field of battle and not a bed of roses. [4]

To marry is to domesticate the Recording Angel. Once you are married, there is nothing left for you, not even suicide, but to be good. [5]

Love is a spiritual coupling of two souls. [6]

In every mystical experience worthy of the name, animus and anima collaborate in an act of love. [7]

Marriage, I repeat, is the extreme case of human relationship. The union of man and woman as husband and wife is the part which makes the marriage. Desire, acquiescence, submission, choice, the decision to wed, depends on personal circumstances determined more or less by context and tradition, and as much wisdom and commonsense as can be summoned. Romanticism may be illusory, and followed by disenchantment. Devotion increases with understanding, toleration and sympathy, and may even overcome bitter disappointments. The openness and trust of a healthy marriage belong to the spirit of truth. Few of us are sufficiently clear and resolved in mind and spirit to achieve this, and it may not even be a conscious, desired objective, though the phrasing of the marriage service is unequivocal.

Feminine and masculine approaches to marriage have differed fundamentally. Physical, practical, social, emotional, and economic interweavings are complex in any age, place, or pair. The human condition, common to both sexes, unites people in need and in delight and can divide when it comes to ways and means and conflicting priorities: fears and anxieties. A good marriage is a partnership, side by side and hand in hand as well as face to face. Understanding and valuing the other's differences tests the spirit of each. Attachment and detachment, dependence and independence, finding the moments of compatible interdependence add a spiritual communion to practicalities.

Is marriage ever primarily a spiritual relationship? Does marriage, with its accompanying domestic preoccupations and problems, strengthen spiritual life? What, if any, is the continuing place for ascetic celibacy as a condition of intense spiritual development? Are the normal responsibilities of spouse and family more liberating than limiting? more life-enhancing than stultifying? What are the particular difficulties, dangers, and strengths in marriage of sexual enjoyment, repression, inadequacy, control? What is sublimation? Of course there are no easy generalizations which can masquerade as answers. Our individuality makes sure of that, and each life and each combination of lives yields what is unique of itself. Our opportunity is to make the best of it.

This collection of studies is focussed on women, and in no sphere of life is the feminine more distinctive than in marriage. For centuries, marriage (almost always involving motherhood, for childlessness held the reproach of being barren) was pre-eminently a woman's life. The unmarried tended to be thought incomplete, perhaps eccentric. Virginity, as indicating chastity, has psychological, physical, and social importance. Marriage was, and continues to be, a practical arrangement, but of inexhaustible interest in the permutations and combinations apparently available. The opening of educational and professional opportunities, together with techniques of family planning, have transformed the scope of life for both married and unmarried women. Household machines help in the speedy dispatch of menial tasks. There is time to pursue wider interests and activities as well as to improve things at home, and, best of all, enjoy family life. Social attitudes are slow to change but the leadership of outstanding women in all spheres has promoted political and legal emancipation which in turn widens opportunity. Husbands need not feel threatened by such developments; there are immense advantages on all sides, as many discover to their credit. Lord Denning (formerly Master of the Rolls and a Law Lord) once said that in the eyes of the law, a married man and woman were one, and that one the husband. In his career as an Appeal Judge he made a series of remarkable judgments which are changing this. The vote, which recognizes the will and voice of women in electing representatives, was the prime achievement of the women's suffrage movement, whose leaders included married women, Dame Millicent Fawcett, for example.

None of these developments has changed the essential functions of motherhood: the bearing, nurturing, and up-bringing of children. Marriage is the preparatory and sus-taining context, and the spirit of the relationship will influence the children as well as parents, for better or worse. Mothers have unique responsibilities and opportunities for which few of us, in retrospect, were sufficient. The infant's need for care and attention appeals to the feminine psychological pattern of desire to care for and to please another, to be needed and to respond, to become depend-able. It offers a path of increasing reciprocal perception and devotion to the growing child, and to the career and experience of the husband and father. These relationships, unless or until they are outgrown, will be the sphere of life which most women see as their priority, where their love is most deeply expressed and their hopes more or less realized.

Marriage normally involves the new couple in making a home for themselves and for future offspring. For the romantic, it is where dreams come true, or turn into nightmares. For the realist, it is where adult life is more fully assumed. Simple or grand, transient or permanent, whether it is in a palace or a stable, the place of new birth is the place of incarnation. The new baby will grow, and is potentially a spiritual as well as bodily being who may, in time, embark on marriage.

The spirituality of marriage rests on that of the individuals so joined. It is in our humanity, feminine or masculine interacting, that its special potentialities await discovery. If we are blind or ignorant of spiritual life, we cannot consciously cultivate it, though it may be nurtured in us by the care of others. The qualities upon which marriage thrives are analogous to the requirements for spiritual health: sensitivity, listening, good organization, enjoyment, ever increasingly concentrated devotion. But in marriage there is also likely to be unexplored, unexploded, unpredictable reactions which test our poise and balance in disturbing, unexpected ways. Sexuality and passion are needed to draw people together, but the fire can destroy as well as refine.

In the language of the gospel, we may be sustained through grace. The apostle Paul found glorious phrases in which to reiterate this spiritual gift, in letters to friends at Philippi, at Corinth, wherever on journeys he had paused to share and expound what he had learned and experienced.

Jesus went with his mother and his disciples to a wedding at Cana in Galilee. When the wine ran out, his mother, Mary, appealed to him, and, in spite of an apparently discouraging reply, she persisted, and told the servants there to follow Jesus' orders, whatever they were. Stone water pots, used for ritual washing, were to be filled with fresh water which, when drawn, had become finest wine: water into spirit.

Much later, when questioned as to the destiny of a woman repeatedly widowed within one family of seven brothers, Jesus' reply was interesting. The questioners were Sadduccees, who denied the possibility of resurrection and who supposed that wives belonged to their husbands. What of this woman, who had been the wife of seven, to whom did she belong? Jesus replied that they had mistaken both the scriptures and the power of God "who is not God of the dead but of the living," and that "in the resurrection they neither marry nor are given in marriage, but are as the angels of God in heaven." (Matt. 22:30). This is a high degree of spirituality, but for those who seek the Himalayas of spiritual experience, Everest beckons.

There are marriages in which intuitive sympathy is attuned to the point where verbal exchanges play a comparatively small part. Others where talk is the twin spring of unity in duality. Perhaps a root of many difficulties is in disparity of expectation and need which leads to loss of confidence and spontaneity, losses which cannot be readily retrieved. Detachment and objectivity, sought through meditative and contemplative prayer, clear the inward vision. Passion may become compassion which leads towards the spiritual virtues of humility and patience, fortitude and mercy, faith, hope, and love. It is easier said than done. "We die to each other daily,"[8] but there is life after death, resurrection after crucifixion. We may learn to realize that we too are among those in need of forgiveness, for we know not what we do. We may know disaffection, but also moments when music sounds and when water becomes wine.

Anne Lamb, writer and teacher, is a native of England, born in Sussex in 1926 and educated at London and Cambridge Universities. She later taught at St. Leonard's School, St. Andrews, in Switzerland, and in Deptford. In 1952 she married Kenneth Lamb and went with him to the United States where he was a Harkness (Commonwealth Fund) Fellow at Harvard and at the University of Minnesota. Anne attended Radcliffe seminars with Professor Helen Cam and Professor George LaPiana. Their first daughter was born in Boston in 1955. After returning to London that year, Kenneth joined the BBC as Talks Producer, later becoming Head of Religious Broadcasting and, in 1969, Director of Public Affairs. Two more children, a son and a second daughter, were born in London. Anne became an armchair critic of BBC programs, a part-time teacher, a writer, and a volunteer in various activities for church and education. From 1980-86 she conducted adult education classes at the Marylebone Institute in the writings of T.S. Eliot, and is now preparing some studies of Eliot for publication. She edited Jeremy Taylor's *Holy Living* and, in cooperation with her husband, wrote *Hope*. Now teaching Divinity at Francis Holland School in London, she belongs to Chelsea Old Church, is a Trustee of St. Gabriels Trust, the Church Colleges Trusts, and of the Delegacy of Goldsmith's College.

That Power who exists in all beings as the Mother,
Reverence to her, reverence to her, reverence, reverence.
                                                    Bhagwad Purana

The Spirituality of Motherhood

Qahira Qalbi

Love spirals forth from the womb of Being; and so it is that each of us, every living creature, comes to this earth plane. The life force, issuing forth, is never so strongly felt as in the woman giving birth to her baby.

All my life I have had a quiet and deep gratitude that I was born a woman, but it seemed to be a privilege, especially, to be a mother. The experience of conception, which is the power of love; of pregnancy, the power of feeling; and birth, the power of thrust, is a course in motherhood and humanness both. There is an infusion of Spirit that fits us for the work to come--rearing the human race. We have heard the expression "the spirit moved him," or "the spirit moves in us." Never is this more true than in the whole drama of childbirth.

The womb is designed through eons of time to contract and expand and, with a hundred pounds of pressure, eject its nine-month tenant with powerful thrusts. Women are infused with this power; it is our inheritance from the universe. This all-pervading, permeating force is the breath that breathes us. Moment by moment we are filled with the very spirit we seek. It is the original impulse behind our every action: our birth, love-making, running a business, cleaning the house, building a bridge, getting out of bed in the morning, and most of all it is the triumphant spirit instilled during childbirth.

When the womb begins its contractions, and as they gradually get stronger and stronger, the woman experiences a cosmic power that seems to be beyond her, yet in a real way is her. The power is oh, so tangible, yet by control of the mind and the breath she can experience a partnership with spirit, even more, a oneness that is akin to a great initiation.

Tsultrim Allione in *Women of Wisdom* says that "initiation is an active choice to enter into darkness."[1] So does the woman birthing her child enter into the darkness of creation, the darkness of pain, the darkness of possible death, by choice and love in order to bring forth a new light into the world. Initiation is always a step into the unknown.

There are many steps taken into the unknown, and we may notice that some of these come unbidden, unasked for, and unexpected like birth and death. An initiation is also the beginning of something new, something different, a chance to do something in a way it has never been done before like our marriage, a new business, beginning a spiritual path. Other important initiations are our first tooth, our first step alone, beginning school, a severe illness, retirement, the death of a spouse or loved one. In each we are free to do things in traditional, tried-and-true ways, or we are free to explore and expand the horizons of humanity's knowing. So it is with childbirth.

Before the swimmer has ever braved the ocean waves, he knows but little of the feeling of vastness, the enormity and power of this ocean being. The same is true for the woman facing the birthing of her baby. Both are prepared by their interest in what is to happen. This step into the unknown, if there be no fear, is part of the fabric of our being. The pioneer, the explorer, the scientist, the mystic, all are within us awaiting the command, "Go!"

The mother to be has read, listened, contemplated, meditated, and drawn from within herself some primordial assurance that she, too, as her ancestors before her, can give birth. This assurance and the calming peace it brings can be deeper than she has ever felt before. If the ill winds of 'old wives tales' do not frighten her, then the joy of anticipation sets in, together with a delight in the coming of her child.

During birth itself other qualities are being forged in the woman as surely as steel is forged in the fire. There is patience in the process and endurance and fortitude in the face of the strong and stronger-growing contractions. There is diffusion of the sudden panic that arises after an intense contraction, and surrender to the assuring voice of the one who reminds her of her breath.

No one can sufficiently capture in words the euphoria, the gratitude, and the total delight which can follow a natural birth. The 'high' of these moments is spiritual to the utmost, while remaining utterly physical. Although difficult times may follow, this experience of bliss has been woven, it has been 'stamped,' in the woman's being and she will always be able to recall it.

Many qualities develop as the mothering career stretches into months and then years. Following the first uncertainty is the certainty, the quiet knowing, that she knows better than anyone the subtle nature of her child. The healer within us all is nurtured in the mother by the growth of her child. Especially when her child is ill, the mother's love pulls gradually from within her the knowledge of how to be healing. Hazrat Pir-O-Murshid Inayat Khan, a Sufi mystic of this century, said this about love:

Is love pleasure, is love merriment? No, love is longing constantly; love is persevering unweariedly; love is hoping patiently; love is willing surrender; love is regarding constantly the pleasure and displeasure of the beloved, for love is resignation to the will of the possessor of one's heart; it is love that teaches man: Thou, not I.[2]

A baby is totally dependent, yet it can call forth from us years of service and mold our personality to love as surely as a skillful craftsman. The cry of a newborn pierces the heart as deeply as a heartfelt prayer, and slowly but surely the mother and father who love become obedient servants. In the Western world we shy from the word 'obedient,' yet my Benedictine friend, Brother David Steindl-Rast, reminds us that the Latin *obaudiens* means "thoroughly listening." Again the Sufi mystic says, "The best way to love is to serve."[3] Obedient servant: what better training can one receive on any spiritual path?

The words of the beloved Sri Swami Rama, "You can never know how much God loves you until you have a child,"[4] reminds me of the phrase so often given in consolation to someone going through the fires of life: "God tests most those whom he loves most." Certainly parenthood is not only a very real spiritual path; it is a test, an initiation. Since nature itself is a sacred manuscript, can we find there an analogy of this trial by fire called motherhood?

Let us for a moment enter the consciousness of a lump of coal hidden deep in the bowels of mother earth.

What does this lump know of diamondhood? Certainly nothing. It is black, soft, burnable, quite dispensable. But the divine alchemist is at work: pressure is applied for centuries on end; heat, tremendous fire, unimaginable initiations are going on unseen, unheard, undreamed. And finally, after eons of time, the insignificant lump of coal is transformed. Did the alchemist love this lump more or less to subject it to such tortures? Will the diamond lack forgiveness remembering all it endured? No, it probably will be too grateful for the loving care it receives as a diamond.

We humans are exquisite. We are free to feel any way we like about our past or future, about our joy and pain. Many people seem to have chosen bitterness, anger, resentment, self pity. It is hard to imagine that anyone would willingly choose this, yet we experience it in ourselves. Could it be that we have, as free human beings, fallen into a trap of unknowing? Have we forgotten that pain brings transformation?

> Out of the shell of the broken heart,
> Emerges the newborn soul.[5]

The experience of childbirth cannot help but change a woman and prepare her for what is to come. At no other occasion is another human being so thoroughly and comppletely a part of us as during pregnancy. The woman is led step by step along the path of love, and anyone who is close to her is invited to walk along.

We speak often of good mothering, conscious of the child's highest good, but good fathering is equally essential to mankind. Men have wished they could also have the experience of giving birth, but they can gather its portence only vicariously, the depth of its meaning only through relationship. But by osmosis the father is also changed, especially when he lives intimately with the mother's process. Feeling, through love, the father has a spiritual experience akin to his masculine nature. He takes giant steps in his awareness to all life forms and most especially to his own inner mysterious nature--the divine feminine. We are all designed to blossom forth as humans with a perfect balance of these two forces--masculine and feminine, the sun and the moon. The tremendous experience of birth is a catalyst for this balancing transformation.

Spiritual Practice and Motherhood

Often young mothers feel they are missing something 'spiritual' in their life because meditation, sacred dance, retreats, and group prayer are difficult to do since the birth of their child. But spirit and matter are not separate; they are opposite ends of the same pole. Matter may be called dense spirit and spirit fine matter; in other words, matter is a state of spirit. The invocation of the Sufis is a reminder of this oneness:

Toward the One
The perfection of Love, Harmony, and Beauty
the Only Being,
united with all the illuminated souls
who form the embodiment of the master
the spirit of guidance. [6]

Thus bearing and rearing a child is a glorious spiritual path because it makes us guardians of the most exquisite product of spirit into matter that exists: a human being. We are all created in the image of the Only Being. When a baby comes into our midst, God, the formless Only Being, is again born in form. Our soul is to God very much what the sunbeam is to the sun. Everything is spiritual, comes from spirit, returns to spirit. The sunbeam is not less an expression of the sun though it shines only briefly on our kitchen floor. Spirit is no less than spirit though it lives briefly as us.

"Mothers don't need to meditate." When I first read those words (so long ago I have forgotten where), I cried. How could it be? I have since lived to understand their meaning and their truth. Mothering is a meditation, the most complete concentration. Caring for a child is transformative: an immature, somewhat selfish, childlike creature called a bride becomes (through a process of pregnancy, labor, and mothering), a mature, mostly compassionate, keenly perceptive, somewhat madonna-like woman.

Psysiologically speaking, there are hormones called prolactin and oxytocen, produced by the body during gestation and nursing which predispose a woman (mammals) to create a place (nesting instinct), and to 'mother' her young and even the young of other mothers. Nature readies us to feed and protect and want to care for the young of the species. Emotionally and mentally (if there are no drugs) we are more alert and 'tuned in,' and would sacrifice ourselves, generally, for the good of our children. How many mothers who could not swim a stroke have dived into a pool to save a small child? And no one will ever know the endless hours mothers spend by the side of a sick or injured child. These characteristics, of course, do not belong only to the woman who has reared a child, but to all humans who have the opportunity to mature and unfold their hidden qualities of nurturance.

Growth is getting in touch with one's limits, one's failings, often painfully so. We know too keenly the times we did not measure up, did not come through with flying colors, but instead weakened, ran away, lied, fell short of what we could have done. But we learn soon enough that there will be another chance, an opportunity to do it again and better. In the mothering career those times come often and sooner, rather than later. So mothering is an intensive, exacting art which makes of the artist a creator, sustainer, healer, and forgiver.

Nurturing

One of the most obvious spiritual practices on the path of motherhood is the development of the woman's ability to nurture. From caring for her helpless baby, through the years of the child's growth, the woman expands her ability to nurture to include all living beings.

For some women having babies and rearing children is an integral part of their purpose in life; for others it is not. But as citizens of planet earth we are all responsible for each other. We are not only our 'brother's keeper,' we are brother and sister to each other; we are each other.

New life forms are an extension of all that has been before, with the potential for being greater--greater expressions of love. We may ask "What is love?" but when we live the answer, we need not ask the question. While rearing children we have an opportunity to daily live the answer. As idyllic as this sounds, it is the answer to the human dilemma of suffering and pain. When life is lived

from the vantage point of the depths of our soul, and forgiveness and love are a way of life, when resentment
cannot take root because the soil of our being is too
finely cultivated to admit such a seed, then what? Then
love will be all we are. There will always be problems to
solve and mountains to climb, but the way to solve and
climb will evolve.

We need only trust our power within; the innate
power to nurture and heal is magnified when we recognize
and utilize it. We all know how a gardener nurtures plants
and flowers, carefully pruning them and loosening the soil
that has become crusted, giving each plant the right amount
of water lest some get too little and others are drowned.
There is full sun for the sunflower, shade for the violets,
while others need a little of both. Bark and leaves and
mulch help these to grow, while this one over here just
blooms and blooms, seemingly fed on neglect. The gardener,
the mother, develops the skills to care for each.

Emotional nurturing comes from one whose emotions
have been tempered in life's fires over and over, deeply,
in the gut level. Mothers see their children torn open and
sewed together, burning with raging fevers, covered from
stem to stern with poison oak. These things are mild on
the yardstick of misery, but a woman who emotionally
survives is strong and at moments even indominable. She
has seen the impossible happen over and over and learns
truly that there exists the finest attunement of all--the
spirit which lies at the foundation of her nurturing.

Love

At the turn of the century a disease called marasmus
was taking the lives of hundreds of babies in orphanages.
Care for them was given--diapering, feeding, bathing, and
so forth--yet they were mysteriously dying. Somewhere
along the way an observation was made: those babies
singled out to be rocked and cuddled and given individual
attention had a very high survival rate. It was discovered
that mothering love was the missing ingredient.

Love is the key to growth. Love is spontaneous,
creative. A woman truly learns about love when she becomes a mother. She learns that it cannot be dealt out in
portions, but is always giving, and more than is asked.

St. Paul, in the letter to the Corinthians says it this way:

Now I will show you the way which surpasses all the others. If I speak with human tongues and angelic as well, but do not have love, I am a noisy gong, a clanging cymbal.

If I have the gift of prophecy and, with full knowledge, comprehend all mysteries, if I have faith great enough to move mountains, but have not love, I am nothing.

If I give everything I have to feed the poor and hand over my body to be burned, but have not love, I gain nothing.

Love is patient, love is kind. Love is not jealous, it does not put on airs, it is not snobbish.

Love is never rude, it is not self-seeking, it is not prone to anger; neither does it brood over injuries.

Love does not rejoice in what is wrong but rejoices with the truth.

There is no limit to love's forbearance, to its trust, its hope, its power to endure.

Love never fails. Prophecies will cease, tongues will be silent, knowledge will pass away.

Our knowledge is imperfect and our prophesying is imperfect.

When the perfect comes, the imperfect will pass away.

When I was a child I used to talk like a child, think like a child, reason like a child. When I became a man I put childish ways aside.

Now we see indistinctly, as in a mirror; then we shall see face to face. My knowledge is imperfect now; then I shall know even as I am known.

There are in the end three things that last: faith, hope, and love, and the greatest of these is love. [7]

How does a woman grow while mothering? Let us see.

Situation	Mother Growing in Love
A. Baby cries and cries, falls asleep after mother walks the floor with him for hours. Mother exhausted, sleeps an hour. Baby awakens crying.	A. Does: get up, hold and nurse the baby, walk some more, (even for days and nights to come) until she is quietly resigned. Could: scream, cry, shake the baby, etc.
B. Toddler being toilet trained relieves himself on carpet while grandma glares reproachfully. Mother frustrated.	B. Does: lead the child to the bathroom assuring him he is all right, and the carpet can be cleaned up. Could: yell at toddler and spank him to show grandma she is punishing him.
C. Seven-year-old girl lies about breaking Mommy's favorite antique teapot which she accidentally broke. Mother is sad and angry.	C. Does: assure the child that she is more important than the teapot, even though it was precious, and so need never lie. Could: smack the child for lying. Take the child's birthday money to pay for the teapot.
D. Teen comes home three hours after curfew, no phone call home. Mother waiting, anxious and fearful.	D. Does: Listen patiently to his side of the story. Tells him she's happy he's safe and how worried she was. Reminds him to call collect. Perhaps share a snack before going to bed. Could: explode, yell ground him for a month and not really listen to him.

E. Son, a passenger in auto accident, in intensive care, head cut open and bleeding, teeth jammed in jaw, two legs broken. Four other teens also hurt. Mother standing at bedside in emergency room.

E. Does: stand by her son and tell him he's in good hands and that she will stay with him. Reassure other children until their parents come.
Could: fall apart, faint, dissolve in tears of anguish. Talk of suing the driver.

There is probably no closer or more intense relationship than mother and child. This very flesh and blood, now alive and moving around, is dearer than one's own self. It is the future you. No human quality goes untouched, often stretched past the limit. Love grows under severe conditions, because it pummels, exalts, crushes, refines, and defines our beingness. If we are anything at all, we are love.

Love in abundance comes to the woman who has given in abundance. It is awesome. As the years flow by mothers think little of all they do; they just do it. Finally all the seeds they've planted come up everywhere and in everyone from the family members to the train master in India. One day a 'window' opens, only a crack mind you, a 'window' to how much God actually loves us, and it is as if a tidal wave poured in: incomprehensible, totally overwhelming, shattering. And love, cultivated through the years of nurturing, now must be for everyone, everywhere, all the time. No more, no less. An always-known idea becomes a reality.

Gentleness

In this world there is nothing softer or thinner
    than water.
But to compel the hard and unyielding,
    it has no equal.
That the weak overcomes the strong,
That the hard gives way to the gentle,
This everyone knows, yet no one acts accordingly.[8]

A mother will soon find that because she loves her child, she will temper rules with freedom, firmness with gentleness. The greatest form of power is gentleness. True gentleness comes from selfless love. It is tuning deeply to another person's feelings and acting out of regard for them. In honoring another person's pride we are honoring our own. In speaking gently rather than shouting, in listening quietly and long enough, we bring to an angry, troubled situation the mercy and compassion to heal the wound. Out of gentleness and harmony will come what most of the world longs for: peace. What better reason for mothers to raise their children gently?

Guidelines, law and order, rules and regulations all have their place, and in an unnatural, life-in-the-fast-lane society, they are needed. But there will come a time, and for some it is now, that mutual trust, faith, and unconditional love is a reality. When we will live from the depths of our being rather than on the surface, we will find the need for authority vaporizes. Some might think this Utopia, might find this to be the ideal, the goal for human unfoldment. But it is rather the beginning. The fact of having a human body does not necessarily mean we are fully human. 'Hu' means, in part, divine—embodying the Godlike qualities in manifestation. 'Man' comes from the Sanskrit *manus,* which means mind. When we are truly human we will live life in harmony with the divine mind, which will guide us towards perfection. There should then be no more killing, no more pollution, no more harming each other. We will guard every person's pride, love our neighbor as ourself. All axioms will be part of our everyday life—not the end of living, but the real beginning.

We know this intuitively when we look at our children and plan for their future. Our children are us in the future. Where does all this expansion of love lead to if not a more superb person? We have been told through the ages: "The past is gone; the future is not yet here." Then the only reality that is upon us is now. The only hereafter is 'here' after we transform to still another form of light.

The Sufis are fond of saying, "Die before death and resurrect now." We are all dying every moment, dying to our own fears, our own false concepts of ourselves, our own limitations. But we know this already, haven't we been told? Let us die willingly and resurrect gloriously, spiraling into the future, consciously joining all those who believe and trust in the ultimate goodness of humanity, and serving with love and patience those who do not. The Sufi mystic, Jelalludin Rumi, says it beautifully:

> From the moment you came into the manifest world a ladder was given that you might escape. From mineral substance you were transformed to plant, and later to animal. How could this be hidden? Afterwards, as man, you developed knowledge, consciousness, faith. See how this body has risen from the dust like a rose? When you have walked on from man you will be an angel, and done with this earth your place will be beyond. Pass, then, from the angelic and enter the Sea. Your drop will merge with a hundred Seas of Oman. Leave him you called 'Son,' and say 'One' with your life. Although your body has aged, your soul has become young. [9]

Understanding

Daily living with children and watching their efforts to grow and learn gives us a deep understanding of their struggles to match our steps, follow our example, learn, expand. There is so much for a woman to note; she cannot help but grow in understanding. When love guides the teacher, she is so much more able to see the problem clearly, and guide usefully. One cannot help but note that the many choices of life are at our disposal. By teaching and guiding her child, a woman learns to choose more clearly:

create	destroy
nurture	shatter
cultivate	undermine
love	instill fear
patience	impatience
understand	belittle
serve	ignore
selfless	selfish
tolerant	intolerant

Even more than the love we give our children--all children--is the bridge we are building to the future.

What we do here and now will be, must be, surpassed. The idea of future, the perception we have of time and space are in reality eternity. There is something thrilling, awesome, about the thought that eternity is not out there somewhere waiting for us, but is now, this very moment. We need not look forward to it; we are living eternity now. These truths are gently instilled in our children at quiet times. During the course of everyday life, spiritual food in the way of guidance, listening, loving is constantly there.

Now that my children are older, the truths I taught them are coming back to me multifold. One of my children said, "I listen to what I say to other people and I know it's what I learned from you!" The greatest joy comes from seeing the seeds of love and beauty sprouting through the next generation.

The saddest moment is seeing history repeat itself because lessons were not learned: the child that follows in the drinking parent's footsteps; a child abuser who was himself abused. There is a line in a Sufi prayer, "You, my Lord, will right the wrong."[10] If there is anything at all good we can do in this life, it is correcting in ourselves the mistakes our parents made with us, in not perpetuating a way of being that we realize was not helpful to us as we were growing. Motherhood is a time for appreciating and reevaluating. The mother remembers how she was nurtured by her mother and father, and also remembers what she didn't like and what hurt. It takes courage to do things in a different pattern from our parents, our grandparents. It takes wisdom to know what to keep and what to discard. But we don't need to fear being perfect. Our children will have our mistakes to correct and their children theirs. But we will accelerate the process of perfection. We will realize the purpose and fullness of Jesus' words, "Be ye perfect, even as your Father in heaven is perfect."

Conclusion

The desire of life to reproduce is stronger than the limited human will to fulfill human desires, no matter how noble. There are those who have no inclination to have a child; they should be respected. But for the many who long for a baby, our love and encouragement is deserved.

The world can never have too many loved and wanted children. We are witnessing in this day what happens when young women choose a career over and above a family. To do this is neither right nor wrong, good nor bad. There is no need to judge the decision; it is the result which is interesting to witness: women in their 30's and 40's bearing their first child, women seeking a man who will father their baby without marriage, women hiring surrogate mothers to bear their children, multiple births due to the use of fertility drugs.

There is an age to come when humans are human and we live as we are designed to live--free from the bondage of self--when our lifespan will be marked once again in the hundreds of years. Peace will be a way of life, and war a distant memory. There will be no need for birth control or talk of population explosion. There will be balance, in ourselves and in our world.

But we cannot wait until this comes about. Dreams are for those who sleep. We must live the future now. We must live as though it has already happened. This means each person's unique ideal of the future will be the way the present is lived. As we pursue the ideal, the ideal is manifest. Then comes the realization spoken of by Hazrat Inayat Khan, "Shatter your ideal on the rock of truth."[11]

Our ideal is limited by our understanding of what Life/God is. As we are willing to explore further horizons, so will the ideal change, grow, be refined. We only know as much as we need to know of life's great mysteries. The more we do realize the more responsible we must be for what we know. As we integrate our ideal, we are illumined by it. Others are encouraged and inspired to live more idealistically.

The spiritual mission of the human being is to make God a reality. Not only do we entertain many religions, but each of us in ourselves is a religion. To come to blows over religion, or God, or whatever we choose to call the nameless and formless, spaceless and traceless, the very breath that we breathe, is so incredibly unnecessary. Yet more wars are fought over God than all other reasons put together.

The imprint of peace begins in the womb and even before--in the life lived in unworldly spheres. A further impression of peace is part of the 'coded information' in the mother's voice as she sings her lullabys. We are all a product of our realization; all that makes us laugh and cry tells the secret of our knowing or unknowing. So the babe at the mother's breast is learning to work for its food; it feels the human body as its comfort and thus experiences satisfaction.

On a spiritual path one may discover that the feminine principle embodied in motherhood is a stepping stone to our Christ-self, our Buddha-self, our divine self. Being a mother physically is not necessary to uncovering our illuminated self, or else most childless masters, saints, prophets would not be remembered today. So the state of motherhood lies as a seed within us all. It is the qualities of love, compassion, patience, tolerance, service, enhanced by motherhood that lead to illumination. A friend once told a true story about himself. His job was routine and he knew it well, so he would have conversations with God while he was working. One day he asked God why he couldn't be illuminated like others (who were writing books about their illuminations). God answered, "You are already illuminated. What are you doing with your illumination?"

The greatest resource the world (and perhaps the universe) has is the human being. All praise to parenthood and those pioneering mothers and fathers who burn in the light to give light to the world. The essence of spirituality is the spiritualization of matter and the materialization of spirit. What finer resource material than babies; what better guardians of this divinity than mothers!

It is the answer to this very question which predicts how much more light and insight we receive. Like the horizon it is endless, always more and more and only less and less as we forget who we are and why we're here. Have you noticed how matters of life and death make us think more about these great questions? When your good friend dies, don't you suddenly want to live life more fully?

It is also true when a new baby comes to live with us. Things that were once so important no longer are. A deeper meaning to life makes our life richer and fuller.

Qahira Qalbi, also known as Jalelah Engle Fraley, was born July 10, 1933 into Sufism. Both her parents, Bhakti and Fatha Engle, were on the Sufi path, and her father was secretary to the great Sufi mystic and saint, Hazrat Inayat Khan.

Involvement with La Leche League International, childbirth education, Right to Life, Hospice and especially the teachings of the Sufis, have given Qahira a life-supporting view. She is a Minister in the Universal Worship, a healing conductor in the Sufi Healing Order, and for the past eleven years has guided individual and group retreats on behalf of the Sufi Order in the West. She has headed Sufi centers in Los Angeles and the vicinity since 1970. Qahira has traveled to New Zealand, India, Europe, and Israel and leads tours to some of the special places in the world for Sufis, such as Turkey and Egypt.

Married to Tansen-Muni for thirty years, Qahira is the mother of six children and the grandmother of four. She and her family live in a small avocado orchard in southern California where she guides individual retreats whenever she is not travelling.

*Handle even a single leaf of a green in such a way
that it manifest the body of the Buddha.
This in turn allows the Buddha to manifest
through the leaf.*

Dogen

The Spirituality of Food

An Interview with

Abbess Koei Hoshino

Abbess Koei Hoshino was interviewed by the editor at Sanko-in, a beautiful, old wooden Buddhist temple in the quiet outskirts of Tokyo where the nun is head of the temple *(Jushokusan)* and master teacher *(sensei)* of the art of *shojin ryori* (Zen cooking).

Jushokusan, please tell us the history of this beautiful temple in which you live and work.

The history of this temple goes back to the period of the northern and southern dynasties (1336-1392), so it is quite old. But during the age of Japan's civil wars (1482-1558) it burned down. The present buildings in which we sit were restored in the year nine of *showa* (1934), about fifty years ago. So we trace the physical aspect of the temple. But we also trace another aspect of a temple--that of the lineage of the *jushoku,* the head of the temple. The lineage of the *jushoku* of this temple goes back to Kyoto. All have been trained at the chief temple of the Rinzai sect of Buddhism in Kyoto, the Donke-in, also known as the Bamboo Palace, founded in 1439. My teacher, Abbess Soei Yoneda, also received her training there from the age of seven. And it is from the unique tradition of cooking of that temple that my own work derives.

What is shojin cooking?

Shojin cooking is the vegetarian cooking developed by Zen Buddhist monks and nuns as an aid to improve their practice of meditation and a spiritual life, through eating only the simplest and purest foods. The word is composed of the Chinese characters for "spirit" and "to prepare."

Is there a difference between the shojin cooking of other temples and that of this temple, Sanko-in?

Yes. No doubt you have heard about *Zenkojisan*. They were princesses, the daughters of the Japanese emperors, who entered temples in Kyoto, which was then the capital of Japan. These temples had the title *gosho,* meaning a kind of palace, because of the princesses who lived there, either voluntarily or by force. It was considered a great honor to have them and so special foods were prepared for the royalty who often was the abbess. Thus the food from these temples, including the Donke-in temple in our lineage, was a blending, an interweaving, of the culinary practices of food for royalty (gentle, elegant, refined, beautiful), and the traditional Zen ascetic discipline (simple and direct). For us it is an important and unique point since our temple cooks food for the public as part of our teachings of Buddhism.

So for you food preparation is an integral aspect of your spirituality?

Oh yes. Every day we rise at 5 A.M.; every day we practice meditation and read the sutras (dialogs and sermons of the Buddha); every day we carry out the chores of the temple; and every day we prepare, serve, and eat food. Cooking, cleaning, doing zazen, sleeping, bathing, sitting, all come under the term *gyojuzaga.* This is a Buddhist term which means, "the four cardinal behaviors" of walking, standing, sitting, lying. Every aspect of life is spiritual practice. In Zen we say, "always, everyday life." This means that everything in life is training. That's how I have lived my life. So I never think of cooking as something separate.

What principles do you use in preparing and cooking food?

Ingredients are selected and prepared with the guidance of the three virtues, balanced with the six tastes. Zen prohibits the killing of any living thing and so we do not use meat, fish, eggs, or dairy products.

Please explain the three virtues.

The three virtues, or the three qualities, are lightness and softness, cleanliness and freshness, precision and thoroughness. They are listed, along with the six tastes, in the *Zen'en Shingi,* the oldest regulations for a Zen monastery, written in 1102. There it tells us that if the cook neglects the three qualities and the six flavors, it cannot be said that she serves the community.

And what are the six flavors?

They are difficult to translate, especially the last, but the six tastes are bitter, sour, sweet, hot, salty, and delicate.

In ordinary non-vegetarian cooking it is said that there are five tastes: sweet, salty, sour, bitter, and spicy. Those are the general tastes we experience. To this Zen cooking adds one more to make six. It is *tanmi.* We can translate it as a delicate taste, a quiet, and gentle taste.

So what does this really mean when it comes down to eating a meal? During the meal we experience the first five tastes and enjoy them. But after the meal, we experience what we call "aftertaste." It is a feeling, a mood of gentleness and quietness, along with the usual feeling of satisfaction. This is the sixth taste.

Do you mean that food alters one's consciousness?

Oh yes. It's a completely spiritual thing. If you are disturbed about something, if you're angry, you won't notice something so subtle. But the sixth taste, the feeling after the meal, is really the most important point of the entire meal.

It seems, then, that the cook is a key element because her spirit will also be in the food.

Exactly! It is necessary to be in a certain pure spiritual condition or psychological state to cook correctly. Of course since we are human, our thoughts change quickly and we may not always be able to maintain that state. But we should always try to achieve that purity when we prepare food.

Is this evident in the taste of the food as well?

Oh yes, it comes out in the taste of the food. Thus cooking is part of one's spiritual practice, part of one's training. Zen teaching says, "Allow your self and all things to function as a whole." When we eat food prepared in this careful way, with the six flavors, then we receive three graces from the food. First, we become healthy in mind and body; second, we have the ability to be thankful for all things, and to maintain this state of mind; third, we are able to work for others with our mind and body. We will be able to give to others. Those are the virtues we receive.

Sensei, when you prepare food, do you think of those who will eat it?

In the beginning of the process, I think of those who will be given the food. But then, as the process of preparing food takes over, there is *mu* (nothingness), as we say in Zen. I don't think of anything. The mind enters a state in which it is not caught up in anything. It is then that one is able to do one's best in cooking. So, if you are thinking, "Let's prepare this well for others" or "Let's offer our affectionate heart in preparing this food" you will know your practice is still shallow. When you are doing your best, you get to the point where you are just *doing* your best, not thinking of it.

Can you give an example of this state of mu or nothingness in cooking?

All right. Let us use the dish called sesame tofu. It is a difficult dish, made from ground sesame, water, and arrowroot. It must be stirred for a very long time, and it is hard work. When you are stirring and stirring with all your might, enough of the heavy batter for fifty people, it's so hard that you want to give up being a human being! But in the midst of the stirring you are not thinking of anything. All your attention is on the sesame. You just keep stirring and watching until the heat begins to soften the mixture and it becomes elastic. You just keep looking into the pan and stirring until the sesame tofu tells you what to do. It gets heavy again and then soft again until suddenly the surface swells up and leaps forward making a clear sound. It tells you that it's ready. Then as you quickly respond and remove it from the heat, a wonderful, delicious aroma comes floating up and you know with your whole body that the sesame tofu is done.

You see, you are cooking something difficult over a very high flame, so if your attention wanders even a little, if your mind jumps to something else for even a moment, the sesame will burn. So you put everything you've got into it. You are completely one-pointed on what you are doing. Do you understand better?

Yes. You've made it wonderfully clear. Though you are speaking of focusing on sesame tofu, you mean we should apply that same careful attention to everything else.

Yes. It applies to everything: selecting the ingredients, chopping the vegetables, cooking the food, laying the trays, setting out the chopsticks, arranging the flowers, spreading the cushions. This complete attention is what constitutes the spiritual practice. It must be understood not just with your head, but with your body. Our tradition insists that cooking involves the whole person. For hundreds of years the Zen monks and nuns have been taught to wash the grains of sand from the rice with such attention that not a single grain of rice is washed away. At no time may we allow our mind to wander as we clean the rice. This spiritual attitude to preparing food--being totally present to what you are doing--is valid anywhere in the world and in anything you may do in your daily life.

I have noticed that much attention is placed on the aspects of each season in your way of life, in the types of food you prepare, and in the decoration of the temple. Is this so?

Yes. One of our rules states that the monk or nun who is the *tenzo,* the cook for the community, must take care to choose produce of the four seasons. I think we Japanese are very sensitive to the four seasons; certainly it is a central point in Zen. When we live in each moment we cannot help but be aware of the fresh green leaves and wonderful breezes of spring, the sunny flowers and grasses of summer, the red and yellow trees of autumn, the pure

white snow of winter. The changes refresh us. The beauty
inspires us. A shoji screen opened to see the pink flowers
of the cherry trees in the garden are a delight; a spray
of green pine and a few cones arranged in a vase cheer
our hearts on a cold day, a glance of a bright red branch
as we look into the autumn garden makes us happy. So
should we cook. We should be surprised by the food and
moved in our heart.

But only the quiet mind can see the real things and
be moved by them. Look now at this tape recorder. It is
rectangular, right? And this teacup is round, yes? And in
this stove the fire is red. We don't make a mistake and
think that the flame is black or that the teacup is rectangular. Our training is to really know that this is red
and this is round. What does this mean? If your mind is
always fussing about things, if your mind is continually
busy, if you often think of things that irk you, if you
think a lot of heavy thoughts, you won't be able to see
things clearly; you won't be moved by the beauty of things.

Therefore you have to always be training your mind.
You must always maintain your mind so that you see
things clearly. For instance, the buds on the willow trees
come out fresh and green. Everyone who looks at the buds
thinks that they are fresh green. But the point is to really
know that they're fresh green, to know it clearly. In Zen
we have the saying, "The flower is red and the willow is
green." To be able to perceive that clearly, one must constantly practice awareness.

**And cooking, requiring awareness, is thus part of that
practice?**

Yes. Some of us are very skillful cooks, some of us are
very awkward. It does not matter. It is only important to
put all of yourself in the cooking--all of yourself. All of
yourself must be at that very moment, so that you have
the sharp, quiet mind needed for cooking. The problems of
the troubled world must not come in at all. Nothing should
be allowed to disturb the cooking.

**Sensei, may we return to the idea of the seasons? How do
we practically relate to the seasons in our spiritual practice**

of cooking?

The obvious thing, of course, is to cook with seasonal ingredients. In our modern world seasonal products are often available year round. Yet serving frozen green peas in January is not the same as serving sweet, young, green peas, fresh out of their pod, in June.

In shojin cooking we are guided by the five methods and the five colors. This helps in seasonal variations also. The five methods refers to the ways of cooking. They are: boiling, grilling, deep-frying, steaming, and serving raw. The five colors are green, yellow, red, white, and black (that is, purple). We try to balance these variables with vegetables and sea plants according to season. Of course the shapes and colors of the dishes are changed according to season as well, and a small branch of flowers or leaves is an extra enjoyment for the eyes.

We try to include the entire person in the joy of eating food. First we experience the environment of the room in which we will eat. Then we see the food served. We see the color, the shape, the contrast to the plate or bowl. Then we smell the aroma of the food. Then we feel in our mouth the textures of the different courses. Each texture will produce a different sound to our ear when we chew the food. And of course we taste the various flavors as we eat. Balance and harmony in all of these elements is essential so that the important sixth taste, the after-taste, the feeling we receive from the food, is achieved.

Sensei, it is considered one of the natural functions of women to nurture. This seems part of her nature as well as part of her spirituality. Does your work in cooking for others relate to this aspect of womanhood?

In a broad sense, yes. But to just cook without meaning is not at all the same as cooking as one's spirituality, so that one becomes rich in heart. The latter way of preparing and serving food is the way of nurturing.

When it comes to food, it's the same the world over: it's women who do the cooking. When we examine various religions we find that those engaged in ascetic practices are not those engaged in preparing the meals. Usually the ones who prepare meals do not do the spiritual practices. All the priests of the various religions, including those in Japan, have others to do their cooking. It is only in the Zen sect that the priests also cook and consider it part of their spirituality. So in most places of the world the preparation of food is given to the women.

How can women learn the deep spiritual significance of preparing food? Where do we begin?

Ah! One must begin where one is. Now I am sitting here. It does not help me to turn now to the right, now to the back, now to the left. Now I find myself here. I must not think it would be better if I were facing a little more in this direction.

The place in which you find yourself now is a given. You must not complain that you are not in another environment. So first of all you have to do your best within those limits. And when you do your best in your given environment, you will succeed.

For example, let's say you are making a stew, a dish which exists everywhere in the world. You find that you don't have any carrots. Well, then you must try to make the stew as best you can compensating for the lack of carrots, perhaps by adding another ingredient. In cooking this problem comes up frequently, and the solution seems to develop naturally. If we do our best, we will succeed. This is very important in cooking, as in life.

Next, you must have a strong desire for spiritual growth. Speaking in Buddhist terms, we say you should arouse this *hosshin,* good resolution. Then you must have an awareness of what is involved in cooking. This we have been discussing. We need this awareness also.

Often we feel that cooking so many meals is a drudgery, and it becomes very difficult to see cooking as a means to spiritual development.

Yes, that seems to be true both in the East and the West. Rather than being told that preparing food is a spiritual exercise, women must awaken that fact in their own consciousness. When all is said and done, what we do when we prepare food is maintain life. If we don't eat, we die. We eat to live. Each of us has to understand really well that by preparing food we are sustaining life, which is something very important, something wonderful, something precious.

This life we maintain is the life of the mind and spirit as well as the life of the body. The spiritual life is naturally fostered by living and working the way we have been discussing. We know deep inside that it is true.

Let us take the family as an example. A woman wants her children and her husband to be healthy and happy. This is her fondest wish and her constant prayer. She wants them to grow in health and happiness. She brings her prayer into reality by making good food for them. The food is very important, but the prayer, the feeling behind it, is more important. We must value and nourish that feeling. The Sanko-in's motto emphasizes this point: *Chori ni kometa aijo*--Cooking with love.

Every day you prepare and serve such meals. Then the day comes to an end. You look at your sleeping children; you think of your husband. You feel love for your family and I wonder if you don't feel yourself to be warmly happy. That's the point. That's what I want to explain. It's not something you have to think about; the instant you see your family you feel how wonderful it is. You don't need to dwell on things, ponder things in a certain way. Intuition is enough, and intuition will guide you.

While eating the temple food I was inspired by the great variety and freshness of the vegetables, the exquisite beauty of the dishes. But I wonder about those who cannot afford the best ingredients. What about them?

Once again, you must do the best with what you have. When you can't get the best ingredients, you do your best within the limitations. That is the guiding principle. As in all of life, you must be flexible. And if you are poor, then make up for it by being rich in heart.

For breakfast we nuns have a bowl of rice gruel and one pickled plum. We might also have a slice of pickled radish. The Western parallel might be a single slice of bread. Even so, we are rich at heart. Thus eating becomes training--learning to eat one's food appreciatively, as if it were a lot.

In meals there are two sides to the issue: those

who make the food and those who eat the food. Till now we've been speaking of the cook, but let us now touch on the other side. Here the important point, as we have said, whether one is rich or poor, is that we eat so we don't die. We only need a certain minimum in our stomach each day. That gives us a feeling of satisfaction. The one who eats the food needs to accept with a loving heart that which is given, and see that receiving the food is also part of spiritual training. We learn gratitude, appreciation, how to accept love, while gaining energy from the food.

If you don't have much, you musn't become pessimistic and say there is nothing you can do because you can't afford much. There is always something you can do. You must begin to think how you can make something good and beautiful with what you've got. Let's say you have only one slice of bread and some milk and you must feed four people with it! You wonder what to do with it. Remain open and think with love. If it were me, I might tear up the bread into pieces and put it in the milk and make a warm soup of it.

When you do your best to prepare food with the desire to give those you love something tasty to eat, then strange to say, it always turns out delicious. Things like this are cause for great joy.

On this topic is also the idea of waste. In Zen cooking we are very careful about not wasting anything. Remember the daikon radish you were served? Well, daily we serve this dish at the temple. We peel the radishes and make the pickles. When you have thirty to forty guests a day the peelings pile up so high! I thought that was wasteful. I looked at them for a long time and decided we must do something about it. So I began to do research in pickle making. After learning the process, I realized it would be good to pickle the peelings in rice bran and salt and push them down in the mixture with the pickles. We did this and got very delicious pickles. Just eating plain rice with those pickles on it is very good. And I feel that the peelings, which were normally thrown away, are very happy to have joined the group of food!

This type of thing has power to make us confident in our thinking. When we put energy into what we do, we will be successful. Remember that preparing food is training for the spirit.

Thank you, Sensei, for your explanations. I should like to ask one further question, not direclty related to cooking, but by your words, of great import. What is the role of zazen (meditation) in your spiritual life?

Since I entered a temple where zazen was the specialty when I was young, it was said that when we did zazen our minds would become very calm and that a wonderful power would come forth in us. We were taught this way, and I practiced so. But I really did not know--really know with my whole being--that it was true until recently. My abbess, Soei Yoneda, was very kind to me and actually brought me up to this life since the age of eighteen. Fifteen years ago she had a heart attack and was told she would live only another six months. She had diabetes and heart trouble. Thanks to our lifestyle, our spiritual practices, and our vegetarian diet, she was able to live for another fifteen years. Nevertheless, I viewed her loss as something terrible and feared that day more than anything. As she was nearing her death, I was very sad; I was actually frantic. My position in this big temple, however, means that I must guide everyone else. So I had to do something. I did my practice of zazen very much then. I did it as if my life depended on it. And each time I sat down to meditate, my sadness suddenly went away and I experienced deep peace. It supported me through those days and has supported me since then.

I feel that my training was wonderful, and even though I am still green at it, I am glad I have been trained this way. When I give myself up to the protection of Zen, then any sadness, any anger, any joy, have no influence over me. I am not bothered by anything. I am able to become my self really, not disturbed at all. Zazen is the place where we experience the truth that our entire life-- our praying, our working, our cooking, our playing--is all one.

Venerable Koei Hoshino is abbess of Sanko-in, a Zen nunnery and temple in the Koganei area of Tokyo. She chose to enter the world of meditation, work, and strict training in 1951 when she was eighteen years old. Hoshino began training as a novice in the Rinzai sect of Zen Buddhism under the abbess Soei Yoneda. After completing her novitiate in the temple and her studies at the university, she assisted the abbess in forestalling the closure of the temple by offering the temple's unique vegetarian food to the public as a means of support, as well as a means of propagating Buddhist teachings. Later as assistant abbess, she helped Abbess Yoneda in writing *Good Food From a Japanese Temple,* a book of recipes and philosophy from the 600 year tradition of cooking, published by Kodansha International. Named abbess after the death of her long-time teacher, Abbess Hoshino performs the temple ritual, teaches meditation and Buddhist philosophy, and continues the work of preparing food for temple guests. She also is the only teacher of traditional shojin cookery in Tokyo. Abbess Hoshino is the founder of the International Vegetarian Association, and as such travels to many countries discovering other vegetarian traditions and promoting the principles of food preparation she so lovingly practices.

Everything harmonizes with me, which is harmonious to thee, O universe. Nothing for me is too early nor too late, which is in due time for thee. Everything is fruit to me which thy seasons bring, O nature: from thee are all things, in thee are all things, to thee all things return.

Marcus Aurelius

Women and Nature:
Time of the New Dawning

Brooke Medicine Eagle

Mother, you gave us our very cells, you who are the deep, deep nest of all your children that ever have been, are now, and will be. You nurture and renew us. Our true mother, Mother Earth, we thank you for our life.
Father, you share with us the spark of aliveness, you who are the Light that shines within us and all our relations from the beginning to the end. Father Sky, we thank you for our life.

It is well that I have been asked to talk with you about woman and nature, and the potential for deepening our spirituality through nature. Spirit is father, sky, light, creation, the spark that ignites and lives within us all. Nature is mother, earth, womb of all possibility, nurturing and renewing place where we receive our bodies. These are our true parents.

When light reached into the dark, ever-present womb and pulled forth two-leggeds, not just dust was made real, but starlight as well. We humans are earth and sky. We can be represented as a cross, a blending: Mother seen as looking across the horizon, Father as looking up. They cross at our heart.

Thus Spirit lives within Mother and within each of us. Father Spirit is not angry and vengeful as some of the old books would tell us, and certainly has not given up and left, as some modern thinkers propound. To stand quiet in Mother's beauty is to immediately recognize the aliveness that abounds around you. Spirit is incredibly alive, moving and dancing and singing in Mother's beauty.

Before we can say we have finished what is begun here, you must take yourself to a quiet place of Mother's beauty and see the life around you. Sit upon Mother. Balance and quiet yourself and consciously join yourself with the circle of all that is alive. If you find this difficult in the beginning, look at every tiny thing you see around you as you sit there, and picture it dead, as though its life is gone: no movement, no sound, no breeze. Every blade of grass, every tree lifeless, every four-legged, all the crawlers, the waters stagnant and putrid, the wingeds fallen and still. Then bring yourself into contrasting reality, and really see the life dancing around you. Breathe in the aliveness and find it in yourself. Feel and listen to your heart beat. Stop doing anything about breathing, and let yourself be breathed. Remember, then, the words "Father is alive within Mother Earth, within me and all things" and give thanks for life.

When you have experienced this, then the remainder of what I say can be real within you rather than merely words.

Our present challenge is to awaken and embody Spirit within us, rather than to leave earth or our bodies to find Spirit. We are entering the time of the nine-pointed star, the star of making real upon earth the golden dream of peace that lives within us. We understand that finding heaven is not going somewhere else, but co-creating it here upon this beautiful earth. We are completing the cycle of the eight-pointed star, Venus, star of the heart, where the lesson has been about ourselves as the cross between sky and earth, and about letting the light and love of Father and Mother join at our hearts and shine forth unrestricted. Having understood and taken within us this knowing of Spirit, we can then use that light and love to manifest a peaceful, abundant, harmonious world around us.

In doing this we have a strong ally in our elder sister, White Buffalo Woman, mysterious holy woman who appeared long, long ago to the Lakota people bringing the sacred pipe and seven sacred rites. Her message, as was Creator's message in the beginning, is of oneness: Spirit lives within everything and thus we are related to all things through Spirit. Spirit is the vibration, the hum, the movement of everything from the tiny atom of a rock to the spiral growth of the tallest tree and the playful fun of children. Mother has her own special hum, as do all things. Her vibration, eight cycles per second, is healing and renewing to us when we experience it. In this modern world we have cut ourselves off from this song of Mother's body, alienating ourselves from her spirit, by producing noise and vibration to surround ourselves: electriticy, motors, radio waves, interference of all kinds. Thus we feel the necessity to go into Mother's vastness to reconnect ourselves with the renewing and nurturing of her spirit.

Inipi--Purification Lodge

One of the sacred rites Buffalo Woman gave is *Inipi,* Purification Lodge, more commonly known as the sweat lodge. Although there have developed many forms of using the lodge, there are some basic elements. A lodge is built of willow and covered with hides or blankets until it is pitch black inside. Earth is taken out of a center hole, where hot rocks are placed to create steam from the water poured upon them. When one enters the small opening, one must crawl upon hands and knees, thus humbling oneself. (Humble does not mean abject or pitiful; it comes from the same root as *humus,* and means "of the earth"). Thus we are coming close again to Mother Earth as we come within her dark womb, sit upon her, and feel her spirit song. The heat from the rocks causes us to relax and surrender, to let go and open, to release what we hold. This is a very powerful form of healing since it allows us to release all that which separates us from Mother and from Spirit, makes us safe within the womb to open to the new and amazing possibilities that lie within us. Norma Cordell, who carries a Nez Perce lineage, reminds us that the first sweat lodge is our mother's womb from which we emerged new into our physical world.

Our challenge in this time on earth is not to figure out and create some new invention, but to heal ourselves, become whole, by surrendering to the larger life, the source of all life, within and around us. My friend, Nancy Swanson, gave me a new perspective on Darwin's theory of survival of the fittest. Rather than the masculine interpretation that the fittest was the one who could fight the best, the deeper and more useful feminine interpretation is of fitness as the one who fits with, and thus is in harmony with, all around--the one who surrenders to the larger life of all our relations. When we emerge from the purification lodge, clean and clear of body, emotion, mind, and spirit, we emerge reborn and new into the world. We come again with the eyes and heart of a child, as the great masters have said we must do to recognize the life of Spirit within us and all things. In entering and leaving the lodge, and often in the ceremony within, the phrase "all my relations" is used to remind us of our deep and real connection with all things so that we remember to pray for all things, not just for ourselves.

Hanblechi--Crying for Vision

Buffalo Woman also gave the rite of Hanblechi, Crying for Vision, through which one retreats from daily life to Mother's quiet, leaving behind clothing, food, and often even water, to clear oneself and call vision to oneself for the people. Messages come from Mother's children around as well as from Spirit within. One of my elders often tells stories of guiding 'city folks' on a vision quest. Occasionally a person would come down from extended time in a sunlit, grassy, forest meadow and report that nothing happened. "Nothing happened?" My elder would then point out all the things that had likely brought the lessons that came from each and every thing around. "Did you notice the soft grasses, how they sway in harmony with the slightest breeze, yet how soon they spring back upward when the heaviest of footsteps move away? Did you know they even break up concrete with their gentle strength? And did you notice how the trees are deep rooted in Mother Earth to stand the high winds? Those who are not are toppled and gray. Did you learn from the rocks near whom you sat, who are the teachers of patience? Did you hear the sweet song of the aspen leaves above you? Did you feel Father Sun describing the cycles of the larger life in his continuous movement across the sky? Did you notice the ant people: how cooperative they are, how each one does his job with vigor? Did you see especially that ants do not kill each other on the freeways of their life?" And so he chided them and made them laugh at themselves for their foolishness and blindness.

I smile, remembering my beginning vision quest when I learned amazing lessons from the winged ones. I was sitting high above Arrow Creek, my back toward what we call the Castle Rocks where Absarokee (Crow) people have been vision questing for centuries. I sat upon a rock out-cropping, flat and somewhat grown over with soft grasses. Beside me a small pine tree at finger tip's reach shaded me. From there I could look far down to see the miniature purification lodge by the creek and my helpers small as ants around our camp. Above me the grassy hill sloped up to another lone rock about four feet high, standing alone. I had heard the tales of animal, bird, and spirit helpers coming to my elders, and in my beginning excitement I kept looking around for something to happen right away. I sat and waited, not even remembering to call to the spirits for help. The long, hot day wore into thirsty afternoon; I relaxed and softened. Just then a magpie flew into the tree near me. I snapped to attention and watched every move, waiting for his message. But he simply sat and sometimes hopped in a very regular magpie way, and said nothing. The only unusual thing was that he was nearly within arm's reach and paid absolutely no attention to me. Soon he flew off. Quiet again. Then in the blue skies stretching out away from me, I saw two dark dots--big birds flying strongly toward me. As they drew closer and glided down into the cliffs below me, I identified them as a pair of golden eagles, majestic and beautiful. I found myself wishing they had come closer, so I stilled myself again. Before long, into the pine tree flew three chickadees, small twittering birds who are at home sitting upon or hanging from the branches. They did their chickadee thing without notice of me, again hopping remarkably close.

Well, now I could see that an interesting sequence was developing, and I studied the 'medicines' (meanings or powers) associated with these three birds. The magpie for me represents the buffalo with whom he is symbiotic. Magpie sits on Buffalo's back, getting fed by the grubs there, and at the same time acting as an alarm for short-sighted Buffalo when the bird sees something far off and flies squawking away. So Magpie made total sense to me since my blessing for this quest had come in a sacred Buffalo Lodge, dedicated to the nurturing power of the feminine. I acknowledged and gave thanks for all these things in my life. My thoughts then turned to Eagle, who flies highest and sees farthest, representing Spirit Above. He also reminded me of my name and the accompanying assignment to touch Spirit Light and carry it across the sky, sharing it. Thus Father Spirit spoke to me again through his high-flying wingeds, an obvious message and reminder. The chickadees, too, made sense. Upon this very mountain our last braid chief (an old-time chief with traditional braided hair), Plenty Coups, had vision quested as a young man, and the power he received was that of the chickadee, whose smallness and gentleness allows her to be anywhere without disturbing whatever is happening, hearing everything, knowing much. Plenty Coups died just before I was born, yet I have always felt close connection with his fatherly energy. I gave thanks and honor to Chickadee.

The most fascinating thought now was, Who will come next? Four is a very significant number among Indian peoples so I was anxious and impatient again. It didn't take long for the next wingeds to come in. I heard a whir of wings above my head and up the hill. Turning around to my left, I was disgusted to see five pigeons fluttering and landing upon the big rock, about fifteen feet from me. Pigeons remind me of big cities and the noise and confusion I hoped to escape upon this quiet hillside! Then too, there was the time in El Paso when I walked under the cornices of a downtown building in a new white outfit and a pigeon dropped a very unwelcome message to me! So I turned my back on them, wondering why the magic number four had been left out and why pigeons, of all things? Aggravated by their clucking, I looked around again to see one of the five sitting upon the very nearest edge of the rock. Then he dropped off the rock into gliding flight directly toward me, and disappeared into thin air. I looked everywhere, unable to accept his midair disappearance, but could find no other explanation. Glancing back at the rock I saw my four 'magic' birds. Pigeon had spoken again! Of course, I felt chagrined and chastised for my impatience, for my judgment, for holding onto the past instead of opening to the present with joy. In that moment I forgave the El Paso pigeon and gave thanks for the humor and gentleness of the lessons: a gift of the mysterious unknown through Mother's winged children.

The Sacred Pipe: Oneness with All-My-Relations

When the mysterious holy one, White Buffalo Woman, came to the Lakota people and gave them the sacred pipe, she spoke to them, and now to all of us, in this way:

> With this pipe you will . . . send your voices to Wakan
> Tanka, the Great Spirit, who is your father and grand-
> father. . . . With this sacred pipe you will walk upon the
> earth; for the earth is your grandmother and mother, and
> she is sacred. Every step that is taken upon her should
> be as a prayer. All the things of the universe are joined
> to you who smoke this pipe. When you pray with this
> pipe, you pray for and with everything. . . . Every dawn
> is a holy event, and every day is holy, for the light comes
> from your father, Wakan Tanka. You must always remem-
> ber that the two-leggeds and all other people who stand
> upon this earth are sacred and should be treated as such.
> This will take you to the end.[1]

I spoke earlier of approaching the world with the eyes and
heart of a child. That leads to other stories and thoughts
about Mother Earth's many peoples.

Teachings from the Four-Leggeds:

A student once told me a very touching story of
her encounter with a bear. Elaine was about three years
old, out with her father cutting trees in a mountainous
area. Her dad had pointed out the caves upon the mountain-
side nearby, warning her that there might be bears there.
Soon she wandered while playing and found herself at the
mouth of one of the caves, which she entered. There was
a bear in the cave, lying in the sun near the entrance.
The hungry little girl recognized her as a mother bear;
the nursing mother invited her to suckle. She was happily
walking forward when the blast of a gun sounded behind
her. The bear spouted blood and died. Elaine's father ran
to her, so thankful for having saved his child from the
bear that was about to eat her. She was broken-hearted
and shocked because she knew Mother Bear was peaceful
and nurturing and loving. Father and daughter's stories
differ to this day because Elaine experienced the truth of
the bear's gentleness and love.

This same childlike knowing and loving relationship
was instilled in Lakota children when the old ways were
practiced. When a woman found herself pregnant, she began

to spend more and more time upon the land, harmonizing herself with all her relations. After the birth, she then spent many more months taking the child into nature and teaching the brotherhood of all creatures--otter, frog, water bird, deer and coyote and squirrel--learning the lessons and powers that each had to give, and most importantly, calling them 'little brother' and 'little sister.' Our elders understood that we are not fully human unless we stay close to Mother and in good relationship with all her children. Yet so often now in the wider culture children are laughed at for their wise understanding that trees and wind and kittens and clouds all talk!

For me personally, cats are amazing models. They have a deep understanding of the physical world and of the efficient use of energy, which is the warrior's central challenge. Their strong sense of self, their total relaxation when at rest, their magical purring, their lithe ease of movement and incredible leaps all speak strongly to me. I would like to share with you a teaching I received from two kittens that lived with me several years ago.

§

My look-alike cats Heeta (Loving Child) and Nochita (little Night Girl) have come in to curl up with me as I dry myself by the fire. They have been with me steadily since their birth, and long before they were born they had come to me in a waking dream. They have made their magic known to me, as I have watched for it since Eldest Grandmother told me how the feline people understand and make profound use of the rhythms of life, of the vibrations which underlie all things on earth below. She said, "They know how to travel on the humming, leaving their bodies behind." Although I had no idea exactly what she meant, and though others sometimes scoffed at her, I knew she had planted a seed that would bear fruit in time.

Coming home after a drenching walk on a cold evening, I sincerely wish to learn of travelling an easier way, so I say to the big kittens as they crawl up on me, "Show me this medicine of yours." They don't acknowledge hearing me, and yet they do a very unusual thing. Heeta lies on my upper chest over my heart, stretching herself across

me in a most uncatlike position, with her chest glued to
mine, front legs down over my left side and hind legs over
my right. With her head on the opposite side, Nochita
then does the same over my solar plexus, my luminous
fibers. Then they simply begin their contented purring, or
so it seems until I notice that their humming becomes
gradually and enormously full without growing louder; the
whole room and my own body begin to vibrate and pulse
with the rhythm of it: wa waa waa waaaa. I have experienced this only once before when my elder chanted with
me in special tones: "The Great Spirit and I are one, the
Great Spirit and I are one . . ." on and on until this
same kind of 'warping' happened, and I traveled through
many marvelous places, exquisite beyond words.

And then I am free on their purring, far outside
the house, moving rapidly and at the direction of my
thoughts. I go far across the great water to a wise old
one who is growing blind, and I work on her eyes. With
my right hand I lay fine fish gut on her cataracts, winding
and circling it from the center, left and outward until it
covers the surface of her eyeball. I blow my breath on it
in steady, even, deep breaths until it just begins to dry.
Then, with infinite care I lift the thread off her eye,
unwinding inward with my left hand until her eye is clear,
the cataract coming with the lifting.

It is complete. I kiss both her eyelids goodbye and I
am moving like a blur through space/time. I open my eyes
in bed to pat and thank Heeta and Nochita. They rise and
stretch, going into the kitchen for a drink.

When the next trading vessel comes, there is joyful
news of their wise one's renewed sight, and a package for
me that no one else understands: an iridescent abalone
shell filled with dried fish for Heeta and Nochita.[2]

§

In his wonderful little book *Kinship with all Life*,[3] J.
Allen Boone tells stories of his experiences with the incre-
dibly intelligent and communicative dog, Strong Heart, and
of lessons given to him by many other endearing creatures.
Another book I highly recommend is *In the Shadow of a
Rainbow*,[4] the thrilling and moving experiences of a Yukon
Indian who is befriended by Nahani, a huge, silver, female

wolf pack leader. There is a saying among this particular tribe of Indians that when you have a special, close, and long-lasting friend, you 'stand in the shadow of a rainbow' with them.

Many of our animal friends, including domestic animals, have so much to teach us. We all know stories of 'man's best friend' the dog: his faithfulness, courage, intelligence, bravery. My Chow dog, Empress Silky Bear, is a wonderful and loving being. I was busy working with a large group of people at the time she was very near the end of her first pregnancy. I had massaged and worked with her, relieving her young back of the burden of all those puppies within her, and was looking forward eagerly to their birth. Silky came to me in the middle of my work and took my hand; she grasped it gently, her canine teeth holding the palm of my hand. I petted her and then tried to go back to work, but found that her gentle clasp was also very powerful. It hurt my hand to try to pull away. She gently but firmly took me down the trail and across the meadow to her bed under the house where she immediately proceeded to birth the litter. Of course, I had wanted to be there!

Another sweet and wonderful little animal taught me a very important lesson of Spirit a few years ago. It was Autumn in the high country and I lay down to rest with my blanket on a bare spot at the foot of a huge aspen. The sun was shining down and I felt more peaceful than I had in many months. Hearing a slight rustle next to me, I turned my head to see a fat little ground squirrel happily making her way toward me. I realized that the bare spot and little hole I was lying on was the entrance to her home. She continued toward me, even though I moved to better watch her approach, and I felt sure she would hop upon me and explore around trying to find her door. Just then I remembered a message I had been given often as a child when rabies and other animal diseases were epidemic, "Don't let them near you; they might bite you and give an awful disease." Suddenly fearful thoughts occupied my mind and at that exact same moment the little ground squirrel screamed in terror, herself feeling fear and danger, and ran in panic to hide. When I realized that my fear had instantly communicated to her, that I had destroyed a potentially beautiful encounter by recalling my old programs of fear, I cried. I shall not forget that lesson from Spirit through the little animal; I'm sure that same instant wordless communication is consciously or unconsciously felt by all other creatures, including the two-leggeds.

Dhyani Ywahoo recounts times with her gentle Cherokee grandmother when mountain lions would come and rub on her legs like great kittens. When I was a child I told my mother that heaven is just like our home in the wonderful Montana wilderness, except that in heaven the animals are not afraid of us. I still believe this to be true, and am working to release all fearful thoughts from my mind and replace them with peaceful and loving ones. As we all replace fear with love within ourselves we do our part toward recreating the Garden of Eden on earth, making heaven real right here and now by embodying Spirit within ourselves.

Big Medicine from Tiny Fliers

So often we two-leggeds deny that wisdom can be gained from any of Mother's creatures. We hold ourselves higher, better, more intelligent, more important than them, and refuse to look upon them with open eyes. Reptiles and insects are two very specific examples. Yet the reptilian part of our brain is the source of the mechanism of feeling which keys our memory for recall; my elders say it is the 'tape recorder' Mother Earth gave us to use and that we are denying our own incredible powers of memory by using mechanical devices outside ourselves. Lizards remember how to regenerate their limbs, and I believe this ability as well lies in the reptilian, or old brain, of humans.

In the past few years, I have opened myself to the world of insects and been given profound lessons there. When I lived in Oklahoma in an open studio, insect people took that opportunity to show me their beauty and diversity. Each night for the whole summer a new beetle or moth would show itself to me, lighting under my desk lamp to give me excellent viewing. There were simple brownish moths whose elegantly patterned backs gave me designs for rug weavings; shiny black beetles with cardinal red wings; delicate iridescent yellow-gold fliers, and tiny green shimmering bees. They reminded me that there are more insects upon Mother Earth than all other kinds of beings put together, and that they have been here for much, much longer than two-leggeds; they know how to live well upon our Mother. The most stunning insect to show herself to me was a moth shaped like a simple miller with a tiny head and an exquisite furry collar, below which descended the flowing cape of her wings. She was radiant white with a collar that looked as if someone had poured cranberry juice over it, which had then spilled down upon her snowy cape, fading into lighter and lighter pink until the very hem of her garment was again radiant white. She was beautiful beyond words. It was clear to me as she regally showed herself that she was a princess, a tiny improbable princess, but one nevertheless.

The lineage of southern seers that has come to me has strong connections with the insect world, and often insects come as messengers or omens from that shamanic family. The women of that family communicate with me through insects that are so shiny black they have a copper-gold iridescence and often gossamer wings. One day in a telephone conversation with someone close to me about a dream I hold dear, I felt my dream had been crushed by his negative attitude, and crying said, "I feel like the egg of my dream has been stepped upon." Finishing the conversation I went outside to talk with my friend, Caer, who was hanging wet clothes to dry in the New Mexico sun. Behind her I noticed a lovely, tiny, turquoise egg lying on the rocks and sand of the driveway. I assumed that she had found it and laid it there to take in when she returned to the house. But when she almost stepped on it I asked her about it. "What egg?" was her reply, and I knew that it was the egg of my dreams being returned, beautiful and whole, to me. When I picked it up and took it to my car, there on the window was an exquisite insect I had never seen before. She was like a huge flying ant, shiny black with copper-gold iridescence and clear wings with veins of copper. To me it was the women of my seer's family come to return my dreams.

The men of that same lineage signal me through blue-green insects; some are an inch tall with long, bent legs, and some are like beautiful scarab beetles. Last year I journeyed to the Tulum ruin on the turquoise Caribbean coast of Quintanaroo, Mexico. In the center of the ancient plaza is a temple dedicated to Itsa Ma, the Descending God, the one Father Spirit sent to be with us on earth. At the top is an image of Father God, Kulkulkan, as a king. Under him is a man, head down as though being birthed, with his right hand reaching to Father God and his left hand reaching down to us on Mother Earth. He is the one our people call Elder Brother and Dawn Star, the one who journeyed all across the Americas two thousand years ago teaching the way of love and uniting the peoples under the light of Father Spirit.[5] His names remind us that he came before us to show the possibilities of a whole new time to come, just as the dawn star presages a new day. He was the beginning of our shaman's line of seers, bringing spiritual light to those in darkness.

As I stood near the temple of Itsa Ma, listening to the waves and waiting for the old Maya man I was to contact, I noticed beside me a tiny, radiant light. Looking down at its source, I saw an exquisitely beautiful beetle, about the size of my little fingernail. Its iridescent colors echoed the beauty of the turquoise sea beside us; its light shone warmer and brighter than I had ever felt or seen. It was unmistakably the Dawn Star's energy. With it came a message to remind my people in the North of the truth of their stories about Elder Brother from long ago, and the urgent need to bring ourselves together again in the spiral of love and light under Father Spirit that will bring our people to health and abundance once again. Then he flew away toward the sea, leaving me awed and filled with light.

Hummingbirds have some of the most powerful medicine of the wingeds. As all good flight scientists know, hummingbirds cannot fly; they defy aerodynamic principles! But tiny and delicate as they are, hummingbirds are able at any moment to fly in any direction, reminding us to be flexible and 'on our toes.' They live, trusting, on the very edge of life. A good friend of mine who has an aviary of these tiny birds from around the world told me something quite astounding: if you go into the aviary and startle a hummingbird into fight, then do not feed him a droplet of nectar when he settles down again, he will be dead of starvation by morning. He lives that close to the edge. Hummingbird's beauty, quickness, courage, as well as her defiance of what we think we know to be true are profound lessons for all of us.

Dragonfly, too, is seen as powerful medicine since she has that same ability to instantly move in any direction, and demonstrates even more flexibility and adaptability by living in all the mediums of earth--water as a larva, land and air as an adult.

Wisdom of the Deep

Our water creatures, fish, dolphins, and others, have much to teach us. My friend, Lalo, recounts a true adventure he had while swimming off northern California. He swam and played at the joining of a river and the ocean, enjoying the mixing of the waters. Being an excellent swimmer, he paid little heed to warnings about the currents until he found himself very far out and having a difficult time making it back to shore through the undertows. Difficulty turned into panic as he fought against the currents until he was exhausted and pulled under. Desperate and confused, he was swirling around under the water when several seals came to him. Between them they nosed him up and helped him forward until he was through the rip tides and into safe waters. Then they left him without further ado.

Dolphins have demonstrated something we are finally beginning to use in the form of underwater birthing, creating relaxed, alert, playful, highly intelligent children who dive and swim, totally at home in water. Dolphins also share a profound lesson with us two-leggeds, who through our manipulation of the world have caused grave damage and pollution. They do not have an opposable thumb and so cannot manipulate, yet they live a beautiful, free, harmonious, and mutually supportive life, having developed the additional brain lobe that we humans have. The great whales, too, have these same lessons and more for us.

Will we learn the lessons of harmonious living from them, or will we insist on killing our brothers and sisters for the products they provide? We must listen with open minds and hearts to the words of Chief Seattle:

> If all the beasts were gone, men would die from great loneliness of spirit, for whatever happens to the beast

also happens to man. All things are connected. Whatever befalls the earth befalls the sons of the earth.[6]

From Out of the Earth

One of my spiritual benefactors named Younger Brother is a plant shaman. As children, both he and I experienced much craziness among the two-leggeds around us; while I turned to animals for love and learning, he turned to plants. A very special understanding he gave me is that plants love us.[7] I had never thought of it in this way, yet I see them every day giving themselves for our nourishment, our healing, our spiritual awakening, the warmth of our homes and fire. He reminds me that the flowers and grasses and trees came before us, creating a cycle of oxygen and clear air without which we cannot exist. He calls Tree People the teachers of Mother's law; where we destroy them we very quickly destroy the very breath of our lives. The master Jesus, our Elder Brother, used parables of grape vines and fruit-bearing trees often as he gave his great lessons. He spoke lovingly of earth as Mother, the creatures as brother and sister, and Father God's caring for the least sparrow that falls.

In our modern world, the community of Findhorn has shown us the enormous abundance of huge, magnificent plants that come as we acknowledge and work with the spirits, or devas, of the plants. We learn in many ways that we must honor and use well the green ones Mother gives us. An enormous number of people use refined plants such as cocaine and alcohol to damage their lives and those around them. Peyote cactus, used in a sacred way in the Native American Church is, on the other hand, opening the way of Spirit and healthful living to a unified pan-Indian group of people across Turtle Island, creating the most unification we have seen among native peoples since the Dawn Star's spiral of light centuries ago. Many people abuse tobacco, forgetting that its medicine is the uniting of all things, and thus they die from cancer and lung disease. Tobacco's spiritual use is in Buffalo Woman's sacred pipe, each pinch added with a prayer which includes two-leggeds, wingeds, those with fins, the green growing ones, the stone people, those who burrow and crawl within the earth, the ancestors and the children to come, and all things in the great circle of life. We must awaken and learn the clear lesson Father Spirit and Buffalo Woman are asking of us: that we mature and step into the great circle of harmony with all our relations.

I must also speak briefly of the stones, gems, and crystal people. We are now finding more and more beneficial uses for these beings, from gem elixirs for treating diseases to the powerful energy of crystals that can be programmed for specific uses. Once I was spending time with Dhyani Ywahoo, a loving and gifted healer from the Cherokee tradition. She spoke of programming the pulsing energy of crystals for healing, for ancient information, for protection, and many other things. Finally she said, "We set our especially big clusters for peace, except in the winter when we set them for warmth." What a wonderful practice, and how efficient a use of energy: warming ourselves with crystals rather than killing our trees to provide our warmth!

My own experience is that crystals act as transformers. We are told that a new tone, a new vibration, is being set on earth to lead us into a golden new time. Since crystals are used as transformers in everything from radios and wristwatches to computers, I feel they are also acting to transform this high new energy into an immediately usable form for us, possibly helping with the transmutation of our very cells into a new kind of harmonious, loving being.

From these stories and lessons I hope you hear again and again the call for a conscious surrender into the greater circle of life to listen to the full and healing voices, touching Spirit through Mother.

Hunkapi--Making of Relatives

Another of Buffalo Woman's sacred rites is the rite of *Hunkapi,* the Making of Relatives. Through this rite one takes someone who is not a blood relative to be a part of the family. The first and most obvious *hunkapi* is marriage. However, when the Lakota people made the vision real, they enacted a larger level of the rite. They took a neighboring people, the Rees, to be their family and so remind us of the larger understanding of all two-leggeds as family

with each other. The rite's deepest symbolism is the remembrance of Father Spirit within each other and all
things, the oneness which brings true peace. The Lakota
holy man, Black Elk, has this to say to us:

> Through these rites a three-fold peace was established.
> The first peace, which is the most important is that
> which comes within the souls of men when they realize
> their relationship, their oneness, with the universe and all
> its powers, and when they realize that at the center of
> the universe dwells Wakan Tanka, and that this center is
> really everywhere, it is within each of us. This is the
> real peace, and the others are but reflections of this.
> The second peace is that which is made between two in-
> dividuals, and the third is that which is made between
> two nations. But above all you should understand that
> there can never be peace between nations until there is
> first known that true peace which, as I have often said,
> is within the souls of men. [8]

I perform many ceremonies to make relatives, creating the
opportunity for people to recognize their oneness with
each other. Among my native people, it is customary to
adopt as family those who are special to us, and that
beautiful rite is being extended to people of all cultures. I
truly believe that we two-leggeds are now being asked to
do a great *hunkapi,* one in which we consciously adopt all
Mother and Father's children as our family. This year I
have conducted a ceremony to pray for the trees that are
being destroyed so wantonly and dangerously, and for the
creatures and plants that we are making extinct by the
hundreds per week. Part of those ceremonies is always a
form of *hunkapi,* consciously remembering our oneness
with all things. This is what my spiritual benefactor calls
'the third attention'--holiness. It is keeping one part of
our attention upon this kind of oneness.

Another aspect of Buffalo Woman's message is this:
we are one with all things, and thus what we do to any
one of Mother Earth's creatures we do to ourselves. The
pipe she brought represents that oneness, with its red
bowl symbolizing the fire of life (or the blood) of all our
relations through Mother, and its stem representing the open

channel to Father within and around us.

Thus our elder sister's call to us is one of creating good relationship, through recognizing and honoring spirit and aliveness in all things. It is a call to the feminine within us, that part which carries this relationship aspect. And as we chose female bodies, we accepted the charge to model and teach and require good relationship among earth's children: two-legged, four-legged, winged, those who crawl and swim, green growing ones, and rock people, all peoples. Buffalo Woman is calling in her accounts with each of us: are we living the oneness in our daily lives, and are we bringing the message of spirit and oneness that she modeled for us as women?

There are two practices here that bring up the balance on our side of the account. The first is to under-stand that Mother lives within us. Mother's mind lives in our belly, in our center. This may seem strange as you read it, since we have been told to numb ourselves to the feelings that occur there, to lock our stomachs in tightness to prevent them sagging. And we have done as was modeled and told us, cutting ourselves off from Mother's life within us. We must reconnect. To do this takes time and practice, so let us begin.

First, loosen your clothing and reach down, finding your navel, and then an inch or so below it, finding your center. In order to be more accurate, use this image, given me by my mentor, Moshe Feldenkrais. If you were to stick a huge pin through yourself and want to spin evenly around it, you would put it through your center. I am speaking of your actual physical, weight-distribution center, and it lies there beneath your navel. Stand in front of a mirror if you want to see, but primarily you must 'feel' that place which is your center. Pull and release your belly with your muscles and keep feeling until you find what seems to be your center. This is where Mother lives within you, the place of the invisible umbilical cord which connects you with her, and thus joins you with all her children as well. It is here that we will learn to truly live the law of oneness.

Let me give you an example that came to me. I was given vision to create a ceremony to block the cutting of trees in the Amazon and other such acts as threaten the life and breath of the children of earth. In meditating on the trees, part of our family and so necessary in the cycle that brings us the breath of life, I realized that for many of us saving the trees is a logical or mental thing, something we think about and decide. I realized that Tree people are usually seen as something outside us, not truly felt as related. If we can actually begin to feel our relationship to them through the cord that connects us to Mother and all her children, then we will have the same experience of the trees that we have of our children who come from our bellies and with whom we have that invisible cord of love as well. If someone were to suggest killing a group of our children, it would not be an intellectual question, one for us to think about and judge and decide. It would be an obvious "No! Unthinkable! For no reason!" And as we feel our same deep connection and relationship with trees through our belly, we will respond deeply and differently to the question of their decimation. It is through this center of ourselves that true relationship will be experienced and lived, not through our minds where we seem to be stuck at present.

So reach down and find your center often. Do it frequently enough that you can begin to feel it internally, rather than having to find it from outside. Pull the muscles inward often so you begin to feel your belly and tone it. My spiritual benefactor asks me to "press my belly against the world." In doing this I think of my belly as the head of a drum upon which everything vibrates. If the head of the drum is loose it doesn't resonate, and if it is too tight it cannot resonate. It must be toned, and your attention must be there to pick up the resonance, the song within you created as your surroundings vibrate there, giving you another kind of knowing.

The other practice concerns our use of the moon cycle, the cycle of our menses. We are presently reaching toward a whole new time on earth, a flowering of the tree of life. The dawn star has long since faded into the pale morning light, and golden day is close at hand--yet much still lies within the womb of mystery, in the womb of Buffalo Woman. We are being called to bring forth into reality what is waiting there for us, to awaken ourselves in the dream. And finding the dream is the function of the moon cycle, especially for the daughters of the earth, whose blood expresses itself with the tides of moon's pull.

It is now that I speak to the feminine, the nurturing and renewing power within all, and especially I call to those who chose a female body, for we express Grandmother's pull most eloquently. Your moon cycle determines the thinness of the veil between you and the great mystery. As the new moon comes toward you, the veil thins, becomes gossamer and transparent. You feel the openness and sensitivity that begins to increase. You pay closer attention to where you allow yourself to be, the energy in which you are immersed, for you imprint very deeply in this receptive time. What you wish to receive, create, and magnify, you choose to surround yourself in now. You turn toward beauty, peacefulness, song, and thus call vision for a radiant, harmonious life for your children and the children of seven generations. You refine what your attention is given to until the blood comes and you retreat into the peaceful beauty and quiet of the Moon Lodge, leaving behind for a few days the everyday world: going within to center, paying your attention to the womb, to Mother's mind within you, and on then into the great mystery waiting there. In the moon lodge you remember your vow to use this transparent veil in calling vision for your people, praying, "Not for myself alone, Great Spirit, do I ask this vision, but that all the peoples may live."

This information received as the menses begin is the clearest human picture from within the womb of the great mystery, from the unknown of our future. Among our dreaming peoples, the most prophetic dreams and visions (of the coming of the white peoples and other such almost incomprehensible changes) were brought to the people through the moon lodge. In other words, the most useful information that can come to us in a time when we are unrolling an incredible new future comes from each of us women who use our moon time well. Conversely, for each of us who do not honor this time, much is lost, including the respect of others for our bleeding.

My call to you is to begin now to honor your moon time, to come together in small hoops (or perhaps eight women) and create a moon lodge, a communal women's retreat and meditation room for the beauty, for the quiet, for the transparent veil. Dedicate yourself to the quest for vision that will guide us and our families at the time. Within this lodge keep a large and lovely book for recording

your visions, dreams, imaginings, and intuitive flashes.
Make possible also a simple art expression for another
kind of record. These expressions will unify the information
and make it available to all who come there; the dream
will begin to unveil itself through strands woven from
many women's dreams. The weaving created through the
gatherings of shared vision on the new moon and the gatherings to actualize those visions during the full moons,
and from the records, will create a fuller tapestry, more
easily understood and made real in the ordinary affairs of
life. For this is the ultimate action--making the dream of
peace real in the 'everydayness' of our lives.

Grandmother's cycle and Mother's mind within us
assist us then with the task of coming again fully present
into the world, when at the full moon we are at our most
powerfully attentive and aware and present for action in
the world. During the days following the first flood of
clearing blood whose potential for life we gift back to
Mother, the flow gentles, wanes, slows, and completes
itself; we integrate the vision within ourselves and ready
ourselves to come forth. From the womb of Buffalo Woman
we carry new creations to join with the light, and birth
takes place. The dream is made real in the beauty of the
earth.

This call, then, is for honoring the deep function of
Mother's gift of life blood within us, to bring forth vision
and make it real for our families at a time when vision is
so important for us and for the healing of Mother. The
honoring of this cycle within us will then be more than
empty form and words; it will be given new life for men
and women alike. And wonderfully, we will notice healthier,
more comfortable menstrual cycles and birthing.[9]

These are simple, ancient ways, powerfully useful
when put into practice. Your feeling may be one of not
knowing what to do; the line of feminine teachings may
have been lost to you. Yet Mother's truth is always within
us. Be willing to discover it within yourself. Reach back
across the gap. Be willing to not know, to reach into the
unknown, the great mystery. Then you and we are following
the model Buffalo Woman gifted to us--we are carrying
the water of Spirit to all the people through our own
bodies. We are nurturing and renewing at the most profound
level.

Her-Alone-They-Sing-Over: Puberty Rite

Another aspect of woman was given when Buffalo Women sent one of her rites in vision to a man named Slow Buffalo, who saw and made real the rite called Her-Alone-We-Sing-Over, given as a young girl comes into womanhood through her first blood. This powerfully beautiful puberty rite reminds the young girl that she is now like Mother Earth and can bring forth children, can live through herself the renewing of the people. She is highly honored at this time by all the people, who also wish to touch her and receive some of the power she is now manifesting.[10] We who have perhaps never been given such a rite, must remember to honor ourselves and the gift of this power of Spirit within us. We must as well find ways to bring this kind of honoring and understanding to our young women, and thus to all the people.

And so we understand that Mother and Grandmother's cycles within us are part of the process of deepening our spirituality and of bringing spiritual gifts to ourselves and to the people. We can be clear and glad as Buffalo Woman turns her eyes upon us. We can sing this song, given to me especially for women in their moon lodge and meaningful always: "We are the daughters of the moon and earth, who live within us and give us birth. We are the turning of the tide; we are the love that lives inside."

As women we have easier access than men have to the life of Spirit and creation if we but refuse to buy into the old stories of Spirit being angry or absent. Creation lives within our wombs; the life of our people is renewed there. It has been shown through recent research that what is necessary for creation of life is first the egg produced by the mother and then something to disturb the integrity of that egg. Sperm from the male was designed to do this second job remarkably well, yet sperm are not the only possible things to break that boundary. When the egg is broken by anything, life begins to unfold! This gives us clues as to the old one's honoring of the feminine as the beginning of all things, and the womb as the most powerful aspect of Spirit within us. Male shamans say that they 'fly off the woman's belly' when journeying to other realms, seeming to mean that the source of power rests there.

Within the native mind there is a remembering of our relationship with all beings from the beginning of earthly time. In the purification lodge we acknowledge the hot rocks in the center as our eldest grandparents--the first things upon earth. Thus all things from one-celled beings to fishes, grasses, reptiles, birds, and mammals come down from them. It is through our bellies, through Mother's mind within us, that we will remember and honor this family tree, past and present.

As we see, there are very many ways to think about Spirit within nature. My examples are brief, yet my hope is that from them you will gain a perspective that gives you the openness and interest to seek the profound lessons so constantly and freely available from Father Spirit within Mother Earth and all our relations.

In black there are all colors.
Where darkness always the light.
Iridescent the raven's wing in sunlight.

Brooke Medicine Eagle was raised on the Crow Indian Reservation in Montana. She is a native earthkeeper, a visionary, a teacher, a healer, poet, singer, and celebration leader. She is also a licensed counselor, a practitioner of Neurolinguistic Programming, a certified Feldenkrais instructor, a ropes course facilitator, and an ardent outdoor adventurer.

Brooke's visions have been documented in. *Shamanic Voices, East West Journal, Whole Life Times, and Shaman's Drum.*

She is currently within a four-year ceremonial cycle, working with planetary circles of people dedicated to awakening the golden dream of peace on earth. Moving toward profound earth healing and individual healing, she asks us to return to the land itself, the ultimate keeper of wisdom.

Brooke travels extensively, offering teaching, ceremony, celebration, and outdoor excursions, carrying to all the ancient light of this land.

God's great power is in the gentle breeze, not in the storm.

"The learned say that your lights will one day be no more,"
said the firefly to the stars.
The stars made no answer.

Tagore

Women and Power

An Interview with

Vivian Jenkins Nelsen

Vivian Jenkins Nelsen, administrative director of the Hubert H. Humphrey Institute of Public Affairs, was interviewed in her home in Minneapolis by the editor.

Vivian, for many years you have been a leader in traditional bastions of male authority--church administration, higher education, and public service. And you have often been the first woman to break ground in each place. What is it like for women in men's strongholds?

Often women have the problem of health when they are the first, or when they are breaking new ground. And then they have to get in there and do more of whatever the men are doing. But men never know when to stop. They get burned out and they keep right on; they get heart attacks and they also get very crazy, very neurotic. They work sick and they expect you to do the same. They never take time for personal emergencies. Work! Even death means nothing. One just doesn't interrupt the flow of work.

There is a woman who works with me whose husband died suddenly at the age of forty-two. There was never a hint of any illness. She was thrown into shock and depression. The prevailing male stereotype is that she was supposed to cry for a day and then go back to work. When she didn't follow this pattern one of the men in the office thought, "Well, after a month she's probably getting lonely" so he asked her for a date. The woman came to me asking me to intervene because the man kept calling her at night, pressuring her to go out with him. When I reported this with great indignation to my own male boss, he saw nothing wrong, except that perhaps the man was a little early in asking. He thought the very best advice for the bereaved woman was to get back to work so she would forget all about her loss! Is that what we want to do? Forget a person who was a part of our life?

I found that such crazy things are the norm for men in the world of business. All of them are ill. High blood pressure, ulcers, and all kinds of stress diseases are there, pushed down, but definitely there. And the effects are part of the environment.

What makes the men get caught that way?

I think it is the way we are socialized, the way we are raised. School does that to us as well as the family, and all of society reinforces it through rewards and sanctions. A few men unlearn that stuff, but it is hard. They must take as disciplined an approach to unlearn it as they took to learn it all.

It was very interesting for me to visit third world countries to see those male values entirely flipped over and find that the countries still could run. On a trip to Egypt with some other business women, a few of us decided to go off on our own. My idea was that we would take a leisurely, romantic ride down the Nile river, watch the birds, and just drift by, seeing the country. Their idea was "What time does the boat arrive? How long is the trip? When do we arrive back at the hotel?" We sat waiting in a grubby hotel courtyard, the air full of dust, flies everywhere, when the guide came up. The other women were so distressed because the boat man would not tell them when we would be back that they decided not to go. He would only say, "When it gets too dark." To him time is when you get done. Throughout the trip it was interesting to see workers deal with Americans who insisted that they must know when and how long and what time. "It says here on the schedule that the boat will be here at nine. Is that right?" And the guide would say, "Oh, yes." Of course there was no boat. I asked a guide why he said yes when no was the obvious response. "Because they **need** the boat to be there." So there are men who work in a different way from the American model and still survive!

In our society what is the basic difference between the way

men use power and the way women use power?

I think the major difference is that women need to have relationships; we are relational-oriented. I think men are raised conversely to be results-oriented, or thing-oriented. That is the major difference. Of course you will find people on both sides, but the prevailing values are 'relational' versus 'thing.'

How does that manifest?

It manifests in every way possible. The difference of the male style and the female style is very real. It is telling people to do things, making them do things, versus negotiating with them. It is helping people to choose what they should do rather than forcing them to do things. The female style lets people choose to do things (within certain limits, of course), rather than using authority to force them to do it and then getting all that energy pushing back at them. But men in business don't understand that, and they don't understand that the women's way is the more healthy style.

For example, my boss (male) tells me, "Don't ask employees if they want to do this. Just tell them to do it!" Or he will tell me that I delegate too much: "You should hold the power more." He feels that he is being a good mentor to advise me in that way. I will say, "I want to have a group that meets regularly, office staff, so they can gripe, get information from me, blow off steam, or whatever they need. It would be entirely their group." My boss says, "Well, OK, but only if you chair the group and keep it all in control." I have heard this sort of answer a number of times in different jobs, and so I now am able to recognize it as a male pattern, a male method.

While I worked in the church I also learned this method. In our Lutheran church each congregation is autonomous. Each is a separate entity, although connected to the larger church. The congregations thus should have much responsibility for initiating and running things. But this is all in theory only; it is all rhetoric. The mother church tells the executives: "You have to be at every kind of meeting, and you have to make sure that nothing gets out of control." In male structures, control is very firmly held by top authority. So I see the way men and women use power as being very different. It is a difference between owning power and sharing it. Men's notion of power is 'power over'--domination and control. Women's notion of power is 'power with'--power shared among all.

When women are working in a male dominated society, how do they remain true to their own selves?

It's hard. It is very, very hard. You have to have a strong center within. This is difficult, however, because on the one hand the environment doesn't allow easily for growth. It's like if I know something is right, then I have always got to be proving it. I can never take chances with anything. I can never make mistakes; I have to be right always because it is my way against his way. Often it does damage to the way I want to be, which is to be open, letting things happen, not always defending the growth process or the change process, and letting people make mistakes as well as making them myself. That's why the male environment is a difficult place to be. You have to be ultimately committed to being broken!

Oh! I didn't expect you to say that! Being broken is part of the process?

That's part of the process.

Yet you still feel that there is a place for women in men's power structures?

Yes. I think that women are the only answer for the workplace. It is so necessary for women to keep the spiritual windows open. I see men and their structures on the way to real destruction--destruction of people. When we look at the workplace now as compared with ten years ago, it has improved, for sure. We can see all the effects of pop psychology: people are more moved by it and more informed by it. But at the same time I think we have a driving materialism now that we have never seen before. The baby boomers are worse than their parents were. They have focused in a very concrete way on material things--things that our folks had only in a general kind of way because they were coming out of the war years and things were scarce at the time. Now materialism has become so intense that there has to be another way of doing things.

Then you think that women can bring, and are bringing, a spirituality into the workplace and into power structures?

You bet. I absolutely know that to be so.

And the difference women are able to make is due to their psychology?

Yes. It is a very profound difference for those who acknowledge it. There are a lot of women who are now removed from the women's struggle. They do not acknowledge their own psychology. They have gotten into the workplace, and so they are now just one of the boys. They don't see themselves in any way different from men because they don't behave any way different. They wear skirts, but if the norm were to wear pants, they'd wear pants. They obey the norms.

But I maintain that there is a battle that goes on within them whether they acknowledge it or not, and whether it is going on in the conscious or the unconscious mind. They are ignoring their own feminine psyche.

There are still expectations that women will be softer than men in the workplace. Women will be the ones that others can really go and talk to. A brother dies and a man has to tell the other men, "Oh well, he was just a fool; we weren't that close." But to a woman executive he can come and say, "God, I'm really broken up; I feel bad." And the woman will understand and be able to comfort him and offer sympathy because she is a woman. Men cannot do that to men. Women get to be the shoulder, the receiver, of a lot of the pain in the workplace that men can't give to each other.

Do you feel that women should keep striving for more power, for higher and higher positions, in the workplace and in society--politics, for example--to change it?

Well, that is interesting. I think some women should, but

it is hard for me to talk about because it is something I personally do not value. People are often telling me to run for public office, but I really don't want to do that. My mother is a public official and I know not to want to do that. I know what it is like. To me somebody has to do it, but there are also other things that can be done to help change the power. I know it is important for women to be in politics. I have seen old ladies and young girls talking about Geraldine Ferraro. I went to a party for her and the women came up to her and cried, "Geraldine, it is so important what you are doing. . ." There was amazing feeling. But to be in public office takes a kind of hardness, a driving, a clawing that I do not admire in women or men. But we must be realistic and acknowledge that in our system that's the way things work. That is how people get to the top. That's why I say I think it is important for some, and probably for all of us in some way.

How do you think that women should use power?

Well, the way we should all use power. That is, first of all, to acknowledge that we all have power, and then to try to work toward a model where we acknowledge other people's power--whether spiritual or intellectual or intuitive or all the other kinds of power that we don't yet respect. I think that we have to work towards really utilizing that power and sharing it. That whole point of view means that things will look very different, obviously, from the way they look now.

Since men are most interested in results, in making a profit, for example, or getting up the corporate ladder, how can a woman with her concept of power enrich the man who is in that framework of mind? How can he even begin to make room for her ideas about power?

Let's use an example. When Japanese motor bikes came on the market, companies like Harley Davidson called them rice cakes! They had nothing but contempt for the Japanese and their products and methods. Guess what? The American company went deep into trouble. They had been a really macho, male company but they were now about to fold. They had to make a real change in the way they were doing business. So the employees bought the company and inaugurated a Japanese business model. It is now working. What is important is that in a funny kind of way the Japanese model of quality circles is very feminine. This is, of course, understanding that Japanese society is terribly homogeneous and terribly male-oriented. But the model of everybody being involved on the line, making decisions along with making the cars, flex time, people being able to switch jobs, and so forth, are all things that the women's movement in this country has long said needed to happen.

What about a company like IBM that is hard-nosed, makes lots of money, makes everyone conform, wants to put everybody else out of business, but is also really successful in that sense?

OK. I think that as a different model pervades the workplace and the consciousness of workers is raised and they realize that they are being limited, it will change things, even at IBM.

Do you think that there is a change in the general mentality of workers?

Absolutely. Because people who came through public schools will be different. Kids don't stand in lines anymore. Kids aren't forced to go separately to bathrooms like when we grew up. All that stuff is changing in one generation just because of the revolution in ideas of some major thinkers in how the schools are done. It will be very difficult for kids who learned in an open school environment (and more and more are), to go to IBM or a similar company and have to wear a suit and conform and have so much control over them. It just will not work. So companies will simply not be able to be as rigid. You see it in the army too. The army is now letting recruits have various lengths of hair and wear facial hair and have more freedom. The young people will not put up with the old ideas. We are seeing this change in a lot of ways. But IBM is going to find that they will not be entirely successful in being able to raise executives up through the ranks that are like little cookies cut out. Now people know there is a different

way. It will take time with big organizations, but it will
happen.

**Is there a price that women pay by being in positions of
power?**

Yes. There are a lot of prices! Women have to choose
often between career and family. If they don't make that
choice then they have to choose between being supermom
and being super-executive. I myself don't have children,
but I see the strain in women around me who do. Women
also have to make a choice between being ethical and
being professional. Those two are NOT the same thing.
They are not the same. In my case the question is Can I
be a good Christian and also be a good business person?
Do ends justify means? Do you lie or not tell the entire
truth to get what you want? The whole Olie North syn-
drome goes on so much in business. You struggle every
time you have to make those decisions in the beginning
and it eventually becomes less of a struggle. Every time
you tell a lie or hold back part of the truth it does something inside you, perhaps not at a conscious level, but it
hurts you.
     One of the other things that women must deal with
is the incredible amount of time one must spend in order
to function well in the work world. Sixty hours a week is
usual, not exceptional. Some people work eighty hours.
And then you have no energy, no fun, because you are
just so tired. I think because of fatigue and long hours
that women who are married probably really curtail their
sex life as well.
     Another thing is that women personalize things.
Being the first one there, or the second woman to have a
position, or something like that means that one is always
on view, under tremendous scrutiny and tremendous pressure.
There is another point and that is how women suffer in
this environment. There is a double standard that goes on.
On the one hand you have to be tough, and on the other
hand you are supposed to be soft. This dichotomy, this
pulling, goes on all the time. You must decide, Is this the
time I should be soft or is this the time I should be firm?
     Another very basic, daily thing to be faced is the
testing. There is testing by men and women both. Men

especially test everything you do, every decision you make, not only the results of your decisions and actions, but your right to make a decision. That is the tough part. That underlying insult is always there. And if the woman is more educated than the men, that produces another tension. Men go through testing too, but not to the extent that it goes on with women. We are always being put in positions, difficult positions, that they hope will show us at our basic. Women are still an enigma in the workplace. Men don't know if they can trust us, so they do terrible things to put us in situations where they can see what we will do, if we will fall apart, stay with the gang, be a team member, or run.

When I first came to the university, men kept swearing and telling jokes in very bad taste in my presence to see what I would do. That sexual harrassment piece is really there. Women then go through a whole stream of 'Did I cause that?' In the work world it is assumed that the woman caused it: she must have sent some secret message in the way she dressed, in the way she handled herself. But it is definitely not a sexual issue; it is a power issue. The male thinks, "If I cannot empower myself in the way that I want with you, then I will force myself on you in a way that is hard for you to say no. If that doesn't work, then I will seduce you. And then you will say what I want you to say because I've made you say it against your will in a non-knowing way." There is an intentional 'stupidness' that men use. We like to think of it as naivete, but it really is a power play. Sometimes when men feel threatened by a woman in authority, they will react in sexual harrassment. They will pretend that women like it, but they are choosing to be naive in order to control.

You said that women test women in power. That sounds rather sad. Why would they do that?

The why of it is fairly straightforward. There is the bottom line that women are not supposed to be leaders and we haven't experienced them as leaders, and so women absorb all the stereotypes about themselves as other groups do too. And the negativity that is part of that is rather significant. The Women's Bureau of the Department of Labor

has done some research on this. There are so few women
bosses that it is a pity. Women don't expect other women
to be bosses and so they don't know how to behave when
they get one. In the beginning my feeling about it was a
kind of confused understanding of the process. I had a
real impatience with it, and when I had my first secretary
tell me that she had never worked for a woman and wasn't
sure she wanted to, I was determined to be the very best
boss that she'd ever had. Well, that puts a strain on the
relationship and it isn't the most authentic relationship
one can have with one person trying to prove something to
the other and the other person trying to disprove it.

The second time that it happened, I received a
letter from one of my staff people saying that I could
advise her but that she would be reporting directly to the
Dean rather than to me because I was a woman. Her line
of reporting was supposed to be directly to me. I confront-
ed it head-on and told the Dean I would not come to
work there unless he got the line of reporting straight. It
did not matter to me how he handled it, but it had to be
handled. That really surprised him and he said, "Well,
really we don't have to confront this. Once she gets to
know you she'll love you." But that was not the issue.
The staff person had a working relationship with me and
it should not be based on whether or not she liked me.
Her working relationship with the Dean was not based on
that. So he said, "Well, it seems to me that you want
power AND authority." I had to reply that one without
the other does not work very well. I did not want to boss
the woman, but I did want to be able to ask her to do
things and know that she would do them for the good of
the order.

That is a long way around saying what my experience has been, but my feelings about it at this point are
a very deep sadness that women spend a lot of time testing
each other and carrying forth stereotypes. It leads other
people to say that women are their own worst enemies,
which is not true, but it does give credence to that position. I think this issue is something that must definitely
be worked on. When women encounter it they have to
share what they are feeling at that time with the person
who is causing it. I found that confrontation to be even
more helpful.

In the long run the Dean did confront the woman and told her that she was going to have to operate as if the two of us--he and I--were identical. And so she did manage that, but only because the top boss told her so. I think that had I probably told her, "Look, this is the way it makes me feel when you write me a letter like this" it may or may not have had the desired effect. But now I am much less nervous about challenging people directly about those kinds of things.

With so many negative aspects to executive positions, why would a woman want to do that?

Actually it is not all negative, but it is more of a struggle than people realize. Young women going into the workplace never have any idea about how hard it is. Yet in my case I am always on a search for meaning, so I won't spend a lot of time on people and activities that ultimately mean nothing either in my life or the institution's life or whatever. And so the times when you can do meaningful things balance off the other negative stuff. It is less a matter of people saying, "Well, you did that job well" than saying "What you did really helped me." That is much more important for me. I would also say that I am a pragmatist, geared to action. So solving problems about things and people as they interact is very satisfying for me. To know you are doing something important, even if the system does not reward you, is very important, very satisfying.

Do you think there is a possibility for women to grow spiritually in the workplace?

You do or you die!

So you have to mature there.

Yes, you have to, or you get stupid. I think maturation goes on anywhere you are. I don't think the ultimate questions are any different anywhere else. They are just framed in a different way in the workplace. But you are still always dealing with questions like Is it for your good or our good? Is it yours or mine or is it ours? Is it for the good of the organization or is it for what I want--my rolex, my Mercedes, or whatever? Those questions go on everywhere. I have done a lot of community work and I know the same thing occurs there. The ultimate value questions are always there. How you treat others, how they treat you.

Would you consider a strong spiritual background an asset for women in positions of power?

Yes, definitely yes. And it can also be a problem. If your spiritual center says that you have to treat people a certain way in order to be ethical, then if the ethics of the workplace are different, you will be clashing all the time. If everything boils down to who's got power rather than who is right in this situation, there will be problems. If your center says that you have to do things in an egalitarian or a fair way and the workplace says that you do things based on a line order or who is boss here, and it is not OK to raise the rightness of questions, then you will be troubled. But I think it's a better trouble to be in than merely floundering with no center, no place to come to. I think a spiritual center is very important from a sense that wherever you are life is dancing around--good things are happening and bad things are happening--and your center is a way of making sense out of that dance. If you don't have a spiritual center, then often things don't make sense to you.

A week ago I went to a funeral of a young man I worked with. We had worked closely on a number of things. He was not able to see his way through some problems and so, at twenty-eight, he hung himself. His violent death was extremely hard on a young woman who was his co-worker. She is now struggling to decipher what his death means. His boss is also spending a lot of time worrying about her style of working with him and how she contributed to his death. So the question of personal values is extremely important. Introspection is necessary.

I think for a lot of people, their jobs are their whole life. Their jobs bring a lot of satisfaction as long as they are able to perform. But when they are no longer able to perform, who are they? They have no identity whatever. Because women are relational, they will not have quite the problem that men have in this regard. They live longer. Men die in alarming numbers the year after they retire. I think that is the basic reason why; they have not learned the social skills to develop intimacy with people. Women learn this early in life and continue to develop it. That intimacy, that caring, both giving and receiving back, sustains us and makes life worth living. Intimacy is a spiritual quality. It is a spiritual facility. It's something that people have worked on for centuries in a very disciplined way to learn to be intimate with their spiritual center, whatever that may be--God, the universe, the environment, or all of them.

But spirituality is also frightening for people. Because I have worked for years for the Lutheran church, I have found people in the workplace very threatened by it. They must have thought that I was going to proselytize them. It is amazing the number of people who felt that my having a spiritual center meant coersion for them. Yet I still believe that we all have to have our own spiritual center.

Since women tend to share power and try to establish a personal relationship rather than give orders and have power over others, how do women avoid the patrimony approach to work, the idea that "I am taking care of my own" like Mayor Daley used to say.

Well, that is a very good question and it is something I do struggle with. In organizations as large as the ones I've been in lately, one does not have to worry about it because one cannot establish personal relationships with so many people. There simply isn't time to have really quality relationships so one simply does what one can. There are enough people to make the mix interesting so it is not possible to dominate the organization in that way.

The problem with the patrimony approach is that it can be very seductive. It can be very dependency building, which is its fault. Because women are accessible in a way that men are not, the staff will bring the woman a lot of personal problems; they will come with work problems also and say, "Fix it. Help me." It is not possible to help everybody, nor is it a style that you want to foster. You want to enable your staff to find their own richness so you give them the time and permission to be able to solve their own problems. That will then hopefully create an independence from you rather than the dependency that accessibility can foster. I have seen people who mistakenly capitalize on this accessibility. I call them Queen Bees; everyone is drawn to the honey. The queen gets rather fat and bloated from all the attention. That's not healthy. You need to be able to struggle with people who say, "Your idea is dumb" and still keep moving and working. We should not constantly need approval to keep us going. We need the ups and the downs, the agreements and the disagreements also, but all of that covered with an ultimate caring that lets people know that we really want things to happen in a good way for them. Whenever I have a choice to make it will be for the empowerment of both of us. It is important that both of us be strong in the relationship whether in the workplace or anywhere else in life.

Vivian Jenkins Nelsen speaks from a multi-faceted career which includes university lecturer, choir director, school board president, organist, and social services worker. Currently she is Director of Administration at the Humphrey Institute College of Public Affairs in Minneapolis.

Born in Nebraska, Vivian attended Dana College where she studied music and art and was the recipient of many awards and scholarships for excellence. She is also completing a doctorate at the University of Minnesota in education, counseling and urban focus.

Always active in the Lutheran Church, Vivian is Program Chairperson for Mission in Communities which is involved in resourcing social justice, global consciousness, peace, world hunger, and refugee settlement. She has taught at Hamline University and the University of Minnesota and has been very active in human relations and community services, particularly for minority groups.

Vivian is a member of the National Council of Negro Women, the Prince of Glory Lutheran Church Council, the Women's Equity Action League, the Metropolitan Cultural Art Center, the Women's Affairs Advisory Board of the Minnesota State Department of Human Rights, and the Greater Urban Parish Board.

A speaker and seminar leader for several school districts, Vivian is presently in Boston with her husband on a six-month fellowship from Harvard University.

How joyous it is to have a perfectly harmonious heart and breath by living harmoniously in the perfectly harmonious energy of heaven and earth.

Mahikari Hymn

Spirituality and Joy

Keiju Okada

Human beings are in essence the children of God; God has given birth to each of us. All of us, in the depths of our hearts and minds, in the depths of our souls, possess a shining, divine nature. This nature is called our true self. It is connected to God's eternal life force; steeped in that life force the true self has life. Made in such a way that it is able to receive unlimited joy, our true self receives as the glory of heaven God's boundless love, goodness, and beauty.

This divine nature is truly our real essence. In Japanese it is called *hito,* which means "human being," but also means "possessor of part of the divine nature of God." Thus anyone who develops this divine nature, anyone who, receiving God's power, devotes herself to God in a truly humble and obedient way is able to manifest these inborn powers of the child of God and the one who possesses part of God's nature.

Spiritual growth, then, means the purification of our spiritual condition, that is, the elevation of our spiritual level. It is the polishing of our true self so that God's nature shines forth from us. It is the manifestation of our innate powers as a real child of God. When we grow spiritually, we are that much more able to do the will of God, we have taken one step closer to God, and we become a cheerful and lively child of divinity filled with God-centeredness.

One sign of our spiritual growth is gratitude. Everything is bestowed on the children of God, from our lives to our bodies. God grants us our daily food and so nurtures us. He freely grants us his precious light. We must be grateful for the glory of serving God, for coming closer to him. Our gratitude to God and our desire to repay him must become ever deeper. Then our entire life will be directed towards him.

In our scriptures, the Goseigin, we learn that it is through our gratitude that we will achieve joy in life:

> *Hito,* you do not live by your own power but are granted your life. You must learn to be thankful for everything . . . and the proper way to express thanks. This is the correct attitude and is very important in the establishment of a relationship with God. Try to make people live according to this principle of God. Thus people will be able to lead lives of joy, and thus they will realize that this is a marvelous way of changing one's life to a life that is based on the righteous law directed towards God, that is, to a life of joy. [1]

Unfortunately, human beings are apt to take things for granted. We take our surroundings for granted; we even take so noble and holy a being as the great God for granted. But we must be truly grateful that we are able to know the joy of living each day, receiving the blessing of God's protective light.

Another way to grow in spirituality is to do God's will and follow his plan for all creation. For a woman particularly, to progress on the spiritual path, she must display or manifest on an ever greater scale the essential qualities and distinctive character with which God has endowed her. Although there is no difference in the ultimate spiritual state of men and women, there is the principle according to which the universe was created that says, "Fire burns due to water and water flows due to fire." From this principle, differences come into being. That is, the respective characteristics of men as men and women as women.

Let me explain. The principle that fire burns due to water and water flows due to fire was formulated at the time of the creation of the universe. It is one of the principles for the order and prosperity of the entire creation. For fire to burn well, there must be air, which is one of the functions of water. Water is horizontal. Water does not flow without the function of fire, which is vertical. If fire and water do not come into harmony with each other, the power of production does not come into being. When water and fire are joined to form a cross, however, the power to produce, to give birth to spirit, is produced.

When a man and a woman are joined in a cross, a child is born; the power to give birth has come into being.

When a company president and his employees are joined in a cross, the company becomes harmonious, and the marvel of achieving superb business results is produced.

Women and men thus have opposite natures; man is fire and woman is water. When man and woman are in harmony with each other and cooperate with each other, the power of the cross comes into being; that which was thought impossible is accomplished before one realizes it, and the world is allowed to fulfill the holy will of God.

The most distinctive characteristic of woman is her role of activating the essential nature of man, which is fire. Woman is water. Therefore woman must be humble and pure like water. Just as water flows to the lowest point, women must be complete in their practice of humility. In Japan we have the expression, "just like clouds or water, moving on without becoming attached to anything." So too, it is important for woman to be obedient to the divine arrangements of God, just as water never loses its properties wherever it may flow. Water never forgets its nature, but always obeys the arrangements of God. When one pours water into a vessel, it conforms to the shape of the vessel in the twinkling of an eye. Truly this is the real form of woman.

One of the important aspects of this divine teaching is that fire is primary while water is secondary and subordinate. As man is primary and woman is secondary, man as the function of fire has the responsibility to take the lead. Woman must help man by performing the function of water. If she does not do this, the work of man will not come into being. The holy role of water is necessary.

For a family to be prosperous, the father must work hard and the mother must encourage and urge him on in his activities. This is the function of water. If women did not exist in life, men would not be sufficiently active. Man literally does not burn when woman is absent. Therefore God gave man a desire for sexual love as a part of his divine plan and brought about the development of the physical world by stirring up man's desire to compete.

In the undertaking of building a heavenly civilization that is peaceful and full of joy, men alone will not do. The undertakings of men are activated by the function of women. Therefore, when men are able to fulfill their role, it is thanks to women. If there were only men, only fire, no doubt everything would end up in conflict. We see this principle also in the relationship between a man and his wife. A man has to leave the home and perform the function of yang: positive, left-sided, fire, vertical. The woman takes care of the home, the children, her husband, performing the function of yin: negative, right-sided, water, horizontal. When they do this, fire and water with their opposite natures come into harmony with each other, and the heavenly world is in accordance with God's will.

In today's society with its sudden changes and violence, both in the home and on the local level, the display by women of their special characteristics is the way to make manifest a heavenly society, and ultimately the way to build a heavenly civilization for mankind.

Because water obeys the divine laws, it never loses its essential nature. Therefore God grants it an important role. We have been given the precious teaching: Because the spiritual essence of water is always centered on the will of God, it will never know destruction throughout eternity. God will give it eternal life.

For all human beings, natural virtues are important; for women particularly, feminine virtues are necessary. We have a traditional Japanese expression, "a woman's help." When the husband accomplishes something big for the world, when a child is brought up to be a wonderful person, this is due to the womanly virtues. What women need to learn is to abandon all thought of trying to show themselves off to best advantage, and instead polish their womanly virtues. The virtues of woman as woman do not exist in the world of men.

To be specific, one virtue for woman is refinement. another is perfection as wife and mother. These virtues show themselves in exquisite femininity, in the way one walks or sets out a rice bowl. This is not general education or knowledge; it is part of the nature of woman. It is important to cultivate these womanly charms for the spiritual growth of oneself and society.

So by following the will of God, by conforming to our nature, and by purifying it ever more and more, we will live in joy and help create heaven on earth. Truly a life that is led in accordance with the will of God is the highest form of human happiness. To do one's best to share that happiness with others is love, sincerity, salvation.

So by following the will of God, by conforming to our nature, and by purifying it ever more and more, we will live in joy and help create heaven on earth. Truly a life that is led in accordance with the will of God is the highest form of human happiness. To do one's best to share that happiness with others is love, sincerity, salvation.

The many great calamities of the world, like earthquakes, volcanic eruptions, airplane disasters, are atonements for sin. They are increasing all over the world because as the human heart becomes drier and drier, society also dries up. It becomes desert-like and brutal, and great confusion reigns. But if one individual begins to purify herself, her family will gradually come to radiate bright light, then their society will become cheerful, and by and by the whole country will become cheerful. By not getting caught up in the world of phenomena, by uniting with God's soul, by making one's heart like God's, by praying (which means to ride God's will), by practicing God's laws, changes become manifest in the world of phenomena and one is led to a world of light.

For instance, those who complain of pain, unhappiness, or illness are in reality being made to undergo a practice for the purpose of purification. If they can master the thinking that allows them to accept and even enjoy these purifications, they can then take great steps forward on the path to God. Thus an unhappy person should enjoy his unhappiness. A poor person should be poor in joy. If they do this, their trial ends quickly without suffering, and they are quickly saved. If they realize that they have negative karma, that they are erasing that karma now, and if they are grateful for the chance to do so, they will be able to overcome the trials of life with ease.

In other words, if we leave everything up to God, if we think only of fulfilling God's will, the doors to the future will open and our destiny will be brighter. If one really unites with God, joy is all there is for such a human being. The joy and happiness that then fills the heart becomes the source for even greater joy and happiness.

We children of God, having been endowed with eternal life, must, through repeated incarnations, serve God and little by little divinize ourselves. For children of God this is the greatest joy. In order to do this, we must elevate the nature with which we are endowed. We must cultivate humility of heart and the virtue of modesty. We must give up judging others and cultivate the mental attitude of always giving room to others and treating them with love and sincerity. We must perform selfless service for others and our own duties with joy and pleasure and treat every minute of every day as something precious.

As we are taught in the Goseigen, if we burn with enthusiasm for the righteous laws, if we do not neglect to be mentally prepared to march forward one step at a time, and if we do not neglect actual practice and devotion, we will be transformed into a person that is thankful and joyous.

It is important to live with a heart full of love for God, to endeavor to come into contact with the holy light of God, to live each day in joy and gratitude with a cheerful heart, to serve with a heart that is gentle and warm, and with a humble heart conscious of our unworthiness of the help we receive from him. When we acquire the custom of attending to divine things properly in our daily life, we are able to cheerfully enjoy life from the heart.

To do acts of good in secret is also important. When people are watching it is easy to do good and avoid evil. But when we are alone and no one is watching, it is important to be able to value oneself. If we know our value as a child of God, we will be able to do good in secret. Our founder has taught us that if one does not show others that she has done good, and does good in secret, God will use her for great purposes. If one is going to do an act of good, it is better to do it in secret.

As God lives in heaven, he leads a life that is always full of joy. The world of the righteous God is the world of heaven; therefore God can be said to be joy (divine energy). God is joy, and joy is the path to heaven that brings the energy of God to oneself. God is trying to build a heavenly civilization on earth through his children. Therefore it is extremely important to fulfill his will to make manifest a heaven on earth that resembles the divine world.

There is a nest of selfish desires in the heart and soul of every person. We should not live our daily lives for the satisfaction of those desires. For us children of God, to serve him is an irreplaceable joy and a true happiness. There is nothing so important for humanity as the purification and elevation of its spiritual nature. Unfortunately, the majority of people limit this infinite spirituality, this divinity, that they have received from God. They daily poison their spiritual nature causing their soul-spirit to atrophy. People today neglect to elevate their spiritual nature. They are daily swayed by their self-love and idleness. They emit evil attitudes of resentment, jealousy, envy, and hatred. They are tarnishing their soul-spirits and their hearts--sullying their brilliant nature of their own accord.

What I would particularly like to stress is that in the world of faith, dissatisfaction and discontent that stem from selfish desires are taboo. Selfishness results in ugly disputes and quarrels. It interferes with God's important work, and leads to the sin of forcing people who are following the true path to lose their faith. Thus it is extremely important to always purify ourselves of selfish desires and to attune our vibrations to God.

In essence spiritual joy is the same as the joy in our everyday lives, but the joy that comes from materialistic satisfaction and puts worldly desires at the center of things is quite different from spiritual joy. When we serve God wholeheartedly, when we think only of the happiness of the children of God, only of the future happiness of mankind, when we serve God through our occupation, work, or study, then we become able to know real joy in our lives.

We must become people of shining light. We must live our lives in gratitude and service to God and become a person of sincere altruistic love abounding in kind concern for others. For those who live in light, joy and peace will daily increase. It is the Parent God who extends the hand of salvation to people seeking salvation and thus saves them. The joy of praising and directly serving God, who does all things for us, is a joy that knows no substitute. If we are able to entrust everything to God, to devote our whole self to God, we have nothing to fear, nothing to seek, and we gain warmth and tranquil peace in the loving arms of God. This is the condition of eternal spring in which we are united with God in joy, in which we praise him.

With the goal of establishing a heavenly civilization, women must help to spread God's light and the attitude of divinity over this earth. I would like women to utilize their special characteristics of water to flow horizontally and spread the love of God to ever broadening horizons. We know that God is joy. Therefore if one is a child of God, one can experience keen and limitless joy in one's heart.

> When you come to breathe in God's light with your whole body, you will be filled with joy. When you are filled with joy upon joy, it is as if God is living in you.[2]

Reverend Keiju Okada is the spiritual head of Sukyo Mahikari, a world-wide religious movement with headquarters in Japan. She is revered by Mahikari members as the living representative of God on earth. In 1959 Kotama Okada, Keiju's father, began the new sect following a profound spiritual experience. Keiju participated in the difficult early work of spreading the teachings with her father, whom she accepted as her spiritual mentor. At his death in 1974 she took over the work of teaching, healing, and

purifying those who came for help. Known as Oshienushisama, "great teacher," she warmly guides the 400,000 followers of Sukyo Mahikari by her writings, her sermons, and by traveling to centers around the world. She officiates at all services in the beautiful Mahikari shrine in Takayama, Japan. An adept in many of Japan's traditional arts, particularly the tea ceremony, she works with Japanese leaders to preserve those ancient skills. Keiju Okada has recently completed a biographical compilation of stories about the life and work of her father.

Even on earth the world is transformed
by those whose minds are established in the vision of oneness.
Bhagavad Gita

Transforming Energy

An Interview with

David Fish

D r. David Fish was interviewed by the editor in London. During the conversation his friend, Justin O'Brien, was asked to comment.

Dr. Fish, what is your definition of spirituality?

Briefly, for this is at best a provisional idea, I would equate spirituality with a search for meaning and purpose beyond the usual values and meanings of career and status, family life and enjoyment, serving that understanding by integrating it into one's living. Some individuals come to this naturally, but most of us have to connect with a teaching if we wish to intensify this process.

What sort of a teaching?

Some traditions hold that there are several major formalized ways, making their appeal to different temperaments. These approaches usually reflect the major types of functionings found in man: the physical, emotional, and mental. So, for example, a man or woman predominantly emotionally polarized will be attracted to a path with an emotional emphasis. This is well illustrated by the four traditional approaches to spirituality. One is the way of the fakir, who attempts to develop a will over the physical body and transform energy into a certain quality. The second is the way of the monk who attempts to transform his emotional nature by identifying with emotions that incarnate higher qualities. Third is the way of the yogi who attempts to control the mind, or the realm of thinking. These three ways often require one to move out of life into special conditions. The fourth way is for those who wish to continue in ordinary life and simultaneously work on the different sides of one's nature. Indeed on this path one's ordinary life situation, that is, the very trials and tribulations of the day provide the material for one's work. This strong relationship with life means it is essential to be psychologically sound and well able to meet the demands of everyday reality. Perhaps surprisingly this cannot be taken for granted.

This is a great simplification of the different approaches because there is overlap, and all work to some extent on the different sides of human nature. But we can see that central to all of them is the idea of transforming energies.

Aren't all these energies the same?

Yes, at one level all energy is the same, but there are also different kinds of energies with different qualities and implications. There are physical energies, heat, gravity, electricity for example and different physical and psychological energies such as emotional and sexual. It might be helpful here to touch on another concept. We can see very clearly in ourselves that energy in relationship to itself can be active, passive, or resisting, or a more subtle combination of both--perhaps the most interesting possibility-- in terms of a deeper relationship with oneself or others. There is the traditional symbol of the male representing the active force, and the female the receptive. The child would be the reconciling or third force. Yet in any man or woman each of these forces can be experienced, and any transformation of ourselves involves the interaction among all of them.

How do you consider sexuality relates to spirituality?

If spirituality is about the transformation of energy and one of the major energies is sexual, then sex plays an integral part in spirituality. If we disassociate sex as a function and consider it as an energy, you see what a great power it has over people. It affects us in body and mind, pervading many human relations. The transmutation of sex energy relative to perception and spiritual work can be seen in the world's religions in the observation of celibacy and so forth. It has been said that in man it naturally plays a part in the realm of the mind in terms of the transformation and regulation of psychological energy. Used in this way the sexual energy has a very fine potential. But we more commonly see its degenerate manifestation in emotional instability and violence. I have the impression at times of sexual energy, the attraction between men and women, the interaction of higher and lower energies within oneself and the relationships of planets to each other as one enormous play of energy.

Are the differences in male and female connected to this transformation of energy?

I believe there are innate differences between men and women although conditioning does play a very significant part in our final persona. This difference in men and women, distinct from conditioning, creates a dynamism that brings forth a need for each to be more sensitive and open to the way the other essentially perceives reality that can lead to both coming to a much deeper understanding of our meaning and purpose on this planet.

Perhaps saints come to a state where they transcend the differences in being male or female, but there appears to me a more natural inclination of each sex to view things differently or with greater sensitivity in certain domains. J.G. Bennett, a philosopher and spiritual seeker who explored this idea, suggested that women often have a more real appreciation of what is taking place in the present. I would go along with this.

What is its counterpart in men?

Seeing the potential in a situation. Which is perhaps partly why men often appear more theoretical and abstract, or get locked into arguments that lead nowhere.

Could you say more about the differences between the sexes in relation to spirituality?

One of the things I feel is that women, both in the way

society conditions them, and in being mothers, have a sense of what it is to serve, which is an essential part of spiritual growth. A man, on the other hand, is conditioned into a more artificial role. Masculinity is equated with being active in a relatively coarse and external sense, of controlling, and being the originator of, his actions. Many men appear a caricature, man aping manhood, rather than having an essential foundation in that which is real in himself. This is the antithesis of the direction of spiritual work which is about becoming real. So instead of being the best sportsman, a successful money-maker, famous, interesting, and so on, what is required is not something superficial but an inner quality of being which requires a special kind of inner containment whilst still being open to the requirements of external life. Thus if man embarks on a spiritual quest his transformation only takes place to the extent that, in addition to his own efforts, he is receptive to a higher influence. He has to discover a very different attitude and openness which is receptive so that he can allow a finer, more active force to act through him, and be at its service.

Women seem less burdened by this type of egotism. They are less alienated from an understanding of their true place in the scheme of things which we see on reflection as one of absolute interdependence with all that surrounds us.

Of course, I am guilty of gross generalization here. Many of these statements need considerable qualification. I should have distinguished at the outset that when I talk of woman, I am speaking from a spiritual rather than a psychological or social perspective. I am assuming, and in general speaking of, a woman who is fairly grounded in those qualities that I perceive as intrinsic to the female archetype. For example: receptive, nurturing, a greater sensitivity for relationship and integration.

This generalization is particularly vulnerable at present when women's roles are undergoing radical revaluation. Many are unable to live according to old stereotypes whilst the new ways are unknown. There is always the problem that in rejecting the conditions, essential qualities are misinterpreted and woman becomes alienated from the gifts that belong to her essential nature. There is a need for the deepening of awareness so that, whilst refusing a subservient position, she does not become contemptuous of her own values. In asserting independence one needs to be inwardly secure enough not to have to control. It seems an especially difficult time for modern, emancipated woman because there are no integrated roles to model on. Modern woman is not given an understanding of a real purpose and role in the way that those in some traditional cultures have retained. Many women that I encounter in my practice are disoriented and confused. There is a loss of being grounded that a normal woman has (that men tend to lack). There is a confusion of levels; important as women's liberation is on its own level, the real question for women--as it is for men--is a more fundamental liberation, that is, a liberation from the slavery of oneself, such as vanity, anger, criticism, and so on.

The practical life for a woman, including motherhood, occurs naturally, existentially, and essentially. Women can easily become still and, by nature perhaps, are very receptive. I feel there is a more direct access to spirituality for women because it is less a creation of something artificial. Man fulfills his role more awkwardly. He is not essentially a father, but only existentially. A woman is more naturally a mother than a father is a father. A man, generalizing from my own experience, learns to relate to a baby, whereas woman instinctively relates to it. Maybe a 'natural' or 'unspoilt' woman has a more direct access to essential values; with man it is as if something more is required to make the connection.

Would you say that receptivity, which you feel is natural to women, is an essential aspect of spiritual growth?

Yes, certainly. I feel that in terms of spirituality we really are infants. The actual moments when we are in contact with what can be described as spiritual, or a higher influence, are very brief and need to be constantly refreshed by our endeavor to open a state of receptivity so as to attract a force that can work in us, bringing authenticity and meaning to our whole being.

Can you give us an example of what you mean by the basic difference of perception of men and women?

All right. Let's say that after I left you I share my impressions of you with my wife. I assume I have a clear
picture of what transpired, but my wife might say, "Didn't
you realize she reacted strongly to your thoughts about
so and so?" She will be much more immediately in contact
with what was happening, with the 'here and nowness' of
what was going on. One aspect of spirituality is this
deeper awareness of the here and now. Generalizing again,
women have a greater facility to read things more through
their feelings and body, and thereby be in touch with the
texture of the situation, whereas men are more inclined
to filter impressions through the process of thought. In
modern Western life, though, this distinction is not as
clear as it was. Contemporary spiritual teachers frequently
find women just as much taken by their thoughts as men.
Nevertheless I am not equating our customary feelings to
spirituality. When I am more open and perceptive, I can
feel when you are listening to me. I can see it in your
face when you are only 'thinking' about what I am saying.
When I am relatively centered, in my body, I can also
feel how you are feeling about what I am saying. Normally, though, I am only reacting to what is being said. To
get in contact with a finer quality of perception there is
a blending of the energies of thinking and feeling and
the body. When someone speaks with this inner relation
there is an unmistakable authenticity. There is a flavor
of freedom in the way they are expressing themselves. A
relaxed poise in the body seems to be essential for this
possibility to arise; one is a bit freer of the distorting
tension of one's egotism. Although men and women start
from different domains there are the same requirements.

One aspect of the egotism that men are given to
is holding up a bigger front. The idea of being in need
seems harder for men to admit to. When perpetuating
one's image of oneself, one is cut off from help, from
another quality of being. Women perhaps more readily
admit to being in need.

And that is a good thing?

I think so. Our usual viewpoint is over-full. We are full
of being capable or incapable, in one way or another. To
meet the need we undoubtedly have, we have to make

room, play a lesser role, allow ourselves to be incomplete, unknowing. We have to accept being insufficient. Something has to melt for something else to be.

Perhaps women have a difficulty in relating to men. I notice that while they may have a more real perception about something, they cannot always convey that to a man, because his force is more dominant. She may have great difficulty conveying her insight, especially if she doesn't cling to her point well enough. Women tend to mistrust their perceptions in front of the force of men's non-understanding. She may have a much better quality of understanding and appreciation of a situation, but to manifest her perception is difficult. Some of this is for the reasons feminists have outlined, but some of it appears to be of a more intrinsic nature. So while women may sense the nature of a situation, men reinterpret it. When men listen to women they often reinterpret what she says on their own terms, or else reject it. Men's thinking or perception is more accessible to a woman than a woman's is accessible to a man.

A woman's determination, however, can be very strong. It is said that the Prophet Mohammed had doubts about his mission throughout his life, but his wife, once she understood his destiny, was unswerving in her encouragement.

What do you think, Justin?

Justin O'Brien: I think a woman is much more relational than a man is. She has a tangible understanding of things. A man tends to be more abstract. Consequently she has a greater problem of loneliness than man does. A man can be entertained by his ideas more easily than a woman can. She likes to be with people and express herself towards people more than a man does. He can put up with his thoughts, work with a mental task for a long time. I am not saying that a woman cannot do that, but I find that a woman needs more sensory support. She likes to hear words. She is also quick to pick up the tonal quality of a word along with its meaning.

David: She is more emotional, then?

Justin: Well, there is a sensuousness about a woman and

it is because of that that she stays close to the concrete. Emotions are not moved by the abstract; they are moved only by the concrete. A woman can zero in on a person with a discernment that is incredible; she can grasp all the details that comprise an individual. She is really oriented so much to the individuality of things; she is a natural artist in that sense.

Women's problem in spirituality, as I see it, stems right out of that. She is more devotional by nature, and from that springs the problem of dependency. For her the struggle is learning independence, learning to be detached, learning to be concerned without becoming totally identified with the situation so that she has to experience all the pain that might be there as well.

A man is usually just the opposite. He tends to get so detached and abstract that he loses an empathy with the situation. Because man is so conditioned by his upbringing and society, his competitive edge is very sharp, making it quite difficult for him to be self-effacing in any way, which is quite easy for woman.

David: Right. And I see it is necessary to side-step one's perpetual efforts to maintain one's image of oneself. I felt very much as you were talking, Justin, that what is required is a kind of wholeness to the way we perceive ourselves and others. We are always out of balance. By letting go a little and coming back inside and seeing what is maintaining the imbalance, even while manifesting, a relationship is established between active and receptive parts of one's nature so that we are both active in a certain way while being receptive. We can feel the situation emotionally without being swamped by a particular emotion, and listen without being carried away by our thinking.

Rather than being stereotypes of man and woman, we would have the possibility of melting and being much more open and free, much more able to include intuitive possibility, classically identified as being feminine, and also have a certain drive, which might be considered masculine. We could then experience and contain much more of any situation. We could experience making tea, driving the car, making love, and not be totally absorbed in these actions which require another special kind of activity or aliveness.

I feel our experience of ourself is naive. Our inner world is largely unseen. We are not brought up to be sensitive to what is taking place within us. I was brought up to learn about things outside myself: to kick a ball out there, to study things out there, to compete out there. That is very far away from this much more inclusive vision of being present to, witnessing, deeply experiencing the moment in which all this is taking place.

What is the goal then? Is it to integrate our own self, our masculine/feminine parts? Is it to integrate a masculine person and a feminine person so that together they can do something for society? What are we striving for in spirituality?

I must go back to the idea that spirituality is about discovering what has more meaning in our experience and learning how to live that. I think that a man and woman in their relationship provide an extraordinary kind of dynamic situation that helps to give a special possibility to evolution, individually and for mankind. The potential is there because there are different qualities in the way we perceive things. Also, blending with someone else psychologically and discovering more about the other may give us a finer way of understanding reality.

As I speak to people about spirituality, it seems they often do not know why they are on a particular path, or why they are striving so hard. They just know that something keeps pushing them forward. They didin't know what it was they were looking for, but they kept seeking. Eventually an inner conviction said, "This is it" and they knew they were onto something right for them. What is this something that pushes us?

People are moved towards a spiritual path by one of two things, usually a mixture of the two. One is a deep dissatisfaction and the other is a vision of something higher.

In the 60's, for example, many people in their teens and early twenties, as part of a larger cultural trend, looked beyond society's customary values and aspirations to question the very fundamentals we had always accepted. Some experimented with Eastern religions, meditation, and the new humanistic psychotherapies. They had a taste that there could be more to life than the consensus reality. Though in retrospect this period appears adolescent, I enjoyed it enormously; it did break ground. For many people it was an introduction to new ideas, to something higher. With respect to the hedonistic side of that time, I think it is important to make a distinction between a need to be happy and a much deeper need which may be spiritual. In the spiritual approach one is preparing oneself to be of service to something higher in some way. To learn to be happy is something else.

Do you mean that one is selfish and one is selfless?

In part, yes. To be happier is not necessarily more spiritual. Nevertheless if you attempt to integrate a spiritual dimension in your life this brings about a deeper fulfillment.

Then you see spirituality as a kind of service?

Absolutely. It must be service to the community, to the planet. If it is about an evolution of meaning, and since we are part of the very fabric of the planet, then it has to be about serving on this very planet. Obviously, warfare, hate, greed, and all those negative things do not serve the planet.

It is a good question to ask what we are doing here, even at this discussion at this moment. To the extent that we begin to come together, then a better quality of energy arises at this moment; we then have fresh thoughts, feelings, and ideas. Incidentally we did not come to this by trying to be happy, but our previous spiritual work probably reflects in our capacity to be here in this way, as a channel in a tiny way increasing the quota of goodness in the world.

It sounds as if you are saying that growth in spirituality is growth in love.

Absolutely. And this may be our hope for the planet and its people.

Justin O'Brien: I think we grow in stages of awareness. At one time I had organized my life around certain things that I liked and disliked. Eventually I grew impatient and dissatisfied with it. There was something gnawing at me, an impulse to go on. So I began to expand, revise, refine. Other things then came into my awareness and I began to organize my life around those. New habits, letting go of old ones. There were changes in the things I knew and the things I loved. My knowledge and my love were searching and went through qualitative and quantitative changes. So I see that spirituality is the pursuit of knowledge and love which combined gives one an awareness of the meaning of life and of oneself.

When that grows, one discovers that it cannot belong to you alone. You feel a sense of wanting to share it. You realize that you are not an island unto yourself. But that awareness is very uneven; it comes and goes in spite of our efforts to stabilize it. We only realize that we must continually grow. Accepting that, one can break through some of the rigidity of the ego, which tries to plateau too early in life and wants to stop the growth process.

Something will always come that forces us beyond the parameters of the rational mind. It is intelligible, but not rational. People call it the mystic experience. I think it is possible for that to be incorporated into our more mundane experiences. We travel on a spectrum, so to speak. Gradually we see that there is no sharp break between the natural and the supernatural, but that all life is a continuum. But there is a definite threshold that must be crossed. That is where the spiritual practices come in. They help us to cross the threshold and continue growth.

In here comes the role of pain. It is the signal that tells us when we have reached the edge. It shows us we must reconnoiter. Pain tells us something is wrong and must be looked at. Then we must struggle until we can discover what it is and correct it. There is a terrible process of discovering, there is a phase of your spirituality, when you must let go of many things you thought were necessary. You do not banish them; rather it is an internal adjustment so that your attitude towards them must change. You can no longer cleave to them. It is a recognition not just of the flux of life, but your recognition of the flux of life with no regrets. Some people get caught there. They will not release their memories of things they've missed, chances that are gone, or things that have been taken from them by nature. They won't let go of that and so they cling to the past. This stops their growth and causes pain. So pain in this instance shows us that we are holding unto something which is not meant to be held. This is an inner insecurity which one must pass. In Christian mysticism it is called the dark night of the soul. But it occurs in every spiritual tradition. It is the painful letting go of those attachments which are good. (It is easy to let go of the bad ones.) The struggle is going through that.

That refers to what you have been saying earlier about receptivity, doesn't it David? Trying to reach transcendence and realizing that we have lots of baggage to get rid of?

David: Yes. There seems to be a paradox in that one must make very great efforts, which is activity, to learn to be free from the very activity which maintains our identification with thoughts and feelings which we seek to free ourself from. It is our identification that makes baggage of our thoughts and feelings.

Justin: I think that the struggle, perhaps especially for men, is to learn to be gentle with life. In spirituality bullying will not work. That is the ego again. One cannot 'stake out' transcendence and forcefully grab it. There must be a gentleness which opens a new awareness. The quality of love changes then and one can love without trying to possess.

David: One of the best definitions of love is "to allow." It has been said that real marriage occurs between a man and a woman when each totally accepts the other. That is a very high thing. If we could be unconditionally open, cultivate an attitude of acceptance to others, and accept the place of the higher and lower in ourselves, we would enter a whole other domain of perception. But we don't love that way. We don't accept the other totally.

We don't even accept the way another eats his soup! And so our energy is spent trying to change each other.

I, too, am interested in the idea of pain and suffering. Pain is a signal, but it is also the very medium by which something is transformed. In life you can cheat at everything, but one of the facts of spirituality is that there is no fooling. No cheating is possible at all. There is very little in life that we can say that about. There is a difficulty in accepting what I discover about myself as time goes on. I recognize much that I don't like, that is unacceptable, and feel the weight and the power of something that may be deeply rooted. Yet in other moments, I am permiable and able to sustain being with the pain of seeing what I am. It is only through the pain of bearing what I am and am not, that I am transformed, redeemed. A new quality of energy arises and something is redeemed. It seems to me that is where growth occurs--where I manage to suffer differently. I suffer for something.

Our fear of suffering and our fear of fear is a big barrier to our growth. We are held back by fear of pain. Nothing in our upbringing tells us that suffering is an integral part of life, and by bearing it in a different way it could be the very medium by which we can come to something really worthwhile. It is the very thing that I have spent my whole life trying to avoid that I must confront if I am to go forward in depth.

Is suffering something we must do ourself or can we help each other with it?

We can help each other do it ourself. We are finally alone in our suffering.

What kind of transformation occurs as a result of this suffering?

When energies are transformed there can be at times a direct and tangible impression of a strong but fine energy permeating one, which has the qualities of love and intelligence. In my experience the essential prerequisites are a very sensitive awareness of one's body. This awareness, or more specifically, this attention, facilitates the possibility of directly experiencing the energy of the thoughts and feelings at the very moment they are happening.

This is not to be confused with the manipulation of energy, or thinking about it; it is not a change of mood. It is a qualitative change in consciousness. This action which is the concern of the heart of spiritual traditions in a sense marks the parting of the ways between psychotherapy and the spiritual path.

So first I search for a qualitatively different awareness of my body. I come into a relationship with it. Most of the time I am lost in thought, I have been talking for twenty mintues without hearing what I am saying, or I have been obsessed by feelings of one kind or another. There is no relationship between that part and the rest of me. Grounded in my body I begin to feel a relationship with more of the whole of me.

Does spiritual work entail striving for this integration, or does it take place after this integration has been achieved?

Spiritual work cannot take place until there is a coming together within. We make those efforts, but we never do any spiritual work. I think all spiritual work is given; our role is to create the conditions to allow another possibility. Everything is given. We do not make our bodies, or our thoughts, or our ideas. All is given. We have nothing of ourself. A very special quality of humility, vigilence, and sensitivity is required. It is a tangible feeling when ordinary striving melts and we are still, dynamically open. Then we may notice that a great thing is taking place.

David Fish, D.O., M.R.O., M.B.Ac.A., is married with two children. He has established a multi-disciplinary holistic practice, including a stress management and educational program in Kensington, London. He qualified in Osteopathy and later in Acupuncture, and has studied the Alexander Technique for the last ten years.

Working with disturbed adolescents in Canada, he received his first training in Gestalt and group psychotherapy which led to his later exploration of both individual psychotherapy and group analytic psychotherapy.

David became increasingly interested in the spiritual dimension of psychological processes. In this direction the

teachings of G.I. Gurdjieff have been a strong influence in developing his understanding. He continues to be actively engaged in a living spiritual tradition. He has a particular interest in the cultivation of awareness of the body as well as the mind in psychological and spiritual discipline.

He is currently engaged in the completion of a book on creative living in the eighties which explores a holistic approach to living, and all aspects of health care (Roxby Press). David enjoys being with his family, running, skiing, and boating.

We are all members one of another.
Ephesians 4:25

The Fulness of Man-Womanhood

Mother Tessa Bielecki

There can be no feminine spirituality, psychology, or theology without the masculine. The integration of masculine and feminine is so fundamental that the feminine may actually be described as "capacity for the masculine" and the masculine as "capacity for the feminine."

This complementarity is clearly indicated in the Chinese philosophy of yin and yang. These notions are so ancient, no one knows precisely where or when they originated. Yin stands for the feminine, the intuitive, the contemplative, and is represented by the moon. The Chinese character for yin also stands for shade, the earth, and the belly. Yang stands for the masculine, the rational, the active, and is represented by the sun. The Chinese character for yang also stands for light, for heaven, and the head.

Within the Judaeo-Christian tradition, we find a similar insight in the Book of Genesis. God said, "Let us make mankind in our image and likeness" (Gen.1:26). In this biblical sense, 'mankind' or 'man' is in no way limited to the masculine, but instead refers to the whole species, or 'humankind.' This is clearly indicated in the next passage "God created man in his own image. In the image of God he created him. Male and female he created them" (Gen. 1:27). Yin-yang complementarity is surely the clearest and deepest meaning of this controversial passage from the first book of the Bible. Our most ancient tradition insists that masculine and feminine together--and only together--are the image and likeness of God.

Within the Wisdom tradition one dimension of the godhead is called wisdom, Sophia. In this tradition, wisdom is feminine and coexistent with God before creation, "an aura of the might of God and a pure effusion of the glory of the almighty" (Wis. 7:25). Considering the Chinese connection between light and masculinity, the Biblical linkage between light and femininity is significant:

> She is the refulgence of eternal light,
>   the spotless mirror of the power of God,
>   the image of his goodness.
> And she, who is one, can do all things,
>   and renews everything while herself perduring.
> And passing into holy souls from age to age,
>   she produces friends of God and prophets.
> For there is naught God loves, be it not one who dwells
>   with wisdom.
> For she is fairer than the sun and surpasses
>   every constellation of the stars.
> Compared to light, she takes precedence,
>   for that, indeed, night supplants . . .
> Indeed, she reaches from end to end
>   mightily and governs all things well.
>
> Wisdom 7:26–8:1

This passage must be understood in its original and deepest sense which is both mythical and mystical. From the perspective of Catholic orthodoxy it must also be related to that tradition which calls the second person (or dimension) of the trinitarian godhood the Son, in fact, "the only begotten Son of God."

The Yin-Yang of Carmel

The yin-yang complementarity in the universe is strikingly evident in the history of my own Carmelite tradition. Since I have written of this extensively elsewhere, I will merely summarize here.[1] We see the masculine principle in the geography of Mt. Carmel, which reaches and stretches itself out of the feminine earth into the heights of heaven. (Carmelites have the distinction of being the only religious order to name themselves after a mountain!) Although the spirituality which grows out of the desert is rugged and virile, the geography of the desert is markedly feminine with its wide open spaciousness abandoned to the ravishments of sun and wind and rain.

Elijah the prophet is the spiritual father of the Carmelite tradition, in whom every Carmelite sees himself as in a mirror. He is the dramatically masculine archetype, phallically symbolized by fire. The mother of Carmel is Our Lady of Mt. Carmel, Mary, the Mother of Jesus. Carmel lives and breathes Mary because she represents another ideal and provides crucial feminine balance to the fierce Elijan spirit. The femininity of Our Lady of Mt. Carmel is aptly captured in the symbol of the cloud, composed of air and water, in which she 'appeared' to Elijah.[2]

Although the first 12th century Carmelite hermits were all men, they were deeply devoted to Our Lady of Mt. Carmel, dedicated their chapel in her honor, and named themselves after her. They were also radically in touch and in tune with Mother Earth, as early Carmelite sources indicate.

St. Teresa of Avila, the 16th century Spanish Carmelite, is the only woman in the Church ever to reform an order of men. In order to accomplish this she exhibited a strong animus in a life of prayer that was both militant as well as matrimonial. In her *Way of Perfection* she told her nuns: "I want you to be strong men." According to one of her own friars, "a breath of warrior energy animated her." But Teresa's life, loves, and mystical writings clearly show an utterly feminine woman, wisely aware of both the strengths and weaknesses of her femininity, eagerly willing to be complemented by the strengths of the men in her life, especially St. John of the Cross.

Like St. Teresa, his madre and mentor, John considered himself a conquistador of the spiritual life. And like Teresa, John, too, is a Mystical Doctor of the Church who outlines the Carmelite path as an arduous ascent up the slopes of Mt. Carmel.

This masculine-feminine complementarity in Carmel reaches its apogee in the mystery of Jesus Christ. That feminine dimension of the godhead we call wisdom unites with the masculine Jesus, and the Christ emerges as the fulness of man-womanhood. The androgynous nature of Jesus Christ (not to be confused with the man Jesus) remains to be explored.

It seems natural and inevitable that the Christian spirit of Carmel, which reflects such masculine-feminine balance throughout its venerable history, should result in a mixed community of men and women called the Spiritual Life Institute, my own small monastic community of hermits founded in 1960. Our community recaptures the spirit of the mountain and the desert, Elijah and Our Lady, John of the Cross and Teresa, and lives according to the primitive

Carmelite ideal in a meaningful contemporary way.

Yin-yang integration is no mere academic question in my life, then, but a burning existential necessity, as I live out my life in community with eight men and six other women on the contemplative Carmelite path.

The Feminist Mistake

The "feminine mystique" criticized by Betty Friedan in 1964, led women to identify rather exclusively with their feminine qualities, allowing all-male, half-men to balance and complete them by being their masculinity for them. Romanticism and the domestic confinement Friedan called "the confortable concentration camp" are based on this extreme feminization of women. Women reacted against the mystique. Suffering from a lack of equality in an over-whelmingly masculinized culture that considered them inferior, they organized the Women's Liberation Movement. Great good has come from women's quest for liberation, including deeper development of women's talents and more effectiveness in shaping society. But the women's movement has also evidenced tragedy and pathos.

Anne Wilson Schoef, author of *Women's Reality,* and Megan Marshall, author of *The Cost of Loving,* reveal evidence of distress and disillusionment. Betty Friedan herself speaks of "nervousness" in the women's movement, an "unarticulated malaise, disconcerted silence and uneasy murmuring," "troubling symptoms of distress." In *The Second Stage,* written almost twenty years after she helped launch the first stage of women's liberation, Friedan boldly asks: "Will we find that the women's movement is, in fact, harboring some incurable cancer, dooming it to imminent death?" What is this "incurable cancer"? Could it be a "blind spot in feminism"? Friedan is courageous in her analysis: "Insofar as the new feminist mystique is defined by reaction against the old feminine necessity, it could suppress important parts of our personhood--breeding a new problem that has no name."[3]

This new problem has a very clear name: "contempt for the feminine." This contempt may well be the greatest damage done to women by dominance of the masculine over the centuries--a contempt tragically implicit in much of the propaganda of the women's movement.

A recent questionnaire asking women their responses to the new image of the liberated woman indicate some unhealthy attitudes. One woman, for example, pretended to be enthusiastic about the new image in public because she was ashamed to admit she was happy taking care of her home and her children. At least she was aware of her pretence in hiding her real joy. But how many repress it altogether in face of the collective contempt?

This contempt for feminine values has had a devastating effect not only on women themselves but on men as well. In their disorientation, women experience confusion and delusion about the nature of womanhood, a loss of identity, anxiety, insecurity, and estrangement within themselves. The tragic alienation of women from their femininity is often accompanied by a deep sense of guilt because it is a betrayal of woman's own birthright.

The Masculine Trap

Out of this alienation, guilt, and contempt for the feminine, many women make another feminist mistake by falling into the masculine trap. Misinterpreting equality, these feminists slip into a kind of envy of men (Freud's penis envy), and become like men themselves, failing to meet the challenge of true equality. Ironically these masculinized women, though liberated from one style of male domination, simply move into another style of the same male dominance. By taking this unfortunate misstep, women show that subconsciously they agree that their feminine qualities are inferior and thus end up reinforcing the already overly masculine character of our culture.

What is meant by the masculinized woman? Such a woman values doing more than being, which kills the creative genius of the feminine. Performance-oriented, achieving, and self-proving, the masculinized woman engages in a busy display of pseudo-masculine activity. She does not want to be receptive. In anger and aggression, the women's movement has impelled her outward in a premature way by its belief that outward action is superior to inward being.

Over thirty years ago this same criticism was made by one of the first and most balanced liberated women, Anne Morrow Lindberg, wife of famed aviator Charles, a mother, author, and world citizen. "In our recent efforts to emancipate ourselves, to prove ourselves the equal of men," she wrote in her incomparable classic *Gift from the Sea*, "we have . . . been drawn into competing with him in his outward activities, to the neglect of our inner springs . . . Why have we been seduced into abandoning this time-less inner strength of woman for the temporal, outer strength of man?" Lindbergh then concludes with an impassioned plea that outlines the vocation of every woman: "Woman must be the pioneer in this turning inward for strength. . . she has always been the pioneer."[4] Swiss psychoanalyst Carl Jung insisted that the creativity of woman (necessarily responsive and contemplative) can never come to fruition if she is caught in an unconscious imitation of men or identification with the inferior masculinity in her own unconscious.

In addition to contempt for the feminine, some members of the women's movement show contempt for men through anger, aggression, hostility, and reverse discrimination. The issue of sexist language is a good example. In the name of 'inclusive language,' some women recommend using the feminine in place of the traditional masculine. In this way they seek "neither equality nor justice, but retribution. . . . The position is rather like that of small children: You did this to me; now I want to do the same to you."[5]   Ironically, in their excessively female focus, these feminists comit the same 'sin' of which they accuse the 'patriarchal' church. The result is a curiously reversed double standard: patriarchy is repressive, while matriarchy is holistic!

The anger of many feminists has led one enlightened gentleman to call them 'fuminists' instead. Many such fuminists remind me of the heroine in Cole Porter's muscial comedy Kiss Me Kate. In a memorable scene Kate sings "I Hate Men" and describes how they are "a boring lot" who only cause her "bother." This negativity toward men, the feminist verbal attack on men, and the effort of many women to separate themselves from men, only increases the persisting problem.

The Soft Male and the Deep Masculine

How do men respond to masculinized or man-hating

woman? They often react with brutal aggressive masculinity or else succumb to the softness of their anima (their feminine consciousness) and retreat into an inferior-passive femininity. No one has dealt more openly with this 'soft male' than Robert Bly, the contemporary American poet, who goes about the country giving workshops on Male Mysteries and What Men Really Want. Bly recognizes the significant growth in the American male over the past twenty years: an increased thoughtfulness, gentleness, and feminine consciousness. But he is disturbed by the lack of freedom in the 'soft male' population. There's something definitely wrong. Many of these men are unhappy and un-energetic, life-preserving but not exactly life-giving. Why? Twenty years ago, when men looked to the women's move-ment for leads, did the newly liberated women indicate they wanted soft men? Bly concludes: "Young men for various reasons wanted harder women, and women began to desire softer men. It seems like a nice arrangement, but it isn't working out."[6]

Why isn't it working? Why is the soft male unener-getic, unhappy and unfree? Like the woman betraying her own birthright and tragically alienated from her femininity, the soft male has also betrayed his birthright and become alienated from the 'deep male' who may be likened to the fairytale character Iron John. Bly retells the ancient story: "Every modern male has, lying at the bottom of his psyche, a large, primitive man covered with hair down to his feet. Making contact with this wildman . . . hasn't taken place in contemporary culture."

Bly insists that every real man must find his deep nourishment and radiant spiritual energy not in his feminine side but in his deep masculine. This masculine depth must be distinguished from the shallow masculine, the macho masculine, or the snowmobile masculine. One of Bly's greatest contributions is his description of positive male energy, a description sorely needed in our time when masculine energy is so often depicted in purely negative terms. Referring us back to ancient Greece, Bly calls this positive male energy 'Zeus energy':

> The idea that male energy, when in authority, could be good has come to be considered impossible. Yet the Greeks understood and praised that energy. They called it Zeus energy, which encompasses intelligence, robust health,

compassionate authority, . . . good will, leadership--in sum, positive power accepted by the male in the service of the community. The native Americans understood this too, that this power only becomes positive when exercised for the sake of the community, not for personal aggrandizement. All the great cultures since have lived with images of this energy, except ours.

In a similar vein, Lee Robbins turns to positive masculine myths for a feminine spirituality. Robbins, a doctoral candidate in psychiatry and religion at Columbia University and Union Theological Seminary, sees the need for both men and women to connect with these masculine myths in order to broaden, deepen, and complement the re-emergence of ancient feminine values in our time.[7]

Gender Differences

Another shortcoming of the women's movement is the gender confusion that reduces everyone to 'unisex,' a sexlessness or false androgyny in which we are all considered indistinctly masculine and feminine without any gender differentiation. Man-woman differences are blurred if not negated; differences falsely attributed to upbringing and cultural conditioning or reduced to mere anatomy. Masculine and feminine have become more and more dangerously mixed in this century. A new synthesis can only come from a radical understanding of our differences. Feminist extremists who believe that the only difference between men and women is biological, and that in every other way they are equal and born with the same potentialities, walk on perilous ground.

Our differences begin in our bodies surely, and there we find our first clues. But the biological difference between man and woman is so fundamental that it does not stop with the body but implies an equally fundamental difference of psychic nature. As Jungian psychology teaches us, no matter how strongly we believe in the ultimate union of both masculine and feminine elements in each individual, so long as we remain in our biological bodies, we are predominantly either male or female. We forget this at our peril:

> Disaster awaits a woman who imitates man, but even a
> woman who aims at becoming half man, half woman, and
> imagines she is thereby achieving archetypal "androgyny"
> will certainly be inferior on both counts. A woman is
> born to be essentially and wholly a woman. [8]

And so is a man born to be essentially and wholly a
man.

Recent scientific evidence demonstrates masculine-
feminine differences as they begin in the body and then
effect an equally fundamental difference of psychic nature.
For example, Dr. James C. Neely writes in his study
entitled *Gender:*

> Male and female hormones differentiate the sensory and
> motor processes at different rates and different times
> and this leads to certain nerve connections for boys and
> certain nerve connections for girls which, in turn, lead to
> varied behavior typical of the sex. In boys, this becomes
> rough-and-tumble play. In girls, the emphasis is on fine
> movements, dexterity, and audiovisual sensitivity. [9]

It is not within our scope to cite further examples. The
point is simple. Every cell in the body of a man has an
XY set of sex chromosomes. And every cell in the entire
body of a woman has an XX set of sex chromosomes.
Men and women are sexually different in their entirety.
A man is a man in his whole self, not just in some parts
of himself. And a woman is a woman in every part of
herself, not only in her body. One of the most frightening characteristics of our age is the urge to destroy
these differences and to reduce everything to a horrible
sameness in the cause of equality.

What, then, are these masculine-feminine differences
that must not be destroyed but recognized and even celebrated? [10] The feminine is tender and receptive while the
masculine is strong and productive; the feminine focuses
on inward being and nurturing while the masculine focuses
on outward action and training; the feminine displays a
'skip-step' intuitive reasoning while the masculine displays
step-by-step linear reasoning. This 'woman's intuition' is
definitely not irrational, as so many men falsely assume,
but simply a different kind of reasoning. The female
brain tends to arrive at the same conclusions as the male

brain but skips steps in the rational process. Greater awareness of these masculine-feminine differences can lead to less frustrating and more complementary man-woman relations.

Gender Equality

We must be careful not to make false dichotomies. Both men and women share certain human qualities but in a manner appropriate to their gender. It is important to stress the mutual sharing of these fundamental human qualities. Well-balanced men have feminine qualities such as tenderness, receptivity, and intuition. Well-balanced women have masculine qualities such as strength, productivity, and linear reasoning. But receptive qualities in a man are feminine in a masculine sort of way, and are therefore differently nuanced than the same qualities in a woman. Masculine qualities in a woman are nuanced in a feminine way. Deeper exploration of these nuances would be helpful.

We can also describe gender differences and equality in terms of being and doing, unconditional love and conditional approval, affirming and firming. The feminine side, in both women and men, has a receptive sense of being. The masculine side has an expressive sense of doing. The first says, "You are good just because you are." The second says, "You are good if you do good and avoid evil." Obviously both approaches are needed, and equally so. The affirming voice that responds to the goodness of being with unconditional love is feminine in both men and women. The firming voice that attends to the character of our actions with conditional approval is masculine in both men and women. Obviously both qualities are necessary for wholeness, and equally so.

Having looked at our bodies to demonstrate masculine-feminine differences, let us look at them again to demonstrate our equality. "The receptive ovum is a symbol of inward being, and the assertive, vigorous, goal-oriented sperm cells are symbols of outward action."[11] Yet when these two unite, they provide equal numbers of chromosomes. While having different orientations, they are indeed equal. We all recognize that in the creation of a new human person, the male and female, the active and the receptive, are of equal importance. This is also true in every creative act, intellectual and emotional as well as physical. It is important to note here that receiving is not passive or inert. It is active in a unique way. Receiving is just as active as producing, though in a more interior way--as any good woman or any true contemplative knows.

It is easy to ascertain how far we are from this genuine equality, as individual persons and as a society. We must ask ourselves which of these two sets of qualities we value most in ourselves and in others: tender and receptive qualities (feminine) or strong and productive qualities (masculine)? Obviously we need both sets of qualities for the fullness of life in ourselves and in our culture. But most of us are incapable of a balanced response because of the overly masculine nature of our cuture. Our American culture, oriented towards work and performance, teaches us higher regard for strength and production. In other words, even though we may value feminine traits, we still consider them inferior to our masculine traits. Because of the tough individualism of the Puritans, our American character is extremely masculine. We are driven outward into work and action (a masculine emphasis) and away from the interior life (a feminine emphasis). We even find it difficult to keep the Sabbath and observe one day of rest out of seven:

> Six days of outer work and one day of inner being, though not equal in quantity, are equal in quality. But few of us really feel it. As a result, the feminine side of life and civilization--and women---are having a difficult time with equality.[12]

Anima and Animus

Every man has feminine qualities within him and every woman has masculine qualities within her. Carl Jung called the feminine element in man the anima and the masculine element in woman the animus. Both of these are archetypal figures representing two modes of consciousness within the psyche of every human person.

No one of either sex is one hundred per cent male or female. The two elements co-exist in every personality in an infinite variety of proportions. Because all men and women are mixtures of anima and animus, it is difficult to find anyone who is a pure example of either.

The precise nature of anima and animus remains elusive. Jung indicates that "the animus corresponds to the paternal Logos just as the anima corresponds to the maternal Eros." He clearly stated that he did not intend to give to anima and animus "too specific a definition." He uses Eros and Logos "merely as conceptual aids to describe the fact that woman's consciousness is character- ized more by the connective quality of Eros than by the discrimination and cognition associated with Logos."[13]

Within this framework, Jung leads us to deeper understanding of man-woman differences. The animus dis- criminates, focuses, differentiates, and defines. The anima sees relationships, makes whole, values, reaches out. The animus is characterized by focused awareness and is asso- ciated with the light of consciousness. The anima is characterized by diffused awareness and is associated with the darkness of unconsciousness.

If we are to be whole human persons, a marriage between anima and animus must take place within us. Both animus and anima function as a bridge between our conscious life and the unknown world of the unconscious. When we contact our contrasexual side, we move into the depths and get in touch with fundamental sources of new life. When either the anima or animus is dominant in the conscious personality, the opposite pole acts as an inner personality, compensating for the outer personality and exhibiting the characteristics lacking in the conscious per- sonality.

What does it mean, then, for a woman to integrate her animus? The animus brings light into the darkness of her diffused awareness. The animus brings a power of dis- crimination and understanding, a focused concentration to her depths. Irene De Castillejo gives a helpful image of the animus, once again related to light:

> I personally like to think of my helpful animus as a torch-bearer: the figure of a man holding aloft his torch to light my way, throwing its beams into dark corners and penetrating the mists which shield the world of half- hidden mystery where, as a woman, I am so very much at home.
> In a woman's world of shadows and cosmic truths he makes a pool of light as a focus for her eyes, and as

she looks she may say, "Ah yes, that's what I mean," or "Oh no, that's not my truth at all." It is with the help of this torch also that she learns to give form to her ideas. He throws light on the jumble of words hovering beneath the surface of her mind so that she can choose the ones she wants, separates light into the colors of the rainbow for her selection, enables her to see the parts of which her whole is made, to discriminate between this and that. In a word, he enables her to focus.[14]

And what does it mean for a man to integrate his anima? The anima helps a man's individuation process by moving him into the depths of the unconscious and revealing new sources of life which nourish his development. The anima enriches his emotional life and enlarges his capacity for love and relationship.

John Sanford, an Episcopalian priest and Jungian analyst, describes the role of the anima in terms of lunar darkness and earthen moistness:

Masculine consciousness has been likened to the sun, and feminine consciousness to the moon. At noon everything is seen in light outline and one thing is clearly differentiated from another. But no one can stand too much of this hot, bright sun. Without the cool, the moist, the dark, the landscape soon becomes unbearable, and the earth dries up and will not produce life. That is the way a man's life becomes without the fertilizing influence on him of the feminine. Without a relationship to his inner world, a man can focus, but lacks imagination; he can pursue goals, but lacks emotion; he can strive for power, but is unable to be creative because he cannot produce new life out of himself. Only the fruitful joining of the Yin principle to the Yang principle can stir up his energies, can prevent his consciousness from becoming sterile, and his masculine power from drying up.[15]

When a man or woman successfully weds the anima or animus within, the result is the integrated, balanced, whole person we describe as androgynous. Energized by the interplay between both the masculine and feminine poles, the androgynous person flows through life in a creative balance between action and receptivity, control and surrender, analysis and synthesis. June Singer, a Jungian analyst who wrote a lengthy study of androgyny, pictures the possibilities: "Without a sense of disjunction, the person will become at once tender and firm, flexible and strong, ambiguous and precise, focused in thinking and diffused in awareness, nurturing and guiding, giving and receiving."[16]

It is important to note that the marriage of animus and anima must take place deep inside every man and every woman. This interior oneness is greatly helped by healthy understanding and profound mutual respect between men and women--and tragically impeded by alienation and polarization between them.

The Shadow Side

We have been looking at the positive aspects of both masculine and feminine, the angelic dimension, the light side. When masculine and feminine qualities do not inter-penetrate and balance each other, they tend to break down into their negative aspects, the daemonic dimension, the shadow side.

How can we describe the shadow side of the masculine? Without the balancing provided by the feminine, outward action becomes blind activism, productivity becomes raw domination, strength becomes hardness, training becomes dehumanized regimentation, linear reasoning becomes narrow, uncomtemplative thinking, and goal orientation becomes insensitivity to persons.

How can we describe the shadow side of the feminine? Without the balancing provided by the masculine, tenderness becomes softness, receptivity becomes passivity, surrender becomes cowardice, interiority becomes inertia, intuition becomes irrationality, diffused awareness becomes ambiguity and confusion, person-orientation becomes an inability to see the task through to completion.

Two other daemonic dimensions of the feminine relate to one another. When deprived of the balancing pro-vided by the masculine, eros becomes possessive concupis-cence and nurturing becomes devouring. In primitive woman the devouring side of the feminine is more obvious, but less dangerous, because primitive societies always provide rites to contain it. But in our contemporary society, this devouring is more hidden (in the respectable disguise of mother love), and therefore becomes more deadly. The enveloping, possessive, destructive feminine is seen in the story of the Borgia princess who "night after night put a drop of poison into her lover's soup, and day after day, won the wonder and admiration of the court by wearing herself to skin and bone in her indefatigable ministering to him. . . . she had to reduce him to being all hers, like a helpless child, before she could pour out her tenderness upon him."[17]

Turning again to the positive side, we must praise the capacity of the feminine psyche for total devotion. A mother in defense of her child stops at nothing. When a mature woman's love has been purged of possesiveness, she will risk everything, even her reputation, to save the one she loves from destruction. The shadow side of this strength is blind devotion to a 'cause' or a person.

If the animus--the unconscious masculinity in a woman--is not brought to conscious awareness in her, it can be destructive, since the animus is charged with the numinous power of the unconscious. In the same manner, if the anima--the unconscious femininity in a man--is not consciously integrated into his life, it also erupts destructively. What does this look like?

In a woman, the negative animus often surfaces as unfounded opinion. While pretending to be reasonable, the argumentation is not all that logical. Controlled by the negative animus, a woman's opinions are not very well thought out but merely passed on ready-made from parents, books, churches, or other authoritative sources of conventional wisdom. Yet they are held with determined conviction.

When the same phenomenon takes place in a man-woman wrangle, the negative animus "may cause the woman to tell the man what he ought to do, or to make some generalized assumption whose lack of validity is perfectly obvious to the man, yet upon which she pontificates with the most maddening assurance. This unrelated pseudo-thinking chills the atmosphere, producing an alienation of feeling which is greatly worsened by the dictatorial manner in which the pronouncements are made."[18]

What happens when a man acts out of his negative anima, that is, his poorly developed or unintegrated anima? "The negative anima within a man results in moodiness and touchiness. The man can be filled with resentment and sentimentality. The poorly developed anima disrupts his personality because it represents an unintegrated emotional life."[19]

Many man–woman conflicts are archetypal clashes between the woman's negative animus and the man's negative anima. Either one can trigger the clash. If a man is moody and withdrawn (acting out of his negative anima), the woman's negative animus may attack with a nasty remark. If a woman offers an irritating irrational opinion (acting out of her negative animus), the man's negative anima may respond with sarcasm. Then man and woman are separated by a thick wall of blind autonomous thoughts and feelings arising from the unconscious. They do not really touch each other at all but merely react to one another as blind archetypes.

Asceticism and Mysticism

Just as we cannot separate the masculine and feminine in any human person but must allow them to interpenetrate and enrich each other, so we must appreciate the essential unity of the ascetical-mystical life. At its best, classical Christian spirituality has always emphasized the intimate connection between asceticism and mysticism. William McNamara O.C.D., the Carmelite priest who founded the Spiritual Life Institute, outlines the delicate balance: "Obviously, there are positive and negative sides to the spiritual life, times to resist and times to yield, times to gain control and times to let go, a world to deny and a world to affirm."[20] As McNamara describes the human adventure as the reconciliation of the yes and the no, the yin and the yang, the *ish* and the *esh* (Hebrew words for earth and water), the reconciliation of masculine and feminine in asceticism and mysticism is implicit.

But exactly what do we mean when we say 'asceticism' and 'mysticism'? The words mysticism and contemplation are essentially the same and may be interchanged. One whole series of definitions relates mysticism to life: living in the now, living in the present moment, living on the spot where you are. Another series describes mystical experience in terms of vision or seeing: beholding the manifold in the one, seeing everything against the background of eternity, seeing things as they really are. This seeing begins with a long, loving look at the real and ends in a long, loving look at the Real. In other words, whenever we take a long, loving look at any reality--a rock, a cricket, or a chrysanthemum--we eventually come to see the Reality of God as he reveals himself in rockness, cricketness, and chrysanthemumness!

These first descriptions of mysticism are deliberately nontheistic because most often our initial mystical experience is not explicitly theistic but more inchoate or confused. As we grow, our experience becomes more overtly theistic. In this higher stage, it is more appropriate to describe mysticism as loving experiential awareness of God, a pure intuition of God born of love, or as the classical literature states, transforming union with God.

Viewed in this manner, we come to see mysticism as the fulfillment of all human desire. Asceticism is a means towards this end, a passionate preparation for divine union: union with God, unity within ourselves, communion among all human persons, oneness with all that is: animal, vegetable, and mineral.

Asceticism is best understood when we look at its Greek root, *askesis,* a strong, masculine word which means "training." Through our asceticism we train ourselves the way a soldier trains for war or an athlete for his contest. Both military combat and the athletic contest are ancient biblical metaphors for the life of the spirit, as relevant today as ever for both men and women.

Understood in this way, asceticism is clearly more masculine, outward, active. It involves practical training, the practice of virtue, and a certain mastery and control of ourselves. This requires grit, effort, and determination. Mysticism is clearly more feminine, interior, and responsive, involving grace, receptivity, and surrender. The two must go together. Without the foundation, the scaffolding, the groundwork which asceticism provides, the mystical life cannot flourish. On the other hand, without the feminine letting go, the yielding, the surrender of the mystical, asceticism is a ladder leading nowhere.

The Feminine Soul and Social Change

In the Christian tradition, the soul is always feminine in relation to God. The very word for soul in many languages is even a feminine word: *psyche* in Greek, *anima* in Latin,

alma in Spanish. In his exquisite mystical poetry, the Spanish
Carmelite, John of the Cross, says "You make my soul feel
like a woman."[21] Does this mean that it is easier for women
to enjoy the mystical life? In many ways, yes, precisely
because the higher reaches of the mystical life presume
more feminine qualities--inwardness, receptivity, tenderness.
Only the genuinely strong man, the 'deep man' who has
nurtured his feminine side, is capable of the surrender
mysticism entails.

Like John of the Cross, only the authentically integrated man can allow God to make his soul "feel like a
woman." This response is no diminution of masculinity but
an enhancement of it. John of the Cross is not the only
example. St. Bernard of Clairveaux called himself the bride
in relation to Christ the bridegroom and considered their
love a mystical marriage. St. Augustine, the Prince of Mystics, surrendered to God's overtures of love with an intimate
prayer of surrender: "You called, and you cried to me, and
you broke open my deafness. You sent forth your beams
and shone on me, and closed away my blindness.   You
breathed your fragrance upon me and I drew in my breath,
and now I pant for you."[22] There was nothing weak or effeminate in any one of these giants from the Christian mystical
tradition.

Some people consider the mystical life an illusion, a
luxury, or a pleasant pastime for those who are "into that
sort of thing." Some critics go so far as to call it an
escape or a cop-out, an irresponsible evasion of pressing
world problems. On the contrary, any authentic mystical
life is not an isolated affair but the source of realistic and
responsible contemplative action in society. In fact, the contemplative life may be the only hope for the future of our
perilously endangered planet.

Look at our contemporary world situation. Our society
moves at a frenzied pace, faster and faster, resulting in
severe fragmentation, alienation, and neurosis. Education
has deteriorated into mere utilitarian training for "making
a fast buck." We have lost our deepest archetypal symbols
and our roots in nature, in community, and in the home.
Where are the integrated personalities and the uproariously
happy people? We degrade sex, woman, and matter and
become obsessed with violence, control, and domination. We
rape our land, pollute our air and water, and neglect the

needs of our neighbors near at hand and around the globe.

These characteristics of our contemporary way of life are far from being unrelated. They are all manifestations of one central fact: an impoverishment of the human spirit, a loss of vision, in short, a crisis in contemplation. The non-contemplative nature of our contemporary culture is yet another example of our collective contempt for the feminine.

Masculine Spirituality and the Lion-Christ

When we reflect on the many problems in our world today, we see the predominance of masculine valuing which needs to be rebalanced by the feminine. Instead of placing an exclusively high premium on the more masculine values of freedom, success, and achievement, our culture must learn to respond in a more feminine way with cooperation, inter-dependence, and community responsibility. In contrast to this predominantly masculine valuing, we see precisely the opposite in the subculture of contemporary Christian spirituality. Partially as a reaction to patriarchal church structures, many of the feminine characteristics of spirituality are being stressed: community harmony, affective equanimity, and psychological androgyny.

Our effort to balance an overly masculine institution with an overly feminine spirituality has created some serious problems, however, and high among them are mediocrity, "the bland leading the bland," the emphasis on "peace at all costs," and a tendency towards "nesting" and ennui. The damage of this feminine imbalance may be called 'spiritual emasculation.' If we refuse to listen, or listen with hostility, to the genuinely masculine voices of spirituality, we may sever ourselves from our biblical roots and seriously distort the revealed image of God.

Our unbalanced feminine valuing, with its attempts to neuter God-speech, actually threatens to 'domesticate' God:

> God is preached continually as a fuzzy but familiar being not unlike ourselves, a safe guarantor of the human enterprise in good times and a sympathetic but powerless bystander when disaster strikes. This lopsided incarnational view achieves what Canaanite Baal paganism could not: the reduction of the mighty, mountain-shattering El Shaddai to a convenient and harmless household God.[23]

Over thirty years ago, in a remarkable essay on the role of women, the masculine voice of English Dominican Gerald Vann expressed the same concern before the problem became as acute as it is today. Vann insisted that the concept of the fatherhood of God is not intended to exclude the qualities we associate more especially with mother-love such as gentleness, sympathy, understanding, and tenderness. Rather it is indeed these very qualities which are implicit in Christ's likening of himself to the hen gathering her chickens under her wing in that heart-rending Gospel passage where Jesus weeps over Jerusalem (Mt. 23:37). But we must be aware that the concept of God as mother is inadequate because it does not elicit enough holy awe:

> Were we to think of God in terms of Motherhood alone we might more easily form a radically erroneous idea of what that Motherhood should mean for us, and might fall into the pseudo-religion of escape, of protection from life, of petting and rest.[24]

Is it not this very feminine emphasis on petting and rest that leads Robert Bly to exclude that "kind young man named Jesus" from his images for the positive male energy he calls 'Zeus energy'? Is it not this very feminine imbalance that leads Jungian analyst Helen Luke to criticize women for their "sentimental religiousity in which the spirit of Christianity is lost indeed"?[25] Is it not this imbalance that leads C.D. Keyes, Episcopal priest and professor of philosophy at Duquesne University, to criticize the church for her loss of vision and virility? "The Church tinkles instead of thundering. It would rather squeak than roar." When people knock on the church door, he laments, they are greeted with a "grin sickening enough to compete with Alfred E. Newman's picture on the front of Mad Magazine."[26] What is the masculine voice of spirituality that must not be tuned out because of renewed sensitivity to the gentle and feminine tones of the divine voice? It is a wild and dangerous and shocking voice, "the voice of Jesus as he speaks in embarrassing Gospel passages rarely preached or any longer understood. It is the call to leave family, home, and possessions for the sake of the Kingdom of God (Lk 18:29). It is the summons for the violent who 'bear it away' (Mt. 11:12). It is the call, not to peace, but to the sword (Mt. 10:34)."[27]

It is the voice of Jesus "going wild in the temple and whipping everybody," says Robert Bly. It is the voice of tiger and earthquake, says William McNamara, because "God is not nice; he is not a buddy, an uncle, or a mascot; he is an earthquake!" When we pray, he continues, "we enter the cave of a tiger and jeopardize our safety in a life-or-death situation. The true man or woman of prayer, passionately devoted to the untamable God, is therefore an irrepressible wild one who finds it impossible to be casual or glib about prayer."[28]

It is the voice of a roaring lion, as we learn from our own sacred scriptures. The "Lion of Judah" (Gen.49:9) is an ancient title for Christ. The prophet Hosea describes the Lord "who roars like a lion" (Hos. 11:10). In the New Testament, the Book of Revelation juxtaposes the image of the sacrificial lamb with the image of the triumphant lion (Rev. 5:5). C. S. Lewis immortalized the image of Christ the Lion for us in Aslan, the hero of his *Chronicles of Narnia*. Aslan is the Turkish word for lion. Throughout the Chronicles Aslan is clearly depicted as an untamed lion.[29]

The deeply masculine voice of Jesus is not the chirping of a grasshopper, according to C.D. Keyes. In a lyrical passage full of enough Zeus energy to satisfy Robert Bly a hundred times over, Keyes describes the Eucharist as "that incredible drama that replays the resurrection." Picture a banquet with the guests assembled and full of anticipation:

> The guests await their host only to find that he comes crashing up through the floor and riding into the heights. He burns a hole in the room by coming suddenly, not gradually. He does not come in flat-footedness, but in holy awe. He is not from among the guests. He is the miraculous Rider on his way from the abyss to the heights and back again. . . .The Eucharist does not greet a grasshopper, but a thundering, flaming horse ridden by a regal clown who startles and shatters with happy sublimity. Liturgy must speak only with a roar, not a chirp, with the thunder of uncanny art, not a tinkle. The lion of the Tribe of Judah has roared. Who dares to answer with a squeak? [30]

God the Father and the Virgin Mother

Many women (including myself) find the image of God as Mother theologically and spiritually inadequate because it is too limited, too culture-bound, and too sexist. [31] These women continue to image God as Father and object to the implication that they are thereby perpetuating patriarchal dominance. They demonstrate how it is psychologically and spiritually unsound, and perhaps dangerous, to try to alter people's fundamental images:

> Images are not metaphors to be interpreted; they represent profoundly personal perspectives. And we do not choose our images. They reverberate from something within us deeper than intellect or external forms. They carry heavy intellectual, emotional and spiritual freight, much of which will be threatened if we jettison the particular images that empower us.

Might it not be safer, and more effective, to keep the deeply rooted masculine image but enrich it be redefining it? For example,

> Father can be returned to its essential meaning as the seminal, generative impregnator. Taking God as Father in those terms, we can see both creation and redemption as impregnations, and God's seminal acts as crucial for the conception and birth of new life in Christ. The idea of God impregnating the world with his Spirit is entirely compatible with the nurturing tenderness that too often is associated only with the image of maternity.

This understanding of fatherhood drastically undercuts the arrogant patriarch view of fatherhood because, "except physiologically, impregnation on the basis of coercion rarely generates new life. It is instead destructive. The divine impregnation, however, is freely given and willingly received. God courts; he does not rape."

Every creative act involves both the male and female in equal importance. Where, then, is the feminine, as God impregnates the world with his spirit in both creation and redemption? The feminine is present in Wisdom, who was present at the dawning of creation (Wis. 9:9). The feminine is present in the Holy Spirit, who is considered feminine in some Christian traditions. The feminine is present in the human soul God impregnates. And the feminine is present in the one we call 'The Woman,' the Virgin Mary, without whose responsive "yes" the Word could not have become flesh.

It is ironic that in this age of heightened awareness of the feminine, the cult of the Virgin Mary is not stronger. This may be due in part to the poor iconography of Mary which too often presents her in vapid sentimental imagery. But there is perhaps a deeper reason. May it not be due to the contempt for the feminine we discussed earlier? More precisely, due to our collective contempt for the feminine way of receptive devotion? The neglect of Mary may also result from the fact that modern woman has lost contact with the archetypal woman in herself.

In the Roman Catholic tradition, Mary reveals to us the very motherhood of God. Every summer on August 15th we celebrate the feast of the Assumption of Mary into heaven. This Marian mystery, felt in the depths of the Catholic soul for centuries, was declared an official dogma by Pope Pius XII in 1950. In a letter to Father Victor White, Carl Jung called this event the most important religious development for four hundred years. He considered the Assumption the integration of the feminine principle into the Christian conception of the godhead.

We call Mary 'the new Eve' because she is not only the Mother of God but the mother of all humanity and a revelation of the archetypal woman within us. We revere her as model of the ideal woman today as yesterday and as always. In this veneration we value her as both virgin and mother. Mary teaches us the deep compassionate wisdom that comes of experience, the wisdom a woman learns through her body, and in particular through her motherhood. She also teaches us another wisdom, the fresh, untarnished, virginal wisdom of the girl. Mary exhibits a richly miltifaceted personality as virgin, daughter, bride, and mother of God. Rediscovering her mystery helps show us the multifaceted fecundity of the feminine.

A New Beginning

The world desperately needs a new women's movement. It must not be based on contempt for the feminine like "the giant misstep" of the previous movement. As we have seen, this contempt for the feminine has led not only to contempt for the masculine, but to tremendous gender confusion resulting in the masculinized woman, the soft male, and an unhealthy obscuring or negation of fundamental man-woman differences. The expression 'woman's movement' is actually a misnomer, since what we need is truly a new human beginning, involving men as well as women. This new beginning cannot be based on politics and power-playing between men and women, on "obsolete power games and irrelevant sexual battles that never can be won," according to Betty Friedan. The new beginning must be based on a new axis: not on the sociology, psychology, and biology of masculine and feminine, though these are indispensable.

The foundation of the new beginning must be profoundly metaphysical. What is the nature of the human person? What is the nature of the masculine? The nature of the feminine? What is the nature of God, in whose image man and woman are created? If we do not understand the nature of the human person--masculine, feminine, and divine--then we cannot understand our roles and responsibilities in contemporary society, because what we do only follows from who we are. It is one thing to be equal, but quite another to be the same. If the nature of man differs from the nature of woman, then we need not be compelled to function in the same roles, and this includes priesthood.

"Eve did not know who she was. That was, and still is, the beginning of the nameless problem."[32] Did Adam know himself any better? Does he now? Both men and women need to run the risk of radical self-knowledge. "Knowing ourselves is something so important," St. Teresa advises, "that I wouldn't want any relaxation ever in this regard, however high you may have climbed. . . For never is anything else more fitting than self-knowledge . . . without it everything goes wrong." As she astutely continues to develop her teaching, Teresa insists more dramatically that "all our trials and disturbances come from our not understanding ourselves."[33]

Our metaphysical search for deeper self-understanding must be grounded in humility and awe: humility in the face of the awesome mystery of God--God as revealed in the wisdom tradition, God as revealed as father and mother, God as revealed in the mystery of the trinity, God as revealed in the androgyny of Jesus Christ, God as revealed in the lion-Christ and the virgin-mother Mary.

Our new beginning must avoid all anger, hostility, and competition. There can be no question of ultimate superiority and inferiority. Men and women must come to a new understanding of their equality and a mutual appreciation of their complementarity. Both men and women have strengths and weaknesses, angelic and daemonic dimensions, a light side and a shadow side. Where man is weak, dark, and daemonic, he must humbly look to the feminine, the anima, for strength and angelic light. Where woman is weak, dark, and daemonic, she too must look humbly to the masculine, the animus, for her balance.

Only the rediscovery of feminine values can insure the spiritual transformation, indeed the very survival, of our world. But at the same time we must not undermine the value of the strong and positive masculine energy needed for the future of our planet. Our future depends on the fact that we all begin anew together as contemplative men and contemplative women, creating a truly contemplative culture. Our culture will not become whole if we imbalance the value of masculine or feminine, just as we will not become whole without balancing the yin-yang of our ascetical-mystical life.

Once woman has lost her feminine way it can only be found through conscious and painful sacrifice. And when man has lost his masculine way an equally painful sacrifice is involved in his quest for the deep masculine. The new beginning so desperately needed will only come into being if both men and women are willing to make this painful sacrifice and pay the high price of transformation. As T.S. Eliot wrote in *Four Quartets,* this "costs not less than everything." Who of us has the courage to pay such a price? The prospect is frightening. For this reason men and women need to support one another with love, respect, and profound appreciation.

The Patient Way of Seeds and Tears

Years ago I found this exquisite feminine poem:

> The earth woman wears a necklace of corn;
> Her body is a planted field, a reaping ground;
> 'Learn,' she says, 'the patient way of seeds.'

As it is the nature of earth to receive the seed, to nourish the roots, to foster growth in the dark so that it may reach up to the light, so it is the nature of the feminine. "We are on the earth and clothed with it," says St. Teresa. We think of the body of earth and the body of woman as one and compliment woman by calling her 'earth mother.' Woman is the symbol of rebirth, regeneration, and renewal for the entire planet.

The masculine trap. Contempt for the feminine. The superiority of masculine valuing in our contemporary culture. How long will we continue to worship the bright light of the masculine sun and become estranged from the patient way of seeds buried in the dark earth and from the re-flected beauty of the silver light of the moon in the black of night? How shall estranged woman find her way back to herself, to the archetypal woman, to the deep feminine within her? "The way back and down to those springs and to the roots of the tree is likewise the way on and up to the spirit of air and fire in the vaults of heaven." [34]

Air, fire and heaven—symbols of the true and deep masculine, the masculine who also knows "the patient way of seeds" by sowing them into the body of the earth and the earthen body of woman. Fertility imagery is universal and sempiternal, whether we refer to physical fertility or the spiritual fecundity of virgins, singles, and celibates. Whatever the vocation, the masculine sows the seed and the feminine gives it a body.

The feminine way out of her estrangement, then, leads by way of the masculine. And the masculine way out of his estrangement to his own deep male leads from the spirit of air and fire in the vaults of heaven back and down to the feminine roots of the tree and the springs of water of life.

The water of life springs from our tears. But so many women today have forgotten how to weep that they have lost the meaning of tears. And men have seldom known the meaning of tears. We all must weep. This is not a sign of weakness but a badge of human strength. We must weep alone and we must weep together. And when men and women have learned this primordial lesson, then perhaps they will learn to laugh together.

Mother Tessa Bielecki is the co-founder (with Reverend William McNamara, O.C.D.), of the Spiritual Life Institute. Formed in 1960 with a mandate from the visionary Pope John XXIII, it is a small ecumenical monastic community of men and women who embrace a vowed life of contemplative solitude according to the primitive Carmelite spirit of Teresa of Avila and John of the Cross. Mother Tessa is Mother Abbess of the Nada Community, with hermitages in the high desert of Crestone, Colorado and deep in the wilderness of Kemptville, Nova Scotia. Mother Tessa has lived a contemplative life of solitude and silence for twenty years. As an 'apostolic hermit' she also leaves the hermitage several weeks each year to share the fruits of her contemplative experience through lectures, retreats, workshops, and ecumenical conferences. She also writes in the Institute's quarterly, *Desert Call*.

I am He, you are She
I am song, you are verse
I am heaven, you are earth
                              Ayurveda

Relationships and Spiritual Growth

Charles Bates

Love is the organizing principle of the universe. It is the attraction that brings things together and keeps them together, forming ever greater wholes. Human love is a metaphor for the bonding creative energy of the divine. For this reason, the relationship of one human being with another is the means for spiritual development. Relationships are experiences of the cohesive energy of existence. Since we are all involved in relationships, it is important to be aware of how to tap them as a resource to self-unfoldment.

The magnificent possibilities for development through relationships are infrequently modeled in great spiritual and religious traditions. Hinduism is one religious source that takes on this task. In the inner teachings of Hindu mythology, the union of fully realized divine persons serve as role models for women and men. Their relationships are as varied as the complex human psyche, yet they demonstrate how relationships can and should be used for self-realization at various times along one's spiritual path.

Radha/Krishna, Sita/Rama, Parvati/Siva, and Lakshmi/Vishnu are a few of the divine couples that model various types of love intimating human expressions of spiritual unfoldment. Radha and Krishna epitomize pure, selfless love, as well as love in separation. Since a permanent relationship between them is not possible, they have no hope of receiving anything from each other; they love in the knowledge that love is their only reward. This is in contrast to Sita and Rama's ideal relationship of loyalty and devotion in marriage. Their union is a symbol of queenly fertility and kingly virility fostering the perfect reign of peace over all that is within and without. Lakshmi and Vishnu are elegance and grace. She is royal authority; he operates through righteous rulers. As a royal couple, Vishnu appoints his agents while Lakshmi empowers them with authority. Parvati and Siva represent the two poles of our involvement in the world and with an ascetic life. Siva, god of extreme asceticism, and Parvati, tempting house-holder goddess, unite to live a life of reconciliation, inter-dependence, and harmony in sexuality and spirituality.

As we learn from the divine partners, relationships are the keys that unlock the doors to our spiritual nature. My Gurudev once said to me, "We are already divine; we must now become human." We can do this 'becoming human' only with each other. We cannot become human alone. We need each other so that we may evoke through the psyche the hidden dimensions that lie deep in our soul.

Steps to Maturity

All human relationships, especially those that are significant to us, move us to self-unfoldment. This unfold-ment takes place through life. Here then lies the purpose of life. Life is a theater for our discovery, our exploration, and our maturation. This way of seeing it is quite dissimilar to what we think of life. Ordinarily we think of life as something to be thoroughly understood and controlled, a task which constantly eludes us.

As a theater, life provides what is indicated in San-skrit by the word *upanishad,* meaning "a near approach." This idea means that the totality of truth cannot be con-tained in human experience or even in the mind. The divine, like life, is too complex in its potentials (realized or unrealized) to be understood. The infinite is therefore bounded and made finite by life. Life provides a place for us to interact with reality in manageable portions. These finite experiences give us a view of infinity from many different sides. The limiting of the infinite within perceiv-able, finite boundaries means that the human condition manages a gradual evolution towards a perfect actualization of its spiritual potential. The 'near approach' is the ability to frame truth by approximation and proximity.

This idea is presented to us in the generic model of the trinity, a model represented in all great theologies. The expression of the model as discovery, exploration, and maturation is a way of organizing our use of the process preserved and taught in the trinity. Discovery is the ability to limit, frame, or bound the unknowable into knowable portions--speaking the truth of reality into existence. Exploration is the ability to bond with and become intimate with its limits. This is done through experimentation within the limits; one eventually becomes identified with the limits as one's own identity. Maturation is the ability to assimilate the experiment and accept one's development inside the limits. It is a creative movement from an essential symbiosis of identification to an eventual maturation of conscious responsibility and separation through individuation.

Along with the trinity comes a fourth element which completes the human learning strategy. This fourth state is transcendence. It is expressed in our lives as the motion toward the new horizons we have opened through our discovery, exploration, and maturation.

It is not possible to skip levels of development. There is no escape from life; therefore there is no escape from self-discovery. It is essential to acknowledge this fact in order to make meaning out of life, for meaning places order in each stage of our human experience of existence. Life is a theater.

Femininity/Masculinity

Our interface with life is significant. Our conscious relationship with the divine, with nature, and with each other is important as we move through life making spiritual potential potent. Our view of the psyche is crucial. We see the psyche as composed of two principles: feminine and masculine. These two principles form a whole, a dynamic process composed of two primary behaviors viewed as polarities. The feminine and the masculine operate as different core organizing principles. The feminine is the organizing principle associated with bonding or cohesion. The masculine principle is the organizing principle associated with individuation or separation. When expressed in human form, femininity as a reality view comes into being as predominating in women, and masculinity as a reality view comes into being as predominating in man. This reality view polarizes an individual's world view in diverse ways from the onset of birth. Since the bonding principle is the feminine aspect of the psyche and the dynamism for bonding takes place in relationships, we can schematize the relatedness of the two poles of feminine/masculine to spiritual development. We bond due to attraction, explore through experimentation, mature by assimilation, and then separate through individuation and press on through transcendence. Relationships are key in this cycle.

According to Carol Gilligan's book *In A Different Voice,* there is a difference between female psychology and male psychology, between their internal world view and external behavior. She points out that a woman's perspective on what is valuable in life will be different from that of a man. Through Gilligan's assessment of work done by Nancy Chodorow, Gilligan holds that since the primary caretakers of children are women, the first role models are women. Chodorow writes,

> . . . girls come to experience themselves as less differentiated than boys, as more continuous with and related to the external object-world, and as differently oriented to their inner object-world as well.[1]

Gilligan concludes that,

> For boys and men, separation and individuation are critically tied in gender identity since separation from mother is essential for the development of masculinity. For girls and women, issues of femininity or feminine identity do not depend upon the achievement of separation from the mother or on the process of individuation. Thus males tend to have difficulty with relationships, while females tend to have problems with individuation.[2]

Femininity and masculinity are a whole, belonging to the same continuum, but as experienced by us as woman and man in nature, they are radically different. Through the current phase of evolution, we as a species have chosen to develop the outward-turned individuation, the separation side of our psyche. Seeing ourselves as isolated from nature, we developed a separation which allowed us to aspire to the power of an adversative mentality toward nature. This mentality manifests at a human level as conflict between the two world views of woman and man, with the male as the apparent external power holder. We have ended up with suppression of our intrinsic internal identity with nature. This repression, which evolves to suppression if maintained excessively, appears to be part of the learning formula for human beings. We move to excess, €exclusivity, and identifying with each phase until it is generalized into our behavior.

I remember a period when my daughter spent hours in her bedroom completely absorbed in playing with her doll house. Day after day she worked. All other activities were temporarily repressed and disregarded. At some point she dropped her exclusive focus and moved on to something else. She could once again see other dimensions of herself. She began to generalize whatever she had learned, putting it into perspective with her developing ego and moving on to the next phase of her life. Belonging to a group, sexuality, independence, were each in turn then assimilated.

We as a species have been developing the outer directedness of our psyche. We have developed the masculine side of our nature at the cost of our feminine side. Our current situation is a demonstration of that cost. According to von Franz:

> For the development of Western civilization, it was perhaps necessary for the Western mind to have to ignore the mother-goddess for a certain length of time, and to put the whole emphasis onto male development. But ignored organs of the psyche behave in the same way as ignored organs of the body. . . . If we ignore certain vital nuclei in the psyche, they will cause illness in the system.[3]

In moving through the levels of development by way of our relationships with each other, we carry with us the dysfunctional 'toxic waste' of human evolution. According to Dane Rudhyar in *Rhythm of Wholeness,* "These toxic waste products may combine, lead an unnoticed life of their own, and often poison the 'water' and 'air' (the collective psychism) of a cultural whole."[4]

Integration

We must not despair. We are like an apprentice and some of our work yet needs refinement. We will assimilate, drop our exclusive identification with our outwardly-turned awareness, see other parts of ourselves again, integrate into a new whole and move on. However, in this current dilemma of humankind we must separate the residue of toxic waste from the valuable product of our unfoldment. As woman and man our maturation and transcendence rests upon our ability to live with the dilemma posed by Nicholas of Cusa: *coincidenta oppositorium,* the coincidence of opposites. Opposites or polarities coexist. But opposing forces integral to a continuum cannot be eliminated as a solution to the conflict. To remove either of them would destroy the integrity of the whole. The dilemma they present when pursued triggers our awareness to the next level of development. The solution lies in embracing the continuum.

The human dilemma is a stage of development where bonding and individuation, feminine and masculine, unite and force the issues of transcendence. In this, the dilemma juncture of unfoldment, transcendence is brought into the awareness by the intuitive insight that paradox is a whole. Now, from this perspective a vaster reality can impact human existence. Our task now is the healing of the separation while preserving the differentiation of the sexes. The relationship of woman and man is the form of the healing act. What does it look like? Viewed one way, the female develops her masculine and the male develops his feminine, each being mindful to keep dominant their original predisposition toward the feminine or masculine. As Robert Johnson says,

> When we talk of women's acquiring . . . masculinity, we must understand that we are not striving for an equal amount of masculinity or femininity within ourselves . . . One must be a woman with masculinity backing her up, or one must be a man with femininity backing him up. The masculinity in a woman is a minority.[5]

I personally view it another way. One evening I led a discussion group that explored spiritual development. I mentioned that when women are strong and aggressive, they are expressing their masculine side, and when a man is compassionate and tender he is expressing his feminine side. Theresa O'Brien disagreed. She had recently seen a London museum exhibit whose theme was Faces of Women. In the sculptures she saw every quality on the continuum of the psyche, from strength and determination to tenderness and compassion, and yet the various portrayals were

all decidedly female. Theresa said that the faces showed
what strength and aggression looked like when expressed
by a woman. I realized then that I had discounted the
fact that women have intrinsic strength and aggression. I
realized that each place on the continuum has all other
places present within it like a holograph. In wholeness all
points must be recognized as present within one's own
self. Typically they are denied, feared, and shoved off to
a remote corner of the other-than-conscious mind where
they are left to fall, projected, onto someone else to act
out for us: let men be aggressive; let women be yielding.

The integrated wholeness has many dimensions and
is therefore different from the unconscious symbiosis we
experienced in earlier human existence. In unconscious
symbiosis we were undifferentiatedly identified with nature.
In this experimental swing of individuation we have separated from nature. Our only hope is to return like the
prodigal son, wiser from exploration, mature, and capable
of contributing as nature's equal partner.

Relationship as Mirror

The question still remains, How do relationships
serve as the means for spiritual unfoldment? There will
always be repressed, newly emerging, or suppressed dimensions of the mind, some coming forth as aberrant attitudes
or dysfunctional behaviors. All of these are invisible by
their nature. It is by relating to another that we go into
partnership with nature so these dimensions can be made
visible. Nature has provided a brilliant means on her side
in bringing the unexplored mind forward. This means comes
in the form of our ability to project our subjective unknown
upon an objective known. One of the Vedic prayers states,
". . . that which is the plenum and the ancient goal, that
remainderless form in which this entire world shines like a
serpent in a rope." Carl Jung's explanation and use of the
phenomenon of projection is also well known. Projection is
how we get our insides outside to learn. It is a strategy
to make visible what is not visible. Since we are almost
exclusively focused outward in our awareness, who and
what we are within ourselves is largely invisible. We utilize
our preoccupation with the external world to hold our projections. The world then appears 'as if' it were as we

thought. In actuality the external world can serve us by continuing to evoke even deeper and deeper aspects of our essence as we interact with it and mature over time.

The partner in our relationship becomes a screen upon which we can project and eventually make vaster dimensions our own. We serve each other through relationships as a self-uncovering device. For example, at an earlier point in my relationship with my wife I was under the impression that she made me have emotional responses. I blamed her for *making* me angry and thought her responsible for my pleasure as well. Eventually I came to realize that I was responsible for my own emotional responses. Her actions were essentialy neutral; I gave meaning to them and then responded to that meaning. In addition to being angry I could choose to laugh, cry, deflect, blame, listen, or whatever. Without the relationship, where I encountered my short-sightedness, I would not have been able to recognize, assimilate, and transcend my limits. In this light relationships are a powerful learning design. We cannot awaken without each other. We cannot become human alone.

Relationships thus help us discover our hidden self. The other person, through his act of participation in our lives, holds many keys that can evoke growth from the sprouting seeds of our potential. We aid each other in surfacing that which is next to be made known. We are already whole in potential, but that potential must be actualized. In a relationship one obtains feedback not possible in isolated existence. A partner evokes, and at times provokes, thinking and experiences that one would not be able to contact through personal abilities. In relationship we put ourselves in situations and encounters that make us stretch. We discover ourself in ways we could never have thought possible.

Relationships also serve as a proving ground for us to access our true knowledge. We challenge each other to contact and accept our limits, dysfunctional attachments, and unresolved residue of life as we prepare to take our tentative next step into the unknown. One way to assess what we need to explore as new learnings for our development is to look at our dark side. We discover our dark side through what we consider to be dark in others.

One of my students has, since childhood, feared

being abandoned. She experiences her life as a series of situations where others leave her. In actual fact, she is the one who constantly entertains the option of leaving and often does. Her dark side--abandonment--is so seductive that to this date she still lives in the idea that others will leave her. This fear translates as anger and is projected on others. What we find intolerable in others must be investigated as a reflection of the actual dark side of ourselves. We do this in order to be empowered by our understanding of the nature of our self. Integrating all sides, light and dark, also creates them as a functional potency which we may or may not choose to use. The strength of our intolerance, hate, and fear indicates that we are in touch with a dimension of our suppressed self.

Relationship is so powerful because it gives us 'hands on' access to the present, and therefore the ability to shape the present and reshape a future. In every situation, we have an opportunity to act from our current level of wisdom rather than compulsively reacting from past habit patterns. This creates relationships as the ongoing opportunity to break the chain of dysfunctional habituation. In our relationships patterns play out before our eyes as what works and what doesn't work. Our view of our partners, and our experience of joy and sorrow with them, is what we have created. In attempting to control the pleasure and pain of our growth we seek to avoid conflict and pain in relationship by manipulating externals, as if the conflict and pain were being imposed upon us. We must reconcile this dilemma. It looks as if we are healing a split, but actually there is no split to heal. In thinking that the split exists we live the split. This is why our pain is so insidious. As long as we think in this way, there is no way out of our boundaries. When we try to push conflict away or push it down, it only becomes stronger because our compulsive resistance affirms its existence, empowering it. The only way out is to live in the reality of our obstacles and contemplate them. As we contemplate and eventually assimilate our obstacles we can walk through them because we now understand their nature as our own.

As we study ourselves by what is evoked in us by others, we can choose to live at the cutting edge of our self-determination and self-definition. We have the assignment, keys, and mapping in each other. Our parents, our children, our neighbors, our significant others, and all of humanity can be raised to the sacred by being seen as an expression of our next step.

We are each representative of points on the continuum of human reality. We create our identity by bonding with the point we represent so much so as to become it. We then regard that place as a living metaphor of what it means to be that type of person. Developmentally, when it is time to discover a dimension of ourself and we cannot access it on our own, we are unconsciously drawn to another human being who serves as the living metaphor. Eventually through the maturation that emerges we transcend the polarities we have created and embrace the opposites as wholes--wholes that are our own self. Dilemma making us real. Dilemma making us whole.

Tantra

In the ancient yogic path of tantra, divinity itself is tapped as a personal resource for human development. The divine characteristics are brought into our human existence by anthropomorphization so they can be assimilated. There are dimensions of genius, insight, and power at the divine level that are essential to successfully traverse the path of spiritual realization. By framing the divine in an understandable form, the attributes of divinity serve the practitioner's aspiration for transpersonal wisdom.

Tantra uses relationships as a road into the mind. It utilizes the relationships of goddess to god, of divinity to humanity, of creator to creatures, of universal energy to every aspect of manifest nature.

Through tantra and its study of energy, we understand that love is the practical, all-pervasive force of creation. By releasing our narrow thinking about love, we come to see why love has been recognized by the great seers as the ultimate energy of the cosmos. Love is that which holds or unites. It is the attraction that the electron has for the nucleus in the atom, that hydrogen has for oxygen in a molecule of water, that pleasure has for pain in desire, and that women and man have for each other in relationship. It is therefore the energy of wholes. It is the energy of true existence.

In human beings that cosmic attraction is manifested

as sexuality. Sexual energy is nature's equivalent to spiritual energy. Sex that is freed of mental obstacles is one of the most easily accessed emotional stimuli available to us. It is one of the most powerful ways two persons can reach out and touch each other in spirit, body, and mind. For a few sex is not the path, but for the vast majority it is the primary way to discover our inner depths and dimensions. Yet humankind in its development has made a casualty of sex. Centuries of social evolution have polluted our ability to contact each other in truly vulnerable and expanding ways because of societal and personal dishonesty around sex. Sex can thus be an obstacle to our development, but it is not the fault of sex itself. Our personal history and society's past injustices keep us frightened and separate from one another, especially at subtle levels. We have lost our ability to understand sex as a metaphor of the union of the universal mind. We truly mirror the union of the universe in creation in our relationship with each other, yet we stop ourselves short of letting grace descend upon us and seeing each other as divine.

Tantra gives us a fresh view. In its practice we utilize ourselves, our imagination, and each other as living metaphors for the divine. The metaphors are taken on by the practitioners under the supervision of an adept. Tantra uses actual relationships in present life associated with cosmic imagery, the memory of relationships in mental practices with cosmic imagery, or a mixture of the two. Thus external life, inner dream imaginings, or a combination of both are used as tools to examine and discover what is in the mind and what lies on the pathway to the soul. We seek to find out what creation is and how it comes into existence. In doing so, we explore how things come together by consciously bringing the divine into the mundane in order to deepen our power of insight.

Our human emotions are enormously powerful. They can serve us in transcendence; they have the ability to transport us to great heights. Emotional power is used to fuel the transport. Devotion is one way to generate enormous emotional intensity. Tantra utilizes that power of devotion and channels it for our spiritual maturity. Through emotional intensity, which is guided by specific devotional concentrations, the practitioner is transported to expanded dimensions of the universal mind. In so doing, the mundane mind is also affected by proximity so that when the individuals return to ordinary awareness, an expanded capacity is experienced as being awakened in them.

Feminine and masculine principles in tantra are seen as currents or pathways of energy. The partners provide each other an opportunity to actualize latent spiritual potential. In the view that women and men need to bring forth the whole of their being, and much of it is submerged in the unconscious, they can use the other as a resource that would be a means to evoke their invisible dimensions. As living metaphors they each can have a practical experience with the unknown until they can begin to recognize it in themselves.

As a team, woman and man awaken and embrace polar opposites in themselves instead of holding and suppressing them and becoming estranged from each other. They can then each experience the feminine and the masculine from their own femaleness or maleness. By suppressing anything, when it is developmentally time for it to come forward, we create a dark side in our minds that expresses itself as severe dysfunction, usually projected, as we have seen, as fear or self-righteous anger onto another person. In tantra, natural drives are allowed and encouraged to come forward in a disciplined way, channeled to realize spiritual potential through human existence. Tantric practices attune to biological and psychological drives and orchestrate an alignment toward their conscious perfection.

What was once deeply buried in the unconscious mind is elicited and discovered. She says, "Through you I find Him in me." He says, "Through you I find Her in me." Through each other they evoke their own experience of wholeness.

As we heal our female/male schism and value our inner resources, we will understand and value the profound depths of human union. Between mature partners the personal bonding through the emotional intensity of sex can explore vulnerability in security. Women and men alike usually hold back from being consumed by the fire of life and the flame of spirit. But life is a rehearsal for the vulnerability of transcendent surrender. With a partner to explore emotional truth, we can become strong enough to be vulnerable, thus loving the divine as a developed, mature, fulfilled human being. We then become a master through completion rather than a believer through suppression.

We honor the ultimate as well as the relative through the vehicles of our body and imagination. The ultimate becomes a real life experience--something very different from mere ritual. Thus charged by touching our divine selves, we are energized and begin to light our own path through accepting the gift of grace eternally present for us.

In tantric practice, the woman sees herself as an aspect of the Divine Mother of the universe. She is in union with the corresponding great male Ascetic of the universe. They both represent Shiva and Shakti, the ultimate male and female principles of the cosmos, by whose union all is manifest and held in existence. Relationship and bonding are the vehicles for this transferrence to occur. The empowering transferrence takes place by taking the other energy pole within ourself with the divine reflection we embody at that time. It evokes the holographic memory and leaves lasting in us our own holographic movement to power our continuing development. It (the practice and transferrence) symbolizes and makes real the mystical marriage of God and human. The sacredness of human is offered at the feet of the divine. Woman and man achieve the status of goddess and god by tapping the divine as a resource and awakening those qualities within themselves. They worship each other as sacred beings who hold something great for each other. In truth they embody the couple in the Visnu Purana (1.8.15) of whom it is said:

> He is speech; she is meaning
> He is understanding; she is intellect
> He is the creator; she is the creation
> He is all males; she is all females
> He is love; she is pleasure.

Summary

We each, woman and man, have different assignments from nature and from society. Sometimes they are at variance with each other. As a result of these differences, we have cultivated greater expertise at particular points along the continuum of the human psyche. Neither group has a corner on excellence in any one dimension, but as a rule we each have developed one side of the continuum more than the other. The female biologically understands surrender (through the functions of menstruation and child-bearing), and the male biologically understands aggression (through competition and validation). Socially the female's worldview stems from bonding while the male's worldview stems from individuation. As a result of these pressures we tend to develop our faculties differently. Looking at the feminine/masculine continuum holographically we see how it is possible for us to develop and make real the potentials that are dormant within us while utilizing and living from our original perspective as woman and man.

Hiding does not work. Having someone to blame in our stead postpones our enlightenment. Lovingly and with commitment we must correct ourself where we find ourself missing the mark. Our 'self-correcting device' can be the questions: Am I being authentic? Does my external behavior match my inner values? Because of our loyalty to our defense system, authenticity and the willingness to challenge our values when needed is difficult. Having a teacher or mentor who has our best interest at heart is more than valuable in this case. Our path must be self-disciplinary (commitment), self-responsible (acknowledging ourself as the source of our experience), and self-corrective (with a monitoring mechanism that serves as a reality check).

Effective movement on the path to self-unfoldment is due to the skill of conducting experiments and the ability to assimilate the learnings from those experiments. In this way the integration essential to enlightenment can take place. We explore and mature in order to actualize spiritual potency. Seeing and honoring our differences can bring us into balance as a world community in a species-oriented relationship. Our difference holds our unfoldment and salvation. Women and men as generalized world views find the other gender's cutting edge relatively easy because each already is what the other is attempting to be. We are at the threshold of an expanded, innovative way of being. Each of us, by embracing our full human self through experiments in relationship, will emerge consciously whole, able to say with Sri Aurobindo, "The answer to the puzzle of life is not in its rejection, but in its fulfillment."

The woman will be a whole being, embodying bonding and individuation from a feminine perspective. Man, as a whole being, will embody individuation and bonding from a masculine perspective. With her current psychological development fully honored and intact, woman then explores assertion, directionality, separation, individuation, ownership, self-validation, ego strength, self-correction, total responsibility, and power as dimensions of her path. With his current psychological development fully honored and intact, man then explores receiving, emotion, attachment, bonding, care, waiting, yielding, sharing, surrender, and vulnerability as dimensions of his path. Together they commit to waking up to truth and the unfoldment of reality.

Charles Bates lives in St. Paul, Minnesota where he is president of GEMS, a stress management, human communications firm, and founder/director of the Twin Cities Yoga Society. His early interest in the fine arts gained him the B.F.A. degree from the Minneapolis College of Art and Design. His travels and professional training programs led him into the fields of chemical dependency treatment, family therapy, sales communications, and counseling. He is a certified practitioner of Neuro-linguistics and an alumnus of the Gestalt Institute of Cleveland and the Herbert H. Humphrey Institute of Public Affairs. He has served as faculty at both schools. Charles has been a student and teacher of Eastern philosophy and self-care practices for nearly twenty years. He continues to give seminars, workshops, and retreats in various aspects of yoga and human communications as well as business and private counseling throughout the country. He is also adjunct faculty at the College of St. Catherine in St. Paul. Charles is author of *Ransoming the Mind: An Integration of Yoga and Modern Therapy,* published recently by YES International Publishers.

You shall love the nothing
Flee the self
Stand alone
Seek help from no one
Let your being be quiet
Be free of the bondage of all things.
                    Mechtild of Magdeburg

Spirituality and Freedom

Sarah Eagger

The issues within freedom for women are changing. They are moving from the external, political ones to involve internal aspects of consciousness. We are becoming aware of the spiritual, psychological, and behavioral areas within woman herself. The socio-cultural doubts of whether women could perform as well as men have largely been dispelled, however other, more subtle, influences obstructing a female's path to freedom are being revealed.

Archetypes and Models

The role of archetypes in the psychological development of women is being revived as a key to wholeness. Myth and symbol are very relevant to the development of a positive psychology for women. Within both the Greek and Indian traditions the goddesses are seen as those with wealth. This wealth is not physical (although it may be symbolically represented as such), but spiritual. It is a sign of her completeness, the richness of her femininity, her power to sustain life: the earth mother. It would appear that women have become impoverished due to their lack of self-awareness and their sense of self as an object. This has meant that we see ourselves as objects rather than as those with the wealth to sustain the world. Time is encouraging us to move away from this object consciousness and take personal responsibility for the fact that we, through our own ignorance, have sold ourselves short. Certainly the more powerful psychological theories of our time have contributed to this sense of impoverishment. Freud tended to describe women in terms of what they lacked anatomically. This perspective maimed women and made them inferior. In his view they suffered penis envy, were masochistic, narcissistic, and had inferior consciences. If competent, self assured, and accomplished they were exhibiting a "masculinity complex." Jung, on the other hand, describes women as feminine conscious personality with a masculine component called animus in their unconscious and men as a masculine conscious personality with a feminine anima in their unconsious. These terms have had popular currency but there are further developments of his theory that are inherently oppressive. He sees the feminine personality as characterized by receptivity, passivity, nurturing, and subjectivity whereas the masculine personality is characterized by rationality, spirituality, and a capacity to act decisively and impersonally. Jung believed that a woman's capacity to think was inferior, and if she was competent in the world it was only because she had a well developed masculine animus, which was, by definition, less conscious and inferior to man's. The functions of the animus that Jung emphasized were those of being hostile, driven by power, and irrationally opinionated. He didn't see women as inherently less creative, but as less able to be objective or take action. Generally he saw women as they served and related to men rather than having independent needs of their own. He discouraged women's striving to achieve and felt that taking up a masculine profession was doing something not wholly in accord with her feminine nature.

Those things which have been "taken away" from women either through society, men, or psychological interpretations have up to now been the main issues addressed by political action. As we move into the spiritual realm the question "What have I done to sell myself short?" becomes more implicit. When addressing things of the spirit we have to acknowledge that we are more than the bodies we live in. The area of "psyche" applies to both male and female, and on many different levels the man within woman and the woman within man is becoming evident.

Biological Evidence

Neuro-biologically, what was once thought to be instinctive is now recognized as learned behavior. The belief that the social behavior of men and women is a natural extension of some predetermined biological set is being challenged. Most significant are the split-brain studies, (principally by psychologist Dr. Robert Ornstein at the

Langley Porter Institute in San Francisco), that have identified that certain skills or conceptual and intellectual abilities are associated with specific anatomic locales of the brain.[1] Descriptive words and phrases which we culturally call male originate in the left brain and those we culturally call female originate in the right brain.

Left Brain	Right Brain
Day	Night
Intellect	Intuition
Time	Timelessness
Active	Receptive
Explicit	Tacit
Analytic	Synthesizing
Propositional	Aesthetic
Lineal	Non-lineal
Sequential	Simultaneous
Focal	Diffuse
Verbal	Spatial
Causal	Inductive
Argumentative	Sensory
Masculine	Feminine

The implications of this are profound. It means that each male with a functioning right hemisphere has available to him the abilities which are culturally considered to be female. Similarly, the qualities of masculinity are available to each female through her left hemisphere. Our culture creates prototypes of male-ness and female-ness by subtly and continually rewarding different behavior in boys than girls.

Beyond the Brain

It is to the inner part of the human being, to the "psyche," which these brain hemispheres subserve, that we now need to turn our attention. One could postulate that as this innermost part is spirit and able to survive death or even to exist in other lifetimes, the experience of being either a woman or a man has been available to each of us. We are neither male nor female but something more. As this awareness increases, the concept of androgeny becomes tangible. The archetypes within Hindu mythology of the deities Vishnu and Mahalakshmi show four-armed figures depicting the perfect balance of masculine and feminine qualities. Within that culture, folklore about the time when earth was paradise describes the differences between men and women as slight. Harmony is seen within the self and externally in nature. This can be contrasted with the extreme polarization of masculinity and femininity today and the external discord and destructiveness of the human race. Changing the current socio-political climate of our world is profoundly linked to balancing the masculine feminine aspects of the self. We need to move from polarization towards maturity.

Barriers

What is it that prevents us from regaining this equilibrium? Strong identification with either body type places us in the limitation of being either male or female. A lack of balance implies overemphasis to either superiority or inferiority. If we are neither of these, then we are free. Clearly the identification and resolution of those things which place us in bondage is not a simple task, yet we also know that misuse, manipulation and artifice is not really what we want. To be true to ourself means knowing, on an inward level, who we are and allowing that to come out of the eclipse of conditioning, both societal and educational. Psychoanalyst, Clara Thompson, wrote in the 1940's that, "Even when a woman has become consciously convinced of her value she still has to contend with the unconscious effects of training, discrimination against her, and traumatic experiences which keep alive the attitude of inferiority."[2]

Becoming aware of the cultural bias is realizing that in some way we are metapsychological beings packaged in a culture. Our spirit cannot be seen, but our bodies are the cultural vehicle for it. It's a bit like selling fresh air in cans. We have to understand this distinction without denial of, nor disassociation from, our bodies. Nevertheless, even though innocently, we have still used the female body to gain things. This eventually leads to abuse. The blatant use of the female body to sell products is an example of our culture's condonation and insidious encouragement.

Strong feelings of indignation or even rage have been aroused in many women as a reaction to the conditioning that our only value lies in how attractive we are to men.

Knowledge is Strength

How do we develop that sense of self which encompasses the true feminine qualities of being a sustainer of life? Again, within Hindu mythology the *shaktis* are powerful women goddesses, remembered for destroying evil and ignorance. Saraswati, for example, is known as the goddess of knowledge. To comprehend spiritual information at the deepest level and articulate it, that is this goddess within. The possessor of that knowledge comprehends it often when no one else can. This kind of self-revelation--where one has the experience of "original thought"--is so very rare in our society of processed thinking that one can feel lonely, 'out on a limb,' or even crazy when stepping the path of self-exploration. As one becomes more connected and clear the clarity of what makes sense and what doesn't becomes evident.

Spiritual education is the key to liberation for women. Women have been discouraged traditionally from being educated because educated women are a threat and don't correspond to the idea of being an object for men. However, men who are developing spiritually are also moving towards ideals of the feminine. So we women must address those things in ourselves that have led to the sellout, rather than blame men. We have settled for less due to our conditioning. Our acceptance has bought with it insecurity. Our conscience feels uneasy as we are holding unto an idea that is dissonant with our true selves. This spiritual inaccuracy causes loss to that true self. The fact that we are taught to consider ourselves as weak has obvious harmful effects, but the same self-depreciation may also be present in men. We have to look deeper. By drawing on the powerful female archetypes we can respond in a truthful manner that will have a subtle but profound role in making society function.

Dependency

The main issue revealed as thwarting women's path

to freedom is her own dependency. Dependent behavior can be defined as the normal infant's way of relating to people. Later, in children and in adults, it seems to be a way of dealing with stress, a reaction to frustration, or a protection against future frustration. There can be affectional, coping, or aggressive types of dependent behavior. Affectionate--by grasping or forcing of affectionate or protective behavior from someone else. Coping--to get help to solve a problem that you can't on your own. Aggressive--by grabbing attention or affection for yourself to prevent others from receiving it. In all cases dependence means a lack of independence. Dependence is leaning on someone else to supply support.[3]   Women often criticize men but it should be recognized that dependent people show aggression by criticizing. It is a common response in those with low self-esteem and anxiety. Anger towards men has also been described as a 'character defense,' a way of defending off dangerous feelings of dependency.[4]

Karen Horney (a renowned psychoanalyst and contemporary of Freud) in a paper called "The Overvaluation of Love," commented that many women in a patriarchal society have a desire to love a man and be loved that is compulsive and driven in its extremeness. They are not able to have good and lasting relations with men; they are inhibited in their work, impoverished in their interests, and often end up feeling anxious, inadequate, and even ugly. In some cases they develop compulsive drives for achievement which, instead of following up themselves, they project into male partners. She draws the distinction between a healthy and spontaneous need for love and one that is a compulsive, self-serving, and neurotic need for love.[5,6]

Clara Thompson also states that "woman lives in a culture which provides no security for her except a permanent so-called love relationship. It is known that the neurotic need of love is a mechanism for establishing security in a dependency relation. To the extent that a woman has a greater need of love than a man, it is also to be interpreted as a device for establishing security in a cultural situation producing dependency. Being 'loved' not only is part of a woman's natural life in the same way as it is part of a man's, but it also becomes, of necessity, her profession.[7]   Elizabeth Douvan[8] also suggests that girls deliberately strive for a lack of definition, a colorlessness, because they need to remain fluid and malleable in personal identity in order to adapt to the needs of the men they marry. This reflects forces that are felt more or less by most girls in our culture. There have also been studies showing that in girls there is a much higher correlation between recognition for achievement and attempts to get love and affection than in boys. Girls are involved in achieving as a way of securing love and approval whereas boys achieve more for its own sake.

By defining personal development holistically and dynamically we see the individual and society, internal and external forces, present and past influences are all mutually interacting and effecting the personality, its defences and symptoms, in a multifactorial way. This shifts the interpretation of women's inferiority from such irreconcilable concepts as "penis envy" to take into account current life situations and destructive attitudes. The conflicting desires of a woman's need to be loved and her equally strong wish to reject that need are one of the major forces that keep her bound. We wish to be both free and safe. Statistics that the mental health of married women is worse than that of single women, or of single or married men may corroborate this. If we both cause and maintain neurosis within ourselves, then there also lie within us the ways, means, and strengths to change it. Hopelessness comes from knowing on some level that making a change in external circumstances will not really do the trick. The paradigm of personal responsibility has more optimism. To become one's own person, to take responsibility for one's own existence is to create one's own life. This shift from other to self makes more energy available to nourish our inner dependency. Freedom and independency cannot be wrested from others, from society at large, or from men; they can only be developed painstakingly from within. To achieve it means giving up dependencies.

The Way Out

Unfortunately, women have tried to break free by imitating the apparently stronger male traits. This has led to high materialistic expectations for success and achievement. In this way our freedom is eroded by the building up of success and eventually backfires. Somewhere along the way we give up our spiritual power. In this situation men and women are equal. We are, as a race, having to face our need to develop spiritually. This has to be done consciously, of our own free will, and not by the force of circumstance. It requires inner work (What are our values? What is success?) and matching our inner and outer worlds. This means exploring androgeny where we are not limited by externals. It means transcending the extremes of materialism, knowing that at the point of extremity that thing becomes its opposite. It means addressing what we have done and what we have allowed to be done to us; taking responsibility for being both manipulated and the manipulator and breaking out of these cycles. Identifying the contradictions within and beginning to work through them is a process. As dependency is a mechanism for defending against insecurity, we must begin to identify what our deeper insecurities are.

Melanie Kleine, (a well known post-Freudian child analyst), speaks of our fear of annihilation as stemming from our infant's ignorance that mother will return and feed us. This fear can be re-enacted in later relationships through a process known as 'fusion.' Fusion, psychoanalytically speaking, is the attempt to recapture a state of primitive empathy (such that an infant has with its mother when there is no perception of individuality), and avoid separateness. To do this means to forgo intuitive and mature empathy. Perhaps the sexual act itself can be interpreted as an attempt to experience fusion, that is, no boundaries between self and other. We can trace the fear of annihilation still further. On a spiritual level it stems from our ignorance and lack of experience of what the self really is. We do not "know," in an experiential sense, what will happen to us if our bodies are destroyed. We fear that if we are separated from our bodies we will no longer exist. As our bodies are external and obvious we tend to identify with them.

This identification overemphasizes the sexuality of that body in order to try and stabilize our identity. This type of identification then extends into other obvious external material things around which we build our sense of self, for example, status, possessions, roles, achievements. The inherent paradox in this type of behavior is that it is the nature of matter to change, to transmute, and yet we look to that for our sense of stability and security.

The Root of the Problem

Intrapsychic conflict arising in the instinctual realm was Freud's analysis of the human predicament. This force for life, 'eros,' with its libidinal energy works in opposition to the death instinct, 'thanatos.' He did, however, also describe the 'nirvana principle' as the tendency of the psychical apparatus to reduce the quantity of excitation in itself, whether of internal or external origin, to zero, or as low a level as possible. Drawn from Buddhism, the term 'nirvana' connotes the extinction of human desire, a state of quietude and bliss. This radical tendency to reduce excitation to zero point is something more than his principle of constancy or of homeostasis. According to that principle, 'constancy' is achieved on one hand through discharge of energy already present, and on the other hand avoidance of whatever might increase the quantity of excitation, and defense against any such increase that does occur. The word 'nirvana' evokes a profound link between pleasure and returning to zero--a link that always remained problematic for Freud.[9]

If we understand, however, that the intrinsic nature of the self is to be distinct, individual, and free, then this resonates with our true reality and is experienced as a lack of psychic conflict (in the deepest sense), and profound pleasure or bliss. This tendency to zero is in fact the underlying motivation for much of our behavior. The pleasure principle is achieved through release from the ego. We seek to emulate this by temporarily escaping from our egos by a variety of physical means. The root of addictive behavior can be seen as the soul's desire to experience this true state of self. To be 'out of your mind' on drugs or to experience 'the little death' through sexual climax are examples.

The addictive, dependent behavior of women in relationships is, in fact, an attempt to reconcile the need to experience constant love and security, from a spiritual point of view, with the illusion that it is obtained through something or someone else. To be able to experience consciously that I am more than my body, more than my masculinity or femininity, or right and left cerebral hemispheres, or cultural conditioning, is in fact to be bodiless, silent, 'zero,' but still intact and whole. This is the essence of spirituality and to experience bodilessness is wholly satisfying. This kind of knowing about my real identity has to be experienced to be of any real use to me. It is something that cannot be just theoretical information. It is the process of spiritual development and requires discipline, and often a lot of pain, to relinquish all the previously held beliefs about what I am. Ultimately it is the only thing that will teach me about my own eternal integrity and freedom.

Filling the Defects

Superceding the Freudian models that the cause of psychic conflicts is due to opposing instincts and objects, Self Psychology, pioneered by Kuhn, sees these conflicts as the 'result' or defects in the self rather than the primary 'causes.' These primary inner conflicts are seen to arise as a result of structural deficiencies, distortions, and weaknesses in the self. The self struggles to maintain its coherence in the face of continual threats to its integrity. The self is seen as a 'particular structure' where goals and values are experienced as a cohesive harmonious unit in time and space, connected to the past and pointing meaningfully into the creative-productive future.

Jung also spoke of the process of 'individualization' where one is becoming aware that one is separate to and different from others, and able to recognize oneself as a whole, indivisible person. Within ontology, a branch of metaphysics dealing with the nature of being, 'self-consciousness' has been described as the awareness of oneself, as a being with a center, who affirms and participates with other beings. The primary security derived from this awareness arises from a centrally firm sense of one's own and others' reality. Therefore it appears we have a structure of the self as an indivisible unit whose conflicts arise due to certain deficiencies.

To begin to replenish those deficiencies is to understand that I have lost my spiritual wealth--my own purity, peace, love, and power. It requires a resolute search for the source of these qualities both within myself and universally. These are the qualities that enable me, as a whole, mature being to sustain both myself and others. They are not qualities that I need from others, rather my own fundamental properties that I share with others. In the same way that the body draws into itself those things of which it is made, that is, water, oxygen, organic compounds, and minerals, the spirit, my 'self,' also draws to itself those things which are primary to it. Our attraction to and need for love, peace, contentment, will, happiness, freedom--for pure self essence, in fact--reflects that this is what I am. Manifested in life, these fundamental qualities blossom into a variety of skills and attributes. They can develop into virtues or power and enhance and enliven any situation with truth.

Let us take, for example, the quality of purity. Jean Shinoda Bolen has developed this theme in her description of the archetype of the 'virgin goddesses,' likening virginity or purity to that quality of being one-in-herself:

A woman who is one-in-herself does what she does not because of any desire to please; not to be liked or to be approved, even by herself; not because of any desires to gain power over another, to catch his interest or love but because what she does it true. Her actions may indeed be unconventional. She may have to say no when it would be easier, as well as more adapted, conventionally speaking, to say yes. She is not influenced by the considerations that would make another trim her sales and adapt to expediency. If a woman is one-in-herself, she will be motivated by a need to follow her own inner values, to do what has meaning or fulfills herself--apart from what other people think. Psychologically, the virgin goddess is that part of a woman that has not been worked on, either by the collective (masculine-determined) social and cultural expectations of what a woman should be, or by an individual males' judgment of her. The virgin goddess aspect is a pure essence of who the woman is and of what she values. It remains untarnished and uncontaminated because she does not reveal it; because she keeps it sacred and inviolate, or because she expresses it without modification to meet male standards.[10]

We begin to see that the things that distress us, our defects, are just that--deficiencies in the primary properties of our true essence. Anger is an example. Rather than a 'thing in itself' or a primary instinctual force, anger is present due to the lack of the experience of eternal, self-existent peace. Hatred is seen as a lack of love, arrogance the ignorance of the true nature of things, greed the inability to be nurtured spiritually. Misdirecting my sense of identity towards my body, until it is derived only from my body, has led to my desire for external validation and reassurance in all that I do.

Freedom From Freedom

It is real freedom to be liberated from these desires and tendencies. It means we lose our fear, both of ourselves and others. It implies a 'wholeheartedness' that Karen Horney describes as the ability to be without pretence, emotionally sincere, and to be able to put the whole of oneself into one's feelings, one's work, and one's beliefs. This gives an emotional mobility to be able to move towards things that are satisfying and away from those things that are not; to be free to succeed and free to love others because of loving oneself. It is being able to let go of the destructive or damaging experiences of the past by realizing the lessons they have taught and transforming them into a potent, motivating force for change. This true, refreshing, spontaneous independence means that we are more emotionally available to respond to any situation or person. Not because of our own needs in a situation but because we have tapped, within ourself, the resources that enable us to do so. These are the resources of the spirit, that begin before masculinity or femininity but can seek expression beautifully through whichever prism they choose. Knowing that they come from me, and that in some sense they are me, means owning them rather than relegating them to some opposite-sexed part of myself. This rise above duality and polarity is the journey back to one-centeredness, one-pointedness, that leaves behind limitations and gently soars towards the ocean of all possibilities.

Freedom is being able to fly.

Sarah Eagger, MBBS., MRCPsych was medically trained in Australia and specializes in psychiatry in London, England. Her various appointments have included the Tavistock Clinic and the Royal Free Hospital. Presently she is engaged in research at the Institute of Neurology and the National Hospital, Queen Square. With a longstanding interest in holistic health, she has also been practicing and teaching raja yoga meditation for ten years.

Dr. Eagger is an active member of the Brahma Kumaris World Spiritual University based in Mt. Abu, India, which has as one of its founding principles the spiritual emancipation and development of women. She has run many workshops on meditation for several groups, including the National Holistic Nursing Conferences, the British Holistic Medical Conferences, and the British Psychological Society's Conference on Eastern Models of Self and Mind.

Dr. Eagger is on the councils of the Scientific and Medical Network, the British Holistic Medical Association, and S.I.G.M.A. An assistant editor of the *British Holistic Medical Journal,* she also travels and lectures in many countries including Australia, India, the United States, the British Isles and countries in Europe. Recently she was filmed for a BBC television production on meditation in relation to self-help strategies for which she also wrote a manual.

In proportion as one simplifies one's life, the laws of the universe will appear less complex, and solitude will not be solitude, nor poverty poverty, nor weakness weakness.

Thoreau

Renunciation and Spiritual Growth

Tenzin Dechen

People come to an awareness of a spiritual dimension in their lives by many different means--some through the experience of great suffering, some through a sense of meaninglessness, some through the experience of a moment of heightened awareness, some through a strong devotional response towards a particular being who represents or embodies a certain spiritual ideal.

What is Renunciation?

However one may become aware of, or develop an aspiration towards, a spiritual path, there is generally some kind of inner movement that takes place. This is characteristically a movement away from a more negative state towards a more positive state. This type of inner movement is the embryo or seed of renunciation, which is not just a matter of giving things up for the sake of it, but rather of a movement towards a better goal.

One may see the Christian view of renunciation as a movement away from the confines of self-centered interests towards the deeper and more fulfilling life of serving one's beloved spiritual master, of trying to practice what he teaches and of trying to help all those whom he loves so much. This inner movement is a joyful experience accompanied by a feeling of freedom rather than of loss or constraint. The external movement of 'giving things up' is just what follows from the internal change. However, to move from love of self to love of others in any real and consistent way is like trying to leap across a chasm which is a mile wide. One needs a bridge. In Christianity the bridge is devotion, where one's love of Christ is greater than one's love of oneself. Through loving and serving him, through practicing what he taught, and through constant prayer, one aspires gradually to develop his qualities.

As a Buddhist one also aspires to develop the qualities of the completely perfect, omniscient, infinitely wise and compassionate being. Such a being is known as 'Buddha' or 'Enlightened One.' The difference between Buddhism and Christianity from a practical point of view, is that there are many more bridges offered in Buddhism. Within Tibetan Buddhism, devotion is seen to be the root of the path, as one receives blessings and guidance from one's enlightened master. However, the guidance and teachings themselves are very extensive, and it is these which, when put into practice, have the power to transform us.

The person whom we refer to as The Buddha, that is the founder of Buddhism in this world, was born about 2500 years ago in North India. He manifested as an unenlightened being who became a Buddha through his own dedicated spiritual practice. Nevertheless, he was endowed with very special qualities from birth. He was of aristocratic lineage, and is said to have been glorious to behold, with an equally beautiful mind and character--naturally kind, compassionate, intelligent, and wise, with great charm and a good sense of humor. At the age of sixteen Gotama, as he was called, won his wife by means of a sporting contest. They married and had a son. Gotama lived with them in the family palace under the care of his very protective father, who took great efforts to keep his son from experiencing or witnessing any of the gross sufferings of life.

Gotama, however, was not at ease in his life of sensuous pleasures at the palace. He felt a need to visit the outside world. He secretly ventured out with his carriage driver on four occasions. On the first occasion he saw an old man; on the second he saw a man stricken with sickness; on the third occasion he saw a corpse; and on the fourth he saw a monk with a shaven head and yellow robe, radiant with inner peace. Gotama was deeply moved by these sights. He realized that what he saw on the first three occasions were the inevitable results of birth in the world of suffering. What he saw on the last occasion indicated a way to free oneself from the craving which leads to such birth. These four sights are known as the 'four signs,' and it is these which led to Gotama's renunciation of the worldly life.

A life which is centered around fulfilling one's

desires may bring temporary pleasures or happiness, but in the long run it only binds one to the wheel of suffering existence--continually revolving from rebirth to sickness, old age, and death, and again to rebirth, by the force of the momentum of ego-grasping. Blindly engaging in worldly life perpetuates ego-grasping which again leads to rebirth in a form pervaded by suffering. The only thing that can cut the root of all suffering is the wisdom which realizes selflessness.

With the determination to achieve this aim for the sake of guiding all beings to enlightenment, Gotama renounced his worldly life. He secretly left the palace at night, and once far enough away, cut off his long black hair and exchanged his princely robes for those of a beggar. He sought teachings from a number of different sages and quickly mastered all that they had to offer. Not satisfied with these attainments he set out on his own. For six years he meditated and practiced austerities which were so severe that they almost led to his death. Realizing that this was useless, he once again accepted food and renewed his meditation practice. Finally, through the power of his meditative wisdom, he attain enlightenment. After this he set about trying to help others deliver themselves from suffering.

It may seem from this overview that renunciation means giving up one's home, job, clothing, and other material possessions, just like the Buddha did. This is completely missing the point. Renunciation is not merely a matter of an external lifestyle. Sometimes it can be very helpful to adopt a so-called 'renounced' way of life but only if it functions to develop or strengthen the inner realization of renunciation. Simply abandoning pleasures and comforts in itself does not necessarily lead to spiritual development, and can at worst be harmful. For example, if one's craving for certain comforts is too strong, or if one lacks any clear purpose, it can cause more misery and confusion to arise in the mind. This would be totally counter-productive to spiritual development. So we need to understand what renunciation really is, and then see how it is helpful, indeed necessary, for any real spiritual development.

Renunciation literally means "to abandon." What is it, on a spiritual path, that we are trying to abandon? According to Buddhist teachings, what we hope to abandon are suffering and the causes of suffering. True Sufferings and True Causes of suffering are the first two of the Four Noble Truths which the Buddha taught after his enlightenment. The third is True Cessations, which refers to the permanent abandonment of different levels of suffering (eventually resulting in complete enlightenment), and the fourth is True Paths, which are the spiritual practices and trainings that lead to true cessations.

Renunciation, in the Buddhist sense, has two aspects. One aspect is the recognition of, and the wish to abandon, True Sufferings and their causes. The other aspect is the recognition of, and the wish to attain, True Cessations. In order to fulfill these wishes, one must engage in practicing the True Paths.

What is Suffering?

First of all we need to understand the nature of suffering. This may sound a strange thing to say given that there is so much suffering in the world: so many wars, so much starvation and sickness, so much general dissatisfaction, depression, and loneliness. However, all these things that we experience to a greater or lesser extent, or that we see going on around us, are only one type of suffering. In Buddhist terminology this is referred to as the suffering of misery. Even a slight headache or a little emotional discomfort falls into this category. This kind of suffering we can easily recognize, and quite naturally wish to avoid, without any spiritual training or insight! The other two types of suffering are more difficult to understand as suffering, and much more difficult to develop the wish to avoid. For this we do need spiritual training and insight.

The second type of suffering is known as the suffering of change. This includes everything that relieves us from pain and satisfies our desires. What we call 'pleasure' or 'relief' is simply the movement from one form of suffering to another. If we are hungry and eat some good food, this relieves us from the suffering of hunger and satisfies our desire for experiencing pleasant tastes. If we continue to eat, however, our stomach will eventually become very painful and even the delicious smell of the food will make us feel sick. So the food in itself is not a cause of happiness. Another obvious example is sitting down. After having been rushing around all morning, it is pleasant to sit down. But continuous sitting will become painful. These things are not in themselves causes of happiness; they are relative to certain conditions.

It is very easy to spend one's whole life chasing after various pleasures thinking that by attaining them we will find contentment. We try to solve our problems in this way, but without any lasting result. Often we find that once we have obtained the object of our desire, our desire changes and we don't want it any more, or the object itself changes, or the object doesn't live up to our expectations, or it soon breaks down, or we lose it, or the reason for our needing it in the first place has disappeared. We are like children trying to catch pretty bubbles in the air. If we catch one it pops, and then we burst into tears because we can't get what we want. And if we do get what we want, this increases our attachment, and the fear of losing our precious object looms up like a horrible monster. Our so-called 'happiness' is continually giving way to misery--to fear, anger, and various other neurotic reactions. If this is the only kind of happiness we have experienced, then we haven't even tasted true happiness. A true cause of happiness does not change its nature, nor can it be the cause of negative emotions and misery; it can only lead to peace.

We mistake the nature of happiness for the nature of suffering, and spend our time chasing after it. Because we are not at peace within ourselves in the first place, we grasp at external objects and situations in the hope of finding a solution. In this way, we neglect the true cause of happiness which is within our own minds, and just make matters worse for ourselves.

What underlies these types of suffering is the third type, which is known as pervasive suffering, or the suffering of composition. Pervasive suffering is the fact that our bodies and minds, and everything which these bodies and minds come into contact with, are composed of aggregates which are contaminated in the sense that they are products of our delusions and past actions. As such they are ready to give rise to the suffering of misery at any moment, regardless of our present circumstances. This is because due to the influence of delusions within our continuum, we have created negative actions in the past which have left negative potentials, or seeds, on our mind stream. All that is needed is for certain circumstances to be present, and these negative seeds will ripen, giving rise to unpleasant situations and painful experiences. There are no external methods of preventing this from happening. Future experiences of suffering and misery are bound to arise in one form or another, at one time or another, unless we have completed the task of removing the causes of suffering from our continuum.

The real causes of suffering are delusions: ignorance, aversion, craving, etc. Ignorance of the true nature of our self causes us to see everything from the point of view of a solid, subjective, self-existent ego-entity, thus giving rise to the strong feeling of 'I' and 'mine.' We naturally grasp onto this 'I' and look to its well-being. We spend our lives continuously trying to make it feel comfortable in every possible respect. If anything comes along that threatens the comfort or well-being of this 'I,' we feel aversion towards that circumstance or person; we want to fight it or run away from it. At all costs we don't want it to diminish the comfort of the 'I.'

By reacting in this way we create negative actions of body, speech, and mind--actions which are motivated by craving for pleasant things and aversion towards unpleasant things. Even if we manage to create only virtuous actions, we still create the causes of having contaminated aggregates, merely because we experience this fabricated 'I' as being a self-existent and solid entity. Until we have removed the causes of this misperception, our continuum is not pure. One also cannot escape the suffering of misery merely by relying on practicing only virtuous actions if the delusions are still present in the mind. Even if one has reached a high level of discipline in this life, such that one does not commit any negative actions, and one has purified all one's past negativities, some downfall could occur in a future life due to the influence of delusions. So it is important to aim to purify the delusions themselves.

Removing Suffering

We may wonder if it is ever possible to remove this

root delusion of ego-grasping ignorance which causes suffering. Because the delusions are not of the same nature as the mind, it is possible to remove them. The nature of the mind is clear, like the sky, and delusions are like the clouds which obscure it. The non-inherently existent mind, which we all possess, is the Buddha-nature. The continuity of this Buddha-nature, when it is fully purified, becomes the Wisdom Truth Body of the Buddha. So the delusions, although they have been within our mindstream since beginingless time, are like the dust on a mirror and can be removed. The job of removing them is, of course, a very big one; in fact it is the biggest of all possible jobs. But it is the only job that is ultimately worth doing. A person who fully recognizes this situation and is fully engaged in the job of delivering himself from delusion has developed what Buddhists call renunciation. Such a person has no attachment for the pleasures of conditioned existence, as he can see that they contain no real happiness; his only wish is to find release from these conditions which he sees to be in the nature of continuous suffering.

While one is engaging in the methods of freeing oneself from suffering, one still has to seek relief from the suffering of misery in the usual ways--such as eating good food, keeping warm, sleeping properly, etc. A renounced person does not deny himself anything that is necessary for maintaining a healthy body and relatively clear and peaceful mind. Behaving in extreme ways and subjecting oneself to unnecessary pain is not part of Buddhist practice. It would only degenerate one's strength and distract one's mind from the main goal, which is to develop wisdom-realizing selflessness. To do this one first needs to develop one's mind by gradually accustoming it to virtue. As one's virtuous tendencies increase and one's non-virtuous tendencies decrease, one's mind will become clearer and more peaceful, and one will find it easier to concentrate. The practice of virtue is based on sound reasoning, not on superstition. According to the Buddhist view there is no person 'up there,' neither Buddha nor anybody else, who decides whether or not you've been a good boy or girl, and what you should experience next, either in this life or the one to come. Everything that happens to us is dependent on a cause and effect procedure. This is known as the law of karma, and concerns the planting of certain kinds of seeds in our continuum by engaging in virtuous, non-virtuous, or neutral acts of body, speech, and mind. It is just a fact of life that virtue leads to happiness and non-virtue to misery, both for oneself and others, whether the result is experienced in this life or in future lives.

The abandonment of non-virtuous actions is itself an expression of some level of renunciation. By abandoning non-virtuous actions one ceases to create the causes of one's own future misery, as well as, and more importantly, ceasing to create present misery for others. The abandonment of the ten non-virtuous actions as taught by the Buddha, and the practice of the ten virtuous actions, is a fairly simple method of purifying negative karma and creating good karma. Merely from the point of view of wishing to protect oneself from experiencing misery in the future it is necessary to practice these. However, if one is a Buddhist one can dedicate this practice to achieve liberation. It will then act as a cause of liberation rather than merely a cause of pleasant circumstances within conditioned existence. And for a Buddhist who dedicates this practice to enlightenment for the sake of all beings, it will act as a cause of that.

The ten non-virtuous actions are: killing, stealing, sexual misconduct, lying, slander, harsh words, idle gossip, covetousness, harmful thoughts, and wrong views. The first three concern negative bodily actions, the next four negative actions of speech, and the last three negative actions of mind. Killing refers to the intentional killing of not only human beings, but any living being, including insects. Wrong views refers to disbelief in the laws of karma and reincarnation.

Renunciation and Vows

Taking various vows serves to strengthen one's practice of virtue. This happens not only since one develops greater determination to practice virtue because of wanting to keep the vows, but also because the vows themselves are said to be a subtle form which is planted in the mindstream and as such increases the karmic results of one's actions. So by taking vows one can purify one's mind more quickly, and thus develop the potential to become enlightened more quickly.

Beyond the ten virtuous actions which are to be practiced by all committed Buddhists, the Buddha explained different types of vows designed to lead to liberation. These are known as Pratimoksha vows. There are four types of Pratimoksha vows for lay people: eight which are taken for twenty-four hours, eight taken for one week, five taken for life, and eight taken for life. A lay Buddhist, whether male or female, can take five precepts for life which are: to abandon killing, to abandon stealing, to abandon sexual misconduct, to abandon lying, and to abandon intoxicants.

So a committed Buddhist can live a normal life, have a job, spouse, children, and home. These vows do not exclude any of the usual activities. Just because someone is a lay practitioner does not mean that he or she is not committed to the path to enlightenment. For people who already have so-called worldly responsibilities and commitments when becoming Buddhists, it is usually best for them to fulfill those responsibilities, and make it part of their practice. If one has no such commitments, then one is free to take monastic ordination as a monk or nun if one feels that this is appropriate.

Monastic vows are many, depending on one's lineage and sex. Nuns take many more vows than monks; the additional ones are concerned mainly with their safety, for example, nun's living situations. There are five types of monastic vows: the probationary vows include five life vows and three changes (or name, appearance, and mind); novices take thirty-six vows; novice nuns wishing to take full ordination take the uncommon novice nun's vows; fully ordained monks take over 200 vows; and fully ordained nuns take about 300 vows. All these vows, whether lay or monastic, are practically the same in all traditions of Buddhism. However I will be referring mostly to my own tradition, that of Tibetan Buddhism.

As a novice nun in the Tibetan tradition, I have taken thirty-six vows. A brief idea of what they concern and how many vows are involved with each subject matter is the following: killing (4), stealing (1), celibacy (1), lying (13), intoxicants (1), time of eating (1), handling gold and silver (1), using luxurious beds or seats (4), singing, dancing, adorning oneself, etc. (7), abandoning the signs of a lay person (1), adopting the signs of ordination

(1), requesting the Abbott (1).

     The practice of any of these types of Pratimoksha vows forms the basis of the path to liberation from conditioned existence. In order to achieve liberation one needs to accomplish three levels of practice: morality, meditative concentration, and wisdom. Without morality one cannot develop a very subtle or powerful meditative concentration, and without developing a particularly subtle and powerful meditative concentration one will not be able to focus one's mind single-pointedly on selflessness, so one will not be able to develop wisdom. And without developing the wisdom realizing selflessness, one will not be able to cut free of ego-grasping. So morality is absolutely necessary for spiritual development.

     If one also wishes to help all other suffering beings to achieve enlightenment, one needs to practice stronger and more far-reaching methods than those needed to gain liberation for oneself alone. The basic practices for this higher path are known as the Six Perfections. They are:

The Perfection of Giving
The Perfection of Morality
The Perfection of Patience
The Perfection of Joyful Effort
The Perfection of Concentration
The Perfection of Wisdom.

     To develop the perfection of any one of these is in itself a vast practice, and altogether they constitute many lifetimes' work. To understand these practices fully, one needs extensive teachings as they are not as simple as they look. Corresponding to this higher form of training are a higher set of vows known as 'bodhicitta' vows. The practice of these vows, together with certain special meditation practices designed to transform the self-cherishing attitude into that of cherishing others, leads to the development of the intense and unshakeable compassionate attitude known as 'bodhicitta.' The word literally means "mind of enlightenment." Generally it is understood to be the motivation to attain enlightenment for the sake of all other sentient beings. Once it has arisen fuly, it pervades every moment of one's awareness and enables one to undergo any suffering for the sake of benefitting another being. Thus it is incredibly powerful. The practice of bodhicitta is the ultimate way of helping others. It is working to free them from the true causes of suffering, not only from the effects of their suffering nature.

Bodhicitta vows exist only within the Mahayana form of Buddhism, which is to be found in the traditions of Tibet, China, Korea, and Japan. The Hinayana form, which can be found in the traditions of Thailand, Sri Lanka, and Burma have only the Pratimoksha vows and the Three Trainings mentioned earlier. Compassion, however, still enters into Hinayana practice to a large extent, though not in the powerful and all-consuming way that it does in the Mahayana.

A Mahayana Buddhist seeks to develop what are known as the three principle aspects of the path: renunciation, bodhicitta, and emptiness. Without renunciation (the wish to free oneself from the true causes of suffering), one cannot develop bodhicitta (the wish to free others from the true causes of suffering). Emptiness refers to the non-inherent existence of the self and all phenomena. Meditation on emptiness is what actually frees us, and as such is the tool of renunciation and bodhicitta. As far as the actual practice of becoming enlightened is concerned, there are two main divisions of practice known as 'method' and 'wisdom.' Method refers to the first five of the six perfections mentioned earlier; wisdom refers to the sixth perfection. Method and wisdom are like the two wings of a bird. Just as a bird cannot fly to its destination with only one wing, so we cannot reach enlightenment with either wisdom or method alone.

Tibetan Buddhism is unique in that it has a living tradition of very powerful meditation practices known as Tantra, or Secret Mantra. All the other practices that we have been discussing up till now are contained in the sutra system. Althought all the sutra practices form part of the tantric path, there is a difference between sutra and tantra which can be characterized as follows: In Sutra the practices of method and wisdom are done separately. One practices wisdom by meditating on emptiness, but meditation on any other object, such as bodhicitta, or any form of practice that does not involve meditating on emptiness, is the practice of method. So at best they can be practiced alternately. By using the tantric path, however, one can practice both method and wisdom at the same time with the same moment of consciousness, so the end result can be achieved much more quickly. There are many symbolic representations of tantric achievements in the form of paintings of deities--often of a male and female deity in union. This represents the union of method and wisdom, the male symbolizing method and the female symbolizing wisdom. In the practice of highest yoga tantra, the subtle mind transforms into the deity, which realizes emptiness as its object. The manifestation as the mandala or holy body of the deity is the method practice and the realization of emptiness is the wisdom practice. The concentration that can be developed through the practice of highest yoga tantra is far more subtle and powerful than any level of concentration that can be attained through sutra practice alone, so it leads to a quicker result.

Devotion forms an integral part of Buddhist practice, and limitless gratitude is due to our teachers who show us and help us to practice the path to enlightenment. In the tantric path devotional practices are especially meaningful, and it is important to train one's mind to see the spiritual master, or lama, as the primordial Buddha. In this way one receives blessings from the Buddha and thereby can develop his qualities more easily. There are devotional practices, prayers, and ceremonies in all Buddhist traditions, and through these one can center one's awareness on the qualities of the Buddha, the teachings and the spiritually realized beings. These three objects of devotion are known as the Buddha, the Dharma and the Sangha--the Three Precious Jewels. Through prayers and devotional practices one can receive much inspiration and spiritual nourishment, as well as create the causes for making progress along the path. Also through the use of ceremonies one can create formal bonds between oneself and the Three Jewels. The various levels of vows are received through ordination ceremonies and initiations, some of which are very elaborate. There are also special ceremonies and methods for purifying any transgressions of these vows. In this way one maintains a direct link with the Buddha, Dharma, and Sangha which operates on a subtle level.

Spirituality in Monasticism

Receiving monastic ordination enables one to train in a relatively basic level of moral discipline which helps one to keep the higher sets of vows more purely. When one understands the great benefits of the vows, it seems that it is no great sacrifice to live within their limitations, for in fact they lead to true freedom. Constantly being under the influence of ego-grasping is itself the most gruesome kind of imprisonment. However, taking vows and practicing the Buddha-dharma does not instantaneously release one from this; one still has to tolerate the sufferings that are generated by ego-grasping. The difficulty is when some delusion arises very strongly and one cannot gain the temporary comfort of acting upon it. At such times one has to remember such things as impermanence: that this feeling or difficulty will pass. All experiences arise and cease. So one can just observe its arising, its presence in the mind, and its departure, without grasping at it. This requires practice, but it certainly is possible to develop an awareness of the basic clarity of the mind, which then enables one not to be disturbed by whatever may arise and pass away within that inner space. There are many other practices which help one to deal in a temporary way with the delusions, in which one actually analyzes the particular delusion that is present in the mind at that moment, and sees that there is no value in it, no good reason to act upon it, and indeed that it doesn't even exist in the way that it appears. Then one can try to cultivate the positive feeling or attitude which is its opposite. In this way one not only deals with the present situation, but one can lessen the power of the delusions themselves, so that gradually one's mind becomes more consistently peaceful.

A monastic lifestyle provides the ideal environment within which to study the mind and to practice meditation. It is very helpful to have a clear and simple way of life that does not encourage self-indulgence nor subject one to unconducive difficulties and complications. Even without the external support of a monastery or a nunnery, the vows themselves act as a very suitable framework within which to develop a constant awareness of one's mental states and so be able to transform them.

Being a monk or nun in itself by no means indicates whether or not one has developed renunciation in the Buddhist sense. It merely makes it easier to develop it. True renunciation is indicative of an advanced level of spiritual development. Most of us who are monks and nuns are just working towards that. Our long, flowing robes and bald heads do not indicate that we have abandoned all worldly thoughts and wishes; rather they are a tool to help us abandon them. This change of one's appearance is really very effective, and over a period of time one can concentrate one's energies more fully on the most meaningful things in life. Our human life is so short, and yet it gives us the precious opportunity to work for real freedom. It seems a tragic waste of time to use it only for fun and games and material comforts which themselves are so easily and certainly lost, at the time of death if not before.

Things of beauty can open the heart and bring warmth into one's life, but when the beauty fades all too often the openness and warmth does also. One needs to develop openness and warmth in all situations and towards all beings, even the ugly and unpleasant ones. A monastic way of life helps one to develop an appreciation of a kind of beauty that flows from within the mind rather than that which appears to come from an external object. When the mind is at peace all things can appear beautiful, even a pile of garbage. However, when the mind is agitated or upset, even a blazing sunset will seem uninteresting. So even 'external' beauty doesn't exist just by virtue of the object.

Although Buddhist practitioners, and particularly monks and nuns, often live in communities, the actual practice is a solitary one. No one else can be in your mind. You yourself have to deal with your own mental and emotional experiences. This does not mean that the monastic life is a lonely or selfish one. Loneliness is something that can be experienced in any situation, whether one is celibate or married with a family. People who are sincerely practicing a spiritual path are often less lonely than people who are not. We have close working relationships with our teachers and spiritual friends, and often such friendships reach much deeper levels than ordinary ones. One is also more easily able to get in touch with a certain 'something within oneself.' By developing deeper awareness one has access to greater reserves of energy, wisdom, and compassion. As such one is able to give more, and to give more wisely, to others. So it is not at all selfish. One is trying first to develop the quality, and then the quantity, of what one can give.

As far as women are concerned, and particularly Western women, the Tibetan Buddhist monastic set-up is in many ways more suitable than that of other Buddhist traditions. The style of life is less formal, and monks and nuns have equal status--which is something that we Westerners can feel quite concerned about. The Theravada tradition in particular takes a heavy view of women, and nuns are regarded as much lower in status than monks. In fact, I believe that in countries where Theravada Buddhism is traditional they do not have any nuns, only female postulants or 'anagarikas.' It is even believed that women cannot reach enlightenment at all but have to create the causes to be born as men in their next life so that they can make it next time round. This attitude is not usually held to be true by Western Theravada practitioners and certainly not by Tibetan Buddhists of whatever nationality.

In Britain, a new order of nuns has been established within the Thai Theravada tradition and the nuns here are given much more credibility than they would have in Thailand. I have friends among the nuns in this new order and know that although their status is more equal to the monks than it would be in Thailand, there are still quite a few differences. The nuns themselves cope admirably with their lower status. In fact this aspect of their life has proved to be a source of great strength to them; they really have to practice tolerance. On an external level their life is stricter than ours is within the Tibetan tradition. I may be a nun and live on my own or with friends, not necessarily in a monastery or nunnery. I can get a job and earn money. For them this would be impossible. They cannot handle money nor own anything much other than their robes and bowl (which are in a sense monastic property anyway). So I still have quite a bit of freedom as a nun, and indeed do get jobs in the city from time to time, wear lay clothes, and grow my hair a little (so as not to shock my employers!). I find this very helpful. In any case, I have to do this sometimes, as within the Tibetan tradition there is no financial support for monks and nuns. Within the Theravada tradition the monks and nuns are 'alms mendicants' and live entirely on whatever the lay people offer to them. This is a very beautiful way of life and has a very powerful effect on those who live this way, as well as on those who give to it.

Although the external lifestyle within the Theravada tradition may be stricter than that within the Tibetan monastic tradition, the inner practice is no less strict. Within the Tibetan tradition there are several more sets of vows to keep which relate to transforming one's feelings, thoughts, and energies. The monastic vows relate mainly to controlling one's actions of body and speech, and though these have a strong effect on one's thoughts, feelings, and energies, they more readily provide the basis for transforming them rather than function as a practice for that end. Our general training is geared to transform every moment of our daily experience into the wish to remove the suffering of all living beings. Even cleaning jobs can be made into a spiritual practice to develop compassion. One example given in the scriptures is that of sweeping the floor while thinking, "I am removing the ignorance and delusions of myself and all living beings; may all be free from suffering." On the basis of this simple practice one can generate a strong motivation to become enlightened for the sake of all beings. A great variety of examples is given in the Tibetan Buddhist scriptures of how to view our daily activities, even down to such things as opening and closing doors. At first one may feel squashed or crowded out by such all-pervading conceptual practices, but gradually the grasping for thought space for oneself subsides and one can motivate more and more of one's life for the benefit of others.

This kind of transformation seems to happen quite naturally when someone becomes a mother, though that intense feeling and concern is limited to her own family. In Tibetan Buddhist teaching many references are made to a mother's selfless love, and we try to develop that kind of love and concern for all living beings. Through an understanding of reincarnation we realize that we cannot point to any living being and say that this being has definitely never been a mother to me in a previous lifetime. Tibetan Buddhists are encouraged to view every living being as a mother from the past, as someone who has been very close to oneself and shown one great kindness and self-sacrifice. In this way we can develop a real feeling for not wanting them to suffer, and the wish to free them from suffering as soon as possible.

In order to guide someone up the slippery mountain passes to liberation, one has to have the strength to do it, one has to have the wisdom which knows the way--not only from maps but from experience--and one has to have the compassionate will to accomplish the task. Thus one works to develop these qualities within oneself so that one can act as a perfectly qualified guide for others. Although one can do much to help others in various ways throughout one's own long path of progress, it is when one's mind finally abides in the sphere of reality, completely free of all obscurations, that one can most fully and effectively help others to attain that lasting bliss--the perfect state of Buddhahood.

Venerable Tenzin Dechen was born in England in 1955. After a traditional upbringing in an Anglican Church boarding school, she worked as an accounts clerk in London and Paris. For eleven years she was in the British Olympic Fencing Squad. In 1976 she went to London University to read philosophy, and in 1979 to Cambridge University to work on her Ph.D.

The study of philosophy and religion eventually led her to her first contact with Tibetan Buddhism. Realizing her attunement with Buddhism, she lived at a college of Buddhist studies in North England to continue her study and spiritual practices. In 1985-86 she visited Bodhgaya, India, and was ordained there as a novice nun in the Gelukpa tradition of Tibetan Buddhism by His Holiness the Dalai Lama.

At present Tenzin Dechen is undertaking an extensive retreat at a Buddhist center in Wales.

She who comes into being through the breath of life from whom the gods all took their birth, the boundless goddess of infinity, who enters the cave of the heart and dwells there, this is that!

Kathopanishad

Feminine Aspects of Divinity

Erminie Huntress Lantero

In recent years there has been growing recognition that the religious language of the Judeo-Christian tradition is over-weighted with masculine symbolism. It took shape in an era of patriarchal domination, first in Hebraic and Jewish society, then in the Roman Empire. As women today become aware of their femininity as a major style of being human, they quite properly resent this. Male theologians have pointed out that masculine pronouns are used for God simply because *some* pronouns have to be used; the statement is annoying, if also reasonably correct. Christianity always taught that sexual distinctions are not really applicable to the transcendent mystery we call God. But the manward aspect of that mystery, the perennial experiences of divine calling, providence, shepherding, communion, made it necessary to continue to speak of God in personal terms. 'He' is at least more adequate than 'It.'

Even prior to the twentieth century, however, there were straws in the wind pointing to feminine rebellion. Mother Ann Lee, founder of the Shakers (1736-1784), claimed to be the second appearing of Christ, 'Ann the Word,' sent to complement the work of Jesus. The Lord Jesus stood before her in prison and became one with her in form and spirit, "my head and my husband, and I have no other." She had already found her earthly marriage intolerable. Mary Baker Eddy, who married three times, also claimed a direct revelation but in less personal terms. In a newspaper interview late in life (1901), she declared that "the manhood and womanhood of God have already been revealed in a degree through Christ Jesus and Christian Science, His two witnesses."[1] "In divine Science we have not as much authority for considering God masculine, as we have for considering Him feminine, for Love imparts the clearest idea of Deity."[2] Her spiritual interpretation of the Lord's Prayer, opening with "Our Father-Mother

God," is used in Christian Science services and must effectively condition any Scientist's religious consciousness.

Mary Baker Eddy went to extremes in denying the reality of evil and the material world, but we find her balanced view of a Father-Mother God right and valuable. There is a bizarre trend today in the direction of a concept of God as entirely feminine. Jokes about this were current even during the Woman Suffrage movement fifty years ago, and a cartoon on "God Made Woman in Her Image," caricaturing Michaelangelo, was recently used by some women's lib members as a Christmas card. The absurdity of such ad-hoc revised symbolism is evident when we reflect that male and female are biologically interdependent, so that neither would make sense without the other. And if we take a close second look at our tradition, both biblical and post-biblical, we will find both. Masculine symbols are dominant and male theologians have frozen them into patterns of abstraction; but the feminine images are also there, awaiting that fuller appreciation for which we were not ready till now. What is needed is to redress the balance by restoring the feminine to its proper importance in the over-all pattern.

There is no need to propose a new twentieth-century charter for this venture. There is one already available, and Mary Baker Eddy did not miss it, in Genesis 1:27.

> God created man in his own image, in the image of God
> created he him, male and female created he them.

The rest of the creation chapter is written in stately prose. This verse is poetic in form, perhaps quoted from a still older tradition. Hebrew poetry follows rules of parallelism, as illustrated in the Psalms. The thought of the first line is repeated in slightly different words in the second, and the third if there is one, or if a further thought is added it is still something implicit in the first statement. "Male and female" is not a change of subject; if he created man male and female, it was because bisexuality somehow belongs to his own image.

This fact was recognized by early rabbinic commentators, one of whom concluded that God made Adam androgynous, later separating him into Adam and Eve. A parallel myth of man's original androgyneity appears in Plato's *Symposium,* where it symbolizes a lost state of wholeness. In our own time it is recognized that while individuals belong to one sex or the other, we are all androgynous in the sense of having both male and female hormones, as well as potential character traits traditionally associated with both sexes.

Some decades ago a Roman Catholic missionary, Joseph Winthuis, returned to Europe from the South Pacific and caused a stir by his diagnosis of the indifferent success of Christian missions over the years, with the social conflicts and dislocations produced by them. The complementarity of the two sexes, he said, dominates the whole world view of these peoples. That a solitary male God without a consort, necessarily incomplete, should claim to be a father who begot a son, strikes the primitive as nonsense; and it seems equally bizarre to the mentality of sophisticated Far-Eastern cultures. Psychotherapists find that even in the West, many suffer neurotic distortions from the lack of an adequate concept or symbol of the feminine aspect of divinity; the over-emphasis on masculine values blocks their capacity for relationship and their road to wholeness.

Perhaps we should say at this point that the Quakers were historically not troubled by the imbalance of sexual symbolism applied to God, because Friends more than most were in a position really to know that God was spirit. If they called him "he," they knew they did not mean that he was a patriarchal despot, an implacable judge, or a leader in crusades against the infidel. To those still nourished chiefly by the Friendly tradition, the whole question may seem irrelevant.

It is only to those of us conditioned by more problematic forms of Christianity, or to those who approach the whole Judeo-Christian phenomenon from outside, that the question becomes important. In the Friends' lifestyle a rare degree of equality between men and women was insured by their realistic acknowledgment of "that of God" in every human being. The Inward Light, a reality present to their individual and collective experience, was no more masculine than it was feminine. Men and women were equally open to its leadings, and the balanced quality of their family life developed accordingly. The problem under discussion would not spontaneously emerge among Friends, except as they are challenged today by unprecedented winds of change.

The Contrasexual Balance

Archeology yields abundant evidence that from Paleo-lithic times, from the Mediterranean lands to the Indus Valley, the ultimate source of life was felt to be maternal. Religion centered in the mysteries of birth, fecundity, and nutrition. The earliest symbols are crude female figurines suggesting pregnancy, no doubt used as fertility charms or amulets to assist childbirth. Burial customs in some places also indicate a belief that the dead would be reborn from the earth. To the primitive mind, woman was the producer of life; the role of the male partner was not immediately apparent.

In the Neolithic period the maternal principle was personified as either a single Great Mother or several goddesses with specialized roles. The Snake-goddess of Minoan Crete was depicted as Earth-mother, Mountain-mo-ther, Mistress of Trees, Lady of Wild Beasts, and Goddess of the Hunt. With the rise of agriculture and cattle-raising in Mesopotamia and Egypt, goddesses such as Ishtar and Isis evolved. The essential role of the male spouse was now recognized, but in Western Asia the god was usually subordinate to the Queen of Heaven, Mother of gods and men, as her servant or son. She was the effective agent in the rebirth of vegetation and the increase of animals or humans; she was the cow-goddess who nurtured kings with her milk; she was also the goddess of the dead, or else her sister. Earth goddesses were usually also moon goddess-es. There were triune goddesses representing the stages of feminine life as the maiden, the mother, and the aging hag-witch, corresponding to the crescent, full, and waning phases of the moon. The Greek Hecate was also defined in triune terms, as queen of heaven, earth, and hades.

In the cosmopolitan Greco-Roman period the Goddess presided over the issues of life and death in a new way. There was widespread syncretism between the various local versions; a long, poetic passage in Apuleius celebrates Isis as including them all. By this time the communal and earthly fertility aspects had fallen into the background. The so-called mystery religions offered symbolic roads to an individual, spiritual type of salvation, release from the flesh and rebirth into immortality. This transmutation took place in the mysteries of Demeter at Eleusis and in Isiac cults throughout the empire. The image of Isis especially was to influence the early-medieval image of Mary; but this is getting ahead of our story.

Moses and the Hebrew prophets encountered matriarchal religion at a time antedating these other-worldly refinements. The indigenous mother-cult of Syria-Palestine was expressed in comparatively crude fertility rites, incompatible with the growing moral sensitivity represented by the prophets. Over several centuries they carried on a heroic struggle to depose Baal and Astarte in all forms, local or imported, to win Israel's exclusive loyalty to a God disentangled from procreative processes. But even as they rejected divinization of the sex principle, they acknowledged a polarity of gender or 'contrasexuality' on the transcendental level in other ways.

The creation story in the first chapter of Genesis seems to be designed in deliberate contrast to the creation myths of Babylon. The battle led by the Sun-God, Marduk, against Mother Tiamat (the salt seas, the watery chaos, the primeval dragon), after which he constructs a universe out of her dead body--also the myths of Ishtar, the morally dubious Goddess who produces all life from her own substance--are swept off the board. Instead, the one God serenely creates a cosmos by his word alone, unchallenged and unresisted. He makes it out of a water chaos called tehom (tiamat, the deep), but this is no goddess. Neither is the resultant earth. Sexuality and fertility are not his attributes but his inventions. Nature is separated off from God and made available for man's use according to divine command, even for man's 'dominion.'

Some Old Testament scholars see this story as a radical secularization of the earth; reduced to a mere creature, it is deprived of the holiness that earlier cultures revered. Critics of the Judeo-Christian tradition are right that it has been read that way, and opened a door not only to scientific investigation but to irresponsible exploitation of earth's resources. The devil can always quote scripture for his purpose. Nevertheless, the Bible contains other passages that instill reverence and a sense of stewardship, and a sensitive reading of the Genesis chapter itself suggests that earth is holy, though in a way that was then entirely new.

The earth of Genesis is a living creature, still mysteriously maternal, cooperating with the Father-God. This actual earth, including (or with her twin sister) the sea, is depicted as a vividly alive mother-being who, unlike mythical goddesses, exists in fact. She brings forth what God commands, forms of life which, like their mother, continue to bring forth. Sometimes God commands, while earth and sea do it; at other times God's creation by word and earth's bringing forth seem to constitute a joint creative act. The discarding of polytheism actually made it possible for man to contemplate more directly the wonder of that continuing miracle, the animate world of nature. According to Genesis this complex structure of creativity, itself a creature, comes initially innocent from the hands of God. The earth, like Mary in the fullness of time, lets it be unto her according to his word, in a gracious, yielding, womanly obedience, an obedience that shares in the primal creative joy.

Later, however, earth becomes involved in the tragedy of Adam and Eve. According to Genesis 3:17ff her original generosity is frustrated and blighted on their account--by God; it did not occur to the writer that it might in the long run be done by man. Eve, the human 'mother of all living,' becomes the next feminine entity with whom God has to deal, this time not obedient but lured into estrangement. The story of our first parents' disobedience is a myth so subtle and rich in ambiguous overtones that even in these times of unbelief new literary treatments of it appear year by year. It may be, and should be, read experimentally in other terms than the traditional. Isn't a certain amount of disobedience necessary to a child's growth? Is the serpent really the devil, or something less sinister? Is God really so naive as to tell them not to put beans up their noses and then be surprised when they do it? or to feel himself threatened by their curiosity and lèse-majesté? Or does he deliberately provoke the disobedience, in complicity with the serpent, because he wants to get the tortuous pilgrimage of human history under way, because whatever it costs, it will be worth it?

In any case, from the wandering sons of Eve he chooses himself a people. He devotes special attention to their deliverance from slavery; their rigorous education through Moses, the prophets, and attendant circumstances; their political development and overthrow; their spiritual refinement in the crucible of exile. The prophets speak of Israel as a son of Yahweh, but at more length as his unfaithful bride. The marital relation between sky-god and earth-goddess, so basic to the fertility cult, is replaced by the marital relation between an intensely ethical God and the community he loves. But the contrasexual balance gives way to precarious unbalance, because Israel is an adulteress. "She did not know that it was I who gave her the grain, the wine, and the oil," he mourns in Hosea 2:8, so she perennially falls back on the earlier-known, less demanding nature gods who care very little about personal morality or social justice. Furthermore, the two Hebrew kingdoms were so situated that they were driven to make repeated defensive alliances with one major power against another, which involved the acceptance of their gods. This too was denounced by the prophets as adultery. Yet even as Israel suffers the whole brunt of Yahweh's wrath, and her existence as a free nation is ended, the prophets promise her survival in the Babylonian exile, reborn to a new and permanent faithfulness.

The post-exilic prophecies of the so-called Second Isaiah and his 'school' (Isa. 40-66) were written after a few Jews were back in Judah but many were widely dispersed. This man sees more clearly than any earlier prophet and lyrically proclaims not only that Israel must have no other gods besides this one, but that only their God exists. (The Genesis creation story was written in the same century, ca. 500 B.C.) This God of incomparable power, beauty, and grace, the sole lord of a marvelous cosmos and of human history, is out to redeem not only Israel but all the world through Israel. The prophet speaks of Israel as the (masculine) servant, whose task it is to teach the world about God, but also speaks of Mother Jerusalem or Zion. Her warfare is ended and her sin pardoned (40:2); the lord has turned from his wrath and reaffirms an everlasting love for the 'wife of his youth' (54:6-8).

Chapter 62 rings the changes on the theme of triumphant marriage in several different aspects; nature, man, and God are caught up in the great reconciliation. The promised land is again fertilized and made fruitful; the returned sons of the land marry her in the spring ploughing (a widespread ancient idea) and God rejoices over his ransomed people as his bride. In 66:7ff Jerusalem becomes explicitly and rhapsodically a mother; all in a moment, before she has any time for labor pains, she brings forth a new nation which will include "all who love her."

But in the midst of her triumph, suddenly it is God who plays the mother role. Earlier (in 42:14) he had declared, "Now I will cry out like a woman in travail"--will gasp, pant, and lash about, destroying any mountains, vegetation or rivers that might hinder the delivery of his people into their own land; it is he that brings them to rebirth. Again in 49:14f he replied to Zion's complaint: "Can a woman forget her sucking child, that she should have no compassion on the son of her womb?" Even these may forget, but he won't. In 66:12ff, the mother role shifts from Jerusalem to God and back again. "For thus says the Lord . . . As one whom his mother comforts, so I will comfort you; you shall be comforted in Jerusalem."

Since the danger of Israel's relapse into paganism is now outgrown, it becomes possible for a prophet to find mother-love even in the austere God beside whom there is no other. But here it is not so much an experience as a hope, a hope which has to be deferred to some future consummation of history. Until then, must all the symbols of suprapersonal motherhood--discarded goddesses, a blighted earth, an unjust society, a faithless motherland, a dubious 'church'--be creaturely, imperfect, even drastically negative? Not so. In the Wisdom literature we find a different answer.

Sophia, the Friend of Man

The Old Testament wisdom literature consists primarily of the Book of Proverbs and two Apocryphal works, Sirach and The Wisdom of Solomon. Wisdom books are as a rule ascribed to Solomon, traditionally the first sage, but usually they are collections from many sources over many centuries. As we have seen, the prophetic books were forged on the anvil of historical crises. The teaching of the sages matured in less troubled times and took a more serene view of God and the world, especially of the individual's ability to live the good life and find himself suitably rewarded by his society and his God for so doing. Job and Ecclesiastes, however, are also wisdom literature, representing protests against the complacent optimism of the more orthodox teachers.

The word 'wisdom' in Proverbs is used with various shades of meaning, referring to proverbial folk wisdom, types of skill or cunning, prudent maxims, moral maxims, kingly capacity for wise rule, or the over-all quality of insight or understanding. When this last is personified, we might suppose it is done only for poetic effect. But one passage, in which Wisdom speaks in the first person, carries theological implications.

> The Lord created me at the beginning of his work,
>   the first of his acts of old . . .
> Before the mountains had been shaped,
>   before the hills, I was brought forth . . .
> When he established the heavens, I was there,
>   when he drew out a circle on the face of the deep
> When he marked out the foundations of the earth,
>   then I was beside him, like a master workman;
> and I was daily his delight,
>   playing before him always,
> rejoicing in his inhabited world
>   and delighting in the sons of men.
>
> Prov. 8:22-31

According to this, wisdom is a created entity, first of God's creatures, who assisted in the rest of creation. If the later verses suggest that she reflects, however 'spiritually,' the earlier image of a goddess-consort, we find that some Old Testament scholars go to great lengths to explain this away. Ancient scholars as well as modern seem to have been uneasy; there are also Hebrew versions which do not have "I was daily his delight"; throughout the last four lines it is wisdom who is delighted, her delight being in the world that has been created. Still, if she was like a master workman, she supplied plans for the cosmic order as an architect would advise a king; and being an adult, her play (given the connotations of the Hebrew verb elsewhere) would be the loveplay from which the universe was born. But the word for "master workman" has the same consonants as a word for "little child," and some ancient translations take it that way. In that case she would be a daughter, God's wisdom in its exuberant beginnings, laughing and playing before him like a child.

Even if the original did carry a fleeting suggestion of marital joys, nothing more is said about it. The principal point throughout the book is Wisdom's affectionate concern for mankind. She is a teacher and counselor, the tireless instructor who teaches man how to live. "She is a tree of life to those who lay hold of her" (3:17), a tree of life and true knowledge in one. She stands in contrast to the "foolish woman," the personification of apostasy, which might involve either literal or symbolic harlotry. In contrast to the furtive revels to which Madam Folly entices the unwary, Wisdom offers a sumptuous feast and invites all passers-by. "The fear of the Lord is the beginning of wisdom" (9:10), fear principally in the sense of reverent awe. Sober as her precepts may sound, her fruits are riches, honor, and long life; in place of false, death-dealing pleasures she offers spiritual nourishment and joy.

The book of Sirach (or Ecclesiasticus) was written in Greek around 180 B.C. It reflects a type of Judaism staunchly devoted to the Law but open to cosmopolitan influences. In Greek, Wisdom becomes Sophia. She is said to be inscrutable, known only to God, yet he has "poured her out upon all his works" and "rained down knowledge and discerning comprehension" on individuals. Again she is a tree, her branches are long life, and her fruit satisfies. To fear the lord is not only her beginning but her full measure and crown. She stands in the heavenly assembly and offers an extended self-portrait:

> I came forth from the mouth of the Most High,
>   and covered the earth like a mist . . .
> Alone I have made the circuit of the vault of heaven
>   and have walked in the depth of the abyss
> From eternity, in the beginning, he created me,
>   and for eternity I shall not cease to exist.
>   Sir. 24:3-9

At first enthroned in heaven, she involved herself with man.

> In the waves of the sea, in the whole earth,
> and in every people and nation I have gotten a possession.
>   Sir. 24:6

The evidence for this is that other peoples also have wisdom literature. But the lord told her to settle in Israel, and her full expression there   turned out to be the Law, the Torah given through Moses: "All this is the book of the covenant of the Most High God" (24:23). (The Torah in turn was personified by later writers as God's feminine consultant at the creation.)

The Wisdom of Solomon is a brief work of the first century B.C., from the cosmopolitan Jewish community in Alexandria; Greek influence pervades the book. It describes Wisdom as a spiritual entity highly exalted, yet living intimately with man. Solomon, that archetypal sage, is said to have taken her as his bride--though if he did, we can only comment that he was not particularly faithful to her. Later chapters describe how she protected Adam, Noah, and Abraham, how she led the children of Israel out of Egypt and educated them. But her universality is also emphasized.

> For she is a breath of the power of God, and a
>   pure emanation of the glory of the Almighty . . .
> For she is a reflection of eternal light,
>   a spotless mirror of the working of God,
>   and an image of his goodness.
> Though she is but one, she can do all things,
>   and while remaining in herself, she renews all things;
> In every generation she passes into holy souls
>   and makes them friends of God, and prophets
> For she is more beautiful than the sun,
>   and excels every constellation of the stars
> She reaches mightily from one end of the earth to the
>   other and she orders all things well.
>
> Wis. 7:25-8:1

Here she is seen unambiguously as more than a "created" being. She is his wisdom, after all, as truly an attribute of God himself as the Word (Logos) or the Holy Spirit; in fact she is identified with both. Greek Logos and Hebrew Wisdom were closely parallel concepts in all but gender.

In the New Testament, though Jesus once implies that he and John the Baptist are children of Wisdom (Luke 7:35), she is otherwise equated with the Logos, which is Christ (1 Cor. 1:24, Col. 1:5ff), and loses her feminine identity. But Eastern Orthodoxy names its mother church in Constantinople *Hagia Sophia,* Holy Wisdom, and a few Eastern theologians have tried to reinstate her as a principle distinct from Christ. There have also been pioneers of the inward ways who took Sophia seriously, notably Boehme and Soloviev.

Jacob Boehme (1575-1624), the shoemaker of Gorlitz, was both mystic and philosopher, as Howard Brinton showed in his comprehensive study, *The Mystic Will.* ('Philosophy' literally means "love of Sophia.") Boehme, while a devout Lutheran, had a profound sense of mysteries in the world of nature which Lutheranism did not account for, and found friends who introduced him to various underground currents of thought. In his reconstruction of the inner evolution of God-universe-man, the heavenly Virgin Sophia plays many different roles. At first an empty mirror of the formless Abyss, she becomes in turn the Mother of God, the Divine Imagination, the model of the universe (like Plato's world of forms), Eternal Nature in its actualization, man's heavenly genius, bride of the soul, and mother of the reborn.

Boehme also speaks of Sophia as an aspect of the divine which he himself has experienced.

> The Virgin has given me her promise not to leave me in my need . . . As I lay upon the mountain at midnight and all the trees fell over me, and the storm beat upon me, and Antichrist opened wide his jaws to devour me, she came and comforted me and wedded herself to me.
>
> I am thy bride in the light [she tells him] and thy longing after my power is my drawing to myself. I sit on my throne, but thou knowest me not. I am in thee, but thy body is not in me . . . I am the light of the mind.

Sophia was the image of God in which Adam was created, which left him at the fall. But she knocks inwardly at the door of man's soul, or "hovers outwardly before him" in the beautiful or awe-inspiring aspects of the natural world, awaiting his acceptance of her as both bride and mother. "As God bears his son the light, as Mary bore Jesus, the virgin must bear the new man. Out of the same virginity from which Christ was born must we all be born."[3]

When American Shaker theologians worked out the implications of their experience of Ann Lee's ministry, they rejected the trinity and asserted a duality, revealed through a dual revelation in human form. "The true order and origin of our existence is from an Eternal Parentage." "As Christ through Jesus manifested God as Father and Power, so Ann Lee by the second appearance of Christ through her has manifested God as the Eternal Mother and Wisdom."[4] They felt that this unlettered blacksmith's daughter's dealings with human problems were such as "only Divine Wisdom could inspire."

Vladimir Soloviev (1853-1900) was perhaps Russia's most outstanding philosopher. Long before he read Boehme he must have known about the icon of Sophia in Novgorod Cathedral, how Russians built temples to her in the Middle Ages and "worshipped this mysterious being as the Athenians once worshipped the Unknown God." His metaphysics as well as his practical religious endeavors were rooted in three visions of Sophia, his "eternal Friend." The first occurred in Moscow on Ascension Day when he was a boy of nine. At twenty-three, as a student in London, she appeared to him in the reading room of the British Museum. He was elated, but grieved that he saw her so dimly; so she directed him to go to Egypt. "He met her this time alone in the desert at dawn, when the transfigured and reintegrated Universe appeared before him in its original splendor and glory"[5]-a vision of "all that was, and is, and ever shall be," with earth's oceans, woods, and mountains visible below him as if seen from the stratosphere, all comprised in one supernal image of feminine beauty.

Thereafter Soloviev devoted his life to the restoration of this fallen world to the transcendent state of unity that God intended. He was the first ecumenist of the nineteenth century, throwing himself into the cause of the reunion of Christendom--principally Eastern Orthodoxy and Roman Catholicism, but intending later to draw in Protestants and Jews. In his youth he envisaged an unbroken progress toward "deification of the world," but his later years were shadowed by premonitions of twentieth-century disasters. He felt, however, that both the dogma of the Immaculate Conception and Comte's "religion of humanity" pointed to a rediscovery of Sophia.

The Holy Spirit as Mother

In the wisdom of Solomon we read: "For wisdom is

a kindly spirit" (RSV), or in an earlier translation, "a spirit that loveth man." A few lines further on, "the Spirit of the Lord has filled the world," and is "that which holds all things together," (Wis. 1:6,7). Wisdom is not only *a* spirit but *the* spirit, the "breath of the power of God," who "enters holy souls and makes them friends of God and prophets" (Wis.7:25ff).

The Spirit of God appears in the earlier Old Testament books in various connections--anything from the fury that empowered Samson to kill a thousand men with the jawbone of an ass (Judg. 15:14f) and the frenzy that fell upon Saul as he joined a company of primitive prophets (1 Sam. 10:10), to the lucid inspiration that moved the great literary prophets. But it is not noticeably feminine (through grammatically it is), nor is it that which holds all things together. Till now, the feminine principle that unifies the world has been Wisdom. Only this late Apocryphal work identifies the Spirit with Sophia, though one earlier passage may have been taken as a hint.

In the Genesis creation story (written 500 B.C.), in the beginning when darkenss was over the deep, "the Spirit of God was moving over the face of the waters" (Gen. 1:2). This has been a subject of heated controversy among committees of translators in conclave. The primitive meaning of *ruach* is breath, and the primitive idea of the breath of God is a powerful wind. The fully developed meaning is that of the Spirit as found in late prophets and psalms, the Wisdom of Solomon, and the New Testament. The New English Bible opts for a "mighty wind" that blew across the waters, accomplishing nothing in particular but heightening the description of chaos. The Revised Standard Version and the Jerusalem Bible keep the traditional rendering, "Spirit of God." This is justifiable whatever the original writer meant, since it was understood throughout our era as meaning that Spirit which was involved in the creation and could be taken poetically as feminine.

Since the Hebrew verb is a general word for all kinds of motion, the RSV cautiously translates it "was moving." But it is used elsewhere of birds that hover or flutter over their young; the Jerusalem Bible has "hovering." A related Syriac verb can mean "brood." The suggestion is that of a mother bird brooding on the mythical cosmic egg, a chaos which hatches out a cosmos. If God as Father created by a word of command, God as Spirit mothers the world into being. The suggestion is stronger if the Spirit is associated with a dove, though this may not have occurred till New Testament times.

In the New Testament the Spirit descends upon Jesus at his baptism in the form of a dove. Centuries before, doves had been the birds of the Mother-Goddess, expressing her gentle, pacific, loving aspects; there is no evidence for direct derivation of the idea, but the coincidence may be noted. The other major manifestation is at Pentecost, in the sound of a mighty wind and tongues of fire that rested on the apostles. To be "filled with the Spirit" was no uncommon state thereafter. Speaking in tongues at Pentecost is said to have meant utterances in languages unknown to the speaker but known to listeners present; later in some of Paul's churches it flourished in the form of ecstatic utterance in no known language. Other manifestations were prophecy and miracles of heaing.

In all this the concept of the spirit is transmuted by the alchemy of a unique series of historic experiences from a broad cosmic principle to a specific dynamic associated with Christ and his resurrection. In our own day C.G. Jung has identified the Holy Spirit with Sophia, and we have seen that he has scriptural warrant for doing so; but to those who have concentrated on the New Testament it must seem a bit strange. We may regard the New Testament phenomena as indicating a specific phase or expression of wisdom/spirit which can and does recur (as in the present Pentecostal movement), but is not applicable to all times and places. The fruits of the Spirit listed by Paul in Gal. 5:22, however, are consonant with universal wisdom: "love, joy, peace, patience, kindness, goodness, faithfulness, gentleness, self-control."

According to John 14-16, Christ promised to send his disciples another comforter, or more accurately "counselor," the Spirit of Truth, to instruct and lead them. This Spirit is surely close to wisdom, but is masculine. In the New Testament the Spirit is masculine where it is personal at all (in Greek it is neuter). What really clinched it in the creeds was that *spiritus* in Latin is masculine. Only in fringe sects whose writings are mostly lost was the Spirit still thought of as feminine. A curious saying from a lost "Gospel according to the Hebrews" is quoted by the Church

Fathers, in which Jesus declares that his mother, the Holy Spirit, took him by the hair and carried him to Mount Tabor.

In any case the all-masculine Trinity became dogma. Even so, the thought of a feminine Holy Spirit recurs spontaneously in circles that probably never heard of it as an ancient minority report. Genevieve Parkhurst, a minister's wife, some years ago was healed of cancer through a vision of Christ. Later, with Glenn Clark's help, she was led into a healing ministry. In her first book she speaks of an insight that came to her "in the silence." "At last I realized that the Holy Spirit is the Mother Heart of the Holy Trinity." We all need a mother's teaching skills; and we need someone "on whose breast our tears may fall unashamed."

> For every yearning God has made provision for its satisfaction. There must be a Divine Mother . . . The Catholic Church, wise to recognize this need, has made provision for such approach through Mary . . . But every Christian should have the mother love of the Holy Comforter.[6]

Mary as Mediator

The most obvious and effective way in which Christendom reinstated the Divine Mother was in the veneration of the Virgin Mary and doctrinal developments around her, both in Eastern and Roman Catholicism. Protestants generally reject all this because the scriptural basis is so slender. The Lucan narrative depicts Mary as accepting the birth miracle in a spirit of obedience and high devotion, but all four Gospels agree that her understanding of her son's nature and ministry was limited (Luke 2:48ff, Mark 3:21, 31ff, John 2:1-12), that (at least on the face of it) she bore other children to Joseph, and became fully a follower of her son only after his resurrection. The exaltation of Mary did not get under way immediately; she is mentioned in the second-century Apostles' Creed simply as evidence that her son was not a merely mythical savior-god like those of the mystery religions, but a man in history born of a human mother.

The earliest Christian feminine symbol was not Mary but the Church--the heavenly Mother Jerusalem (Gal. 4:26f), the bride of Christ (Eph. 5:32), the sun-clothed woman in travail (Rev. 12:1-6). Besides being the new Israel, the Church was the second Eve, mother of all living, mediating spiritual life from Christ, the second Adam; or the virgin mother of those reborn through baptism, nourishing them with the milk of the Logos. But these attributes of Mother Church were also discernible in Mary. She too was the second Eve, who by her obedience undid the disobedience of the first Eve, bearing the Seed that would overcome the serpent as predicted in Gen. 3:15.

The belief in her perpetual virginity, her bodily Assumption into heaven, and her exaltation as Mother of God all began in popular piety before the fifth century, but the title, "Mother of God," was officially affirmed as orthodox dogma only after long controversy, at the Council of Ephesus in 431. From then on, she was increasingly venerated in her own right; like the ancient goddesses she was now Queen of Heaven. The Eastern Church came to associate her with Sophia, whose femininity and primary importance had been maintained by the Gnostics as also by worshippers of Isis (who called her Sophia) all the time the Apostles and early Church Fathers were ignoring her. Even the Roman Church, though to less degree, eventually accepted the association with Sophia sufficiently to use the wisdom readings from Proverbs 8 and Sirach 24 on the feasts of the Immaculate Conception and the Assumption respectively. (Both are in the first person; to most of the faithful, presumably the speaker is Mary!)

Mary's endowment with divine wisdom was less important to Christendom at large, however, than the emotional values involved. In the early centuries of monastic fervor, Mary became the object of the sublimated devotion of ascetics and celibate priests, as she still is. And as church became unequally yoked with empire, enforcing mass conversions of whole peoples, its hierarchy rigidly authoritarian, its theologians defining the trinity in terms more and more abstract, they effectively removed Christ from the sphere of human feeling. Whatever understanding, compassion, maternal tenderness, even earthly humor, the common folk once found in Jesus of Nazareth, they now had to find in Mary. Only she was close enough to their hearts to mediate between them and a remote, relentless deity.

By the thirteenth century in Europe, the devout

humility of the young Jewish mother was completely lost in the majesty of the Queen, who was the true determiner of human destinies since her power to intercede with the Trinity was limitless. Adored by earthly monarchs, nobles, and commoners alike, her chief monument was Chartres Cathedral, but she also dominates most other ecclesiastical art of the Middle Ages. As Henry Adams describes her unforgettably in *Mont-Saint-Michel and Chartres,* she had all the feminine charm, esthetic tastes, and arbitrariness of the great queens of France, but infinitely more power, and a warm personal interest in her humblest folowers. According to the legends she would stop at nothing to secure a place in heaven for her devotees, regardless of their deserts otherwise.

It was around that time that the doctrine of Immaculate Conception was introduced: the tenet that even Mary was conceived in the womb of her mother, Anne, not virginally to be sure, but miraculously freed from the otherwise universal taint of original sin by the retroactive grace of her son. By the nineteenth century it had won general consent among Roman theologians and was announced as a dogma by Pope Pius IX in 1854. The other tenet that Mary was taken up bodily into heaven, defined by Pius XII in 1950 as the dogma of the Assumption, went all the way back to New Testament Apocryphal legends and had long been accepted also in Eastern Christendom. Neither was biblical, of course, but both were admissible under the principle of evolution of dogma. Doctrines merely implicit in scripture and the earliest tradition, it is believed, may be gradually made explicit as the Spirit leads the church into all truth.

Catholic scholars and the hierarchy are in tension with popular piety at some points, though not all. In the last 150 years there have been a remarkable number of "apparitions" of Mary (Paris, La Salette, Pompeii, Lourdes, Fatima), leading to forms of devotion that Rome after initial resistance and careful investigation found it wise to approve. Since most of them were experienced by children or simple folk in uneducated rural communities, the reported words of Mary were colored by the limitations of the culture involved, and strengthened the impression among non-Catholics that Mary is worshipped superstitiously as a goddess. But the fact is that highly educated Catholics too have had profound experiences of communion with Mary, and responsible theologians are clear on the point that she is not and never was a goddess--though historically and psychologically she had to fill the place of the lost goddess in the hearts of many Christians. Theologians and common folk agree that she plays a needed mediatorial role between alienated souls and the God they find so difficult to approach directly. The next dogmatic definition quite possibly will call her "mediatrix," or else "co-redemptrix," since it is believed that she actively shared her son's redemptive suffering on the cross. But rather than a goddess, she is a divinized human.

The Eastern Churches have been more willing than the Roman or Protestant to think in terms of apotheosis: "God became man that man might become divine." But support for it can be found in scripture, and Mary may be regarded as the first human being in whom this miracle is wrought. There have been Christians who would say that Jesus was the first to whom it happened; Paul speaks of him as the "firstfruits" of a new humanity (1 Cor. 15:23). But on the basis that he was essentially God incarnate who came down from heaven, Mary was the first divinized human, the first who totally received him in faith and was transformed by him. She thus became a mediator between the whole Trinity and mankind, Mother of all Christians, and archetype of the church. Her life story of feminine receptiveness to God's gift of himself, her gracious obedience, her suffering love even to the death of the cross, and her humanly incredible triumph, constitutes a paradigm of the way of transformation which any faithful individual is ultimately called to follow. Mary can lead us to God precisely because she is not God; however closely she may reflect and approach the mystery of divinity in its feminine aspects, she is still on our side of the fence.

The Shekinah as Presence in Exile

Still another version of the feminine mediating principle between God and man developed in post-biblical Judaism. The abstract noun *sh'kinah,* literally "indwelling," does not appear in the Bible but the related verb does. Mishkan (dwelling) was one name for Moses' desert tabernacle, the tent of meeting. God's presence was manifested in quasi-physical terms in the burning bush, more spectacularly in the cloud of glory first seen on Mount Sinai, then in the tabernacle and later the temple. In the first few centuries A.D., Aramaic versions of the Old Testament introduce the word "shekinah" (like heaven in the Gospel of Matthew) as a reverent circumlocution for God. In Ex.25:8 the Lord's words, "I will dwell . . ." become "I will let my Shekinah dwell among the children of Israel."

In Talmudic literature from the third century on, she is feminine in more than a grammatical sense. Theoretically she is omnipresent in the world, but more often she is physically localized. The Jerusalem temple was built to be her permanent home. When this temple was desecrated and destroyed, the Shekinah wandered to the desert or perhaps the Mount of Olives, waited vainly a few months for Israel to repent, then for awhile withdrew to heaven. After decades of exile, partial return and the building of a second temple, some say she visited it intermittently. When this too was destroyed in 70 A.D., she moved on to the principal synagogues of Babylon, where she not only appeared from time to time but made herself audible in the sound of a bell. She was believed to be a comforter of the sick, a helper of those in need, and especially tender toward repentant sinners. She would descend and rest upon any who performed good deeds, even if they were pagan idolaters, and would also "rest between" worthy husbands and wives. In this period both the Holy Spirit and the Shekinah are mentioned in the sense of a feminine entity who talks back to God, uring him to mitigate his wrath against sinners. On the other hand the Shekinah can be a disciplinarian herself, and is sent by him on punitive missions.

The full flowering of the Shekinah doctrine, or should we say the Shekinah experience, came about through the complex late-medieval phenomenon known as Kabbalism. This was partly a magical movement and partly mystical in the highest sense; it was somewhat frowned upon but never "excommunicated" by the leaders of Jewish orthodoxy. Since the Shekinah accompanied her people through centuries of exile and mourned with them (she was seen by one mystic in widow's garb by the Wailing Wall), she came to be identified with the ideal Israel, the faithful community which awaited redemption. According to an eminent Jewish scholar, the fact that the Shekinah as a feminine element in divinity "obtained recognition in spite of the obvious difficulty of reconciling it with . . . the absolute unity of God, and that no other element of Kabbalism won such a degree of popular approval, is proof that it responded to a deep-seated religious need." [7] Among all the common folk of Eastern European Jewry, she was felt to be "a wifely and motherly, passionate and compassionate female divinity . . . no mere symbol or emanation, but a great heavenly reality whose shining countenance shoved the theoretical doctrine of the oneness of God into the background." [8]

Eastern Europe seems to have been especially fertile soil for veneration of the feminine principle; but Kabbalism started in Spain, and an especially notable group of Kabbalists settled in Safed in sixteenth-century Palestine. They used to go out in procession at dusk on Friday evenings, into the hills and fields, to greet "the Sabbath Queen." "The Shekinah" is not a widely current expression among Jews of today, but a moving hymn to the Sabbath Queen is still sung on Friday evenings in synagogues around the world.

> Come, my friends, to meet the Bride,
> Let us receive the face of Sabbath . . .
> Come, O Bride, come, O Bride!

In the principal classic of Kabbalism, the Zohar, not only two (or three) but ten attributes or aspects of God are distinguished, some masculine and some feminine. Among them is wisdom, now masculine, paired with feminine intelligence. The ten Sefiroth are thought of as flowing into one another in a subtle, intricate pattern of divine evolution-within-himself, reflected in turn in the physical universe and in man. The tenth and final "face," the most highly evolved, the most expressive, the most humanized, is the Shekinah--who is the kingdom, the mystical community, the queen, the bride. But due to a primordial fall long antedating Adam, the Shekinah is in exile while the world lasts. The banishment of the Jews from Spain in 1492 renewed their acquaintance with the horrors of exile and intensified their sense that the whole of human life is conditioned by it. "Life was conceived as Existence in Exile and in self-contradiction." Redemption and reunion with God could come about only through death, repentance and rebirth. The individual soul goes through many stages of exile, requiring repeated reincarnations. "The exile of the Shekhinah is not a metaphor, it is a genuine symbol of the 'broken' state of things in the realm of divine potentialities . . . To lead the Shekhinah back to her Master, to unite her with him, is the true purpose of the Torah." The fulfilling of every commandment, the performance of all good actions, are to be done "for the sake of uniting the Holy One, praised be he, and his Shekhinah, out of fear and love."[9] In this type of mysticism the emphasis actually shifts to the healing of God through human action, rather than the other way round.

In the Hasidic movement in Poland in the eighteenth century from which Martin Buber derived spiritual nourishment, there was a special emphasis on discerning the Shekinah's hidden presence in morally confusing situations. Men of mystical insight were called upon to clarify them, to lift her "from the very dust of the road" and cause her "to re-approach her Source." Buber wrote a beautiful chronicle, apparently based on fairly copious records, about two gifted leaders in this movement, entitled in English translation *For The Sake Of Heaven*. Leaving aside its fascinating political and historical allusions, the story brings out the relevance of the Shekinah doctrine to marital love. In Judaism, celibacy has never been encouraged; holy men especially are expected to marry. Any true marriage, according to the Kabbalah, becomes a symbolic realization of the love between the king and his Shekinah; it helps to heal the wounded heart of God. This reminds us that we have not yet mentioned the Song of Solomon, that collection of frankly carnal love songs which owes its place in the canon to the fact that Judaism took it as an allegory of the love between God and Israel, while Christians took it as referring to Christ and the Church or to God and the individual soul. It would seem that only those who take the Shekinah seriously are in a position to value the songs for what they are and yet to feel that they belong in scripture.

To return to Buber's chronicle. The younger leader, known generally as "the Yehudi" (the Jew), is genuinely in love with Foegele, the wife of his youth, who bears him three children. But he leaves her for years on end to wander about Poland as a teacher, feeling he is called to do so; as the Shekinah wanders in exile, so must he. Returning to find Foegele on her deathbed, he promises to fulfill her request that he marry her sister, Schoendel. The second marriage results in two more children, but is full of tension and outbursts from Schoendel. She resents his treatment of her poor sister, his serene, maddening patience with herself, and his complete detachment from household problems brought on by his excessive generosity to strangers.

One night the Yehudi wakes and looks out of his window into complete darkness. This is suddenly dispersed by the blast of a heavenly shofar, and he sees "red udders exuding the mik-white light of origin." (The actual Milky Way is probably only the physical analogue of this mystery of the divine world.) He finds himself standing by a pool full of the white radiance. A wave of it takes on the form of a woman's body swathed in a black veil, except for the bare feet, covered with dust and bleeding wounds from long wayfaring. She tells him that it is precisely the holy men, the Hasidic rabbis, who are tormenting and excluding her by their dissensions: "each of you exiles his comrades, and so together you exile me." Her word to the Yehudi himself is: "one cannot love me and abandon the created being." She raises her veil, shows the face of his beloved Foegele, and appeals to him to help her go home.[10]

This vision and his repentance marked the beginning of a greatly enriched ministry of teaching and healing. We may assume his efforts toward reconciliation with the second wife. Just before his death, with his disciples and the five children around him, he once again asks her forgiveness, and she responds with tears.

"Comfort, Life, and Fire of Love"

Sophia, Spirit, and Shekinah may be seen as somewhat different but overlapping bands of the total spectrum of divinity as immanent in the universe and in man. The cosmic aspects are more prominent in Sophia. Spirit and Shekinah are more intimately concerned with experiences of inner life and human relatedness with which we are familiar, but with differences of emphasis. All three are closely related to what Friends call the Inward Light, although Friends have not clothed it in imagery nor thought of it as feminine.

Such experiences have not ceased in our own day. Those acquainted with the techniques of Jungian analytical psychology will know that "active imagination" is sometimes practiced, in the sense of opening oneself to waking dreams or fantasies. Dream symbols come to the surface to speak or act on their own; the conscious mind carries on dialogue with them and works out their meanings for situations in actual life. The fantasy figures are highly personal to start with, but as this road is followed further, universal symbols may break through with numinous effect and fantasy be intensified into genuine vision.

A friend of mine wrote me a letter years ago about a fantasy series of this kind. She had a sympathetic "heavenly Mother" in a gray-blue robe, who treated her as the frightened small child she inwardly was, and helped her deal with an ugly old witch who, as often in dreams, represented some unacceptable tendency in herself. Encouraged to show sympathy to the witch, she fed her with oranges; the creature turned into a cheerful old peasant woman full of folk wisdom. Later a problematic situation came up in my friend's professional life, not the sort of thing folk wisdom could cope with. In the next fantasy the peasant woman split down the back like a chrysalis, and out stepped Athena, goddess of wisdom!

Athena is the Greek equivalent of Sophia; being better known to our culture and portrayed in art, she is more available to pictorial imagination. It was a powerful experience of "august, feminine Authority and Wisdom." "Tears filled my eyes, and although she said almost nothing, her presence was calming and confidence-giving." There were later visitations, but she did not replace the tender Heavely Mother. That a Mary figure and a Sophia figure were both needed has been found true also by others, perhaps because in our culture a discrepancy is felt between wisdom and compassion, between knowledgeability and love.

A more unified dream experience is reported by a Quaker poet, Elsie Landstrom. One Halloween, she took her two small children on a trick-or-treat expedition and they met all manner of hobgoblins and ghosts. At bed-time, after singing the doxology together, the children asked, "What is a *holy* ghost?" On the spur of the moment she defined it as a soft breath or sigh from God toward us, conveying love and hope. Later that night she dreamed of walking down a road to a great cathedral, entering and seating herself on a bench near the altar, on which stood candles and a plain cross.

> Suddenly she was there, the Holy Ghost herself, looking less like a soft breath than anything I had ever seen: a lightning flash of living love, she leaped straight to the center where she lit and spun in flaming red. Tall, with red hair and red shoes, a red and blue gown, every slim inch of her outlined in flame, I knew she had just leapt straight from the heart of the sun, from God himself, to pirouette before me. Every move was pure ecstasy.[11]

In a later dream she asked directions from a woman in a car, to get herself out of a difficulty on a city street which probably stood for some dilemma in real life. The woman stepped out, and became the flaming Spirit, just long enough to let the dreamer know who she was. She then cooled down to a comforting human warmth, took her arm and guided her.

This story reminds me of a medieval hymn to the Holy Spirit which speaks of "comfort, life, and fire of love." The traditional term, "comforter," in the Latin is literally strengthener; it can suggest anything from a soft maternal bed quilt to Luther's ruggedly masculine "mighty fortress." I have heard quite a few sermons recommending that we battle against evil and forget about soft breaths and comfortable quilts; but even these can be life-savers for children and others when sorely beset. Mrs. Parkhurst's experience of the Spirit as Gentle Mother also carried this kind of comfort. Fire, however, is a more ancient and central symbol, and more dynamic. In this dream-vision the flames of Pentecost from above seem to blend with those of the burning bush on earth, associated in the Middle Ages with Mary as well as the Shekinah.

One last word. Nothing in this essay should be construed as recommending a relapse into polytheism. Despite the possible implication by one of the scholars quoted that the oneness of God is only a "theoretical doctrine," the fact that he is one in all these aspects has been and is as much a matter of vivid first-hand experience as any encounter with a specific aspect. The Inward Light's leading into unity would make no sense whatever unless God were a unity. But I believe (to an awesome degree) God graciously expresses himself in whatever aspects are necessary to enable us to apprehend him, through all our ages of cultural change. There is an element of paradox here, but no contradiction.

Erminie Huntress Lantero, Ph.D. was born in 1907 and raised in New England Congregationalism. She received a Master of Divinity from Union Theological Seminary, completed a traveling fellowship at the University of Marburg, Germany and in Jerusalem, and received her doctorate in philosophy from Radcliffe in 1933. She taught at Wellesley and Sweet Briar Colleges, and in 1938 moved to the Quaker residential study community at Pendle Hill where she taught and served as librarian. One of the founders of the Friend's Annual Conference on Religion and Psychology, she also served as the editor of *Inward Light* until 1980. From 1945-60 she was assistant editor of the quarterly, Religion in Life, and from 1961-63 was administrative assistant to the dean and president of Union Seminary in New York. Erminie was married to Peter Lantero, a Roman Catholic from Genoa, from 1947 until his death in 1963. In the late 60's she was research assistant to Dr. McCrea Cavert, General Secretary of the National Council of Chur-

ches, helping to compile a history of the American Church. Her pamphlet on Feminine Aspects of Divinity was published in 1973. Since then she explored world religions, became a Jungian astrologer, and wrote a book on the newly discovered planet, Chiron. In 1983 she retired, for reasons of heath, to a Steiner home for the elderly in Spring Valley, New York, where she recently celebrated her 80th birthday.

And whoever, either now or after I am gone, shall be a lamp unto themselves, and a refuge unto themselves, and shall take themselves to no external refuge, but holding fast to the truth as their lamp, it is they who shall reach the topmost height.
Buddha

Women and Scriptures

Justin O'Brien

If one would interview mystics and saints acclaimed by their cultures as spiritual adepts, one would find hardly an individual to vouch that spiritual growth comes easy. Yet the story of their achievements fascinate us. Their vexations, their inner trials, the opposing circumstances, their impact upon society, all those ingredients that make a biography interesting, enable us to associate with their spiritual journey. Their stories reveal variations, however, that defy an attempt at neat theological categorizations. The desire to evaluate spirituality on an abstract scale by degrees of holiness is never conducted by the saints themselves, but only by their admirers or their detractors. The saint frequently lives an unconventional life, breaking boundaries and forcing society to reconsider its role models. Hence the import of a saint often exceeds our expectations of the spiritual life.

The successful quest for spirituality shows such wide variations in the actual lifestyles of men and women that these are difficult to collate into fixed rules. While institutional religions understandably resist approving those spiritual approaches that do not fit their denominational standards, holy men and women have been known to embarrass church orthodoxy. So how does one learn from the ranks of holy people?

A dilemma recurs particularly in Western women's quest for spirituality: spiritual guidance can be hazardous to her self-esteem. She frequently has to make a choice between society's cultural-religious beliefs about her gender and her own personal feelings about herself. This vexation surfaces acutely in the awareness of women who attempt to control their spiritual destiny.

A principal source of irritation for women has been those historical fonts of spiritual waters, the scriptures of the world. The traditional keepers of these scriptures are men who also claim the final authority for interpretation. Into this established tradition have come new dissenting voices. These voices--it need not be said, mostly feminine-- are bringing fresh reflections upon the interpretive role that gender asserts in the composition of scripture and its social context.

For most male believers, a major basis for religious security arises from the conviction that spirituality, like most everything in the universe, is truly a man's world. For centuries the male spiritual elite--theologians, pundits, priests, rabbis, shamans, mullahs, lamas, and roshis--used their scriptures to justify their privileged positions in society. The Torah and the Gospels, as well as the Qu'ran, are considered by their followers to be divinely inspired words, but words, one should keep in mind, composed from and within the context of a patriarchal culture, and thus unavoidably reflective of those values. In the ambience of patriarchy--a classical worldview that embraces social, economic, political, and religious values stressing male privilege and domination--it happens that women, from its point of view, are subjugated and oppressed. Women believers, on the other hand, have actually achieved religious security from obedience to these conditions. Security does not necessarily promote growth. While men recognize that women's lives demonstrate unique aspects in this cultural context, these differences are given only secondary consideration in spirituality.

Let us take a look at one of these principal scriptures. The Bible is not a series of scientific abstracts, but just the opposite. It narrates stories of Semitic peoples in their searching and struggle for the meaning of life, covering a period of approximately 1,400 years. Their quest has been characterized by theologians as salvation-history, wherein oppressed and sinful people respond in various ways when offered liberation by a divine benefactor. The heroes of these stories have names like Abraham, Noah, Moses, David, Solomon, Sampson, Jeremiah, Isaias, Daniel, John the Baptist, Jesus, Peter, Paul, Stephen, to name a few. Heroines, in comparison, hardly exist. Since the spread of the Bible into the world, it has been the customary interpretation of believers to accept the patriarchal worldview it depicts as the cultural standard, not only in Semitic societies, but throughout the Western hemisphere.

Over the centuries a great deal of social modification has ensued. The description of a Jewish or Christian wedding in the twentieth century, for example, is not the same in every detail as in the times of Moses or Paul. Yet the religious and cultural patterns of modern societies still retain the patriarchal perspective. Women's social status and spiritual opportunities are primarily devised and approved by men. Spiritual authority and the abundance of spiritual benefices have devolved historically since the Greeks upon males as the primary, if not exclusive, agents of achievements and transmission. Even the God of the Bible has been traditionally imaged as male. Would it seem, women inquire, a blasphemy to imagine the divine as transcending gender? Would God be impugned by inclusive male and female characteristics? Is salvation permitted only if one accepts allegiance to God in the male role? A further question may be asked regarding the Bible as a whole. Just as the prophets in the Hebrew scriptures reinterpreted their own traditions, dismissing and rejecting as well as emphasizing and enhancing inherited values, so has the time come in our period of history to place the patriarchal standard into problematic circumstances? As the standard of social intercourse it may have worn out its welcome and, thanks to feminine criticism, we are realizing its limitations. A new quandary then emerges for those whose sole roots for spiritual values reside in the Bible. If one relies upon the Bible for every clue to spirituality, then any questioning of biblical structures sounds subversive.

For many women the Bible is the most authoritative source for their spiritual life. As we have seen, the composition and redaction of the Bible has been the responsibility of those living within a patriarchal social context. Down through the ages this fundamental outlook has been the inspiration that male believers have recounted to indicate the proper place of women in society and spirituality. For the most part, women have accepted this arrangement.

Yet what are women to do when frustrated by the conflict between their religious beliefs about their gender and their own self-discovery? Some, professionally and personally, assert questions that jeopardize their religious and social inheritance. They criticize specific interpretations of biblical texts that assume, and thus support, the male context of spirituality on social and theological grounds.

Some discover how confining and unfair this tradition appears, and later come upon other scriptures, such as the Upanishads, that exalt the feminine person.

Theological speculation and religious ritual have been derived from those texts of scripture that would indicate that women should retain a submissive role. Overlooked and forgotten texts that reveal women in less restrictive light have not been a major concern of theologians until recently. It has been the common practice to generalize many texts and give them an anthropological import. For example, Paul's letter to the Corinthians speaks about the proper decorum and manners of women in a religious assembly:

> But every woman who prays or prophesys with her head uncovered dishonors her head; for that is even all one as if she were shaven. For if the woman be not covered, let her also be shorn; but if it be a shame for a woman to be shaven, let her be covered.   I Cor. 11:5-6

The traditional interpretation of this text is that women must cover their heads since this decree arises either from an exigency of woman's nature or by divine ordination, and because Paul spoke about Corinthian women of the first century, his regulation must be valid today. The expansion of Paul's remark to a local community into a universal proclamation about women's headdress makes as much sense as insisting that Paul had vested interests in a haberdashery. Other problems arise: is Paul's dictum obeyed better by the colossal extravaganzas of Victorian women or by the postage-size doilies pinned on the heads of the women of the Assembly of God? There is neither textual nor logical connection between Paul's utterance and its un-conditional application to women everywhere and for all time. What are exegetes and theologians to do in the face of texts that scholarship alone cannot seem to resolve? What about texts that offer only a negative status quo about women, as well as those that would challenge this presumption?

> I will therefore that men pray everywhere, lifting up holy hands without wrath and doubting. In like manner also, that women adorn themselves in modest apparel, with shamefacedness and sobriety; not with braided hair, or gold, or pearls, or costly array but (which becomes women

professing godliness) with good works. Let the woman
learn in silence with all subjection. But I suffer not a
woman to teach, nor to usurp authority over the man,
but to be in silence. For Adam was first formed, then
Eve. And Adam was not deceived, but the woman being
deceived was in the transgression. Notwithstanding she
shall be saved in childbearing, if they continue in faith
and charity and holiness with sobriety.   I Tim. 2:8-15
2:8-15

For as many of you as have been baptized into Christ
have put on Christ, there is neither Jew nor Greek, there
is neither bond nor free, there is neither male nor female;
for ye are all one in Christ Jesus.   Galatians 3:27-8

These quandaries illuminate a further problem: just
how practically useful is the Bible as a guide for feminine
spirituality? Depicting women in scriptures is one thing;
discerning her nature and possible spiritual options is another. Does belief in the Bible as God's revelation presume
that it instructs women to reiterate in their current spiritual life the same socio-religious values that structured
Semitic societies? Specifically, is the description of women's subordinate role an appeal to perpetuate it forever?
Is this what being faithful to the holy texts means? With
such an approach to the Bible it would be only logical to
insist that Jews and Christians initiate holy wars, extending
the pillage and rape recorded in Exodus. Obviously a civilized person would be repulsed by such an inference. But
the repulsion does not remove the problem: Should believers
today reinstitute the self-image and social status of men
and women found in the passages of the Bible? Does the
paucity of biblical stories enhancing women's role mean
that this absence is normative, ethically and spiritually?
    Confronting the Bible are irreversible changes in
history. The cultural emergence of modernity and the
nuclear age have no antecedents in biblical times; the
attitudes, ambitions, pressures, and general sense of living
today has no exact equivalent in the biblical world. Curiously the enlargement of women's roles and the increased
recognition of new opportunities in society have been
inspired less by biblical resources than by women's hard
struggle in the social, economic, and political arenas. A

tension unavoidably arises between the Bible's description of women and the contemporary assessment of her worth and opportunities.

When the Bible is not appraised as a manual of proof-texts to exemplify a patriarchal society, then there is room for viewing women in other contexts. Discerning multiple contexts permits a differentiation of value judgment. Acknowledging the historical conditions for textual statements clarifies the range for applying these statements. The Jewish community would not cast its reading of the Wisdom literature, for instance, into the political light of Deuteronomy; the Psalms are not legislation. At the same time, the continuity of the people in their history accumulates an overall context for the personal well-being of the community.

One advantage in approaching the Bible overall, viewing the breath of salvation as a wholeness of the person, is that it exerts a corrective pressure upon all forms of oppression that people discern in their communal life. It questions the patronizing of either gender over groups in society, thereby exposing any arbitrary assumptions. If the Bible opposes a sense of justice, then belief in the Bible is fruitless and destructive.

For example, women have known the feelings of being powerless in societies dedicated to personal freedom. Here the Bible can be a source of guidance. Among the multiple themes taken up in biblical stories, one of them involves the perspective of the powerless. Stories of God's concern for widows, orphans, outcasts, the physically handicapped, the impoverished, and the enslaved abound. The afflicted of society are very much included in the biblical concern for justice and liberation. Women could associate their own exile from recognition by society and religious authorities with these various episodes. Thus they can draw upon the Bible's emancipation themes for stimulus to continue their own struggle for personal, social, and spiritual identity.

There is another unexpected critical tradition within the Bible that is not given sufficient attention as a spiritual resource. The prophetic tradition presents a host of protesters to confront the social and spiritual abuses of not only the "pagan," but of the Jewish faithful. From Amos to Zechariah there is a long list of prophets whose writings reveal a distinctive perspective that opposed the injustices of the social and religious status quo. The prophets were keen critics. They denounced society's use of religion to exonerate injustice and prejudice and to entrench privileges of power over the less advantaged.

What these writings provide in their spirit and rationale is both precedent and incentive to examine the forms and policies constituting spirituality today. The reason for resisting the canonizing of particular texts is that they themselves reveal limitations. They relate to specific problems in a specific era--crucial problems at that time, but not exhaustive of every instance of injustice. The acerbic judgment of a prophet does not necessarily extend to every form of oppression in that community. Obviously the prophets selected certain issues to denounce or praise; others they left untouched. They were sensitive to the enslavement of the Jewish people by foreign empires, but neglected to protest, as neither did Paul, the Jewish family's use of slaves. Is it safe to assume that because other instances of oppression are not denounced they are therefore tacitly approved by the prophets? If this tradition is more than merely an historical episode, then its prophetic spirit is an encouragement to examine the current forms of spiritual orthodoxy for their enrichment, as well as for their deformation.

The Bible speaks to one's path when it stirs the mind and heart to life. Scripture can shake our sense of reality, stirring our longing for life, beauty, truth, and goodness. It requires less our submission than our enlargement of soul to recognize its self-worth. It must relieve our anxiety about the fragmentariness of living and beckon us to wholeness.

Scripture, however, cannot be the highest court of appeal for spirituality. No revealed writings can. The greatness of the Bible, as well as other scriptures, lies not in its composition and proclamations but in its power to induce the reader and listener to fulfill themselves from its message. Once, when I was completing research at a library belonging to the New Church of Jerusalem, I asked one of the church officers, an energetic and intelligent young man, if the people in the community meditated and explored consciousness as Emmanuel Swedenborg, their founder, charted it. He replied that it was most unlikely.

Why should they bother since it had all been done already by their founder in the eighteenth century and was vividly described in his writings? Apparently many people are satisfied to treat scripture as an armchair traveller's brochure: read about it but don't visit.

Scripture can be viewed as one of the many important companions that we meet along the way of our life's destiny, a companion which offers us an encouraging word, suggests a route, and displays a rough map. This encounter illuminates the meaning of our experience, provided we pay attention. Our weariness with the many insoluble moments of not knowing what to do about the confusion of life can fade almost like magic. We feel refreshed. Scripture has this power to renew when it reflects our most profound desires. It is a precious map; it is not the territory. It offers only a guide to where the treasure lies, leaving the details of how to get there to us. As a trusted companion it can reveal much about ourselves but it becomes a peril when we substitute it for the private work of self-discovery.

Spiritual growth, then, does not necessarily result from reading and believing in scripture. Faith in the biblical word cannot be equated with the realization of spirituality. Memorizing a biblical text is not the same thing as realizing that text in our concrete daily life. The profound meaning and direction of life is not a duplication of biblical stories. By itself the Bible cannot serve as the only resource for human wisdom any more than as the sole source of astronomy when it describes the heavens. At best, it is naive to use scripture as the only means for spiritual guidance. God does not reside in a book. Genesis and the Wisdom books assert that God is found by means of learning about reality. Only by engaging in life's problems, living in the world and drawing upon its values, does one begin the long, twisting road to understanding the meaning of God and of ourself.

The objective discrepancy between the biblical account of women and that of the ever-changing contemporary scene demands that women cross-examine both. They must perform the interrogation by themselves. It is a spiritual inquest, one that hopefully illuminates evidence to assess in the unending journey of self-definition.

For this task, full of wonder and pain, there are

certain aids and principles that hasten the marvel of self-discovery and its attending freedom. The aids have proved sound over the centuries. They are useful only if the traveler finds a resonance with them. Not all will be suitable at once; they require adjustment to one's lifestyle. But since they come recommended by historical persistence, they are worth more than a glance.

First is the recognition that health and spirituality belong together. Taking care of one's body is imperative. A spiritual program that undermines health is spiritually destructive. It almost seems banal to mention, but it is a fact of our hectic world that women are as guilty as men in abusing the elementary requirements for sound health. Adequate sleep, nutritious food, sufficient exercise, and relaxation are the staples that, if neglected, imperil one's overall health and spiritual vitality. Occasionally one has to step back and ponder: What am I doing to my body? Since my body is an extension of my mind, what I do with my body redounds upon my mental outlook. It is amazing how melancholy and nervous behavior lessen when bodily requirements are met. Too often one's concept of spirituality includes a disregard of the body leading to decreased energy and illness.

The second principle is one's responsibility for the formation of personal identity. Spiritual growth does not entail the vigorous diminution of the ego, for without it one could hardly entertain a serious possibility for spiritual fulfillment. One's individual responses to life, the way one judges life's experiences, derive from, as well as instill, an intimate sense of identity. Self-worth and personal ambition reflect one another. When women think they should disqualify themselves from spiritual attainment out of a restrictive sense of modesty, then the result is mediocrity, a sense of unworthiness, and a threatening, scattered life. Healthy spirituality, on the other hand, instills a vibrant sense of self-direction. Forming a strong sense of personal worth is not necessarily equivalent to self-aggrandizement. The candid assessment of one's talents, together with an attitude of positive engagement with life's ambiguities, and a refusal to be less successful about life than the sages and saints, signify some of the elements composing the spiritual formation of personal identity.

The various spiritual practices are designed not to

embellish the personality's complacency in its holiness, but to confront oneself with ever more and richer reality. All spiritual practices are attempts at personal insight which liberates one from self-imposed boundaries. The finite personality reaches out to the unknown, the infinite. The bruises incurred by growth, it seems to me, have only one ultimate reason: to bring one to the truths about life. Anything less is self-delusion, which is the biggest cause of our troubles. One struggles until shrewdness dawns.

The third principle is the recognition that one's person is not just the result of historical forces and society's standards. Persons possess a life force which may be described as inherent dignity. This quality is neither granted nor abrogated by society. People may abuse it but it is never lost. Historically, societies have been slow to recognize the broad implications of this irreversible truth. In the contemporary world it is insufficiently appreciated in many cultures. Personhood is primary in every human being. Cultural roles and social mores cannot erase this priority; it remains unalterable and must include an equitable share in the cultural good, services, and opportunities necessary for humane survival with dignity.

Women's experience of life is as important as men's. The complementarity of the sexes means that one gender is not considered dependently inferior or instrumental to the other, scriptures notwithstanding. A woman must trust her own experience and not just man's interpretation of it. So many assumptions are embedded in society's ways of treating people that a constant vigilence is demanded to disclose any demeaning of the sexes.

Men and women are variously interdependent among themselves and among each other. We require each other in order to become self-reliant. Society's rules are not made to establish utter conformity but to support sufficient order so that people can become themselves. Personhood does not deny autonomous individuality but realizes that it can take place better in community. People can actually achieve more by fostering ties with the developing community.

But a community remains an abstraction without a material setting. We cannot exist as spiritual human beings without preserving our earthly roots. Finally it comes down to the insight that both men and women are morally responsible to ensure that the universe succeeds. People are not monads, islands of sheer individuality. A certain reciprosity emerges as one recognizes how dependent one is upon clean air, pure water, nutritious crops, and the rhythms of nature. Nature is not inexhaustible in her generosity. No longer a leisurely option, ecology must become a trust, an indispensable obligation, for survival.

These minimum principles are not really subject to the democratic procedure of consent. They are not a temporary preference, but required by the very nature of self-consciousness in either gender. Any lessening of them in political, economic, educational, and spiritual aims or policies dehumanizes all in the community. They belong to the spiritual essence of being human and thus form a foundation for spirituality.

It should be obvious that the comprehension of spirituality, like humanity, is impossible through one sex alone. The marvel of nature is that each gender reveals those characteristics that are variously androgynous to both. How the human spirit expresses these potentials is the particular constellations of temperament, character, and choices that blend into making the individual. Gradually one sees that only by nurturing personal relations with others can certain truths about individual human nature and gender emerge and become understandable. In this way, individuality-in-community comes into being; a paradox but not a contradiction. The various ways discoverable by society for encouraging an interdependence upon genders protects the claim to public and private recognition of individuality. One's interactions are a telling index of one's self-regard. Hence spirituality thrives when there is a healthy recognition of diverse paths. Orthodoxy is not necessarily one-dimensional. A diversity of traditions must prevail if the value of the person is appreciated.

And so the factors are listed. All quite simple on paper and seemingly unspiritual. Yet without them to forge the journey, one makes oneself anemic on a diet of holy dreams. Christian women must resist the temptation to imagine spirituality as a holy fairy tale with Prince Jesus coming to their rescue.

Spiritual growth demands a revision of the meaning of life. It takes place in the face of real experiences, private and social. A spiritual path forces one to pass through a series of predicaments, confusions, upheavals, and readjustments to life. It's never easy. The revisions demanded for growth are more than a change in ideas. The will, emotions, attitudes, relationships, the way one schedules the day, all affect a lifestyle that embodies the uneven growth in self-knowledge. The locus for feminine spirituality can not start in scripture. It begins in the throes of that feminine struggle that finally sees in the heat of life's trials the world's attitude that she still ought not be as free as men because of her gender. Out of this painful insight and her personal struggles of defeat and gain, however tenuous, emerges a clarifying freedom that, assimilated alone though shared with others, disposes a woman to find the ultimate resource in herself.

Spirituality always remains a personal odyssey, a life ripening towards wisdom; a life wherein one gradually loses fear of change, where insecurity and loneliness are whiffs of memory recalled in the laughter of remembrance, where a steady tranquility feels at home amidst the chaos of ephemeral values of the day, where petty anxieties cannot touch deeply, and where one senses more and more a union with creation in its altering manifestations of creative energy. Self-discovery now becomes for her a sacred revelation, not because a church confirms it or that any bible suggests it, but because a woman matures from it into her feminine consciousness of being. The spiritual quest beckons to her to nurture from out of all this complexity of pain and wonder a personal philosophy that kindles a new awareness of life's worth and a celebration of feminine destiny. From the truth of her experience of living she may even hear echoes of the scriptures.

Justin O'Brien, Ph.D. is a theologian, philosopher, and a researcher. Currently he is Senior Research and Education Fellow in Holistic Medicine at St. Mary's Medical School, London, and Director of Education at the Marylebone Health Centre. He holds advanced degrees in both philosophy and theology from American and European universities. He has served on several college faculties,

including Franklin and Marshall College, The New School for Social Research, New York City, Mundelein College, and ten years with Loyola University, Chicago.

Dr. O'Brien's interest in spiritual development, combined with his academic and counseling skills have helped him to formulate principles of a spirituality that integrates body, mind, and spirit. A recognized expert in meditation, he draws upon his personal experiences of traditional disciplines in monasteries, ashrams, and hermitages in America, Europe, the Middle East, the Orient, and India, as well as fifteen years of training with Sri Swami Rama in the perennial spirituality of the Himalayan sages. Since 1972 he has also been a faculty member of the Himalayan International Institute of Yoga Science and Philosophy.

The author of many articles, Justin has also written *Yoga and Christianity, Running and Breathing, A Theory of Religious Consciousness,* and a book on Christianity and the science of yoga to be released by Rutledge and Kegan Paul. He is contributing author to *Meditation in Christianity, Art and Science of Meditation, Western Spirituality,* and *The Spirituality of the Religious Educator.*

If you don't breathe, you die;
If you don't pray, you die spiritually.
Soren Kierkegaard

Prayer: The Language of Love

Mary E. Giles

As I struggle to begin this essay on prayer I appreciate the discomfort of St. Teresa of Avila when she was instructed by religious superiors to write about her inner life for the edification of her sisters and lay folk who sought her spiritual guidance. The natural reluctance to reveal intimate aspects of ourselves was sharpened in Teresa by the fact that, even though she was intelligent and spiritually perceptive, she was not theologically educated. She realized all too well that the Catholic Church took seriously Paul's injunction that women not teach; those who dared speak in Teresa's day often had to explain themselves before the inquisition. Teresa, however, was encouraged to teach by her divine Mentor whose instruction was infinitely superior to a degree from the university of Salamanca or Alcala de Henares.

Obeying the direction of her superiors, Teresa wisely chose not to venture outside the bounds of personal experience. Even when she refers to an event in prayer as happening to "a woman she knows," we recognize Teresa. She shunned the theological distinctions of learned men as too clever for her and of little profit to the uneducated women for whom she wrote. Let theologians write about prayer in their correct (and dull) language; she, Teresa, formed an appealing vocabulary from the stuff of everyday life, brightened by images of groundhogs and water wheels and palmetto plants.

I first heard about St. Teresa of Avila when I was a graduate student of Spanish literature, but not until an unexpected desire for prayer many years later sent me to my library in search of her writings did I read the volume which had rested there untouched. Reading her autobiography opened the door onto a world of unimagined spiritual possibilities.

Even though I did not understand much of Teresa's

autobiography, her words struck me as somehow true. Prayer, she said, was talking with God. That I could understand. And when she addressed God in the ardent language of lovers, I knew I had found in her a spiritual mentor and mother.

Intimidated now by the subtlety of the subject and aware that others are more qualified than I to write of prayer, once again I appeal to Teresa, first to define a point of departure, second for the courage to persevere in the task. The starting point I discern in her example of writing out of personal experience; the courage, in submitting my understandings to the wisdom of Teresa and other "authorities" on the language of love.

§

Returning to that moment years ago when I was inspired to pray, I consulted the autobiography of Teresa and her *Interior Castle,* a work of remarkable artistic maturity as well as a cohesive elaboration of the journey in prayer which she had outlined in several chapters of the *Life.* I resolved to follow her advice about "mental prayer," a kind of praying which, she explains in the *Interior Castle,* begins the journey inward. Indeed, says Teresa, we cannot enter the castle of our soul and embark on the journey to its deepest center where soul and God are united in intimate loving unless we practice mental prayer:

> As far as I can understand, the door of entry into this castle is prayer and meditation: I do not say mental prayer rather than vocal, for, if it is prayer at all, it must be accompanied by meditation. If a person does not think Whom he is addressing, and what he is asking for, and who it is that is asking and of Whom he is asking it, I do not consider that he is praying at all even though he be constantly moving his lips.[1]

We need remember that in Teresa's day women were not encouraged to think for themselves in religious matters, including prayer. Mindless recitation of formulaic prayer was the order of the day, even in convents which supposedly were dedicated to cultivating the interior life. Teresa was espousing dangerous teachings, for a woman, yet she was given to understand in her own twenty-year odyssey of turning inward to God that mental prayer was the essential first step for her nuns, and for all of us, if we are to advance in loving God.

Mental prayer is commonly known and practiced today under the rubric of "meditation," but when I was casting about for direction in prayer, meditation was associated with Eastern religions rather then Christianity. So everything Teresa said about mental prayer was news to me and very helpful. I was immediately attracted to mental prayer, in large part because years of academic study had trained me in the art of paying attention, which is the point of this prayer.

I emulated Teresa in the practice of picturing events in the life of Jesus Christ, particularly his passion and crucifixion. For example, I would see myself present at the crowning of thorns, imagine my feelings, relate the event to my own life, and reflect on its meaning in the larger arena of human endeavor. As a beginner I found mental prayer effective because there was something for my imagination and reason "to do."

Even though it was easy for me to quiet my body and emotions and concentrate on images and thoughts, I did not presume that mental prayer was a subject to be mastered in a given period of time. I did not consider mental prayer in the same category as the preterite tense of irregular verbs in Spanish. Teresa's repeated advice to continue prayer indicated that here was an indeterminable content that would require indefinite practice; thus I applied to prayer the principles of repetition and regularity which undergird teaching and learning.

Prayer may not be a definable content, but in one major respect its practice is similar to both academic learning and art. Prayer, study and art require increasing concentration. In a course on English literature, as students learn about authors, works, movements and how to analyze literature, not only the nature of literature but also its critical methodology become more and more sophisticated. The demands of analyzing a tragedy by Shakespeare are clearly greater than those implied in the study of a fairy tale!

The same need for rigor and concentration is evident

in art. Could we imagine a Leonardo da Vinci taking up brush and paints one day and the next creating the Mona Lisa? Granted, he was a genius, but even the most gifted must train their talent and submit to long, arduous practice to find and refine their artistry.

§

Prepared by years of academic discipline, I heeded Teresa's counsel to practice prayer. I did not slavishly imitate the details of her practice, however, for our lives were very different. She was a nun in a convent in sixteenth century Spain; I, a modern woman with the responsibilities of wife, mother, and teacher. Gradually through experimentation a pattern devolved in which I set aside for prayer a large part of Friday mornings and, as possible, a short time each day, except for Saturdays when all the family was home. I did not have a cell as Teresa did, but the area in our bedroom where I studied functioned as my "prayer space." I sat on the chair or the floor for prayer and used the desk for writing in the spiritual journal I had begun. The atmosphere was conducive to prayer as it was to study with an entire wall of windows that opened to a restful view of the garden and hills beyond. A time and space for prayer suited me because the sense of routine was assurance that in my already busy schedule I would pray regularly.

In retreats and workshops over the years I have always stressed the need for a specific time and space for prayer because these factors were helpful to me. When women objected that it is extremely difficult to find time each day for prayer, especially if they have small children at home (one woman said the only time she could pray was when she took a bath), I would reply that usually we make time for what we really want to do. That response is valid up to a point: I have come to see that some women are imprisoned by the very routine which freed me from negligence, procrastination, and apathy. More spontaneous than I by disposition, some friends of mine pray "on the wing," like humming birds at the flower--which is not to say that their mode is better or worse than mine. It is just different. Nor do they fail to pray regularly; for these spontaneous prayers, regularity means that they pray frequently rather than at a set time in the same place.

The recognition that practice can take different forms points to the fundamental truth that prayer is unique. Spiritual guides through the centuries say over and over that prayer is different for each person. Prayer must be different because it must be unique and it must be unique because each person is unique. The point is simplistically obvious, yet confusion threatens to cloud our understanding as soon as we outfit ourselves with guidelines, principles, road maps, and in a multitude of ways suggest that what tradition calls the "straight and narrow" road is also uniform.

The fact of uniqueness means that each of us is destined to create rather than imitate prayer. Only if we are liberated from preconceptions of what prayer should be can we create modes of praying that at the moment are the just right expression of our love for God. Freedom in prayer means that we must push beyond rote recitation of words and search out meanings for ourselves, that we speak to God in our own vocabulary, that we listen to guides like Teresa but not strain to imitate them. Freedom means that we are to be adventurers of the heart, charting the strange, "fabulous isles" of which St. John of the Cross sings in his "Spiritual Canticle."

This adventure is risky. I am bound to take wrong turns in prayer, now trying a method that is ill suited to my temperament, now clinging to one prayer when God calls me to another. But these are matters to be found out; what is important is that we travel by the compass of the heart, alert to the desire for God that initiates the journey and enables us to persevere when we cannot see the road ahead.

Rather than suggest techniques for mental prayer, therefore, I prefer to recommend a disposition that is beneficial to prayer in general. The disposition is for solitude. In our society where the market place sets a mood of frenzy and prizes efficiency and profit, there is little encouragement to nourish solitude and silence. Watching students rush on and off the campus, juggling incredibly heavy and conflicting schedules of classes and jobs, I am not surprised they have neither time nor taste for solitude. Even their study goes on in noise--the noise of worry over grades, requirements for graduation and prospects for well-paying jobs.

   We can nourish solitude in many ways. I find inspiration in nature and animals. Recently I was walking across the campus in the late fall afternoon when I caught sight of a furry grey squirrel skimming head-first down the trunk of a tree. Rather than walk by with a thought of "how cute and picturesque," I stopped to watch the squirrel complete the downward journey, scoop up a nut and sit upright with bulging cheek and bright eyes. Then he caught sight of me. No movement. I looked at the squirrel; he looked at me. Then his buddy started head-first down the trunk. Midway he stopped. The three of us looked at one another. Aware of a presence behind me, I turned to see a student who had stopped. Now four of us watched one another. Suddenly a cool October breeze swept across the back of my neck and stirred the leaves on the ground. Did I imagine the conversation or did the squirrel poised on the trunk actually say to his buddy, "Get up here with that nut, friend; we've got lots of work ahead of us." I realized I had interrupted a serious enterprise. I walked on, leaving them to their nut-gathering. It was a small moment, but briefly I saw the world through the eyes of a creature other than myself.

§

   For several months mental prayer was so satisfying it never occurred to me that prayer could be other than what I was doing: consciously quieting myself and focusing my imagination and reason on a subject. I was confident that with mental prayer, devotional reading, and attendance at church liturgies, my relationship with God was splendid.

   Although I had read in Teresa's writings about prayer further inside the castle, my reality was limited to the entry hall. The words I had read about prayer in the inner mansions were just that--words.

   One evening I went to my 'prayer space,' settled in the chair, read a short passage from Scripture, and closed my eyes to imagine the scene selected for meditation. Or rather I was about to close my eyes when suddenly I felt them close and my entire being became quiet, more intensely quiet than I had ever accomplished previously. No image, no thought; just a quieting as if I were wrapped in stillness. I had not caused this wonderful quieting that moved through and around me. The experience lasted perhaps fifteen minutes; then the quieting lifted as unexpectedly as it had dropped 'round me. Something marvelous had occurred, but what, I didn't know.

Some days later I was reading in the *Interior Castle* and came upon this passage:

> First of all, I will say something (though not much, as I have dealt with it elsewhere) about another kind of prayer, which almost invariably begins before this one. It is a form of recollection which also seems to me supernatural, for it does not involve remaining in the dark, or closing the eyes, nor is it dependent upon anything exterior. A person involuntarily closes his eyes and desires solitude; and, without the display of any human skill there seems gradually to be built for him a temple in which he can make the prayer already described; the senses and all external things seem gradually to lose their hold on him, while the soul, on the other hand, regains its lost control.[2]

I recognized the experience as mine and understood from Teresa's explanation that for her (and other authorities corroborate her understanding) this unsolicited quieting called recollection marks the entry into a subtle mode of praying which, because it is out of our control, is called "supernatural." Even though we know there is the phenomenon of recollection, and even though we quiet ourselves in readiness for it, we cannot make it happen; recollection takes us by surprise.

Until this event my awareness in prayer was of what I was doing: quieting the body, saying words, imagining scenes, evoking emotional responses and scrutinizing concepts. Now, in the silence of recollection, I was made aware of God and God's activity; that activity was simply stilling, quieting, silencing me.

This experience of recollection made me acutely aware of another truth of prayer, one almost obscured by my efforts to pray: Prayer is relationship. In relationship two persons are in a process of being present one to the other. In the abstract that truth is obvious, but in practice it is a truth we do not always honor or know how to honor.

In prayer we miss the mark of relationship in two ways. First, as beginners we can be so intent on what we are doing and how to do it, as I was with mental prayer, that we become self-absorbed, losing sight of the fact that prayer is a conversation rather than a monologue. Second, we make of God an object by bringing to prayer expectations about who God is and what God is to do for us. I assumed, for example, that God was a someone "out there" and "up there" to listen to my prayers and grant requests. The consequence of making God an object is that we cannot see God as God is, that is, not until by God we are stripped of the expectations, needs and cravings that stand between us and the Beloved.

The latter observation suggests that God and our relationsip with God is mystery; our senses, emotions and reason cannot catch and contain the presence to whom we stretch out in prayer. This mystery we also discern in human relationships. On marrying, a man and woman embark on a journey of creating their relationship. They may set out with notions of what a marriage should be, but they will discover that the real circumstances of living day in and day out with another person make a lie of preconceptions. A man and woman as individuals undergo uncontrollable psychological and physical changes which the relationship being created through them cannot not reflect. Under the stress of change preconceptions and the expectations they fuel shatter. Thus at no given time can a man and woman define their relationship as a "this" or a "that." Relationship is mystery--that which in this moment is being wrought in word, gesture, and the thousand ways we are present to one another.

So also is mystery this relationship being created with God through prayer. I cannot see now into the deepest corners of my being or know the person of ten years hence whom I am becoming, nor do I understand the One with whom I relate in prayer. My faith is that the moment of relating somehow is creating a living unity--a God-and-I. In prayer I do not produce a commodity; there is no package tied with the ribbons of reason which I hold aloft in proud ownership: "This package is my relationship with God." How-to manuals to the contrary, relationship with God, like human relationships, has nothing whatsoever to do with production or analysis. The point is that praying is creating love for God, and this creating and this loving are mystery.

On this journey in mystery we are bound eventually to travel without agendas, time tables, specific destination or such known modes of transportation as mental prayer. What we can know is that we are destined for the stars and beyond, to travel in the space ship of the heart.

Thus caution is "thrown to the winds" insofar as time and specifics are concerned. There are no five-year plans for loving on the journey, nor are there in human relationship. We do not sign up for a twelve-month friendship or a five-year love affair. We plunge into friendships and love affairs and relationship with God for the duration of our lives.

§

In the months and years after the first experience of recollection, I came to discern in it two qualities which proved to be reliable indications whether prayer was given by God or my own activity. The first quality was its unexpectedness. I did not expect to be quieted by God that day I was about to gather myself inward for meditation, nor subsequently would I anticipate the moments when God drew me ever more intimately inward. The second quality was discernible in the effects of the prayer: refreshed, joyful, peaceful, and above all, caught in wonderment that something so beautiful had happened to me.

A further indication that the prayer is genuinely from God is a sense of certitude remaining afterward which nothing can eradicate. To this day that first experience of recollection is as vivid as the day it occurred, as is the conviction that it came unbidden, an indescribably lovely gift from God.

If that certitude is absent, then I must ask myself the "hard questions." Was I truly surprised? Had I been reading anything or talking with someone about something that could have triggered the event? Was I truly humble, or was there a voice whispering, "You deserved the favor"? If even a little hesitancy creeps into my reply, I should admit that somehow, consciously or otherwise, I authored the experience.

The question of whether an experience originates with God or in us as the work of wish-fulfillment or an overly active imagination is difficult to answer, particularly if we do not have help in discernment from a spiritual director. I am sensitive to the need for spiritual directors because in retreats and workshops on prayer the question inevitably comes up: "Where can I find a spiritual director?" I would like to have a list of directors available; alas, directors are scarce, more available to the religious, of course, than the laity. Nonetheless we are not entirely without spiritual direction if we take for a friend a volume like the *Interior Castle* or *Contemplative Prayer* by Thomas Merton or the perenially reliable two-part treatise by St. John of the Cross entitled the *Ascent of Mt. Carmel* and *Dark Night of the Soul*. For those who are unsure if they should remain with mental prayer I recommend the latter works, in which St. John gives concrete signs for discerning if God is calling us from meditation to contemplation.

Contemplation is the traditional term in Christianity for the reaches of prayer beyond meditation where we do not initiate or govern the prayer but are recipients of God's loving. Recollection is for Teresa and her generation the lowest rung of the contemplative ladder, but it is nevertheless "supernatural" prayer because it comes outside the natural mode of knowing which involves the active use of our senses, imagination and intellect.

The experience of being made quiet is akin to a consciousness which I call attentivenss. Attentiveness is an attitude of being alert to, receptive to, open to. In contrast to "paying attention" during which we push outward to grasp something with the intellect, in attentiveness we are being opened . . . to what we are not sure.

Attentiveness has a counterpart in activities other than prayer just as concentration or paying attention do. Sometimes in the classroom I "see" in students the transition from paying attention to being attentive. Recently in a course on medieval culture we were discussing the theological significance of the Beatific Vision which crowns Dante's journey in *The Divine Comedy*. As the students grappled with terms like 'trinity,' 'incarnation' and 'redemption' I could see turning the wheels of their paying attention. Sensing their struggle with the strange vocabulary, I stopped talking, took up the text and began to read. Dante's poetry swiftly overtook me; I felt poised with the poet before the circles of light wherein he is inspired to see the mysteries of his faith. Attentive to the poem, I became attentive also to the students, hearing stilled their wheels of concentrating. No explication, no questions, no discussion intruded on our attentiveness. When the reading concluded with Dante's completing his journey and turning earthward to share the vision, we remained quiet for several minutes, nourished by the poet's gift--his language of love.

So also in prayer there is this transition from paying attention to the words of a prayer or the meaning of a passage from Scripture as the wheels of analysis are stilled and we are brought to rest in a prayer over which we have no control, a prayer that is simply waiting on God.

The transition, unfortunately, can be complicated by our attempts to cling to mental prayer out of habit or fear of the unknown or because we think it is the right thing to do; we do not understand that God is calling us to a subtle conversation. Thus the question of discerning the transition is important. For assistance in discerning this step from meditation to contemplation, let us look at the thirteenth chapter of Book Two of the *Ascent of Mt. Carmel* where St. John says that if the following three signs are present at once rather than successively, then God is calling us to supernatural prayer:

First, we no longer can meditate or use our reason. That is, no matter how strenuously and for how long we try, we simply cannot pay attention. The mind will not function as it has in the past, and the effort to force meditation can cause headaches and even nausea.

Second, we have no desire to fix our meditation on other particular objects, exterior or interior, and derive no pleasure from prayer or other activities. We do not have a distaste for prayer that is alleviated by a substitute activity such as going to the movies; rather we have lost our taste and ability for mental prayer and know not where to turn.

Third, our only pleasure is in being alone, alert to God. Let us listen to St. John:

> The third and surest sign is that the soul takes pleasure in being alone, and waits with loving attentiveness upon God, without making any particular meditation, in inward

peace and quietness and rest, and without acts and exercises of the faculties--memory, understanding and will--at
least, without discursive acts, that is, without passing
from one thing to another; the soul is alone, with an
attentiveness and a knowledge, general and loving, as we
said, but without any particular understanding, and advert-
ing not to that which it is contemplating.[3]

If we cannot meditate, if we take no pleasure in
meditating on God or anything else, and if we want only
to be alone, resting attentive to God, we should cease
trying to meditate and remain quiet. Our alertness to
God, our attentiveness to God, our receptivity to God, our
being open to God--this attitude or condition in itself is
prayer: God is speaking the divine language of loving in
words that are not heard and gestures not seen or felt.
Instructed in loving, all we can do and are to do is "listen,"
for what and to what we do not understand.

This loving, this prayer, is "dark" because we do
not understand it with the senses, imagination or intellect.
Thomas Merton wrote marvelously clear descriptions of
contemplation:

Contemplation is essentially a listening in silence, an
expectancy. And yet in a certain sense, we must truly begin to hear God when we have ceased to listen. What is
the explanation of this paradox? Perhaps only that there
is a higher kind of listening, which is not an attentiveness
to some special wave length, a receptivity to a certain
kind of message, but a general emptiness that waits to
realize the fullness of the message of God within its own
apparent void. In other words, the true contemplative is
not the one who prepared his mind for a particular message that he wants or expects to hear, but who remains
empty because he knows that he can never expect or
anticipate the word that will transform his darkness into
light. He does not even anticipate a special kind of transformation. He does not demand light instead of darkness.
He waits on the Word of God in silence, and when he is
'answered' it is not so much by a word that bursts into
his silence. It is by his silence itself suddenly, inexplicably
revealing itself to him as a word of great power, full of
the voice of God.[4]

Many like Thomas Merton have been inspired by St. John's treatise to write their own accounts of the dark way that God takes us as we move more discretely in prayer, but no one has mastered the master of the dark night in his gentle proddings on the mystery of God's quieting our physical-psychological being and conversing with the soul in the language of silence. St. John realized that this language causes us pain at the outset because we strain to interpret the darkness that overwhelmes us. He realized that darkness in prayer is a dimension of the larger darkness that overtakes us as we are weaned from relying on people, institutions, rituals and theologies that mediate the divine presence. He realized that God pulls us into an intimate embrace where there is no room for an idea of who God is or a person to mediate God's reality. God is drawing us out of the consciousness wherein we see God in a flower or a lover or a painting or a priest or a liturgy and pulling us into a higher consciousness in which all particular and specific items are seen in God. The shift in perspective is radical, shattering comfortable ways of knowing about God and plunging us into knowing God as God is. Of course our mode of prayer is affected, and of course the forms of prayer that were solacing and useful (mental prayer, for example), no longer serve. The old forms were specific in nature because we molded them from the clay of our experiences, but God's prayer does not fit into those forms because the clay of the divine is altogether different. The darkness we experience in prayer as well as in other aspects of our lives where we are accustomed to seek God--liturgy, symbols, people-- is both the measure and nature of God's love. And the darkness, St. John reminds us, is painful until by God's grace we are able to see the darkness as light. St. John assures us that "although this happy night brings darkness to the spirit, it does so only to give it light in everything; and that, although it humbles it and makes it miserable, it does so only to exalt it and to raise it up."[5]

§

I stated that when I first experienced recollection I was in no way anticipating it, and that even though I may have read of the experience in Teresa's writings, I was

not conscious of it in days and weeks preceding the event.
The fact that we are reading spiritual descriptions of the
inner way as a guide for ourselves, however, presents the
possibility that unconsciously we would like to imitate the
path set forth. As much as I admire and love Teresa, I
remind myself that her prayer is hers and mine is mine.
If I allow her example to dictate my steps rather than inspire them, I am bound to stumble. I must find my own
path which, though it may run parallel to hers, will not
overlay it.

One area where our paths run far apart is that of
the extraordinary phenomena with which Teresa often is
identified. I refer to visions, locutions, trances, flights of
the spirit--the many phenomena she describes in the rooms
of the castle between recollection and the spiritual marriage of the seventh and last mansions.

Why was Teresa's prayer characterized for several
years by these phenomena? Why did she see Jesus and
hear his words? Why was she enraptured with effects
which she vividly describes?

> For when He means to enrapture this soul, it loses its
> power of breathing, with the result that, although its
> other senses sometimes remain active a little longer, it
> cannot possibly speak. At other times it loses all its
> powers at once, and the hands and the body grow so cold
> that the body seems no longer to have a soul--sometimes
> it even seems doubtful if there is any breath in the
> body. This lasts only for a short time (I mean, only for
> a short period at any one time) because when this pro-
> found suspension lifts a little, the body seems to come
> partly to itself again, and draws breath, though only to
> die once more, and, in doing so, to give fuller life to the
> soul. Complete ecstasy, therefore, does not last long.[6]

The simplest answer to the question of why Teresa
suffered ecstasy is that God chose to love her this way.
Scholars have also sought psychological explanation in her
emotional temperament and dependence on senses and
imagination in prayer.

St. John warns that the way of a Teresa is fraught
with danger. He saw all around him in sixteenth century
Spain evidence of the perils that beset those who relied
on what they saw with their physical eyes or eyes of the
imagination or heard with the physical ears or ears of the

imagination. He saw men and women in and out of religious life who were so smitten by the prospect of seeing angels and conversing with Jesus that they imagined supernatural beings in astonishing detail and chatted with them aloud in self-induced trances. John saw also how pride and envy divided convents and monasteries where religious sought to outdo each other in length, intensity, and detail of their visions and confessors boasted to one another about the feats of their spiritual charges.

The prudent course of action, St. John advises, is to resist the phenomena, and failing that, disregard them when against our will a vision overtakes us or we are enraptured out of our senses. What need have we of revelations, St. John asks, when for the Christian the ultimate revelation has been given in Jesus Christ? And do not trouble yourself, he says further, that God will be offended if you resist, for if the experience truly is a divine favor, you are powerless to reject it. Moreover, God sees deeply within your heart that your desire is intent not on specific favors limited by particular forms but on the formless darkness that more and more we intuit is God as God is.

John's advice is as sound and welcome today as it was four centuries ago. Superstitions may change their garb, but they do not disappear; the twentieth century has its share of superstitious beliefs in prophets and visionaries and cultic leaders who betray us with their emphasis on precisely that which we must leave behind in our journey to God. That is, we must drop the baggage of expecting and relying on particular experience such as visions of the end of the world or revelations whispered distinctly in the ear of a self-proclaimed prophet and travel unencumbered through darkness.

In the case of Teresa, whose journey for many years was marked by the phenomena St. John warns against, let us remember that they were a stage which she had to endure. When Teresa is drawn into the innermost recesses of her soul, described in the seventh mansions, therein to meet her Beloved in the beautifully simple union of the Spiritual Marriage, the extraordinary phenomena cease. Her life in the seventh mansions is a harmony of all her energies--physical, emotional, intellectual, and spiritual--and she is a unity of loving with her God. Her prayer is as simple as the unity of the active Martha and contemplative

Mary who symbolize these mansions.

Like all prayer, contemplation is limitless, growing from simplicity to simplicity and purity to purity. By simplicity I mean that the senses, imagination and intellect are bound into the single thread of attentiveness. Purity means that prayer has been cleansed of specific intentions: We love God for the joy of loving and nothing more. As we move from simplicity to simplicity and purity to purity our awareness is deepened and heightened, as is the quality of our love, so that at any given moment we are freed from specific intentions and made single-hearted in our attentiveness; at this moment our prayer is perfect. But another moment comes when the simple is more simple and the pure, purer, though we do not consciously make comparisons with the past or hope for greater things in the future. The moment is complete, hence perfect, in and of itself, and in this completeness we rejoice without thought for the past or future.

Although we cannot control contemplation, we can dispose ourselves to it. The way I dispose myself to contemplation is to read slowly several times a short passage from Scripture until a line or phrase attracts my attention. Then I close my eyes and aloud or silently repeat the phrase, addressing it to spiritual friends whom I 'meet in prayer.' It may happen that suddenly I am absorbed and suspended, not speaking, thinking or moving, my entire being for a moment caught in God. The experience can last for only a second or for several minutes. Usually I am aware of going in and out of absorption, as it were, somewhat like a swimmer who comes up for air. The experience may last for as long as an hour. Sometimes even after having gone about my other activities, I am aware of being absorbed, as if I were doing and speaking from within a bubble of quiet.

I have had to learn not to strain for contemplation. Contemplation is so nourishing that we would like it often; so there is the temptation that we try to make it happen. We can't. I also have learned that psychological rubbish surfaces during contemplation. St. John knew that obscene images and sexual stirrings can occur during prayer, and he advises us to disregard them as much as possible for they are temporary and must be endured. They are no reason to stop praying or cease disposing ourselves to

God's prayer.

I mentioned meeting friends in prayer. Several years ago at a retreat, another woman and I agreed to meet each other in prayer. On Friday mornings we would think of each other as our companion in loving God. Over the years many women and men have joined us. I do not invoke the name or imagine the face of every person whom I know to be present on Friday mornings, but I find that each week one or two friends are particularly vivid and so with them I greet in general all others who are meeting in prayer.

One benefit of this companionship in prayer is that knowing others are praying with me strengthens me to pray when I might succumb to the lure of reading a book or going for a hike. But the greater benefits are those I cannot discern, the ones that issue unseen from the fact of prayer itself. They lighten days when my praying falls victim to the deluge of family and professional obligations and pour into the stream of grace that enables me to pray at all.

Spiritual friends are praying friends, whether we sit together in silence or from a distance gather as one in love or through letters open our hearts to God. For women today whose lives are immensely rich and complex and who do not have the institutional support that was Teresa's, we must create ways of helping each other on the inner way. We all need at least one person with whom to talk about prayer and pray with. I am blessed with several such friends, most of whom are "secular" rather than religious.

Of course opposites such as secular/religious and contemplative/active break down before the force of Unity which through prayer is being realized in loving God. More and more I am aware of this truth as teaching, study and writing as well as relationship with family and friends are becoming prayer. In my commitment to inspire in students love for beauty, truth, compassion and goodness through our study of literature, art, philosophy and religion, each day I am aware of being absorbed, as it were. As I teach and work individually with students I feel as if I am acting from within an absorption that stills me to distractions and magnifies my concentration and attentiveness. I am not aware of addressing specific words or thoughts to

God, but nonetheless I know I am praying. The method and meaning and context of prayer have been transformed from moments of concentrating on God and being made attentive to God into an unbroken moment of awareness within God. This awareness is not being aware of, say, an idea or person or activity, but rather it is a keen sense of purpose--that life is meaningful, that all of my being is meaning, that praying is the expression of awareness of meaning as I create with God meaning through every word, gesture, and thought.

§

I ought not end this essay before saying a word or two of feminist inclination, since this is a collection of writings about women and spirituality. Is there something unique to women as prayers? Frankly, I don't know. If I subscribed to the theory that women by nature are receptive and intuitive, I could make the case that women are thus pre-disposed to contemplation. However, from the perspective of uniqueness, the case is weak before it is argued.

The prudent, generous and wise course is to acknowledge the fact of uniqueness. God calls us to love as the unique person each one is. What can be said to apply to all who hear the call is that the journey in prayer takes us through darkness into the light wherein we see ourselves and God in a wondrous simplicity, a unity of loving.

Mary Giles, Ph.D., writer and teacher, holds a doctorate in Romance Literature from the University of California, Berkeley. She has taught Humanities, Spanish, Medieval Cultures, and Religious Studies since 1964 at California State University in Sacramento. Mary is the founding editor of the quarterly journal, *Studia Mystica* and the author of many articles on literature and spirituality. She is a frequent speaker at both scholarly meetings and at religious workshops and retreats. She also leads retreats on prayer and women's spirituality. Her translation, with critical introduction, of Francisco de Osuna's *Third Spiritual Alphabet* is part of the Classics of Western Spirituality series published by Paulist Press. Her other books include *The Feminist Mystic: Essays on Women and Spirituality, When Each Leaf Shines,* a theology for women's ministry, and *The Poetics of Love: Meditations with John of the Cross.*

Mary is a wife and mother, devoted to her family. In her leisure she enjoys riding her horses and caring for her other animals.

She who sows in tears will reap in joy.
                    Psalm 126

This is how love is:
So what if your head must roll--
What is there to cry about?
                    Kabir

Suffering and Self-Realization

An Interview with

Irina Tweedie

The editor interviewed Irina Tweedie, Sufi mystic and loving spiritual guide, in her home in London and while on lecture tour in the United States.

Mrs. Tweedie, have you found that the spiritual path of women is different from that of men?

Yes, quite different. My teacher, whom I call Bhai Sahib, said one day, "Man needs many practices because the energy in man works entirely different from that in women. I give men many practices. Women need hardly any practices at all. She will reach reality because she is woman."[1]

Just imagine me, how thrilled I was! I thought, "Aha!" but I didn't say anything. Suddenly he sharply turned to me and said, "Oh no, don't rejoice. It is just as difficult for everybody. It is only different."

You see, a woman is nearer to matter than men are. We are made in a different way. We have to produce children out of our physical body, so our psyche and our bodies and our chakras and everything else are made entirely different from those of men. Man uses his creative energy, manifested as semen, to beget children. His energy is transmuted into something else, so it is rather difficult for him to reach a spiritual level. We women hold the creative energy of God in our chakras. We have it already and we keep it. Spiritually speaking, we don't need to get anything else.

For the sake of the children, however, we women need protection, we need warmth, we need comfort in order to procreate the human race. The woman is, therefore, so much more attached to the physical things. We need them. Things like security, money, food, shelter are extremely important to us. It is in our very nature.

We can't help it. And for the sake of these things, I think, women have always accepted being second-class citizens: we needed things that the man can give.

Then the process of bearing and raising a child is important for a woman's spiritual growth?

Yes. Children are extremely important for spiritual development. The birth of a child for a woman is a spiritual experience of the first magnitude. Children are very special; they are magic. And they are definitely a spiritual experience.

What about women who are unable to bear children?

It doesn't matter. I never had children. I had two husbands (not at the same time!) but I never had children. They just didn't come. But for some women to have no children is a terrible psychological suffering, because it is in woman's very nature to desire children. Because children are so important for a woman, they also present the greatest obstacle for her spiritual life. A swami in Dehradun, India told me that according to Vedanta, to have no children is spiritually easier for a woman because children create such attachment. Children represent a tremendous attachment to a mother. How could it be otherwise? They are part of the woman.

It would seem, then, that women need a partner to progress spiritually.

I think man and woman both need partners. Guruji said to us, "I would like to take them together to God. They complement each other." More and more as I have to deal with people I personally see that human beings shouldn't be alone. We need each other. Women especially. Nobody is more; man is not more than woman and woman is not more than man. We are just different. Guruji used to say, "You all swim in the ocean. Who is nearer the shore? And which shore?" No one is higher or lower than another. We are all different, but we need each other.

What is the nature of that relationship?

The relationship is based upon energy. The relationship between the two sexes (or between the same sex on the homosexual level), always has to do with the energy we call kundalini. Kundalini is very powerful; it is the same energy that is at the center of every atom. It is earth energy, and it is considered to be feminine. When two people come together and there is love, or even not love, but just sexual desire, what happens on the energy level? The energy forms a circuit, a closed circuit, between man and woman. They are enclosed in an energy grid which produces beautiful effects. But this circuit or grid can be so easily broken! The least thing can break it. A little bit of hurt, a bit of pain inflicted by one upon the other, and it's gone. It is as if the chemistry wasn't all right. And sometimes the loveliest people leave each other in anger for quite small things.

But basically man and woman are really the same, and on one level of consciousness I often have difficulty distinguishing one from the other unless I pay close attention.

Then at the soul level we are dealing with the same reality?

Absolutely. For instance, my teacher said that in the moment of ecstasy, in the moment of sex, it is the same for man as for woman. He said that the feeling is the same, because it is an explosion into space. The one who is the real enjoyer is the Atman, the higher self. The body partakes only by reflection.

In order to be perfect we must have both the male and the female qualities. Psychologically in every woman is also a man. We have both characteristics. No one is only male or only female. With spiritual progress, the man will not become effeminate, nor will the woman be masculine, but each will become whole, a perfect balance between the two qualities.

Why, they, did God decide to make this division of the sexes?

In order to create the world, one had to become two and two had to be different and separate. As simple as that.

And once the two are different, the pursuit of life is to rejoin them?

Yes, quite right. And that will all happen in millions and millions of years when Brahman takes in the breath.

It appears that all the searching and seeking of life, all the desires and ambitions, all the achievements and hopes, are underneath the obvious, a striving for ultimate unity.

Yes. The whole of life, everything from a stone to the galaxy, searches for unity. If you look at nature, you see that everything tries to look like a human being. In trees you see the human form. Even in pebbles you see somehow a human form. Because we human beings are made in the image of God, we especially look always for oneness. Sufis say that the human being is the crown of creation and seeks unity, unity, unity. We find this seeking in ourselves psychologically at every level.

When we love someone we seek that oneness. We want to be of one mind when we love someone. Finally in the moment of ecstasy there is oneness. And union with God is such fulfillment, such glory, that we are never alone again.

Yet loneliness seems to be a great problem for many women. Is there some reason for it? Does loneliness itself fit into our spiritual development in some way?

I think that on the spiritual path loneliness is definitely a problem, not only for women but also for men. What happens when we really are on the path? To be on the path, using the conventional words, is really, how shall I put it? It is friction. It is the law of nature, like the tide, like day and night, like a pendulum. There is nearness and there is separation. When we are in the state of nearness to that which we call "God" or "That" or "Void" or our "Higher Self" (which are all one and the same thing), then the human being is happy. When we are separated the soul is crying. This very friction is the purifying of the mind. You see, friction creates fire; fire is pain and suffering, and great loneliness. It keeps going backwards and forwards. That is how the mind will be purified.

Women are more lonely than men because they have more longing. We bring into this world two qualities: the will to live, and the will to worship. The will to live is self-preservation. The will to worship is the love aspect embedded in the very texture of our soul. This love aspect is the essence of God. It manifests itself in us as longing. Women have such longing. We often feel an emptiness, a great yearning. There is always a place in the heart of a human being reserved for That. No mortal creature can fill it. We are made in God's image and he is the greatest lover, a jealous lover, who keeps a place for himself. Longing is one of the messages which the soul sends to the human being: "Go home. We must go home to the Beloved."

Who is this Beloved?

The Beloved is a great emptiness! It is a void, terribly frightening to the mind, but responsive. It is at the same time absolute fullness, absolute light. It is the nothingness where everything is. It is the fullness where nothing exists. It is the fullness of love.

A woman doesn't want a friend; a woman wants a lover! The moment of union with God is the most intimate things in the world. At that moment we are united with our Self, with our soul, the Atman, the personal God, the Creator, the constantly drunk one, drunk with his own creation. And that union is bought with suffering.

Must everyone experience spiritual suffering?

Yes. Because there comes a time in spirituality when we have to find absolute happiness within ourselves. It is one stage on the path. This is a process that we all have to go through. People come and say, "Oh, I can't meditate. It is like a brick wall in front of me. I feel quite naked, suspended in the void and nothing is there. God is not there. I cannot pray. I can do nothing. All is dark." About this stage Swami Rama advised, "Get established in the darkness." It will pass.

I remember one day when my teacher spoke to Lillian, the woman who introduced me to him. She was so happy that day; she was radiant and telling him all the wonderful things that happened to her. Bhai Sahib very quietly turned to me and said, "And you?" I just shrugged because I was at that moment in the darkness. "Yes," he said, "union is good, but separation is better. When the human being is happy he doesn't do anything; he's just happy. But when you are alone, when you are forsaken, you are crying and you make an effort. And the Brahma Vidya is such that a thousand years are not enough."

I said, "Bhai Sahib, will that state last?" He answered, "My dear, it will pass; it comes and goes. But don't tell it to pass. Just say, 'Oh beloved, it doesn't matter. I am still faithful. I am still true.'"

So suffering cannot be avoided on the spiritual path?

It cannot be avoided. We have an idea of the spiritual life that is not true. We think it is all beautiful with a master sitting in the Himalayas, and everything lovely and sweet. But it's not like that at all. The spiritual life and its training is hard and crude; it is rough and difficult. You are humiliated, thrown down; your face is rubbed in the dust and you are beaten to nothing.

After my training in India a friend asked me what my training was like. I replied, "Perhaps it is like a steam roller going over you. And what gets up is paper thin and transparent, and there is nothing left."

Of course, I think that women do suffer more. A woman psychologically is much more, I wouldn't say sensitive as that is too crude an expression, but I feel that we are hurt much easier than men. I read somewhere a beautiful poem (I don't remember whose poem) long ago that began, "We women bleed." We have our children with suffering and blood. We bleed for our children; we bleed for our man. There is constant bleeding. Very often just coming back from meditation or going into meditation, I remain half conscious and I feel that a woman is constantly bleeding for one reason or another. I can't put it better than that. I am absolutely sure that a woman suffers more than a man. Also, you see, being a second-class citizen we are constantly pushed down, down, down. There is suffering from all directions: physical and emotional and psychological and physiological and every possible way.

Is suffering good? Is it necessary for our development?

If it is good, I don't know, but I think it is the will of God. It should be like that, that's all. It is the drama of the soul.

Will there ever be an end to the loneliness and suffering?

I don't think so. But this is my personal opinion and should be accepted with a grain of salt. I think suffering is actually a very wonderful thing because suffering is also redeeming. Without suffering how will we know that there is no suffering? That there is joy? Suffering is fire; fire is purifying.

You know, we Sufis have written about this. It is actually in books, though I did not know it, and discovered it only afterwards. We have states, wonderful spiritual states, full of beauty and joy and peace. But after that there is a kind of depression. It is not an ordinary depression; it's something else: this world is oh, so difficult to bear because somewhere else is so much nicer!

How would I enjoy the other states if I wouldn't know that deep suffering afterwards? We have to accept that. You know, there comes a time when illness doesn't matter, pain doesn't matter, nothing matters anymore because there is this infinite joy that you can offer this suffering to someone, somewhere, and say to him or it, "Well, this terrible pain in me I offer to thee. It is a miserable flower, but it's all I have."

What is the role of the teacher in spirituality?

The whole spiritual life is getting rid of the ego. We have to get rid of the ego in order to get anywhere. Two masters cannot live in one heart. Either I or That; either the little self is there, or God is there. (Let's use the word God, because it doesn't matter what we call it). The role of the teacher is to get rid of this little ego. It is a very simple process, but it is very painful. The teacher must erase the ego and it is done through suffering. The master does nothing but his duty to help us get rid of it, but by jove, it is a painful thing. It is crucifixion, absolute crucifixion. The teacher's duty is to turn you inside out, but you are never the same again.

The goal of every yoga is to lead a guided life, to be able to listen. So the master must be able to reach the disciple and vice-versa. It's a two-way process. (Either it is the master, or it is your higher self--they are the same thing). So spiritual training is really analysis, but much harder, much worse, done with yogic power.

Human beings want to run from such power and from such pain, but before a great teacher takes you in his hands and turns you inside out, he will give you something magnificent. He will show you what human beings really are--what they look like somewhere where they are not human anymore, but divine. There is such greatness; you are like a great fire! And from that moment you can never look at another human being without remembering. You will see each human being as part of the Beloved.

How does one find a teacher?

There is a spiritual law which says, "When the disciple is ready the teacher will be there." So going out and looking for a teacher is grabbing the wrong end of the stick. If we aspire, if our torch is lit, in the darkness of the world somebody is bound to see it. Every one of us has only one teacher. Only somebody who has deep karmas with you has the right to subject you to what only a teacher subjects you to. Only one person in the world, the infinitely pure, disinterested one, can do that and not incur karma himself. The relationship with that teacher is a great grace from God based on mutual past karma. It is not something we can accomplish. It is a great grace.

Is meditation important for spiritual growth?

Yes. It is the feminine which *leads* us to spirituality. What is the feminine in spiritual practice? It is meditation.

Is woman's approach to meditation different from man's?

Very much so. Love. I have to begin with love, because meditation belongs there. Love, like everything else in the world, has a positive and a negative aspect; in other words, a masculine and a feminine aspect. The masculine aspect in love is "I love you." The feminine aspect is "I'm waiting for you." Meditation is the feminine side of love. The feminine says, "I am a cup waiting for thee." That is meditation. We are speaking here of love of God, of course. "I am waiting for you. I am here. I surrender to you. I am waiting for grace."

For us women the spiritual life, in one way, is easier than for men. Only a certain temperament of man can surrender like we can surrender. And spiritual life is surrender. Bhai Sahib said, "Women are taken up through the path of love, for love is a feminine mystery." He said we women do not need many spiritual practices. We need only to renounce. Renounce what? Renounce the world. Complete renunciation, which is the most difficult thing for the woman, is necessary. I had to do it--to give everything away. Bhai Sahib said to me, "You cannot say to the Beloved, 'Oh I love you, but this is mine, and so far and no further.'" You have to give everything away, including yourself, in complete surrender.

And to whom do we surrender? We do not surrender to the teacher. That is rubbish! My teacher kept repeating, "You must surrender. You must surrender." And of course I presumed that he meant surrender to the teacher. One really does want to surrender to the teacher, but one does not. One surrenders only to the light within oneself, to one's own highest self. Absolute surrender with love is necessary. You surrender to that eternal part within you; ancient, without beginning or end. That is an extraordinary thing. It is the thing that people do not know. I realized it in deep meditation. When we have self-realization, we do not realize anything else except ourselves. That is why it is called "self-realization" or "God-realization." They are the same thing.

One day somebody here in the group, a young man, told me something infinitely touching. He said, "When I am with my girlfriend, in that most supreme moment of sex, I have a tremendous desire to be one with her." I remember I looked at him and my heart was full of compassion. Poor him. He was hoping to be united to somebody else. There is no such thing as somebody else. There is only you. The realization is always with oneself; it is never with anything or anyone else. It is the same thing as the first experience of the superconscious state. You find yourself in absolute omnipotence, in absolute light, in absolute magnificence, and there is no God to be found! It is shattering. One brings only bits and pieces of memories from it, and one tries to understand those states partially, very little. It takes years. I am twenty-five years at it and I still can't understand it well enough. But I know the more you meditate, the more silent you become. This is a fact. And what you have to say you can speak only in parables.

We start out, it seems, with a concept, an idea of God 'out there.' And then as we grow, and suffer, and struggle, and finally renounce our ideas and our concepts, we have the spiritual shock that it is not out there; it is within.

Yes. And it's here in this world, too. This life and the spiritual life are one and the same. But this is already a step on the path. At the beginning there is the world and there is something else to which we should aspire. But once we progress enough, we suddenly begin to realize that there are no such things as the world and the spiritual life, but that they are two sides of the same coin. There comes a time for every one of us when we are thrown back, as it is said, into the marketplace.

In *Zen Flesh Zen Bones* there is a description of being thrown back into the marketplace. One is amongst the people; one buys and one sells, and this life is then no different from the other. "Barefooted and naked of breast I mingle with the people of the world. My clothes are ragged and dust-laden, and I am ever blissful. I use no magic to extend my life. Now before me the trees become alive."[2]

Great Sufis have always been shoemakers, tailors, potters; they lived among people. Guruji said that in our tradition we are not allowed to go to the monastery or the cave or the forest to meditate by ourselves. We have to live in this world and to realize just the same when the light is closing tightly around us, because it is all the same. God is here, too.

What is this mystic joy that comes after many trials, tears, and struggles that seems to surpass any other joy?

The state of the soul, the plane of the soul, where the soul is, is pure joy. Joy is natural to our soul. When we reach a certain spiritual level, joy and tranquillity are ours. And here comes a great mystery. For all of us on the spiritual path, the first thing we experience is great peace. Joy comes afterwards. First you realize the self and then you realize God. First comes peace which surpasses understanding. It is like the depth of the ocean where there are no waves, but only absolute stillness. Then we realize God which is a void, frightening to the mind. But this void is absolute fulfillment; it is full of love for you, absolute love, unspeakable, absolute bliss.

And then after that nothing really matters. There is no man and no woman. Everything is one.

Irina Tweedie was born in Russia in 1907. She was educated in Vienna and Paris and moved to England at her marriage. After her husband's untimely death she eventually married again to a naval officer. Their happy life together also was shattered at his premature death in 1954, and Irina was plunged into despair and profound spiritual crisis. A friend introduced her to the Theosophical Society where she began the journey which eventually brought her to India at age 52 to the Sufi master who was to completely transform her life. At his instruction she recorded her training in extensive diaries which were to become the inspiration for thousands of readers around the world. At the death of her master in 1966 Irina returned to England where she devoted all her time to teaching, lecturing and conducting workshops. She worked as librarian for the Theosophical Society where she also carried on the spiritual mission given her by her teacher. Having celebrated her 80th birthday, Mrs. Tweedie continues her travels to Germany, Switzerland and the United States, where she speaks to large audiences. She welcomes students to her home in North London where she guides them with warmth, gentleness, and wisdom. Parts of her diary were published as *The Chasm of Fire* in 1979; the complete diary is newly published by Blue Dolphin under the title, *Daughter of Fire.*

I am the greatest truth of all, nothing beyond.
                                        Chandidas

Women and Mysticism

Bernadette Roberts

If we were to remove all mention of women from the history of the world's major religions, the history of these religions would not undergo the slightest change. If, on the other hand, we removed all mention of men from the history of the world's major religions, these religions would cease to exist. What the history of religion reveals is that the evolution or revelation of religious truths, philosophies, and theologies is no different today than if women had never existed, and that the presence of feminine mystics and holy women has never altered the course of religious history or changed its direction in any way. As an historical reality the absence of women in the evolution of religious revelation is a curious phenomena, and one of the questions it raises is the extent to which these religions truly reflect a feminine consciousness, its needs and goals.

That we have always assumed our religions were equally representative of the feminine psyche is an assumption that finds no footing in our religious histories. As solely representative of the masculine consciousness, what this history suggests is that we may not yet have the complete story of the human psyche in its encounter with the divine. Defining religion as both the quest for ultimate truth and the experiential revelation of that truth, [1] a totally masculine revelation poses the question of whether or not there is a difference in the way ultimate truth is experienced and interpreted by women and men respectively. As with any one-sided representation, our religious history leaves open the possibility there may be another side to truth, a side that may have been unrecognized, ignored, or otherwise judged incompatible with the masculine psyche. If there is another side, however, we cannot look to our religious histories to find it. History has posed the question; it does not answer it.

In searching for an explanation of our dominantly

masculine religions, there is at least one place we know NOT to look, and that is to the Godhead, Absolute or Ultimate Truth, which, being void of all distinctions, cannot be said to be either female or male. Being beyond distinctions, the divine would not account for any particularly male or female revelation, experience, or insight. While our religious history would seem to justify the belief (held by many) that revelation of the divine to the male psyche is proof of its predilection or affinity with a masculine God, this view not only contradicts an absolute without distinctions, but automatically excludes women from the possibility of a definitive revelation of the absolute, in which case religion would be a hopeless pursuit for women. But since we hold that the absolute transcends the distinction of gender and any combination thereof, we must look to something less than absolute to account for our masculine religions; look instead to that particular faculty in human beings that experiences the divine, namely, consciousness, self, or psyche. As the unique experiential faculty of all human beings, consciousness is not only responsible for our religions, but responsible for all distinctions and differences that we know of. In our view, the true distinction between men and women is one of consciousness. Thus our primary goal is to point out that particular factor in the psyche that best defines this difference. If there is no distinction between the masculine and feminine psyche, then we have no explanation for the masculine dominance of religion apart from a religiously based suppression of women.

Although it may be tempting to view the evolution of religious history in terms of an unconscious (or conscious) cultural view of women as inferior beings, this explanation does not really get to the heart of the matter. For one thing, this view is not justified by the facts of history; women may have been overlooked, but there is nothing to verify their actual suppression or silencing. Even if we insist on this notion we would still have to account for the reason underlying this suppression, account for its psychological and religious basis. Then too, without an intrinsic distinction between the masculine and feminine psyches there would be no reason why women were not equally represented in our religious histories and involved in the same areas of its evolution. But if we are dealing with two different psyches, and, as we will be pointing out, two different levels of religion, we move directly to the source of our psychological and religious differences, move beyond the merely conditioned level of consciousness to its unconditioned origins. Viewing our religious history in the light of an intrinsic distinction yields a different insight than if this history is viewed as an unconscious cultural suppression of women. Bringing to light the 'other side' of truth (other than the one generally represented by the masculine psyche) yields valuable insight into the nature of consciousness and the distinction between its masculine and feminine experience. Somehow the old argument that in the end truth must be the same for all is not very convincing when ultimate truth reveals itself to men only, or when men only have defined it, taught it, propagated it, are its sole authorities, and historically have defended it with outright wars. Those who do not find this a curious phenomena or who cannot question such a 'truth' should probably not read any further. We are addressing those who seriously question their past and present religious history, and who are open to the possibility of another side to truth, a side discoverable through the recognition of an intrinsic distinction between the masculine and feminine psyche.

The fact that this distinction has never been fully recognized for its religious implications or brought to the fore in our religious histories, does not mean that women have necessarily and whole-heartedly understood or endorsed the masculine revelation. On the contrary, their historical silence may indicate the opposite--namely, that they have never gone along with it. In the depths of their psyches they may never have been able to do so. The women mystics who appear in the pages of our religious histories could hardly be expected to differ with the predominant religious view when their very recognition was unconsciously dependent upon this conformity. Even then, women mystics had no position within their traditional religious framework. Thus if they saw anything that might have contradicted this framework, we can be certain not to have heard of it. (As the more illiterate members of society, they could hardly have checked up on what was being written about themselves).

At any rate, we are not accusing men of suppressing

a side of truth or revelation they do not know is there, or a side they may be incapable of grasping. On the contrary, we hold that the revelation of the divine to the feminine psyche may not be wholly understandable to the masculine consciousness, for which reason it has been largely ignored, not taken seriously, or simply brought into conformity with the masculine psyche. At the same time, the fact that the masculine mentality (along with its particular view of women, or ignorance of them), has dominated our religious histories, not only suggests the male's greater psychological need for dominance, but more importantly, suggests its greater need for religion. These two needs, religion and dominance, are not entirely unrelated, as our history reveals. What we have to face is the fact that any truth that must be vigorously guarded and defended has less to do with the divine than it does with the psyche's experiences and understanding of the divine. Thus while religion can rarely be reduced to the divine or absolute truth, with few exceptions it can almost always be reduced to the human psyche and the extent to which religion serves its needs and purposes. There is nothing the matter with this, of course, so long as religion is not exclusive in its services, or so long as it serves one and all without distinction. Whether or not our religions have done so, is one of the questions raised by its history. Our point is that the masculine psyche, which has dominated the religious scene, does not attest so much to the divine as it does to its own psyche--its particular mentality, needs, goals, and so on. But before we pursue this line of thought any further, we must first say something of what we mean by 'revelation' and how it is used in our present context.

As we know, revelation is always the experiential disclosure of the divine (truth or absolute; it has many names) to an individual subjective consciousness. We have no way of knowing, of course, if the experience of one human being is the same experience of another. We cannot get under each other's skin, and even if we could, we would immediately lose all knowledge and experience of ourselves--in which case we would be nothing ahead. At best, then, all we can speak of is the 'similarity' of our experiences without making claim to having had someone else's exact experience. Although we may say that every experience of the divine is a revelation of sorts, yet the notion of revelation usually centers on the disclosure of something new or previously unknown. Whether or not this disclosure is only new to the individual experiencer, or is a hitherto unknown truth pertaining to all mankind, is the usual drawing line between a private and universal revelation. As ultimate truth, a universal revelation would be unmixed with any masculine or feminine discriminatory elements because the divine is without discriminatory elements. Thus the particular gender of the experiencer would be a matter of total indifference. If we look carefully at our religious histories, however, we discover that universal truths of such a totally ageless, non-discriminative applicability are exceedingly rare--at least there are very few I know of. More often than not, what goes by the name 'divine revelation' bears the stamp of discriminative consciousness in some form or other in that it pertains solely to an individual consciousness (male or female) or to a particular religious, racial, or cultural group of people. Like the divine, however, the hallmark of universal truth would transcend all such discriminatory factors as well as the purely external, historical circumstances that would otherwise limit its applicability to all people. That we have few such truths indicates that somewhere along the line the medium has got in the way of the revelation. Looking at our religious histories, the absence of the feminine medium suggests that either universal truth has not revealed itself to woman, or that it's revelation has not been recognized, grasped, or understood by the masculine psyche. The reason for this we think is obvious: we are simply dealing with two distinct psyches; thus the feminine revelation may not have served the masculine interests and its view of how things should go, or 'be.' But whatever the reason for the dominance of the masculine revelation, one thing we know: women as the discoverers or revealers of universal truth will not be found in the pages of our religious histories.

So far we have only excluded the divine and its revelation as being devoid of any distinction of gender. We turn next to address the notion of a feminine-masculine distinction based on the differences of biological or sexual functioning. In our view, use of the biological argument is more suitable to the animal kingdom than it is to the human

human species, because it is an argument that need not include the human species at all. We cannot give priority to our animal nature when we know that human beings are unique by reason of consciousness, not by reason of what they have in common with animals, plants, and minerals. But the fallacy of the biological argument is that consciousness itself is responsible for the gender distinction--a distinction the animals know nothing about, or would be unable to argue from their purely sensory way of knowing. Left to themselves, the senses know nothing of the biological or sexual distinctions consciousness has made possible to the human mind. Not only is consciousness the primary distinction between man and animal, but consciousness is the faculty responsible for this very distinction, and all distinctions, for that matter. In other words, consciousness is our human distinction as well as our distinguisher. This is why the search for our human differences must be grounded in our purely human uniqueness, and why the only true distinction we can speak of--between male and female--centers on consciousness and not on our animal or vegetative differences.

Unfortunately, when we turn to the study of consciousness what we find is that here too, knowledge of the feminine psyche has been the historical product of the masculine psyche--a psyche that has never had the immediate feminine experience. That men have put themselves up as authorities on the feminine psyche is the most naive form of dishonesty I have ever heard of. What we have to face again and again in all honesty is the fact we can never have one another's experiences, and that what men and women know of one another is based solely on their continuous interaction and relationships. Our knowledge of one another is always outside-in; never inside-out. (Strictly speaking this one-way phenomena attests to the absolute One of the divine that can never create or give rise to two absolutely identical things, even psyches). But if we object to men as authorities of the feminine psyche, we have to admit that until women find their own unique expression in large number and over a period of time, our masculine religious and psychological assumptions will continue to be unconsciously accepted as the only truth there is. To open up new possibilities we need to develop a new eye on old and deeply imbedded religious psychological notions, a uniquely feminine eye capable of divining those traditional assumptions that may not be working for the feminine consciousness, or that strike it as not applicable, or simply as not true. It takes a profound spiritual maturity and self-knowledge to do this.

Although on its more superficial or conscious level the psyche is largely conditioned by its cultural milieu, yet on its deeper unconscious level, consciousness itself is the maker of this milieu. As the mind's inherent discriminator or reflexive mechanism, consciousness creates our social, religious, philosophical paradigms, histories, and cultures. Thus we have to be careful, aware, alert, and responsible for every idea we espouse or reject because this acceptance or rejection will condition the consciousness that creates our cultural environment. So long as consciousness remains, nobody can escape this conditioning. All we can do is examine it and be responsible for it. At the same time, we have to realize that it is the inherent unconscious function of reflexive consciousness to make the divine into its own image and likeness. Although this truth has been cleverly turned around to read that man is created in the image and likeness of God, yet we know that God has no image or likeness and thus, ultimately, neither would man--a fact that would seem to topple the argument. But the paradox of the great image-maker (consciousness) is that this reversal--man made in the image of the divine--is a necessary illusion without which there would be no quest for ultimate truth. If on some rudimentary level of consciousness human beings were not assured of an affinity with the divine, they would not bother to pursue the true nature of this affinity.[2] And without this pursuit, no one can hope to overcome the illusions that consciousness puts in the way of ultimate truth. At one and the same time then, consciousness or self is a great reality and a great illusion-maker, which means our human journey is both a passage through consciousness as well as its gradual unmasking. It is only at the end of the passage, with no illusions remaining, that the illusion-maker falls away. But in the meantime, so long as consciousness remains, it has no choice but to bring its experiences of the divine into its own dimension of knowing and experiencing. In this way, the Absolute that is All and Everywhere is brought into focus and experienced as personally subjective, an experience that is both satisfying and self-serving to consciousness. The phenomena of consciousness is nothing less than the phenomena of the divine at the service of human beings. But as to those for whom this invention has been most self-serving, well that is the story of our religious histories.

But if we can understand how and why reflexive consciousness makes the divine into its own image and likeness, we can get some understanding of why certain cultural views of the divine are reflective of a masculine mentality and its particular way of knowing and feeling. We note, for example, that the divine is often portrayed with masculine attributes, behaviors, judgments, feelings, and so on; and how it always has a curious way of setting up a social order of some kind. Whether this order is that of a religious hierarchy, a caste system, or a privileged religious, racial, or cultural group of people, underlying this order is the implicit (sometimes explicit) understanding that women are either inferior to men or subject to them. It amounts to the same thing. It is mind-boggling to consider how much there is in our world religions that has always been unconsciously (or consciously) self-serving to the masculine psyche. That our traditional views have been solely representative of its intellect and vision is not a happy matter when we consider that these views have been taken as absolute truth--truth on which men and women have staked their lives. But the fact that our traditional views of the divine or ultimate truth can be traced to the masculine psyche is not our major concern; rather our concern is that these views are void of any feminine representation. What difference this makes, or could make, is the question posed by our religious histories.

Earlier we stated that the total dominance of the masculine revelation points to the male's greater need for religion. To discover the psychological factor underlying this greater need we propose to look at the distinctive religious goals that the masculine psyche has envisioned for its ultimate fulfillment. As expressive of man's psychological deficits and needs, religious goals not only explain man's religions, but explain his psyche--how he experiences himself or sees himself. Thus as the vision of perfection and fulfillment, our religious goals are a revelation and expression of consciousness itself; I would even say that our religious goals are the single most important clue we have regarding the true nature of consciousness. In looking over our religious histories I find the following goals to be universally held in common: the experiential realization of oneness with the absolute or ultimate truth; transcendence of the ego or a condition sometimes called 'selflessness'; an unbounded compassion, love, and charity that is capable of giving without receiving, or the ability to give without any egoic return. To truly attain any one of these, of course, is to attain them all. Although these goals are testimony to a common human heritage and its vision of ultimate fulfillment, we must nevertheless question the degree to which these goals reflect similar feminine deficits and needs. Observation does not bear out an equal degree of feminine egoic self-centeredness, which self-centeredness is always proportional to the experiential absence of the divine. Also, in general at least, we do not find women noteworthy for a lack of genuine compassion, or the inability to give selflessly, or to serve others in a most hidden and non-gratifying way. Nor can we assume that women have ever felt themselves truly separate from the divine, or separate from a profound inner center of strength that they somehow know or intuit is beyond themselves. The definition of 'ego' as a sense of separateness--separate from the divine, from nature, from other people--is a masculine definition expressive of its own experience; an experience, I am convinced, that is not equally reflective of the feminine psyche. That the stronger feminine sense of oneness has been cited as evidence of a more 'primitive psyche' or a 'pre-conscious' condition, is just another egoic ruse for assuming ascendancy. But my point is this: the attributes men prize, the goals they aspire to attain through their religious framework, are attributes innate in the feminine psyche--attributes, in fact, that best define the feminine psyche. This does not mean women do not have to strive to perfect a native endowment, or that they have no ego, but it does mean that they experience far less problem in transcending the ego, and less need to go outside themselves to do so. Thus the need for intellectual thought and instruction, interpretation, authority, rules and regulation, rigorous ascetics, rituals and practices--perhaps ninety percent of what we know as 'religion'--are inventions of the masculine psyche and reflective of its own needs. We do not question the validity of these needs and the path it has mapped out for itself, what we question is the extent to which they are equally reflective of the feminine psyche, its needs and goals, and the path it must take.

Putting aside what may be regarded as merely a personal observation, let us look at our religious histories, look at all history in fact, to see if there is any truth to the observation we are making. What history reveals is that the male's native aggressive need for dominance has been problematic from the beginning. Religion is the recognition of this problem, for which reason it addresses itself to the need for discipline and ultimate transcendence of the problematic ego. Without this, there can be no lasting peace, no true relationship between human beings, and even no ultimate salvation. But if the religious goal of transcending the ego is both admirable and imperative for the masculine psyche, what about women? What is their true relationship to religion, or their place in its general scheme of things?

Although we hold that men have a greater need for religion, we also hold that women are more innately or naturally religious, for which reason they unconsciously gravitate to its more profound level, a level that men must work to realize with greater diligence and conscious striving. In simple terms, women are natively more at home in the transcendent areas of religion, while men have the greater tendency to remain on the more superficial levels of religious involvement. As less native to men, it is always a greater fete, of course, when the masculine consciousness breaks through to the transcendent level, which is why we hear more about the masculine breakthrough and why, even today, it is the 'holy men' of our various religions who articulate and propagate the transcendent levels of their respective religions.

While women have no trouble understanding the masculine breakthrough, they are somewhat at a loss to understand its earth-shaking momentousness. In other words, the masculine breakthrough acts to point out much of what women have unconsciously taken for granted; while, at the same time, this breakthrough tells us what men have never been able to take for granted in their own psyches. For women, being faced everywhere they turn with the totally masculine example and authority as well as its particular path, the response is the rather eloquent silence we meet with in our religious histories. While finding themselves in accord with the transcendent level, they may not, however, find themselves in accord with the path and its particular perspective. Here I am reminded of certain feminine Christian mystics who suffered unnecessarily because they felt bound to bring their experiences of the divine into conformity with the traditional masculine view of how these experiences should be understood, interpreted, articulated, and so on. With these impossible and dishonest demands put on her, a woman simply retires into silence--a silence that, unfortunately, has been regarded as total agreement or humble submission. But as we have said, the historical silence of women cannot be construed as whole-hearted agreement or endorsement of the masculine perspective. We see other reasons for this silence, reasons that have yet to be brought to light. As things stand, however, it is thanks to the masculine breakthrough into the transcendental level that we have any recognition at all of women in our religious histories; without the masculine breakthrough there would be no mention or recognition of women having attained the ultimate masculine goal.

As we can see, religion can cut two ways or act as a double-edged sword. On its more superficial level it can become a vehicle for sheer egoic dominance and a vehicle for keeping everyone in their place. On its more profound, contemplative and mystical level, religion can be the vehicle for overcoming or transcending this same ego and its need for a pecking order. For women, this sword has historically only cut one way. Where we meet outstanding women in our religious histories is on its most profound and transcendent level. We do not meet them on the superficial level of egoic involvement or where the power struggle goes on. Thus one reason for the absence of women in our religious histories is this history's involvement in the more superficial levels of religion. While this may be more native to the masculine psyche, it is not the home ground of feminine consciousness. Clearly, our religious histories testify to the presence of two very different psyches and two very different levels of religion--the egoic and the transcendent.

When we turn to consciousness to find the origin or cause of these different levels, what is needed first of all is a complete overview of consciousness. As our unique human experience and way of knowing, consciousness is a multifaceted system that can be studied from a number of perspectives--from the purely physiological to the meta-physical on into the unknown. In these few pages, however, we cannot hope to cover this ground. Thus what follows is primarily focused on the phenomena or experience we call the 'ego.' As I see it, the more dominant male ego accounts for the major distinction between the feminine and masculine psyche; and, in turn, the transcendence or non-transcendence of the ego accounts for the two different levels we find present in our various religions.

As the unique property of all human beings, consciousness, on its most basic level of structure and function, is no different for men than it is for women. As the reflexive mechanism of the mind, consciousness is the mind's ability to bend back on itself, and in this unconscious action the mind not only knows itself but, at the same time, puts its subjective stamp on all incoming sensory data. Without this subjective stamp the intellect could not develop. In the developmental process this stamp is increasing colored with cultural perceptions, values, and judgments which play a large part in conditioning either a masculine or feminine consciousness. But the reflexive mechanism, which IS the knowing-self, is only one side of the coin; the other side of consciousenss is an entirely different dimension of experience, a side we know as the 'feeling self.' While this side is not reducible to the reflexive mechanism, it nevertheless functions in conjucntion with it to compose the entire experiential field of consciousness and its unitary functioning. Together the knowing and feeling self make up our entire human dimension of experience. It is in the particular dimension of the feeling self, however, that I find the major distinction between a masculine and feminine consciousness.

The unconscious action of the reflexive mechanism sets up the subject-object poles of consciousness, responsible for the object-self and the subject-self. [3] But in this same unconscious action of knowing itself (which is a looking into itself), the mind automatically gravitates to a mysterious 'point' in consciousness where the subject-object self converge to a single non-dual experience. It is at this point of convergence that we experience the origin and essence of the feeling self. The most profound and subtle experience of this point or feeling self is one of simple 'being' or 'life'--feeling being or life center. We call this experiential point the 'center' of consciousness; and from this center there arises various experiences of energy, will power, emotionality, and other subtle feelings. This center is also responsible for the experience of psychological and spiritual interiority, a sense of within and without, and the feeling of being a discrete entity or separate physical form. Altogether this center gives rise to a pervasive experience of life--psychic, spiritual, and physical life--and this all pervasive experience IS the feeling self. Prior to its falling away, shattering, or transcendence, this center of consciousness is what I call the ego. Although in the developmental process this experience (feeling self) takes on an increasingly masculine or feminine expression, we must remember that the experience itself is prior to its cultural expression, which expression varies from culture to culture. In other words, consciousness or the feeling self gives rise to culture and its religions. It is not the other way around.

What I call 'ego' then, is the initial center of self or consciousness which, in experience, is the will or self-energy unconsciously centered on itself. What irreversibly initiates the transforming process is the sudden falling away of this center (a shattering that is painful to the will) and the subsequent encounter with a void in its stead. This hole or void in the center of consciousness effects the totality of consciousness--every aspect of the knowing, feeling self--to bring about a totally new type of aware-ness, a radical change of consciousness. From here on there can be no will or self energy (ego) centered in or on itself. Instead all is centered in the divine. Adjusting to this event is the journey to the bottom or innermost center of our being or void, also the highest center, where the divine reveals itself as our abiding true center and the center of all that exists. From here on, the unconscious reflexive mechanism of the mind not only bends back on itself, but also bends back on the divine, the true center that has replaced the ego center. At this point of realiza-tion we also learn, solely in retrospect, the difference between the ego-self and the true-self, the old man and the new man as the masculine saying goes. But just as we do not know the ego-self until it is gone, so too, we cannot possibly know the true nature of the true-self until it, too, is gone. First, however, we must realize the true self in its oneness with the divine, and live it thoroughly in the ordinary events of life, before this oneness--self and the divine--can ultimately fall away, which falling away is comparable to Christ's own death. But since this final death heralds the end of our human journey or the end of our passage through consciousness, it is not our present concern. Rather, our first concern is to come into our mature state of oneness or transcendence of the ego, for it is only after living this egoless state to its ultimate completion that we can even begin to discuss our final eternal state or ultimate human destiny.

Our view of the ego, defined as self-centeredness or as self-will unconsciously focused on itself, is different from 'ego' as it is defined, say, in the Hindu tradition or in the psychological paradigm of Carl Jung. For the Hindu the ego is the 'jiva' or individual self that has not yet realized its oneness with the divine, or realized its true identity as the divine. This ego or individual separate self lasts only so long as this realization is absent. But once realized, all experiences of an individual self as separate from the divine or separate from anything else that exists, simply falls away. Thus for the Hindu, the realized or transcendent state is void of ego, individual self, or jiva. For Jung, on the other hand, the true individual self only emerges in the transformed state. Here the ego (which Jung regards as the totality of self-consciousness) is united or integrated with self (the totality of the unconscious). In this view the ego never falls away because it is responsible for all man consciously knows about himself. It is the totality of reflective self-consciousness as distinct from the unconscious or all man does not know about himself, or has yet to learn. Thus what Jung identifies as ego--the totality of reflective self-consciousness--the Hindu identifies as a false or illusory condition or state of consciousness. For the Hindu 'true' self-consciousness is more in the order of 'feeling-being' rather than the mind's reflexive mechanism, which seems to be Jung's sole notion of self-consciousness. For the Hindu, true self-consciousness is divine consciousness--the experience of divine Being, which divine Being IS itself, consciousness.

What Jung only vaguely got hold of or missed altogether, is the fact that self-consciousness is present in the unconscious before it ever rises to the level of consciousness. Thus true self-consciousness is on the unconscious level of the psyche, and not merely on its conscious level. What this means is that the entire system of consciousness, all its levels including the conscious (ego) and unconscious (self), IS self-consciousness. Man's entire experience of psyche or consciousness is the experience of self on some level or other. This fact not only accounts for the continuity of consciousness across its various levels, but tells us that self-consciousenss goes right on whether we are aware of it (on the conscious level) or not. In a word, nothing can be said of consciousness that cannot be said of self, and all self words are but expressions of this uniquely functional experience we call 'consciousness.'

At first sight the crux of the difference between the Hindu and Jungian view of ego seems to lie in their different view of the individual. Where the Hindu means the experience of an entity separate from the divine, Jung means the experience of an entity who has realized its oneness with the divine, symbolically, at least. The difference is not merely semantic, however. Everything depends upon the articulation of their respective experiences. Thus, for example, I did not encounter any recognizable experience of the divine in Jung's writings, but did, in fact, recognize this experience in certain Hindu texts. For the Hindu, Self is the divine in subjective experience and the only uniquely 'One' there is--not to be confused with the experience of the egoic one or individual. For Jung, on the other hand, neither the unconscious self nor any aspect of consciousness is regarded as truly divine; at best it can only symbolize the divine. In fact, Jung never admitted to any divine at all, even beyond consciousness. All told, we cannot honestly compare his definition of ego and self with that of the Hindu, when by definition and experience, they are not speaking of the same thing. The lesson, of course, is that we must be careful about brushing off our differences as 'merely semantic' when truth lies in the different experiences that underlie the use of similar words.

At any rate, my view of ego is somewhat different from both of the above. While I hold that the entire system of consciousness is the essence and true nature of self, yet I hold that it is not divine, but like everything else that exists, consciousness is also not separate from the divine. Consciousness is that human faculty or function that brings an otherwise infinite all-pervasive divine into focus and centers it in experience of 'being.' Without this faculty, the divine would not be a specific experience; it could not be focused on within or without. In fact it could not be known to the human mind at all. While I do not agree with Jung that the ego is responsible for our entire sense of self or self-consciousness, I agree that the ego is the immature, superficial center of consciousness. And while I concur with the Hindu view that the true center underlying the ego is the divine (and not merely the unconscious or 'self' as defined by Jung) I do not agree that the ego is an illusion of a separate self. On the contrary, if prior to the realized or transcendental condition the ego has not already experienced, glimpsed, or intuited its oneness with the divine, it would not go in search of its perfect realization. Thus it is neither accurate nor sufficient to define the ego as the experience of separateness when, in fact, the ego may have continuous unitive experiences prior to its own permanent dissolution in the realization of oneness.

In the yin and yang theory we have the view that consciousness is composed of two different energies, and that the best of all possible lives is to live with these two energies in perfect balance. As I see it, however, consciousness can only be a single energy--single in its origin and its ending--but which, in turn, can generate a number of different experiences of energy. If we call the singular feminine energy the 'yin,' and the distinctive masculine energy the 'yang,' we can understand how these two energies were discoverable: by the sheer contrast of men and women in their encounter with one another. So long as we are the living embodiment of an energy we can only take it for granted, but when we meet with a dissimilar energy, then we can no longer take our own experience or energy for granted. Thus it is in the encounter and relationship between men and women that we not only recognize our own distinct energy but recognize the 'other' type as well, and the difference between the two. Without denying the attraction between these two energies or the fact they can learn from one another, we deny that these energies can ever be experientially exchanged or shared. What balance can be achieved between them is soley on the basis of the feminine-masculine relationship; and however useful this may be in the process of realizing our identity, it can never constitute that identity. Those who rely on the feminine-masculine relationship for their identity will sooner or later be left with no ground to stand on, for in the process of discovering the true self we must surrender all relationships through which this identity was hitherto known. Only the divine can give us our new identity.

As a specific energy, or as consciousness' own experience of itself, the yin and yang are innately distinct. Even after the transforming process, when consciousness has attained what many people consider to be its highest state--transcendental, unitive, or God-consciousness--this distinction remains. The unique balance achieved in this transcendent state, however, is not between two opposite energies, but between a single unified energy (individual consciousness) and the divine. In contrast to the experience of consciousness, which is the experience of energy, experience of the divine is one of 'no-energy.' Thus the unitive or transcendental condition is the balance between a positive and negative experience of energy, where the divine (no-energy) curtails the egoic energy of consciousness by the sheer void or non-existence of that egoic energy. Thereafter it is the void or no-feeling that keeps the feeling self from exceeding its proper mean, or keeps it from experiencing excessive passion, desires, and so on.

It is important to keep in mind that, in experience, the divine is a 'still-point,' not an energy point. The experience of energy is always and everywhere our 'self'--consciousness or psyche. The notion that the divine is energy or consciousness is just another example of consciousness making the divine into its own image and likeness. Although the divine truly touches upon consciousness and moves it, this movement belongs to consciousness. We might liken the divine to a stone thrown into the quiet pond of consciousness. The stone moves the waters, but the moving waters are not the stone. The cause is not the effect. The illusionmaker, however, has always tended to mistake the moving waters for the divine and to believe that its experience of the divine is the divine. But this is why the falling away of the illusion-maker or consciousness is equally the falling away of the divine. When, at the end of our journey, consciousness or self falls away, the first thing known is that all the experiences we had believed to be the divine, was only the self. This is a shocking revelation, but also a great truth that is revealed.

Because our present interest in the ego is its expression in a religious context, we will assume that the ego has chosen to pursue the greatest good it knows or experiences, which is the divine or ultimate truth. Right off, one of the first mistakes we make is the religious belief that this whole-hearted turning to the divine is all that is required, or that having set our hearts and minds on the divine we are therefore automatically relieved of the ego and its totally self-centered existence. Until the divine has shattered the ego, however, or shattered this energy in pursuit of its own desires and its own vision of the divine, we are still unconsciously wearing our religion on our sleeve--it is still superficial and self-serving.

Unfortunately the vast majority of 'religious people' spend their lives on this egoic level of religion and consciousness. What happens when there is no transformation is all very subtle: unknowingly the ego uses religion to preserve itself, defend itself, change the world for itself, and thus religion becomes the servant of the ego, its cloak and its mask. This is the most powerful position the ego can possibly assume, because it is all in the name of the divine and ultimate truth. And other people believe it. Once again, we have to face the historical fact that religion can be as destructive to human beings as it can be helpful. The difference depends on which way the sword cuts, whether the ego is transcended or not.

The reason so few religious people go through the transforming process is because it is obviously not self-serving to do so. After some well intended beginnings, the ego finds religion so comfortable, secure, and self-rewarding that it sells out to this beginner's level and goes no further. Thus there is no transformation, and no true religion. We need not detail how this lack of egoic transformation and transcendence has affected our religious histories; with one exception, it is the whole of this history. The one area of exception is the contemplative dimension of egoic transcendence, which alone represents the truth and profound depths of religion. We do not hear about this dimension in our churches and temples, however. Those who run them not only find this dimension personally threatening, but the idea of common people getting hold of this profound dimension is often viewed as threatening to the status quo. The unspoken fear, of course, is that the experiential revelation of the divine to subjective consciousness will somehow contradict the traditional belief system. In this matter, not even the divine is to be trusted to get it right. For this reason experiences of the divine beyond the egoic level (sentiment, devotion, emotionality, and so on) are often regarded as suspect and out of the ordinary line up--not wholly to be trusted, in other words.

One egoic ruse that keeps us from aspiring to the contemplataive dimensions is the view that this dimension is a special gift of the divine (or a special placement of birth, as in the Eastern religions), given to a few privileged souls or saints. By putting the transcendent dimension and its saints on a pedestal and out of reach, religion can otherwise maintain a common mental, experiential dimension, the one-dimensional level so typical and indicative of egoic consciousness. Another ruse is the view that contemplatives live in a world of their own beyond the pale of ordinary society; their lives are often seen as selfish, antisocial, and therefore useless to anybody but themselves. This myth is contradicted, of course, by the fact we would not have heard of the profound transcendent level of our religions if these people had not stepped forward to help others realize the same. That there is no value for the 'unseen' or for what cannot be tangibly demonstrated, is a paradox of the egoic level of religion.

But whatever the ruse or rationalization used, the outcome invariably works to maintain the egoic level at all costs. We must not think, however, that this is done consciously or with mal-intent. On the contrary, the ego is ignorance personaified. Egoic consciousness is not something apart from ourselves or something we can put our finger on within ourselves. Rather the ego is the entire (immature) personality and consciousness, everything we know about ourselves--our entire experience. Thus so long as we are living it, we cannot possibly know anything of an 'egoic self.' All we have to go on is the recognition that all is not perfect within ourselves, a recognition that should clue us in to the necessity of going deeper within to find a more perfect dimension of existence. That so few realize it is absolutely imperative for every human being to make this journey attests to the failure of our religions. What presently attests to Christianity's failure in this matter are the many Christians looking to the Eastern religions to provide this contemplative or transcendent dimension. Few of these people have had any idea that a comparable dimension exists within Christianity. While I am happy for those who find their needs being met in the East, this does not make me happy with Christianity.

Putting together what we have said so far, it should be obvious that the absence of women in our religious histories is no great loss. That women have not been involved on the more superficial or egoic levels of their respective religions is indicative of the difference between the masculine and feminine psyches. We really cannot ask what our religious histories might have been (or would be today), if women were equally represented on the masculine level of power and authority. The fact that they are not so represented speaks for itself. Needless to say, if there is no distinction between psyches then our religious histories would have had equal feminine representation, in which case no distinction could have been made in this area. Then too, we have to understand that it does not matter who is in a position of authority--man or woman--if this fact in no way changes our history, or if positions of authority are more disastrous than helpful. In other words, merely to substitute a feminine figure for a masculine figure would net us nothing. What the feminine psyche reveals is that the most profound level of religion has no need for dominance in any form, and that, as a matter of religious history and significance, the silence of the feminine consciousness speaks eloquently for religions's sole validity--its transcendent level.

One more point: while consciousness is responsible for our religions, our religions in turn are responsible for conditioning consciousness. It is imperative to be aware of this circular phenomena and to understand how it works. We must be sure to derive our religion from its original wellsprings, that is, from the unconditioned depths of our own experience of the divine, and not from a conditioned level of consciousness or any secondary source. Change on the conditioned level is merely the presence of a new idea or insight, which is incapable of bringing about true change or of having any lasting effects. But change on the unconditioned level where consciousness emerges from the divine and eventually dissolves into it involves an irreversible change, one that moves outward like ripples on a pond to effect us all--effect us in its own way and at its own profound level. On the surface it would appear that religion has been the cause of war, unrest, and the lack of peace in the world. But if we look deeper, we find no religion there at all. Instead, what we find is religion being used as the excuse, the mask, and the facade for the warring, domineering, authoritative ego.

While women cannot change this fact, which would take an act of God, they can nevertheless be mediums of the divine in pointing up the transcendent, non-egoic, contemplative, and mystical depths that alone is the sole essence of true religion. Short of this depth, all we can do is aspire and pray to become religious people.

Bernadette Roberts has searched for answers to ultimate questions since childhood when her interior experiences seemed to have nothing to do with the Christian beliefs in which she was raised. At fifteen she experienced a breakthrough; she realized that Christ's own interior experience was the experience of God and not merely of himself. From that point on, her own journey was one of duplicating Christ's experiences of life with God.

At seventeen she entered a Discalced Carmelite monastery where she remained for eight and a half years. She left the monastic life because the interior journey was finished: "you cannot go deeper than the deepest" and because the interior movement had turned around to go outward to embrace the wholeness of human existence, this world, and the divine.

Bernadette received a degree in philosophy and taught in high school. Later she received a master's degree in Early Childhood Education. Along with the addition of Montessori credentials and four children of her own, she established an 'experimental preschool' that duplicated Piaget's developmental tasks and Montessori's initial educational experiment. She ended her teaching career in 1975 teaching Child Development in a junior college.

In 1978 Bernadette had what she called 'the experience of no-Self,' which was the dissolution of both the divine and the phenomenal self experience. It was the end of the unitive state she realized in the monastic years. Because she could not find an account of this event in the contemplative literature of her own tradition or in those of the Eastern traditions, she wrote two books: *The Experience of No-Self* and *The Path to No-Self.*

*I found God in myself
and I loved her,
I loved her fiercely.*
            Ntozake Shange

Navia: The Voice of Prophet Woman

Rabbi Lynn Gottlieb

They drink wine in bowls
Annoint themselves in oil
But they are not grieved over
   the ruin of (my people) Yosef.

                              Amos

There arise generations and times in which the nature
of our existence undergoes yet another revelation of consciousness. As the scientist reveals the cosmos, as the
artist reveals the imagination, as the psychologist reveals
the workings of the hidden mind, so the prophet reveals
the nature of justice in her time.

Within the Way of the Nameless Mystery, Jewish tradition believes there is a Caring whose manifestation is
the prophetic voice. The prophet is one who illuminates
the core message emanating from the Caring: we are commanded, called, summoned, moved to lead lives grounded
in love and justice. The call to love *(hesed)* and justice
(tzedek) is a vision of humanity which can transform violence and oppression, greed and hatred into gentleness and
equality, generosity and compassion.

Love and justice are synonymous; they are two sides
of the same whole. That whole, or *shalom,* is peace. Love
and justice balance each other. They are both considered
a sacred obligation on the daily path of peace. The obligation to love and justice require certain behavior. To love
is to act justly. To love is not to oppress the poor, or the
stranger, or the less privileged in society. To love is not
to bear false witness, or stand idly by while one's neighbor's blood is being shed, or withhold the wages of a day
worker until morning. Love is manifested through deeds of
righteousness. Justice, which is required for peace, is

understand as the right of every member in society to a
certain economic base which includes the right to own
land, and the right to maintain the land of one's ancestors
throughout time.

The prophet, in Jewish tradition, is a person extremely sensitive to these commandments. The prophet is sensitive
to spiritual insensitivity. For within the prophet lies an
open heart, a heart which is not afraid to touch pain and
suffering, a heart which is called to make things right, a
heart which rages against the devastation of human lives
caused by evil and ignorance. This rage is not merely
word, but also action. The prophet is not passive; she lives
on the streets. In the midst of the people. And she speaks,
speaks with a poet's voice drawing on the words of the
people.

The love of the prophet for the people is a theology
of ultimate concern, and a theology of hope. Because the
prophet loves life and trusts in the power of the spirit to
heal, the prophet counsels against war, against violence.

> Not by might and not by power, but by spirit alone shall
> all people become free.   Zecharia

The centrality of justice as the measure of love in
Jewish tradition derives from our experience as slaves in
ancient Egypt. Because of the suffering of that generation
we are commanded to remember what it is like to be
oppressed, and so to develop an ongoing sensitivity and responsibility to maintain a society based on justice.

> When a stranger sojourns with you in your land, you shall
> not do him wrong. The stranger who sojourns with you
> shall be as the native among you, and you shall love him
> as yourself, for you were strangers in the land of Mitz-
> ryim.   Exodus 22:21

Finding Women's Voices

History, as life, is not static. A people's fate can
change, sometimes for the better, sometimes for the worse.
And so the dialogue about the meaning of justice must
continue to be a sacred obligation. Jewish tradition pre-
serves this dialogue through the yearly celebration of
Passover. We are required to tell our children about Yitziat

Mizryim, the liberation from ancient Egypt, as if we ourselves were slaves. We must be able to show a sensitivity to the meaning of suffering, and an understanding of redemption, and be able to apply them to issues of injustice facing us in our current lives. Who plays the role of Pharoah today? And who are the midwives who resist oppression and initiate the struggle for freedom?

When the word prophet is spoken, images of Isaiah, Jeremiah, Ezekiel, Amos, and others spring to mind. In this work we reflect upon the spiritual voice of prophet woman. Who was she? Never canonized into a book proper, how do we find her? Who are the women who express the value of ultimate concern? Who are the women who see through the conventions and beliefs and power structures of the privileged classes of their time to the passionate call for justice?

It is already recognized that most women in the world suffer from the institutionalization of male privilege in all spheres of life. This state is commonly known as patriarchy. Jewish women have and still do suffer from this oppression as well. Institutionalized privilege does not easily surrender its power. For the most part, the official interpretors of Jewish law and custom have been men. Women were not permitted to legislate, to give witness in court, to be counted in official prayer quorems (a daily aspect of traditional male Jewish culture), to read from the Torah in public (from Talmudic times, because of the supposed offense to male honor), to initiate divorce, or to sing around men (because it might arouse their lust). Our role was limited. We were designated as nurturers and providers for the family. We did not have time for the scholarly pursuit engaged in by the men. This inheritance of segregation continued to recent times. Within the last one hundred years, and especially in the last twenty, Jewish women have managed a revolution in custom. We now enjoy full sacred status in all but Orthodox Jewish communities. As we integrate ourselves into the realm of the sacred, we ask ourselves: What is the nature of the sacred way of Jewish women?

The Prophetic Voice of Women

The impulse to freedom and the liberation of human

potential is in itself part of the prophetic impulse to justice, and so forms part of the content of the female prophetic voice. As we create an open place for ourselves, part of our work is healing the wounds caused by such a long history of oppression. Healing of the wounds is part of the peace-making process. How do we heal our wounds?

So many women feel invisible. Our story is not told. We open the pages of our sacred texts and we read mostly about the lives of men. The prophet is a woman who breaks the silence of history by speaking women's names into the void. Healing is performed by giving ourselves a past, a sense of where we came from. Knowing our past gives us homelands from which to grow the future. The past gives root to our souls, helps ground our spirits in women's evolutionary herstory, and puts us in touch with women's knowledge and adventure throughout time. Yet how do we find our past? Where do we look for prophet woman?

In search of prophet-woman we must draw on many tools of research: historical, literary, anthropological, archeological, and linguistic. We look both to primary sources within the tradition, and we also make cross-cultural comparisons, looking to the voice of prophet-woman in other traditions. In this work, I would like to examine the role of the prophet-women who were part of the Exodus tale: the midwives Serach, Yohevet, and Miriam. In this context, it is important to understand how much Jewish tradition honors oral tradition. While the Torah is considered the classical and 'authoritative' sacred text, nonetheless it is said that both the written and the oral traditions were given to the people at the moment of revelation. The oral tradition has come to include post- and pre-Biblical legends and laws.

Every generation is commanded to interpret the Torah. In this process of interpretation, meaning is clarified, deepened, expanded upon, illuminated from the shadows and implications in the text which we discover from our own perspective as we also ground ourselves in traditional meaning. The Torah is spiderwoman--unfolding her web of meaning in each generation. The changing tapestry of tales, prayers, and customs is alive and a sign of the vitality of the people. So we turn toward the past, and begin our journey to uncover the voice of prophet-woman in the Exodus tale. Who was prophet-woman of ancient times?

Prophet Woman in Early Israel

Jewish men did not invent the patriarchy, but they participated in its rise, long ago. Patriarchy began to dominate the world scene some time around the year 5000 BCE. Patriarchy spawned many forms, bore many societies through its head, and gradually replaced the predominant world religion which preceeded it by 30,000 years. Before the origins of the warrior kings, we find evidence that wherever people left artifacts, they worshipped the Great Goddess, the Lady of Infinite Forms. Called by a thousand names, her icons are everywhere. She is associated with the rise of humanity to consciousness. In those times women were highly honored because of their ability to speak in her name. A woman was called prophet, or seer, when she performed certain roles. The prophet was an interpreter of dreams and events, a counselor to the people, and to rulers of people. She proclaimed judgments and settled conflicts; upon her rested decisions of war and peace. As prophet-woman she led the people in celebration and lament. She was a poet; she sang the history of her people, she sang praises to the Mother of Life. As prophet-woman she presided in a holy shrine, keeping watch over eternal fires, teaching the young her craft, creating disciples for the future; she practiced the art of envisioning and making peace.

Prophet-women existed among the early Israelites. They were women of power. Devorah, Hulda, Miriam, the wise women of Avel, and Serach all give testimony to the prsence of the female prophetic voice within early Jewish culture and tradition. It is difficult to know exactly how and when women lost their former prophetic status. We know that women held positions of power that were later denied them. It seems likely that women began to lose their ancient tribal powers with the onset of the Israelite monarchy. Saul persecuted women spiritualists. Over time women's spirituality was viewed as demonic and fearsome. The lives and memories of women of power were erased from history. Only traces remain. Yet from those traces we can begin to reimage women's place in pre-patriarchal times. It is an act of historical irony that Jewish women are led to the forbidden icons and foreign tales to gain a fuller understanding of our own heroines. By knowing, for instance, that Queen Bee is an epithet of the Goddess, we can better understand the meaning in the name Devorah, which means "queen bee." Devorah was probably not a proper name, but a title of a woman who served as chief prophet: Devorah, or Queen Bee, who sat on Mount Tabor, Navel Mountain. The mountain, too, is a sacred realm of the Goddess, her navel leading to the underworld. She sat under a palm tree, a tree held sacred by practitioners of Goddess religion. And she was keeper of the fires: Eshet Lapidot. When we see how women from other cultures shared and performed the tasks held by Devorah, we can begin to contemplate her true place among the Israelites, and also begin to get a sense of her spirituality and the spiritual meaning of culture rooted in positive female imagery.

Creating a Tale

In this work I would like to offer a poem called Navia, or Prophet Woman. This poem draws on traditions and images from ancient Goddess religions as positive sources of women's spirituality. This poem also draws on the Jewish sense of justice as it is related in the Exodus story, and as it has become the ongoing heart message of Jewish sacred tradition. As a preface to the poem, I would like to include information on each of the prophetic personas which compose the poem: the midwives Shifra and Puah, Serach, Yohevet and Miriam.

The Midwives
The midwives Shifra and Puah, chief midwives among the Evriim (Hebrews) are the feminine prophetic proto-types of Jewish tradition. They are concerned with life, and are willing to surrender their own lives in order to save women and children from acts of state cruelty. Their acts of courage in the first chapter of the Exodus tale initiate the process of liberation which eventually unfolds in full. Since they were head midwives, we can assume that there were other midwives as well. Puah, or "Increase Hand Woman," and Shifra, or "Horn of Freedom Woman"

are merely the two who have become visible to history. As leaders, they serve as role models for the entire community. Midwives possessed the knowledge of healing herbs to cure the body. They also possessed the power of healing the social realm of human relations. Because of these characteristics Shifra and Puah are honored and given special status among the Israelites.

The midwives are associated with the name of the mystery known as Elohim. Elohim in Jewish tradition refers to the aspect of justice within the Great Mystery. Elohim also refers to the justice of the earth. This is the justice which sides with the powerless and shows concern for those struggling to survive.

In the Exodus tale, the midwives are the enablers of freedom. The image of women enabling other women to give birth is linked in the tale to the people of Israel running through the parting seas. As the seas open, so the womb opens and sends forth new creation. What patriarchal tradition could not do in the Jewish context is make the theological leap to God as a midwife woman. The female motif of midwife, birth, blood, children, parting seas, and liberation point to divine movement and presence. The Spirit is a midwife woman, enabling us to give birth to our own freedom.

Serach--Smells of Time Woman

Serach (not Sarah) is mentioned by name in the Bible only as Serach, daughter of Asher. But in Jewish legend she holds a place as the bearer of redemptive wisdom. Serach knows secrets and she reveals them to those she deems worthy of receiving them. She reveals to Yaakov that Yosef is alive in Mizryim, and so all the family journeys toward its destiny. She knows the mysterious words which will bring on redemption so that, when Moshe returns from Madiam proclaiming himself as redeemer, he is sent by the elders to Serach, who then tests his wisdom. Serach also knows where the bones of Yosef are buried, and how to raise them up from the river Nile. It is said she worked in the grist mills of Mizryim during the enslavement period and that she was over four hundred years old when the people left Mizryim. It is also said that she did not die, but went directly to Paradise like Elijah: she leaped into the other side. Her name means "smelly," and to make sure it is properly understood in a positive light, I have called her "Smells of Time Woman." She is prophet-woman as wise elder, as possessor of the insights which come from age and experience, and so are fully crafted in their wisdom. These are the elements of Serach's tale upon which I draw in respinning her yarn.

Yohevet--Goldencloud Woman

Yohevet means "glory of Yo," which refers to the name Yhvh. She is the mother of Miriam, Aron, and Moses. Some traditions say she was one of the midwives. As in many of the tales, I find that I can expand on the tale by exploring the meaning of a character's name. This is a common device among storytellers. Kavod, the last part of Yoheved's name, refers to the cloud of glory associated with the presence of the Mystery. In the Exodus story this cloud led the people out of Mizryim and formed a kind of house *(sukkah)* of protection around the people. This cloud became known as the wings of Shekinah, the feminine presence or female divine in Jewish tradition. So I have drawn a story of Yoheved, or Goldencloud woman, from the implications of the meaning of Kavod in her name. How did she receive her name? That became the question out of which the story is spun. Yoheved then is prophet-woman in her aspect of hope.

Yehoyah--God as Midwife-Woman

In Yoheved's name, Yo refers to the enigmatic description of the mystery of Yhvh. The letters form the verb "be." The form 'yhvh' indicates an active being, being in the sense of process, of unfoldment. In the Kabbalistic tradition Jewish religion came to acknowledge feminine and masculine aspects of Yhvh. This allowed me to begin looking for the feminine images associated with Yhvy. I began to see Yhvh as Changing-woman of Native American tradition, and as Shakti Lali of Hindu tradition. I began to see the feminine in Yhvh not as the tradition saw it, a passive receptive aspect which receives and reflects male energies, but rather as an active creatrix in the midst of life. In Jewish tradition the creative divine aspect is always associated with the male. To change this perspective I have changed the pronunciation of Yhvh. Although there is a tradition not to pronounce the name, we still refer Yhvh

with the male formulation Adonai or My Lord. I began to
see Yhvh as my midwife.

Originally the name Yhvh was a wordless cry yelled
by women. The support for this is found in the name
Halleluyah, or "praise yah." Traveling to the Middle East
and hearing the ululation spoken at celebration and lament-
ing time by women, I understood the origins of Yhvh. It is
a cry, a woman's cry. It has been described as sounding
like the cry of birds, and the howl of wild animals. It is
a sound of tremendous power and release, of strength and
expression. It fits in with the understanding of Jewish tradition that the Mystery is beyond names. The cry of ululation is used by women during times of giving birth and so
becomes part of the theological context of the Passover
story. God as midwife crying the ululation as the sea
parts and she draws her people through. So I have come
to call Yhvh in the female aspect: Yehoyah, Changing
Woman in her aspect as Midwife.

Miriam--Parting-seas Woman

Miriam, sister of Aron (and Moses?) is called Navia
at the moment she leads the women in dance at the parting
seas. As Rahel Adler has pointed out, "Miriam is identified
as a prophet during a time in which a prophet is known
as a miracle worker, a source of new religious knowledge,
and a poet. Yet she is portrayed as the protector of her
infant brother Moses and as the leader of a woman's
victory chorus repeating a song sung by Moses. The nurturi-
tive role is stressed over the creative."

Here again we must draw on Israelite sources, and
other women's materials to pull a fuller story of Miriam
from what is only hinted at in the text. Again, I began by
looking at Miriam's name. Although Miriam can be understood to mean "Bitter Sea Woman," it can also be understood as "Mistress of the Sea." If we associate this name
with ancient Goddess religion, we come up with the Goddess
as Lady of the Sea. In the Exodus tale, this image of
Yehoyah as midwife woman also carries the image of
Yehoyah as Sea Woman. Miriam as prophet interprets the
word of Sea Woman, Mother of Life. Miriam is midwife
woman and healer, envisioner and celebrant. She brings
new religious knowledge. What does she see? How would
she have told her story?

NAVIA: VOICE OF PROPHET WOMAN

Dedication

As I commit these words to page, my heart and mind, my voice and hands join the cry of women everywhere in the world today. We are living in times of great violence. Women from many cultures and traditions are under vicious attack by the forces of greed. Wherever we turn our gaze, whichever country we look upon we see the faces of poor women, hungry women, women with many children struggling to survive. And we know too that the spirit of women is rising, is on the move. We will not be contained. We are hearing the voice of prophet woman in our time calling us to create her web of caring; calling us to envision the rainbow; caling us to commit our lives to the peacemaking trail. As a Jewish woman, I am aware also that I must reach out to extend my spirit beyond the Jewish kinship ties to make peace with my Muslim and Christian sisters. The truth must be comprehensive, must include all of us. Male theological systems have for so long mirrored us to each other as enemies. Today, in our time, we must create a theology from our own experience and a spiritual vision which mirrors us to each other as beloved friends. We are all children of the earth. Let us, together, find the way to make peace on her ground, to make peace in her skies, to make peace in the hearts of all earthkind.

The Midwives' Prayer

We claim the right not to be driven from the land
We claim the right not to be beaten
We claim the right not to be starved
We claim the right not to be sick all the time
We claim the right not to be enslaved by an oppressor's hand.
We are strong faced women
Our eyes fill the heavens
We are not afraid to stand up
See, we are standing here today
And will not move from this place
until our children
are restored.

Yehoyah
Sacred One of birth and healing
Upon you we call
You who created the healing herbs
Your prophet-woman wears a skirt of many shells
As the sky wears stars
So may our people grow
So may our children increase.

Kol Yohevet

A new Pharoah
who did not know Yosef
came into power over Mizryim.
He announced to his people:
"The Israelites among us
are too numerous
and stróng for us
we must deal cleverly with them now
otherwise
they may increase so much
that in the case of war
they will join our enemies
and fight against us
driving us from the land."
So they appointed taskmasters over us
to crush our spirits with hard labor.
We were to build up the store cities of Pythom and
Raamses
as supply centers for Pharoah.
But the more they oppressed us
the more we increased.
The Mizryim came to dread us.
They began to force us to do labor
designed to break our bodies.
They made our lives miserable with harsh work
involving mortar and brick
as well as all kinds of work in the field;
all the labor was intended to break us.

In those days Pharoah summoned the head midwives
of the Evrim.
(That is the name they gave us

vagabonds, gypsies
so we wore the name and honored
the power of free roamers
My mother was one of the midwives.
The people called her Puah
increase hand woman.
She demanded that each birth become a celebration.
Somehow bread and wine were collected
shells and beads
goat hair blankets and woven baskets were brought.
We would go to the tall grass by the river
with singing and dancing
to bless the mother and father,
we would welcome the newborn child.
A new name among us
renewed hope
life extended.

Yehoyah knew the love of the midwives
and the people increased greatly
and because of their love, Yehoyah
made them great houses.

It was rumored that Pharoah could not sleep
on the nights the Israelite women gave birth.
He would dream of us
turning into grasshoppers
and creeping crawling things
swarming over his bed,
his hands his face
He would wrest himself
from his inner horrors
screaming along
with our birth cries.
So he summoned my mother
and her sister saying:
"When you deliver a Hebrew infant
if it is a boy, kill it
if it is a girl
let it live."
My mother loved Yehoyah
and did not do as Pharoah commanded
and let the boys live

and Pharoah summoned them again and demanded:
"Why did you do this, you let the infant boys live?"
My mother understood his madness well
and said: "The Hebrew women are not like Mizryim women.
They deliver as swiftly as the beasts of the field.
They give birth before a midwife ever gets to them."

Pharoah hung my mother
and my aunt Shifra.
I was a young girl, only ten years in my life.
I buried my mother's body
and planted a cedar twig
over her grave.
Everyday
I would visit her and weep
over the grave.
Because I cried so many tears
the twig grew quickly
into a tree.
One day
a morning dove came to live in the tree.
Much to my surprise,
everything I secretly wished for
the bird brought to me.
Because of the suffering
I came often to the tree
and the bird.
Here I felt protected and close to my mother.
One evening
under the full moon sky
I embraced the tree
and felt my mother's body.
A luminous cloud rose up
and the bird began to sing
From that time on
the people called me Yoheevet
golden cloud woman
because of the seven luminous clouds
which surrounded me
wherever my footsteps fell.
It was a sign of great hope
among the people.

They said it was a sign
Yehoyah was with us.
That Yehoyah heard our cries.

Navia, Healing Woman

Once, we were nothing
but souls on the wind
until she came and gathered our spirits.
She washed our wounds
in the healing waters of her courage
until we found our tongues
singing in our mouths
our eyes
able once again
to see the spirit of the people
an eagle in our vision.

The Birth of Miriam

Goldencloud woman
gave birth to three children:
Aron Moshe
and Mariam Navia
Parting seas Woman
born with a snake wrapped around her
a sun emerging from her forehead
horns like the crescent moon
she greeted her people
as the morning star
shimmers in the dawn
her seafires burned within.
Open
open to your vision of the waters. She sees
Yehoyah, the Midwife Woman
whose strong hands
catch us
as we are cast by the tides
of her parting seas onto earth's open shore.
As her eyes greet the light
she sees a mountain
she sees an eagle flying over the waters
she sees all the people passing through.

Kol Miriam

Navia
truthseeker seeing past
convention
through illusion
to the boney
truth.
Spiritwarrior
down into Tehom's wide abyss
you dive into her well
eat the fruit buried
at her roots
visions draw near
dreams stream through you
and your voice
wet
and open
moves image
into sound
sound into image
snakewoman
your utterance bubbles forth
flowing with words
a rushing river
of exhaltations
with your long snake tongue
slender bird tongue
thick cow tongue
entoning with drum
what your mind's eye
sees.
Parting seas woman
open open
to your vision of the waters.
The future unfurls like a fern
yielding its spiral to the rain.
In the rising spring tide
comes the muddy flood waters
the people
like grains of sand along the river
carried off to distant lands
waves like wings

bearing them to new nesting grounds
an eagle in your vision.
Face east
to the yellow sun
you remember the promise of freedom
and think
the time should be now.

Too many dead
too many dead children
Navia Dolores
Bitter Water Woman
your eyes run down with tears.
Too many dead
too many dead children
you have seen their faces
flesh on fire
bodies burning like funeral pyres
you rub yourself in ashes
tear your clothing
and call to the other women
to mourn with you.
At first they are afraid
but their children are
too many dead
so they sit with you
crying like jackals in the night
a storm rages inside them
it is the rage
of Yehoyah.

What turned You
to look at me
my anger my fits of rage
my loud grieving
what turned You to look at me
I saw You in a woman
hiding herself in the fields
squatting over stone
rocking and groaning out a child
I saw you crying over her
cupping up her cries and drinking them like water
her birth blood rose to Your nostrils

the smell reminded You of Your promise
You said:
    I hear
    the cries of the people
    I will take you out
    of Mizryim
    I will draw you forth
    with wonders
    and a midwife's hand
    I am Yehoyah
    the Midwife Woman.

I offered a prayer
saying
Yehoyah
Sacred one of birth and healing
upon You we call
You who made the healing herbs
Look, your prophet woman wears a skirt
of many shells
as the sky wears stars
as the sea holds drops of water
so let our people grow
so let our children increase.

And I prophesized in Your name
I spoke to the children of Yisrael saying:
People of Yisrael
you pray to the peak of the West
to Isis and Osirus
to Horus and Re
you wait for their sweet breezes to purify you
for their soft hands to soothe you.
but their wind is foul
their hands crust and cannot heal.
We are mud carriers for dead gods
because their people offer thanksgiving to them,
while they embitter our lives.
We build their cities
fill their silos with grain
their overseers belch and sleep
while we lick up bird droppings for a meal.
They instruct us in the wisdom of their scribes

OPPOSITION TO SUPERIORS IS A PAINFUL THING
ONE LIVES AS LONG AS ONE IS MILD
Obedient sons and daughters obey the gods
Only a fool does not know these things.

My kin
let us become a nation of fools
and madwomen.
Mizryim's teachings bring us death
their wisdom causes pain.
We build houses for idols
pyramids for hollow men
our sides ache
we destroy our arms at work
we are wretched through and through.
Yet you lift your face
to stone
and ask for mercy.
You stretch out your arms to wood
and beg for justice.
Can stone answer
or wood speak?
Do the gods heal our children
or comfort a mother's grief?
We serve Mizryim with silver
and lapis lazuli
we carve gods out of carob wood
and fashion ornaments of turquoise
and costly stone
we clear their way up the river to the tombs
and they cover our path with thorns
they rule over us
embitter our lives.
Listen Yisrael
rise up from your long sleep.
Let us set a table for the needy
offer our poor bread to the homeless
and set aside a day of feasting
for Yehoyah has called us
to make a path to the wilderness
where the eagle flies free.
Across the waters She will carry us
over the mighty flood waters

she will bear us
with outstretched arms
and a midwife's strong hand. Yehoyah is like
Eaglewoman
grieving like a motherbird
whose young are kidnapped from the nest.
There will be no end to her grieving
until her children
are set free.

Kol Serach

Every one thousand years
there is born a woman
who does not die
but lives
forever
she comes from the root soul
of the Ancient Mother of Days
When seven such women are born
and seven Houses rise
this circle of knowledge
will be
complete.

With no borders between skin and soil, Serach seemed like an old weed whose thick stalk and web of tendrils reached down deep. She cannot be uprooted. Her flesh was human parchment, a scroll of bones upon which life had enscribed four hundred years. Her mind was clear. Stories she remembered in detail. She knew stillness in the midst of fire and could reach into herself and draw forth just the right gift of wisdom.

When Pharoah, king of Mizryim, enslaved the tribes, Serach was forced to work in the grist mills. Sorrow filled the people; seeing her in chains, they feared for her life. For Serach held the memory of their beginnings, she alone knew the time of their redemption. How could she die?

Squatting by her grinding stone, she raised her head slowly and spread her strong hands in the blessing sign. Even in the fields they could feel the force of her blessing. Even without their drums the women could hold the rhythm for tales with their grinding stones.

Serach opened her mouth. And in the hollow of her first sound, they saw a moment held forever, Yehoyah in her fire, Yehoyah in her word, Yehoyah in her soft eyes. Each listening heart became a letter in her word, became the breath between the letters, became the light in the breath of all beginnings. With this light they could remember the first fluttering fires of creation, streaming into time and space like blood, pulsing into the open space of her abyss. With that fire they beheld the story of the people on the path to the city of peace.

She said: "The homeland is earth, but it is also a dream." She said: "Each one of you will come to understand the gift you must craft within yourself as an offering to Yehoyah. For this gift is need for the dream." Then sitting there she raised the grinding stone above her head and smashed it on the ground, shattering the stone into six hundred thousand pieces. She moved her hands over them like two birds hovering over the abyss. And the fragments became birds and the birds flew to us, each one carrying a mirror. "Gaze upon this," she said, "and you shall see the face of eternity in all which meets your gaze." As each one turned their eyes to the mirror it melted into their foreheads, and each one saw Her, in a moment held forever. Yehoyah, the midwife woman, would enable freedom in their own time. And in that mirror they saw Serach, suddenly an eagle, flying into a small opening in Her seam. That was the last they saw her in Mizryim.

But they say she wanders. And she has been sighted throughout the world at the birth of children, where people still believe that souls of great compassion send blessings to an open heart.

Rabbi Lynn Gottlieb is a story teller. She has been working in her field since 1973 when she began serving as rabbi to Temple Beth Or of the Deaf and the Hebrew Association of the Deaf. She began writing and performing stories of women in the Bible in 1976, and has continued to travel throughout the United States, Europe, Canada, and Israel, telling tales with chant, story, and sign language, as well as leading rituals in peace-making and Jewish celebration.

Since 1983 Rabbi Gottlieb has served Congregation Nahalat Shalom (Inheritance of Peace), which she helped found in Albuquerque, New Mexico. Lynn Gottlieb was ordained by Rabbi Zalman Schacter and Rabbi Everett Gendler in 1980 in New York City.

She is currently working on a book entitled: *Shekinah Coming Home,* A Guide to Jewish Women's Mysteries.

Shine forth your light
to guide and sustain us
prolonging, O Goddess, our days.
                    Rig Veda

Women's Words: Wisdom, Power, Beauty

Sue Woodruff

For me time flows in a spiral. Frank Lloyd Wright gave form to this image in his design for the Solomon R. Gugenheim Museum in New York City. Although I had read about this building, I was still unprepared for the actual experience of walking its spiral path, examining each piece of art from many vantage points. As I moved along, I knew the reality of spiral time in my body. Experiences and events, truths and images which occur at a given moment on the spiral appear slightly altered as I continue my walk. Matthew Fox uses a similar image when he speaks in his text, *Original Blessing,* of the four-fold path we all travel: the Via Positiva, the Via Creativa, the Via Negativa, and the Via Transformativa.[1] As I live and move along this path I am accompanied by women I have met.

§

My grandmothers were beautiful women. Both of them empowered my life with a legacy of ritual and prayer. My mother and her friends relished the sound of words, the weaving of rhyme in poetry. My teachers introduced me to their friends radiant with wisdom. Through each of these women I met others, my women friends, who share their words of wisdom, power, and beauty with me daily.

Virginia, my mother's mother, carried in her body her Pacific Northwest roots. Her French Canadian and native American heritage flowed into her prayer. Each evening after super, Grandma chose one of us to join her in her room for her evening ritual. I treasure the memory of those intimate moments. We carried a pot of tea, two cups, and sometimes a bowl of rice with cinnamon, sugar, and milk. While the tea steeped, Grandma freed her waist-length hair from its topknot. I brushed and brushed her white mane. Meanwhile Grandma began her formal prayers

426 The Spiral Path

with a reading from Grandpa's French Bible. Memorial
cards, yellowing letters, and birth announcements marked
favorite pasages. After the reading came the prayers to
our Mother God in the Chinook jargon of her Columbian
River ancestors. Intuitively I knew that although Grandma
and I might pray very easily to God our Mother, the Sisters
in our parish school would not readily accept this manner
of addressing God. So God our Mother remained in our
home ritual.

Next Grandma led a family litany in English during
which we prayed for each of her thirteen children, her
grandchildren, her sister's family, other relatives and myr-
iad of friends. Birthdays, illnesses, deaths, failed crops,
journeys, new babies, anniversaries, we prayed for them
all. After I had braided Grandma's hair into one long plait
for the night, she would pour two cups of tea and we
would share fears, secrets, and jokes while we sipped.
Then with a goodnight kiss, she would send me on my way
as she climbed into her bed.

My other grandmother, my father's mother Ulla
Belle, often lived far from us. But for a few years, she
came to Oregon living with Grampa on a small farm near
our hometown. Grampa, a nurse in our local hospital,
would pick me up on his way home, and when he left for
work the next morning, I delighted in time alone with
Gramma. During my days and nights with her I learned to
grill cheese sandwiches, to sew on a treadle machine, to
crochet miles of chains, to scatter feed for the chickens,
to eat fresh peas in the garden and to delight in stories.
In place of my despised afternoon nap, she substituted a
new ritual. We climbed upstairs to the big bed she usually
shared with Grampa. We fluffed the pillows and settled in
to read our favorite books. Sometimes she read her latest
novel while I browsed through her lady magazines and
shopped via her many catalogs. I loved it most when she
would read aloud to me. I cried over Peter Rabbit, worried
about Old Mother Hubbard, laughed with the antics of
Winnie the Pooh. Gramma's voice wove magic with the
words of that day's lucky author.

I also treasure the wisdom my mother, Rosie, shared
with me. In our neighborhood my mother and her friends
gathered for coffee and conversation while we youngsters
explored our friends' yard or basement. The young mothers

took time for reading, writing poetry, and sharing ideas in the midst of laundry, shopping, and cleaning. While crawling under tables and hiding behind skirts, I met such women as Maria Montessori, Dorothy Day, Barbara Ward Jackson, Caryll Houselander, Ann Morrow Lindbergh. The words and wisdom of these women lived in the conversations and poetry of my mother and her friends. Later in school I would meet these authors again and welcome them as old friends.

School opened treasures for me. My imagination and spirit feed on new ideas and word feasts. Several teachers shared their love of language by reading aloud to me and encouraging me always to read and then to read some more. As I grew and developed, I began to treasure the wisdom and the power I found in many women's writings. Several became sources of light and strength to whom I returned again and again during the years. Their words of advice echoed in my heart as I faced new situations or reflected on past experiences. Like my grandmother, I gathered the pages of my own prayer book. From time to time I would make a new friend, a writer whose work finally reached my hands through some chance encounter.

§

In my spiral journey through life, I am often brought to a standstill by the utter beauty of our earth. My native Oregon is alive with natural splendor. One of my favorite childhood haunts is Silver Creek Falls. I continue to be entranced by the small creek where I wade while waiting for a rock to choose me. It is a mystery how this tiny stream suddenly falls off the edge of the earth and plunges through mist and spray to the pool below filling it up and spilling over into a new creek.

When contemporary femininst songwriter Cris Williamson sings in "Waterfall," her song about her "endless waterfall" which is "filling up and spilling over,"[2] I am returned immediately to this childhood retreat. Biblical images of living water, healing water, cleansing water, refreshing water spill in on me. I am changed and transported to another level of my being. Mechtild of Magdeburg, a medieval woman mystic, also understood this power of water falling. "Divine love is so immensely great! Great is its

overflow, for Divine Love is never still. Always ceaselessly
and tirelessly it pours itself out, so that the small vessel
which is ourselves might be filled to the brim and might
also overflow."[3] Isn't it only right and fitting that water
falling releases power to light our homes since divine life
falling into us releases power to light our lives?

Along with water, the earth shares great pleasure.
Do you remember mixing up mud pies or squishing barefoot
through the oozing mud? Working up the soil for spring
planting pleasures all the senses. One of my favorite gardeners swears that tasting the soil is essential to understanding it. The smell of freshly turned earth, of land
parched by summer's heat, of soil moistened by spring
rain call to images of our Earth Mother deep within.

Julian, a 14th century anchoress, lived confined
within a small room attached to her church in Norwich.
She is hardly the mystic one would first turn to for images
of earth and of pleasure. But listen to this: "There is a
treasure in the earth that is a food tasty and pleasing to
the Lord. Be a gardener. Dig and ditch, toil and sweat,
and turn the earth upside down, and seek the deepness,
and water the plants in time. Continue this labor and
make sweet floods to run, and noble and abundant fruits
to spring. Take this food and drink and carry it to God as
your true worship."[4]

Centuries later May Sarton, a New England poet,
journaler, and novelist, in her poem, "An Observation,"
notes that "True gardeners cannot bear a glove / Between
the sure touch and the tender root."[5] A contemporary of
my mother, May watched her mother garden as I had my
grandmothers. She reflects upon the significance of what
she saw and of what she also experienced tending her own
garden. The price for this sensitive, sure touch is a scarred
and roughened skin. We "Pay with some toughness for a
gentle world."[6]

A woman May Sarton met while visiting in New
Mexico shares this sensitivity and reverence for the earth.
Edith Warner, a delicate, shy woman from Pennsylvania,
came to live at the foot of the mesa which houses Los
Alamos. Her frail constitution drew strength and healing
from the rough earth, the parched air, and the precious
waters near her home at Otowi crossing. In her journal,
Edith reveals her reverence for her adopted land:

My friend was wrong who said that this country was so old it does not matter what we Anglos do here. What we do anywhere matters but especially here. It matters very much. Mesas and mountains, rivers and trees, winds and rains are as sensitive to the actions and thought of humans as we are to their forces. They take into themselves what we give off and give it out again.[7]

This order and delicate balance of the entire cosmos yields a harmony that offers peace and blessing for all of us. Cycles of seasons; water falling on the earth then rising in clouds to fall again; seeds dying in the dark earth waiting for warmth and new life, these images return me to my spiral path. This first cycle overflows with blessing and open hearts, Mechtild calling me to "Live welcoming to all."[8] Images for this gallery include grapes at the crush pressed down and spilling over; the goddess with many breasts flowing with milk for her people; the miracle of people so moved to share their food that baskets of leftovers are collected.

With the blessing and support from this Via Positiva, we move into the emptiness and darkness that at times engulfs our lives. Each of us experiences these moments of pain; they form a natural part of our lives. This Via Negativa is not to be denied or avoided or glossed over. We must enter into the darkness and embrace it before we can move on and see it from a new perspective. Our medieval beguine, Mechtild, learned from suffering that "whoever is sore wounded by love will never be made whole unless she embrace the very same love which wounded her."[9] Adrienne Rich, a contemporary feminist author, in her poem "Power" speaks of the denial by the great scientist Marie Curie:

> She died a famous woman denying
> her wounds
> denying
> her wounds came from the same source
> as her power.[10]

Emptying out and letting go is a call to prepare for new growth. St. Paul reminds us that Christ emptied himself, accepting death on a cross in preparation for his new risen life. *The Reed of God,* written near the time of my birth, contains Caryll Houselander's wartime reflections on emptiness and waiting. This English woman touched the

pain of my mother and many other war brides waiting for
their husbands to return. In the poem "Pastoral" she speaks
of Mary and of herself as an empty reed, a shepherd's
pipe. Any song can pour through her. She is empty, waiting
to bring music to life when filled with breath.

> Now, if you will, breathe out your joy in me
> And make bright song,   11
> Or fill me with the soft moan of your love.

Within ourselves we experience a pull of opposites not
unlike the tug between magnetic poles: emptiness/fullness,
dark/light, joy/sorrow. Our challenge is to blend, to hold
the tension of these opposites within ourselves. We need
to transform our dualistic worldview into a dialectical consciousness.[12]
     St. Paul tells of the struggle that continually wages
within him. Even when he wants to do what is good, it is
something else he chooses instead. Cris Williamson acknowledges this dual reality and her struggle for freedom in
her song "Wild Things." She urges a return to the darkness.
"But wild, wild things can turn on you / And you got to
set them free."[13] May Sarton, too, describes the inner
struggle that often spills out in our actions through her
poem "The Angel and the Furies." As we strive to maintain
our balance in the swirl of "sudden motions of evil" or
"intimations of good" she reminds us of our humanity.
"Able to bless and forgive / Ourselves. / This is what is
asked of us."[14] But Mechtild shares with us a dream she
had. She is offered a choice between chalices. In one hand
God presents the white wine of consolation and in the
other the red wine of suffering. We choose our drink.
"Blessed are they who drink this wine: for although I
offer both in divine love, yet is the white wine nobler in
itself; but most blessed are they who drink of both, the
white and the red."[15]
     Here emerges another biblical image: the vine and
the branches, the vine dresser who prunes so that more
and better fruit will be produced. Hildegard of Bingen, a
majestic woman and medieval mystic, evokes this same
image visioning the Spirit as employing a pruning sword.
"In the aimless, spinning soul where fog obscures the
intellect and will, where the fruit is noxious and poisonous,
you guide the pruning sword."[16] Hildegard incessantly draws

out the greening power of trees, plants, and even people.

> When a forest does not green vigorously,
> then it is no longer a forest.
> When a tree does not blossom,
> it cannot bear fruit.
> Likewise a person cannot be fruitful
> without the greening power of faith,
> and an understanding of scripture.[17]

Remember the biblical metaphors of seeds, plants, weeds and reeds. "Have people never observed how earthly seed come to growth when it falls to the ground and is soaked by rain and dew?"[18] For new life to emerge nature requires a certain darkness or waiting period. "The consummation of this seed is a greening in the soul that is like that of the ripening world."[19] Should we not also expect such periods in our lives?

Anne Morrow Lindbergh is another woman I met through my mother and her friends. As a young mother, Anne learned well the place of pain and darkness, of emptiness in her life: she endured the trauma of the kidnapping of her baby son. All her money and family prestige could not lessen the pain of unending waiting. She reflects upon waiting and emptiness in her book *Gift from the Sea*. These brief mediations on shells found by a beachcomber speak deeper truths at the heart of many women's lives.

> The sea does not reward those who are too anxious, too greedy, or too impatient. To dig for treasure shows not only impatience and greed but lack of faith. Patience, patience, patience, is what the sea teaches. Patience and faith. One should lie empty, open, choiceless as a beach waiting for a gift from the sea.[20]

Edith Warner meditates on mesas and mountains outside the window of her New Mexican home as she waits for death. She is afraid and says so. An Indian friend advised her. "She had felt a fear once that I did, but she said, 'I am strong in my heart.' Surely that is better than saying there is no fear, no pain."[21] At the same time Edith also draws on the strength of her friend and of the land. In her last Christmas letter, she writes of her dying to her friends.

After weeks in a hospital it is especially wonderful to be
here in Tilano's room. Here he can rub my arm to relax
me and give me of his calm and strength. From the bed
I can see the first light on the mountains, watch the
snowclouds rise from the glistening Truchas peaks, follow
the sunset color from the valley to the sky. I can feel
the mesas even though I do not see them. It is a good
place in which to wait for the passing from a rich, full
life into whatever work lies beyond. [22]

Death is described in rich, yet simple, images by Mechtild,
the medieval beguine. To her God says: "Do not fear your
death. For when that moment arrives I will draw my breath
and your soul will come to Me like a needle to a magnet."[23]
Death is a "rippling tide of love (that) flows secretly out
from God into the soul and draws it mightily back to its
Source."[24] As she ages, drawing nearer to the time of her
own death, Mechtild grows impatient and reminds herself
"a good old age must be full of patient waiting and trusts
in God alone."[25] At the end of her life, Mechtild prays,
"Lord God, close now your treasured gift by a holy end."[26]
        A common mystical reference to this experience of
pain and suffering, of emptiness and waiting, is the dark
night. In a plaintive, mournful tone, Williamson cries "Where
is the light?" as she wanders in the dark. She begs, "Magnetic true-north, show me your face."[27] She describes
"One of the Light" as a "song of my journey, my spiritual
quest for the light which I know exists for me in this
life."[28] Mechtild writes of a lantern gone out. In the dark
its beauty can no longer be seen. "There comes a time
when both body and soul enter into such a vast darkness
that one loses light and consciousness and knows nothing
more of God's intimacy. At such a time when the light in
the lantern burns out the beauty of the lantern can no
longer be seen. With longing and distress we are reminded
of our nothingness."[29] Hildegard ponders how we create our
own darkenss. "Envy drives out all greening power! When
the greedy do not get what they want, they fall into a depression from which they are not lightly lifted. The day
hurries quickly by, they say, "it is always night." If happiness should stand outside, just beyond their door, they say,
"I am accursed." Should it go well with all they undertake,
still they would say, "It goes badly."[30]

The darkness gives way to nothingness, to emptiness, to despair. Simone Weil, a French contemporary of my mother, but a new friend of mine, sees the main value of suffering is to teach us our nothingness. "Grace wills empty spaces but it can only enter where there is a void to receive it, and it is grace itself which makes this void." [31] As a Jew, Simone faced the horror happening to her people. Although at one time she was safely in America, she chose to return to Europe, refusing to take more for herself than her compatriots had. The young woman undermined her precarious health and died in Ashford, Kent on August 24, 1943 of pulmonary tuberculosis and starvation. Adrienne Rich commemorates Simone's life, work, passion, and intensity in the poem "Leaflets" in which a woman is pictured distributing fliers in the pouring rain. The inherent poetry of a life lived wide open, innocent and sincere, is praised and acknowledged.

The theme of suffering and nothingness is further explored by Annie Dillard. After writing her Pulitzer prize winning *Pilgrim at Tinker Creek,* Annie moved West to an island off the coast of Washington State. The fruit of her isolation is *Holy the Firm,* a weave of reflections, insights, and the story of Julie Norwich, a child who is badly burned and airlifted to a hospital. We are forcefully reminded of being created, of living in a world which seldom makes sense. "I sit at the window, chewing the bones in my wrist. Pray for them: for Julie, for Jesse her father, for Ann her mother, pray. Who will teach us to pray?" [32]

What is our response to pain, to suffering, to the dark, to the emptiness and nothingness? We wait. Wait in silence. We embrace the dark then let it go. Into the silence comes the sound of birth, according to Caryll Houselander. One waits empty and open like the beach waiting for the gift of the sea, says Anne Morrow Lindbergh. Each foam-capped wave shelters dark spaces, observes Adrienne Rich. A leaf falling from an autumn tree teaches the art of letting go, writes May Sarton. "If I can take the dark with open eyes / And call it seasonal . . . / Love will endure." [33]

All agree that in some way a new birth comes from this experience. Creative energy is released. This next phase is the Via Creativa. For me this part of the path highlights the image of God as Mother implanted in

me as I joined my Graondmother in prayer. God as Mother
was not foreign to her native language. For years this
image grew inside of me, nourishing my meditation and
prayer. Then one day She broke free and emerged from
the paint I spread on a canvas. Her form in this painting
has a special place of honor in my room and in my life.

As my life unfurled, I followed the path marked out
for me, meeting other women who treasured similar images.
In Santa Fe I finally came face to face with a woman
who had previously existed only as a legend. Meinrad Craighead brought a series of circular Mother God images to
our offices. The vivid colors, rounded forms, interplay of
darkness and light, left me silent. Just recently these
images, together with Meinrad's commentary, were published. I invite you to feast on these luscious mandala
dream forms.[34]

Another woman whose creative energy astounds me
is Judy Chicago. Opening day of her massive Dinner Party
exhibit is a cherished memory. Symbolic plates use graphic
female imagery to honor the thirty-nine women chosen for
this event. Equally impressive is the historically appropriate
stitched runner for each woman. A place is set for Hildegard of Bingen. Her plate carries a stained glass motif.
The runner is a reproduction of Hildegard's own drawing
of the cosmos, a distinctly feminine egg shape incorporating
the four directions with the elements: earth, air, fire,
water.

Dorothy Day was a very special woman for my
mother's circle of friends. Her newspaper, The Catholic
Worker, brought her to their homes. Dorothy and her
lover, Forster, were going to have a child. This very fact
caused her to reflect on being made in the image of God,
a co-creator of this world.

> Forster loved nature with a sensuous passion. I have always
> felt it was life with him that brought me natural happi-
> ness, that brought me close to God. His ardent love of
> creation brought me to the Creator of all things. I cried
> out to him, 'How can there be no God, when there are
> all these beautiful things?' God is the Creator, and the
> very fact that we were begetting a child made me have
> a sense we were made in the image and likeness of God,
> co-creators with Him.[35]

Centuries ago medieval women also meditated on a

maternal God. Mechtild ran to God who reached out and pulled the child up onto her lap. "God is also mother who lifts her loved child from the ground to her knee. The Trinity is like a mother's cloak wherein the child finds a home and lays its head on the maternal breast."[36]

Julian of Norwich is famous for naming not only God, but Jesus also, as mother. She identifies the love of Christ with a mother's loving concern for her children. Hildegard also develops this mother image. She visions God as gifting all people with the call to be co-creators of the universe, to give birth in imitation of God, the Birther. "Just as the creation of God, that is, humankind, never ceases to come to an end, but rather, continually develops, so also the works of humankind shall not disappear."[37]

The call to co-create draws upon our capacity for creativity. Ech of us knows the satisfaction of laboring to bring to birth a creation. Some women experience this, as Dorothy Day did, in the birth of their children. Others, like May Sarton and her mother, create in their gardens food for family and friends, flowers to delight the senses. Some women recognize clearly the role they play in birthing themselves. Joanna Cazden, another contemporary musician, challenges women to take their own courage in hand and create life for themselves. "Take your own courage down off of that shelf. You can sing for the world. You can live for yourself."[38]

Anne Morrow Lindbergh reminds us of the necessity for quiet and contemplation. From this overflows some creative life of one's own: an arrangement of flowers, a poem, a prayer. The importance lies in being attentive and present to one's inner life. "Quiet time alone, contemplation, prayer, music, a centering line of thought or reading, of study or work. It can be physical or intellectual or artistic, any creative life proceeding from oneself. It need not be an enormous project or a great work. But it should be something of one's own. Arranging a bowl of flowers in the morning can give a sense of quiet in a crowded day, like writing a poem, or saying a prayer. What matters is that one be for a time inwardly attentive."[39]

Then, lest we become too self-oriented or introspective, life continues to flow out. We continue our spiral journey by examining our reality and responsibility as a communion of people. This part of the path is called the

Via Transformativa.

We are interconnected and need to recognize our need for interdependence. With the advances of technology, our world, indeed our universe, is shrinking. We must all live together in our global village. Cris Williamson recognizes this interdependence in her song "Sister." "Born of the earth, a child of God just one among the family."[40] We need to lean on each other, to be there for each other. Naomi Littlebear's song, "Like a Mountain" rallies peace workers on many continents. "You can't kill the spirit. It's like a mountain, old and strong: it loves on and on."[41] Edith Warner, friend of many scientists at Los Alamos, knew that they could not return after the war to their own various laboratories leaving the new destructive power in the hands of the military and politicians. Nor could she return to making her famous chocolate cake. Life was different. The memory of Hiroshima and Nagasaki impelled her to search for ways to live together in peace. "So louder and louder blasts echo over the Plateau and my blood runs cold remembering Hiroshima. If the world lived here, all would be reminded frequently that we must catch up with striding science and find a way to live together in the peace that Christmas signifies."[42]

For change to occur, I must change. Adrienne Rich recognizes the energy surge that touches us in this time as people become more conscious of themselves and each other. In her poem "The Parting: II," a woman combs her hair seeking in its tangle the part that brings order. Williamson prays, "Open mine eyes that I may see / Glimpses of truth thou hast for me / Open mine eyes, illumine me / Spirit divine."[43]

Caryll Houselander saw with her inner eye an icon of Christ with arms spread wide over a grey London street. The Russian face, later identified as that of the assassinated Tsar, spoke so clearly to her of the unity of all people. "The austere simplicity of that beautiful face stood sharp with grief. But the eyes and the mouth smiled with the ineffable love which consumes sorrow and pain as rags are consumed in a burning fire."[44] Later in an underground train, she saw this same face of Christ in everyone she met. "But I saw more than that; not only was Christ in every one of them, living in them, dying in them, rejoicing in them, sorrowing in them, but because he was in them, and because they were here, the whole world was here too, here in this underground train; not only the world as it was at that moment, not only all the people in all the countries of the world, but all those people who had lived in the past, and all those yet to come."[45]

Holly Near reiterates this theme of unity and identification when she identifies with a Central American woman, a student shot at Kent State, and a musician tortured by the junta. Seeing herself in others she continues to sing their song, calling for justice and for freedom. "It could have been me, but instead it was you. So I'll keep doing the work you were doing as if I were two."[46]

Mechtild understand this and calls us to pour out compassion on the earth. "When we on earth pour out compassion and mercy from the depths of our hearts and give to the poor and dedicate our bodies to the service of the broken, to that very extent do we resemble the Holy Spirit."[47] Power is given us that we might serve others.

We continue our journey on the path marked out for us. We spiral round and round as we glimpse again and again from new vantage points the images of our journey. The grandeur of nature continues to halt our movement. The pleasures of our earthy life treat our bodies to new delights and enhance memories of past ones. Love overflows in open, welcoming hearts. Eyes open, we enter into darkness. We find in pain and silence the Nothingness we call God. In the dark new life seeks light. We give birth to ourselves and our creations in ever-changing forms. Together we change and grow. Together we seek to build our world in justice and love.

Along the spiral path of our own journey, we have company--women to be with us. Women of long ago like Mechtild, Hildegard, and Julian shower us with wisdom born of a simpler life lived in a closer harmony with the elements. Contemporaries of my mother, Edith Warner, Caryll Houselander, May Sarton, Dorothy Day, Anne Morrow Lindbergh, bring the light of their experience of peace and war, of creation and of emptiness. Women of my day, Adrienne Rich, Annie Dillard, Meinrad Craighead, Cris Williamson, share the insights of their lives through song, poetry, painting, and writing. Each of these women accompanies us on the spiral path as we continue to create ourselves and our world.

Sister Sue Woodruff is a member of the Sisters of the Holy Names. She lives on the west bank of the Wilamette River in her native Oregon. Sue holds degrees in Elementary Education and Language Arts from Marylhurst College and in Curriculum Development from Western Washington State University. She has taught for several years in junior high schools, latterly in open classrooms, and has worked at planning and goal-setting for her religious community. In the larger community, Sue was education counselor at the Urban Indian Council of Portland, and later Assistant Director of the Training and Employment Department. She then became editor of *The Little Magazine* of Bear and Company in Santa Fe while writing *Meditations with Mechtild of Magdeburg,* published in 1982. Returning to Oregon, Sue served on the committee for renewal within her religious community and is currently Coordinator of Ministry for the province. She continues to find wisdom and refreshment in the words of women writers, sharing these treasures with other women and men in workshops about women's spirituality and literature.

Notes

Chapter 1: The Spiral Path

1. Schwenk, Theodore. SENSITIVE CHAOS. (New York: Schocken Books, 1976), p. 20.
2. Gilligan, Carol. IN A DIFFERENT VOICE. (Cambridge, MA: Harvard University Press, 1982), p. 23.
3. Swami Rama. FREEDOM FROM KARMA. (Chicago: Himalayan Institute, 1973), p. 54.
4. Christ, Carol. DIVING DEEP AND SURFACING. (Boston: Beacon Press, 1980), p. 13.
5. Frederick Franck in a lecture, "Art as a Way" at the Marylebone Health Centre, London, March, 1987.
6. Bates, Charles. RANSOMING THE MIND. (St. Paul: YES International Publishers, 1986), p. 64.
7. Gibran, Kahil. THE PROPHET. (New York: Alfred A. Knopf, 1973), p. 13.
8. Dowling, Colette. THE CINDERELLA COMPLEX. (New York: Pocket Books, 1982), p. 21.
9. Christ, op. cit., p. 15.
10. Mary Daly in BEYOND GOD THE FATHER; Carol Christ in DIVING DEEP AND SURFACING; Mary Giles in THE FEMINIST MYSTIC; among others.
11. Craighead, Meinrad. "God My Mother," in Bear & Co. Magazine, Vol III, No. 3, p. 22.
12. Cady, Susan, et. al. SOPHIA: FUTURE OF FEMINIST SPIRITUALITY. (San Francisco: Harper & Row, 1986), p. 12.
13. Swami Rama. BOOK OF WISDOM: ISHOPANISHAD. (Rolling Meadows, IL: Northwest Yoga Center, 1972), p. 5.
14. O'Brien, Justin. "Eastern Spirituality and the Religious Educator," in THE SPIRITUALITY OF THE RELIGIOUS EDUCATOR. ed. by James Lee. (Birmingham, AL: Religious Education Press, 1985), p. 188.
15. Teresa of Avila. THE INTERIOR CASTLE. trans. by Kavanough and Rodriguez. (New York: Paulist Press, 1979), p. 79.
16. For an excellent clarification of the problem and the historical background of meditation and contemplation in the West, see Justin O'Brien, "The Development of Christian Meditation in Light of Yoga," in MEDITATION IN CHRISTIANITY. (Honesdale, PA: Himalayan Press, 1983), p. 33ff.

17. Augustine of Hippo. CONFESSIONS. Book x, cap. xxvii.
18. Underhill, Evelyn. MYSTICISM. (New York: New American Library, 1955), p. 299.
19. Thunder, Perfect Mind, 13:16-14:15 in NAG HAMMADI LIBRARY, p. 271-272.
20. Purce, Jill. THE MYSTIC SPIRAL. (New York: Avon Books, 1974), p. 18.

Chapter 4: Woman's Body and Spirituality

1. Ochs, Carol. WOMAN AND SPIRITUALITY. (Totowa, NJ: Rowman & Allanheld, 1983), p. 10.
2. Waddell, Helen. THE DESERT FATHERS. (Ann Arbor: University of Michigan Press, 1972), p. 77.
3. Genesis, Chapter 21.
4. Meenakshi Devi, YOGA LIFE, Journal of Ananda Ashram, April, 1983.
5. Ochs, op. cit., p. 9.
6. Ibid., p. 105
7. Ibid., p. 69.
8. Sosa, Roberts, et. al. "The Effect of a Supportive Companion on Perinatal Problems, Length of Labor, and Mother-Infant Interaction," NEW ENGLAND JOURNAL OF MEDICINE, 1980, 303: 567-600.
9. Ochs, op. cit., p. 28.
10. Ibid., p. 30.
11. Swami Muktananda. I HAVE BECOME ALIVE. (South Fallsburg, NY: Syda Foundation, 1985).
12. Ochs, op. cit., p. 30.
13. Ibid., p. 11.
14. Ibid., p. 65.
15. Bonysenko, J. "Behavioural-Physiological Factors in the Development and Management of Cancer," GENERAL HOSPITAL PSYCHIATRY, 1982, 4:69-74.
16. Abeloff, M.D. and Derogatis, L.R. "Psychologic Aspects of the Management of Primary and Metastatic Breast Cancer," PROGRESS IN CLINICAL AND BIOLOGICAL RESEARCH, 1977, 12:505-516.
17. Levy, Sandra. "Emotional Response and Disease Outcome in Breast Cancer: Immunological Correlates," The Society of Behavioural Medicine, 4th Annual Scientific Sessions, p. 45.
18. Bonysenko, op. cit.
19. Schwerin, Doris. DIARY OF A PIGEON WATCHER. (New York: William Morrow, 1976).
20. Jackson, Edgar. UNDERSTANDING LONELINESS. (Philadelphia: Fortress Press, 1981).
21. Segal, Bernard, M.D. LOVE, MEDICINE AND MIRACLES.

(London: Rider, 1986).

22. Benson, Herbert with Proctor, William. BEYOND THE RE-
    LAXATION RESPONSE. (New York: Barkley Books, 1984).
23. The Prince of Wales. "Annual Representative Meeting: Presi-
    dential Address: BRITISH MEDICAL JOURNAL, 1982, 284:185.
24. Kubler-Ross, Elisabeth. ON DEATH AND DYING. (New
    York: Macmillan, 1969).
25. Ibid.
26. The Fourteenth Dalai Lama, His Holiness Tenzin Gryatso.
    KINDNESS, CLARITY AND INSIGHT. trans, ed. by Jeffrey
    Hopkins (Ithaca, NY: Snow Lion Press, 1983).

Chapter 5: The Spirituality of Marriage

1. Begehot, Walter. THE ENGLISH CONSTITUTION. (Oxford:
   Oxford University Press, 1968).
2. Coleridge, S.T. AIDS TO REFLECTION. (London: George
   Bell, 1904), p. 88.
3. John Wycliffe's translation of 1 Corinthians 15:44 from the
   first version of the New Testament in English, 1382.
4. Coleridge, op. cit., p 88, 89.
5. Stevenson, Robert Louis. "Virginibus Puerisque," in COMPLETE
   WORKS, Vol 2, Shanston Edition, 1911, p. 292, 297.
6. Jonson, Ben. "The New Inn," Act. 3, scene 2, from Jonson's
   COMPLETE WORKS (Oxford: Clarendon Press, 1938).
7. Bremond, Henri. PRAYER AND POETRY. trans. by Algar
   Thorold, (London: Burns, Oates & Washbourne, 1929), p. 194.
8. Eliot, T.S. "The Cocktail Party," Act 1, Scene 3 in COLLECT-
   ED POEMS AND PLAYS. (London: Faber & Faber, 1969),
   p. 384.

Chapter 6: The Spirituality of Motherhood

1. Allione, Tsultrim. WOMEN OF WISDOM. (London: Routledge
   & Kegan Paul, 1984), introduction.
2. Hazart Inayat Khan. THE COMPLETE SAYINGS. (New Lebanon, NY: Sufi Order Publications, 1978), p. 80.
3. Ibid, p. 128.
4. Swami Rama of the Himalayas in a public lecture in Chicago,
   Illinois, 1975.
5. Khan, op. cit., p. 29.
6. Pir Vilayat Inayat Khan. TOWARD THE ONE. (New York:
   Harper & Row, 1974), p. 1.
7. NEW AMERICAN BIBLE. I Corinthians, 13, p. 1353.
8. SPRINGS OF ORIENTAL WISDOM. (New York: Herder &
   Herder).
9. Rumi, Jelaluddin. THE RUINS OF THE HEART. trans. by

    Edmund Helminsi. (Putney: Threshold Books, 1960), p. 323.
10. Hazrat Inayat Khan, op. cit., p. 167.
11. Ibid., p. 115.

Chapter 8: Women and Nature

1. Drysdale, Vera Louise and Brown, Joseph Epes. GIFT OF THE SACRED PIPE. (Norman: University of Oklahoma, 1982), p. 6-7.
2. This true story is presented in Brooke's adult children's book, THE NAMING. (Unpublished), p. 16-18.
3. Boone, J. Allen. KINSHIP WITH ALL LIFE. (New York: Harper & Row, 1976).
4. Leslie, Robert Franklin. IN THE SHADOW OF A RAINBOW. (New York: New American Library, 1974).
5. For more information on this story see L. Taylor Hansen, HE WALKED THE AMERICAS. (Amherst, WI: Amherst Press, 1963), and Brooke's article "Lineage of the Sun," in THE AMERICAN THEOSOPHIST, Spring, 1986.
6. From a letter of chief Seattle of the Duwamish Tribe of the State of Washington to President Franklin Pierce in 1855. "This Land is Sacred" printed by Dale Jones of the Seattle office of Friends of the Earth.
7. For further information see Peter Tompkins and Christopher Bird, SECRET LIFE OF PLANTS. (New York: Harper & Row, 1973).
8. Drysdale and Brown, op. cit.
9. Parts of this section have been included in "Moon Time" in SHAMAN'S DRUM, Spring, 1986; used with permission.
10. For a full description of this rite, see Drysdale and Brown, op. cit.

Chapter 10: Spirituality and Joy

1. GOSEIGEN, THE HOLY WORDS. First Edition (Tujunga, CA: Bishop of North American Region of Sekai Mahikari Bunmei Kyodan, 1982).
2. Ibid.

Chapter 12: Fulness of Man-Womanhood

1. Bielecki, Tessa and McNamra, William. "The Carmelite Story," in THE TENT OF MEETING TEXTS. (Santa Fe: The Tent of Meeting, 1985), p. 41-50.
2. See the first book of Kings 18:41-46 for Elijah's 'vision' of Mary in the clouds.
3. All Betty Friedan quotations are from THE SECOND STAGE.

(New York: Summit Books, 1981), Chapter 2.

4. Lindberg, Anne Morrow. GIFT FROM THE SEA. (New York: Vintage Books, 1965), p. 57.

5. Gleason, Richard letter to CHRISTIAN CENTURY, July, 1986, p.620.

6. Bly, Robert. "What Men Really Want," NEW AGE, May, 1982, p. 30-37, 50-51. All Bly quotations are from this article.

7. This workshop was given at Wainwright House in Rye, New York on January 24, 1986.

8. Luke, Helen M. WOMEN, EARTH AND SPIRIT. (New York: Crossroad, 1981), p. 273.

9. Neely, James. GENDER. (New York: Simon & Shuster, 1981), p. 273.

10. For my summaries of masculine-feminine qualities I draw heavily throughout this essay on Mary Rosera Joyce's WOMEN AND CHOICE. (St. Cloud, MN: Life Com, 1986).

11. Ibid., p. 172.

12. Joyce, Mary R. "The Women's Movement Tomorrow," ESCAPE MAGAZINE, p. 31.

13. Jung, Carl. COLLECTED WORKS, quoted by John Welch in SPIRITUAL PILGRIMS: CARL JUNG AND TERESA OF AVILA. (New York: Paulist Press, 1982), p. 165-66.

14. de Castillejo, Irene. KNOWING WOMAN. quoted in Welch, p. 170-71.

15. Sanford, John. THE INVISIBLE PARTNERS, quoted ibid.

16. Singer, June. ANDROGYNY. quoted ibid.

17. Bertine, Eleanor. MEN AND WOMEN. quoted in Vann, Gerald. THE WATER AND THE FIRE. (New York: Sheed & Ward, 1954), p. 142.

18. Ibid., p. 136.

19. Welch, op. cit., p. 168.

20. McNarama, William. THE HUMAN ADVENTURE. (New York: Doubleday, 1974), p. 160.

21. John of the Cross. "Spiritual Canticle," in POEMS OF ST. JOHN OF THE CROSS. trans. by Willis Barnstone (Bloomington: Indiana University, 1968), p. 49.

22. Augustine. CONFESSIONS. Book 10, No. xxvii.

23. Arnold, Patrick. "The Masculine Voice in Spirituality," in AMERICA, Nov. 10, 1984, p. 292-94.

24. Vann, op. cit., p. 141.

25. Luke, WES, p. 11.

26. Keyes, C.D. GOD OR ICHABOD: A NON-VIOLENT CHRISTIAN NIHILISM. (Cincinnati: Forward Movement, 1973), p. 7, 19.

27. Arnold, op. cit., p. 294.

28. McNamara, HA, chapter 9.

29. Lewis, C.S. THE LION, THE WITCH, AND THE WARDROBE.

(New York: Collier Books, 1970).
30. Keyes, op. cit., p. 108.
31. Shidler, Mary McDermott, letter to CHRISTIAN CENTURY, July 2, 1986, p. 620. All quotations are from this source.
32. Luke, WES, p. 162.
33. Teresa of Avila. THE INTERIOR CASTLE. Ch. I, Nos. 2, 8, 9; Ch IV, Nos. 1, 9.
34. Luke, WES, p. 11.

Chapter 13: Relationships and Spiritual Growth

1. Gilligan, Carol. IN A DIFFERENT VOICE. (Cambridge, MA: Harvard University Press, 1983), p. 8.
2. Ibid.
3. von Franz, M.L. PROBLEMS OF THE FEMININE IN FAIRY TALES. (Dallas: Spring Publications, 1972), p. 25-26.
4. Rudhyar, Dane. RHYTHM OF WHOLENESS. (Wheaton, IL: Theosophical Publishing House, 1983), p. 207.
5. Johnson, Robert. SHE: UNDERSTANDING FEMININE PSYCHOLOGY. (New York: Harper & Row, 1986), p. 54.

Chapter 14: Spirituality and Freedom

1. See also, King, Avrom E., "Right and Left Hemisphere Skills in Dentistry," in HEALING CURRENTS, The Journal of the Whole Health Institute, Vol. 10, No. 1, 1986.
2. Thompson, Clara, M. ON WOMEN. (New York: Basic Books, 1964).
3. See also Dowling, Colette. THE CINDERELLA COMPLEX. (New York: Fontana, 1982).
4. Bardwick, Judith. THE PSYCHOLOGY OF WOMEN. Study of Biocultural Conflicts, 1971.
5. Horney, Karen. "The Overvaluation of Love, A study of a Common Present-Day Feminine Type," PSYCHOANALYTICAL QUARTERLY, Vol. 3, 1934.
6. Horney, Karen. THE NEUROTIC NEED FOR LOVE. ed. by Harold Kelman. (New York: Norton, 1967).
7. Thompson, op. cit.
8. Douvan, Elizabeth, "Sex Differences in Adolescent Character Process," Merrill-Palmer Quarterly, 1957.
9. Laplanche, J., Pontalis, J.B. THE LANGUAGE OF PSYCHO-ANALYSIS. (London: Hogarth Press, 1983).
10. Bolen, Jean Shinoda. GODDESSES IN EVERYWOMAN. (New York: Harper & Row, 1984).

Chapter 16: Feminine Aspects of Divinity

1. Beasley, Norman. MARY BAKER EDDY. (New York, 1963), p. 304.
2. SCIENCE AND HEALTH WITH KEY TO THE SCRIPTURES, on Gen. 1:27.
3. Brinton, Howard. THE MYSTIC WILL. (New York, 1930), p. 178f, 201.
4. Morgan, John H. "Eternal Father-Eternal Mother in Shaker Theology," INWARD LIGHT, Spring, 1973.
5. Zernov, Nicolas. THREE RUSSIAN PROPHETS (London, 1944), p. 121.
6. Parkhurst, Genevieve. HEALING AND WHOLENESS ARE YOURS (St. Paul, MN, 1957), p. 34.
7. Scholem, Gershom. MAJOR TRENDS IN JEWISH MYSTICISM. (New York, 1961), p. 229.
8. Patai, Raphael. THE HEBREW GODDESS. (New York, 1967), p. 161ff.
9. Scholem, op. cit., p 249f, 275f.
10. Buber, Martin. FOR THE SAKE OF HEAVEN. (New York, 1945), p 228ff.
11. Landstrom, Elsie. "A Lightning Flash of Living Love," INWARD LIGHT, Spring, 1972, p 27ff.

Chapter 18: Prayer, The Language of Love

1. Teresa of Avila. INTERIOR CASTLE. trans. by E. Allison Peers. (Garden City, NJ: Doubleday, 1961), p. 31-32.
2. Ibid., p. 85.
3. John of the Cross. ASCENT OF MOUNT CARMEL. trans. by E. Allison Peers. (Garden City, NJ: Doubleday, 1958).
4. Merton, Thomas. CONTEMPLATIVE PRAYER. (Garden City, NJ: Doubleday, 1971), p. 90.
5. John of the Cross. DARK NIGHT OF THE SOUL. trans. by E. Allison Peers. (Garden City, NJ: Doubleday, 1959), p. 119.
6. Teresa of Avila, op. cit., p. 154-155.

Chapter 19: Suffering and Self-Realization

1. Tweedie, Irina. DAUGHTER OF FIRE. (Grass Valley, CA: Blue Dolphin Press, 1986).
2. Reps, Paul. ZEN FLESH, ZEN BONES. (New York: C.E.Tuttle, 1957).

Chapter 20: Women and Mysticism

1. Our definition of religion as the revelation of the divine or Ultimate Truth to consciousness, is the same definition we use to define 'mysticism' in its broader sense. Although we

prefer to define 'mysticism' in the Dionysian terms of a particular path or via negativa, this definition is too narrow for our present purposes.

2. With Christ, the divine virtually put its stamp of approval on man's image-making relative way-of-knowing; Christ is the fulfillment of consciousness and its longing or need for a God like ourselves, God among us, with us.

    Because our passage through human existence is a passage through consciousness, Christ was the revelation of this passage—a revealtion of consciousness—and how it must be lived by all of us.

3. Needless to say, the subject and object of consciousness are the same—it is the same mind bending back on itself. All awareness or consciousness then, is subject-as-object. If this reflexive mechanism were suspended or put to rest, we could not speak of subject or object, or speak of consciousness at all. Those who dispute this fact are only considering the conscious level of consciousness, whereas we are referring to the unconscious level of physiological functioning where the brain makes consciusness possible.

Chapter 22: Women's Words: Wisdom, Power, Beauty

1. Fox, Matthew. ORIGINAL BLESSING (Santa Fe: Bear & Company, 1983).
2. Williamson, Cris, "WaterFall," from THE CHANGER AND CHANGED (Oakland, CA: Olivia Records, 1975).
3. Woodruff, Sue. MEDITATIONS WITH MECHTILD OF MAGDEBURG (Santa Fe: Bear & Company, 1982), p. 92.
4. Doyle, Brendan. MEDITATIONS WITH JULIAN OF NORWICH. (Santa Fe: Bear & Company, 1983), p. 84.
5. Sarton, May. "An Observation," AS DOES NEW HAMPSHIRE. (New Hampshire: R.R.Smith, 1967), p. 30.
6. Ibid.
7. From Edith Warner's unpublished journal quoted in Peggy Pond Church, THE HOUSE AT OTOWI BRIDGE (Albuquerque, NM: University of New Mexico Press, 1959), p. 18.
8. Woodruff, p. 126.
9. Woodruff, p. 69.
10. Rich, Adrienne. "Power," THE DREAM OF A COMMON LANGUAGE: POEMS 1974-1977. (New York: Norton, 1978), p.3.
11. Houselander, Caryll. "Pastoral," THE REED OF GOD. (London: Sheed and Ward, 1944), p. 39.
12. Fox, op. cit., p. 208-219.
13. Williamson, Cris. "Wild Things" op. cit.
14. Sarton, May. "The Angels and The Furies," A DURABLE FIRE. (New York: Norton, 1972), p. 34.

15. Mechtild of Magdeburg. THE FLOWING LIGHT OF THE GOD-HEAD. trans. by Lucy Menzies. (London: Longmans, Green, and Co., 1953), p. 37.
16. Uhlein, Gabriele, MEDITATIONS WITH HILDEGARD OF BINGEN. (Santa Fe: Bear & Company, 1982), p. 39.
17. Ibid., p. 62.
18. Ibid, p. 121.
19. Ibid., p. 123.
20. Lindberg, Anne Morrow. GIFT FROM THE SEA. (New York: Random House, 1955), p. 17.
21. Church, op. cit., p. 116.
22. Ibid., p. 117.
23. Woodruff, op. cit., p. 80.
24. Ibid, p. 74.
25. Ibid.
26. Ibid., p. 132.
27. Williamson, op. cit.
28. Ibid.
29. Woodruff, op. cit., p. 60-61.
30. Uhlein, op. cit. p. 75.
31. Weil, Simone. GRAVITY AND GRACE. (London: Routledge and Kegan Paul, 1952), p. 10.
32. Dillard, Annie. HOLY THE FIRM. (New York: Bantam, 1977), p. 48.
33. Sarton, "The Autumn Sonnets", ADF, op. cit., p. 43.
34. Craighead, Meinrad. THE MOTHER'S SONGS. (New York: Paulist Press, 1986).
35. Day, Dorothy. THE LONG LONELINESS. (New York: Harper & Row, 1952), p. 134-135.
36. Woodruff, op. cit., p. 109.
37. Uhlein, op. cit., p. 124.
38. Cazden, Joanna. "The Hatching Song," HATCHING.
39. Lindberg, op. cit., p. 56.
40. Williamson, "Sister," op. cit.
41. Littlebear, Naomi. "Like a Mountain," QUIET THUNDER. (Portland, OR: Riverbear Music, 1977).
42. Church, op. cit., p. 134.
43. Williamson, "Song of the Soul," op. cit.
44. Houselander, Caryll. A ROCKING HORSE CATHOLIC. (New York: Sheed and Ward, 1955), p. 112.
45. Ibidl, p. 137-38.
46. Near, Holly. "It Could Have Been Me," HOLLY NEAR: A LIVE ALBUM. (Ukiah, CA: Redwood Records, 1974.
47. Woodruff, op. cit., p. 117.

Bibliography

ALLIONE, Tsultrim. Women of Wisdom (Boston: Rutledge & Kegan Paul, 1986).

ALSTON, A.J. Devotional Poems of Mirabai (New Delhi: Motilal Banarsidass, 1980).

ANDALSEN, Barbara Hilkert, et. al. (ed.) Women's Consciousness, Women's Ethics (San Francisco: Harper & Row, 1985).

ANDREWS Lynn V. Medicine Woman (San Francisco: Harper & Row, 1981).
Flight of the Seventh Moon (1984).
Star Woman (1986).

ATKINSON, Clarissa W. Mystic and Pilgrim: The Book and World of Margery Kempe (Ithaca, NY: Cornell University Press, 1983).
Immaculate and Powerful: The Female in Sacred Image and Social Reality, Vol. I, Harvard Women's Studies in Religion, (Boston: Beacon Press, 1985).

AUROBINDO, Sri. The Mother. (Pondicherry, India: Sri Aurobindo Ashram, 1979).

BANKSON, Marjory Loet. Braided Streams: Esther and a Woman's Way of Growing (San Diego: Lura Media, 1985).

BOLEN, Jean Shinoda. Goddesses in Everywoman: A New Psychology of Women (New York: Narper & Row, 1984).

BRUCHAC, Carol et. al., (ed) The Stories We Hold Secret: Tales of Women's Spiritual Development (New York: Greenfield Review Press, 1986).

CADY, Susa, et. al. Sophia: The Future of Feminist Spirituality (San Francisco: Harper & Row, 1986).

CAMERON, Anne. Daughters of Copper Woman (Vancouver, BC: Press Gang Publishers, 1981).

CAREY, Ken. Vision (Kansas City, MO: Unison Press, 1985).

CATHERINE OF SIENNA. The Dialogues translated by Algar Thorold (Rockford, IL: Tan Books, 1974).

CHERNIN, Kim. Reinventing Eve: Modern Woman In Search of Herself (New York: Times Books, 1987).

CHRIST, Carol Womanspirit Rising: A Feminist Reader in Religion edited by Judith Plaskow (San Francisco: Harper & Row, 1979).
Diving Deep and Surfacing: Women Writers on Spiritual Quest (Boston: Beacon Press, 1980).

Laughter of Aphrodite: Reflections on a Journey to the Goddess (San Francisco: Harper & Row, 1987).

DALY, Mary. The Church and the Second Sex (New York: Harper & Row, 1968).

Beyond God the Father (Boston: Beacon Press, 1973).

Gyn/Ecology (Boston: Beacon Press, 1978).

DOWNING, Christine. The Goddess: Mythological Images of the Feminine (New York: Crossroad, 1984).

ENGELSMAN, Joan Chamberlain. The Feminine Dimension of the Divine (Philadelphia: The Westminster Press, 1979).

FIORENZA, Elisabeth Schussler. In Memory of Her: A Feminist Theological Reconstruction of Christian Origins (New York: Crossroad, 1983).

GILES, Mary E. The Feminist Mystic and Other Essays on Women and Spirituality (New York: Crossroad, 1982).

When Each Leaf Shines: Voices of Women's Ministry (Denville, NY: Dimension Books, 1986).

GILLIGAN, Carol. In a Different Voice (Cambridge,MA: Harvard University Press, 1982).

GOLDENBERG, Naomi. Changing of the Gods (Boston: Beacon Press, 1979).

HALL, Nor. The Moon and the Virgin: Reflections on the Archetypal Feminine (New York: Harper & Row, 1980).

HEYWARD, Carter. Our Passion for Justice (New York: The Pilgrim Press, 1984).

HILLESUM, Etty. An Interrupted Life: The Diaries of Etty Hillesum, 1941-1943 (New York: Pantheon Books, 1983).

HUNGRY WOLF, Beverly. The Ways of My Grandmothers (New York: William Morrow, 1980).

HURCOMBE, Linda. Sex and God: Some Varieties of Women's Religious Experiences (London: Routledge and Kegan Paul, 1987).

INAYAT, Taj. The Crystal Chalice (Lebanon Springs, NY: Sufi Order Publications, 1980).

IYENGAR, Geeta. Yoga: A Gem for Women (Bombay: Allied, 1984).

JULIAN of Norwich. Revelations of Divine Love translated by James Walsh (St. Meinrad, IN: Abbey Press, 1975).

KENNETT, Roshi Jeiju. The Wild, White Goose: The Diary of a Zen Trainee in two volumes (Mt. Shasta, CA: Shasta Abbey, 1977).

KINSLEY, David. Hindu Goddesses: Visions of the Divine Feminine in the Hindu Religious Tradition (Berkeley: University of California Press, 1986).

LAKOFF, Robin Talmach and Raquel L. Sherr. Face Value: The Politics of Beauty (London: Routledge & Kegal Paul, 1984).

MAITLAND, Sara. A Map of the New Country: Women and Christianity (London: Routledge & Kegan Paul, 1983).

MAYORGA, Nancy Pope. The Hunger of the Soul: A Spiritual Diary (Los Angeles: Whitmarsh & Co., 1981).

MOLLENKOTT, Virginia Ramey. Women, Men and the Bible (Nashville: Abingdon, 1977).

The Divine Feminine: The Biblical Imagery of God as Female (New York: Crossroad, 1986).

MOLTMANN-WENDEN, Elizabeth. Liberty, Equality and Sisterhood translated by Ruth Gritsch (Philadelphia: Fortress, 1979).

A Land Flowing with Milk and Honey: Perspectives on Feminist Theology (New York: Crossroad, 1986).

NURBAKHSH, Javad. Sufi Women (New York: Khankiquaki-Ni Matullahi Publishers, 1983).

OCHS, Carol. Women and Spirituality (Totowa, NY: Rowman and Allamheld, 1983).

PAGELS, Elaine The Gnostic Gospels (New York: Vintage, 1981).

PAPA, Mary Boder. Christian Feminism: Completing the Subtotal Woman (Chicago: Fides/Claretian, 1981).

PERERA, Sylvia Brinton. Descent to the Goddess: A Way of Initiation for Women (Toronto: Inner City Books, 1981).

ROBERTS, Bernadette. The Experience of No-Self: A Contemplative Journey (Boulder, CO: Shambhala, 1984).

The Path to No-Self, 1986.

REUTHER, Rosemary Radford. New Women, New Earth (New York: Seabury Press, 1975).

Mary, the Feminine Face of the Church (Philadelphia: Westminster Press, 1977).

Religion and Sexism (New York: Simon & Schuster, 1974).

Women of Spirit, edited with Eleanor McLaughlin, 1979.

Sexism and God-Talk (Boston: Beacon Press, 1983).

RUSSELL, Letty M. Human Liberation in a Feminist Perspective: A Theology (Philadelpha: Westminster Press, 1974).

The Liberating Word, 1976

Feminist Interpretation of the Bible (Oxford: Blackwell, 1985).

SAYERS, Dorothy L. Are Women Human? (Grand Rapids: W.B. Eerdman's, 1971).

SCHAEF, Anne Wilson. Women's Reality: An Emerging Female System in the White Male Society (Minneapolis: Winston Press, Inc., 1981).

SEN, Ramprasad, Leonard Nathan and Clinton Seely, trans. Grace and Mercy in Her Wild Hair: Selected Poems to the Mother Goddess (Boulder, CO: Great Eastern, 1982).

SHARMA, Arvind. Women in World Religions (Albany: State University of New York Press, 1987).

SMITH, Margaret. Rabia the Mystic and Her Fellow Saints in Islam (Cambridge: Cambridge University Press, 1984).

SOELLE, Dorothee. The Strength of the Weak: Toward a Christian Feminist Identity (Philadelphia: Westminster Press, 1984).

SPRETNAK, Charlene. The Politics of Women's Spirituality: Essays on the Rise of Spiritual Power within the Feminist Movement (New York: Avelior Books, 1982).

STARHAWK. The Spiral Dance (San Francisco: Harper & Row, 1978).

Dreaming the Dark (Boston: Beacon Press, 1982).

STONE, Merlin. When God was a Woman (New York: Dial Press, 1976).

TERESA OF AVILA. Collected Works, translated by Kavanough and Rodriguez, two volumes (Washington, DC: ICS Publications, 1976, 1980).

THERESE OF LISIEUX. Autobiography, translated by John Clarke (Washington, DC: ICS Publications, 1975).

TRIBLE, Phyllis. God and the Rhetoric of Sexuality (Philadelphia: Fortress Press, 1978).

TWEEDIE, Irina. Daughter of Fire: A Diary of a Spiritual Training with a Sufi Master (Nevada City, CA: Blue Dolphin Press, 1986).

UNDERHILL, Evelyn. Mysticism (New York: New American Library, 1955).

WALKER, Barbara G. The Woman's Encyclopedia of Myths and Secrets (San Francisco: Harper & Row, 1983).

WARNER, Marina. Alone of All Her Sex: The Myth and Cult of the Virgin Mary (New York: Alfred A. Knopf, 1976).

WILNER, Eleanor. Shekhina (Chicago: University of Chicago, Press, 1984).